£17-00
Book Sale 92.
KT-511-537

An Introduction to Numerical Methods for Differential Equations

James M. Ortega
Department of Applied Mathematics and Computer Science
UNIVERSITY OF VIRGINIA

William G. Poole, Jr.
BOEING COMPUTER SERVICES COMPANY

PITMAN PUBLISHING INC.
1020 Plain Street
Marshfield, Massachusetts

© 1981 James M. Ortega and William G. Poole, Jr.

Pitman Publishing Inc.
1020 Plain Street
Marshfield, Massachusetts 02050

and

Pitman Publishing Limited
39 Parker Street
London WC2B 5PB

Associated Companies
Pitman Publishing Pty Ltd., Melbourne
Pitman Publishing New Zealand Ltd., Wellington
Copp Clark Pitman, Toronto

All rights reserved. No part of this publication may be reproduced, stored in a retrieval system, or transmitted in any form or by any means, electronic, mechanical, photocopying, recording and/or otherwise without the prior written permission of the publishers. The paperback edition of this book may not be lent, resold, hired out or otherwise disposed of by way of trade in any form of binding or cover other than that in which it is published, without the prior consent of the publishers.

Printed in Great Britain by
Antony Rowe Ltd, Chippenham, Wiltshire

Library of Congress Cataloging In Publication Data

Ortega, James M., 1932-
Numerical methods for differential equations.

Cover title: An introduction to numerical methods for differential equations.
Bibliography: p.
1. Differential equations—Numerical solutions—Data processing. I. Poole, William G. II. Title. III. Title: Introduction to numerical methods for differential equations.
QA371.065 515.3'5 81-817
ISBN 0-273 01686-5 AACR2

Contents

Preface

The need to solve differential equations was one of the original and primary motivations for the development of both analog and digital computers. The numerical solution of such problems still requires a substantial fraction of the available computing time on existing computers. It is our goal in this book to introduce numerical methods for both ordinary and partial differential equations, although the concentration is on ordinary differential equations, especially boundary-value problems.

We treat initial-value problems for ordinary differential equations in Chapter 2. Chapters 3 and 4 consider finite difference methods for linear and nonlinear two-point boundary-value problems, respectively. Chapter 5 introduces Galerkin and collocation methods. Chapter 6 deals with eigenvalue problems. In Chapters 7 and 8 we deal with initial- and boundary-value problems for partial differential equations.

As a minimum background, the reader is assumed to have had a first course in computer programming, which has probably used some elementary numerical methods for numerical integration, curve fitting, and so on. We also assume a solid background in the calculus and in linear algebra and a first course in differential equations. Some basic facts that we need from these areas are collected in the appendices and further background material appears in the text itself. Students with this minimum background will require a full year to cover the book completely, although a one-semester or two-quarter course can easily be taught by eliminating some topics.

The solution of differential equations requires techniques from a variety of other areas in numerical analysis. For example, the solution of linear boundary-value problems by either finite difference or projection methods ultimately requires the solution of systems of linear algebraic equations, and a self-contained treatment of this subject is given in Chapter 3 when it is first needed. If the differential equation is nonlinear, the resulting algebraic equations are also nonlinear, and the solution of a single nonlinear equation and systems of nonlinear equations are treated in Chapter 4. Similarly, polynomial, spline, and least squares approximation are introduced where needed as tools for solving differential equations. Students who have had a one-semester course in numerical methods can use much of this material as a review and can concentrate on differential equations. In this case, most of the book can be covered in one semester.

Since most of the main topics of a first course in numerical methods are covered, the book also can serve as text for such a course. Indeed we view the book to be basically for this purpose but oriented toward students primarily interested in differential equations. In fact, we have found this organization, which may seem rather unorthodox for a first course, to be more satisfactory and motivating than the usual one for a rather large number of students. Thus the book can be used for a variety of different audiences, depending on the background of the students and the purposes of the course. From earlier versions of the manuscript, the authors have taught successful courses ranging from the first numerical methods course for juniors and seniors in mathematics and computer science to a numerical differential equations course for first-year graduate students in engineering and the sciences.

A few model problems are presented in the first sections of most chapters, and in some cases a rather complete derivation of the equation is given. We do not mean to imply that these sections are sufficient to teach the difficult art of mathematical modeling, but they are included to give some motivation. These sections can be covered very quickly or omitted completely without loss to the remainder of the book, or expanded upon if the instructor wishes to stress modeling aspects.

The style of the book is on the theoretical side, although rather few theorems are stated as such and many proofs are either omitted or partially sketched. On the other hand, enough mathematical argumentation is usually given to clarify what the mathematical properties of the methods are. In many cases, details of the proofs are left to exercises or to a supplementary discussion section, which also contains references to the literature. We have found this style quite satisfactory for most students, especially those outside of mathematics.

The solution of differential equations on a computer is a large and important part of what has increasingly come to be called scientific computing. To place our subject in this larger environment, the introductory chapter, Chapter 1, gives an overview of scientific computing. The computer science topics discussed briefly there are not pursued in detail in the remainder of the book, although at various places we indicate that a particular technique would be useful in practice.

The development of numerical methods for solving differential equations has evolved to a state where accurate, efficient. and easy-to-use mathematical software exists for solving many of the basic problems. For example, excellent subroutine libraries are used throughout the world to solve the initial-value problems of Chapter 2, linear equations of Chapter 3, and eigenvalue problems of Chapter 6. The reader is advised to examine the supplementary discussions and references at the ends of all sections for information on available software. Some of the exercises require the reader to write programs to implement some of the basic algorithms for these same problems. The purpose of these exercises is not to develop usable software but, rather, to have the reader experience what is involved in coding the algorithms, thus leading to a deeper understanding of them. The development of accurate, efficient, and easy-to-use software is beyond the scope of this book.

We owe thanks to many of our colleagues, anonymous reviewers, and students at the College of William and Mary, North Carolina State University, and the University of Virginia who made useful comments and suggestions on earlier versions of the book. We are also indebted to numerous secretaries for their expert typing (and retyping) of the manuscript.

1 The World of Scientific Computing

1.1 What Is Scientific Computing

The thousands of computers now installed in this country and abroad are used for a bewildering—and increasing—variety of tasks: accounting and inventory control for industry and government, airline and other reservation systems, limited translation of natural languages such as Russian to English, monitoring of process control, and on and on. One of the earliest—and still one of the largest—uses of computers was to solve problems in science and engineering, more specifically, to obtain solutions of mathematical models that represent some physical situation. This is the general area called *scientific computing.*

There is now hardly an area of science or engineering that does not use computers for this purpose. Trajectories for earth satellites and for planetary missions are routinely computed. Aerospace engineers also use computers to simulate the flow of air about an aircraft or other aerospace vehicle as it passes through the atmosphere, and to verify the structural integrity of aircraft. Such studies are of crucial importance to the aerospace industry in the design of safe and economical aircraft and spacecraft.

Civil engineers study the structural characteristics of large buildings, dams, highways, and so on. Meteorologists use large amounts of computer time to predict tomorrow's weather as well as to make much longer range predictions, including the possible change of the earth's climate. Astronomers and astrophysicists have modeled the evolution of stars, and much of our basic knowledge about such phenomena as red giants and pulsating stars has come from such calculations coupled with observations. Ecologists and biologists are increasingly using the computer in such diverse areas as population dynamics (including the study of natural predator and prey relationships), the flow of blood in the human body, and the dispersion of pollutants in the oceans and atmosphere.

The mathematical models of all of the problems mentioned previously—and of most of the other problems in science and engineering—are systems of differential equations, either ordinary or partial. Thus, to a first approximation, scientific computing as currently practiced is the computer solution of differential equations. Even if this were strictly true, scientific computing would still be, and is, an intensely exciting discipline. Differential equations come in all "sizes and shapes," and even with the largest computers, we are nowhere near being able to solve many of the problems posed by scientists and engineers.

But there is more to scientific computing, and the scope of the field is changing rapidly. A variety of other mathematical models also arise, each with its own challenges. Data reduction—the condensation of a large number of measurements into usable statistics—has always been an important, if somewhat mundane, part of scientific computing. But now we have tools (such as earth satellites) that have increased our ability to make measurements far faster than our abilities to assimilate them; fresh insights are needed into ways to preserve and use this irreplaceable information. In more developed areas of engineering, what were yesterday's difficult problems to solve even once on a computer are today's routine problems that are being solved over and over with changes in design parameters. This has given rise to an increasing number of computer-aided design systems. Similar considerations apply in a variety of other areas.

Although this discussion begins to delimit the area that we call scientific computing, it is difficult to define it exactly, especially the boundaries and overlaps with other areas.† We will accept as our working definition that *scientific computing is the collection of tools, techniques, and theories required to solve on a computer the mathematical models of problems in science and engineering.*

A majority of these tools, techniques, and theories originally developed out of mathematics, many of them having their genesis long before the advent of electronic computers. This set of mathematical theories and techniques is called numerical analysis (or numerical mathematics) and constitutes a major part of scientific computing. The development of the electronic computer, however, signaled a new era in the approach to the solution of scientific problems. Many of the numerical methods that had been developed for the purpose of hand calculation (including the use of desk calculators for the actual arithmetic) had to be revised, and sometimes abandoned. Considerations that were irrelevant or unimportant for hand calculation now became of utmost importance

† Perhaps the only universally accepted definition of, say, mathematics is that it is what mathematicians do.

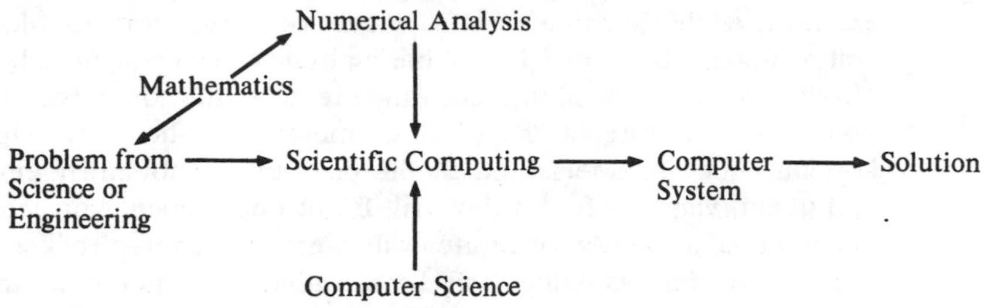

FIGURE 1.1 *Scientific Computing and Related Areas.*

for the efficient and correct use of a large computer system. Many of these considerations—programming languages, operating systems, management of large quantities of data, correctness of programs, and so forth—were subsumed under the new discipline of computer science, on which scientific computing now depends heavily. But mathematics itself continues to play a major role in scientific computing: it provides the language of the mathematical models that are to be solved and information about the suitability of a model—Does it have a solution? Is the solution unique?—and it provides the theoretical foundation for the numerical methods and, increasingly, many of the tools from computer science.

In summary, then, scientific computing draws on mathematics and computer science to develop the best ways to use computer systems to solve problems from science and engineering. This relationship is depicted schematically in Figure 1.1. In the remainder of this chapter, we will go a little deeper into these various areas.

1.2 Mathematical Modeling

As discussed in Section 1.1, we view scientific computing as the discipline that achieves a computer solution of mathematical models of problems from science and engineering. Hence, the first step in the overall solution process is the formulation of a suitable mathematical model of the problem at hand. This is a part of the discipline in which the problem arises; that is, engineers devise models for engineering problems, biologists for biological problems, and so forth. Sometimes mathematicians are involved in this modeling process, at least as consultants, but, unfortunately, the art of mathematical modeling has increasingly fallen outside the purview of present-day mathematicians.

The formulation of a mathematical model begins with a statement of the factors to be considered. In many physical problems, these factors concern the balance of forces and other conservation laws of physics. For example, in the formulation of a model of a trajectory problem—which will be done in Section 2.1—the basic physical law brought to bear will be Newton's second law of motion, which requires that the forces acting on a body equal the rate of change of momentum of the body. This general law must then be specialized to the particular problem by enumerating and quantifying the forces that will be of importance. For example, the gravitational attraction of Jupiter will exert a force on a rocket in Earth's atmosphere, but its effect will be so minuté compared to the earth's gravitational force that it can be safely neglected. Other forces may also be small compared to the dominant ones but their effects not so easily dismissed, and the construction of the model will invariably be a compromise between retaining all factors that could likely have a bearing on the validity of the model and keeping the mathematical model sufficiently simple that it is solvable using the tools at hand. Classically, only very simple models of most phenomena were considered since the solutions had to be achieved by hand, either analytically or numerically. As the power of computers and numerical methods have developed, increasingly complicated models have become tractable.

In addition to the basic relations of the model—which in many if not most situations in scientific computing take the form of differential equations—there usually will be a number of initial, boundary, and side conditions. For example, in the predator–prey problem to be discussed in Chapter 2, the initial population of the two species being studied is specified. Boundary conditions are usually a natural part of the problem; for example, in studying the flow in a blood vessel, we require that the flow cannot penetrate the walls of the vessel. In other cases, boundary conditions may not be so physically evident but are still required so that the mathematical problem has a unique solution. Or the mathematical model as first formulated may indeed have many solutions, the one of interest to be selected by some side condition such as the solution be positive, or that it be the solution with minimum energy.

In any case, it is usually assumed that the final mathematical model with all appropriate initial, boundary, and side conditions indeed has a unique solution. The next step, then, is to find this solution. For problems of current interest, such solutions rarely can be obtained in "closed form." The solution must be approximated by some method, and the methods to be considered in this book—and increasingly in practice almost to the exclusion of other classical approximation methods—are numerical methods suitable for a computer. In the next section, we will consider the steps to be taken to achieve a numerical solution in a general way, and the remainder of the book will be devoted to a detailed discussion of these steps for a number of different problems.

Once we are able to compute solutions of the model, the next step usually is called the *validation of the model*. By this, we mean a verification that the solution we compute is sufficiently accurate to serve the purposes for which the model was constructed. There are two main sources of possible error. First, there invariably are errors in the numerical solution. The general nature of these errors will be discussed in the next section, and one of the major themes in the remainder of the book will be a deeper understanding of the source and control of these numerical errors. But there is also invariably an error in the model itself. As mentioned previously, this is a necessary aspect of modeling: the modeler has attempted to take into account all the factors in the physical problem but then, in order to keep the model tractable, has neglected or approximated those factors that would seem to have a small effect on the solution. The question is whether neglecting these effects was justified.

The first test of the validity of the model is whether the solution looks at all reasonable. For example, if the problem is to compute a rocket trajectory where the expected maximum height is 100 kilometers and the computed solution shows heights of 200 kilometers, obviously some blunder has been committed. Once such gross errors are eliminated—which is usually fairly easy—the next phase begins, which is, whenever possible, comparison of the computed results with whatever experimental or observational data are available. Many times this is a subtle undertaking, since even though the experimental results may have been obtained in a controlled setting, the physics of the experiment may be different from the mathematical model. For example, the mathematical model of airflow over an aircraft wing will usually assume the idealization of an aircraft flying in an infinite atmosphere, whereas the corresponding experimental results will be obtained from a wind tunnel where there will be effects from the walls of the enclosure. (Note that neither the experiment nor the mathematical model represents the true situation of an aircraft flying in our finite atmosphere.) It is the experience and intuition of the investigator that is required to make a human judgment as to whether the results from the mathematical model are corresponding sufficiently well with observational data.

At the outset of an investigation, this is quite often not the case, and the model must be modified. Usually this means that additional terms—which were thought negligible but may not be—are added to the model. Sometimes it requires a complete revision of the model and the physical situation approached from an entirely different point of view. In any case, once the model is modified, the cycle begins again: a new numerical solution, revalidation, additional modifications, and so on. This process is depicted schematically in Figure 1.2.

Once the model is deemed adequate from the validation and modification process, it is ready to be used for prediction. This, of course, was the whole purpose. We should now be able to answer the questions that gave rise to the modeling effort: How high will the rocket go? Will the wolves eat all the rabbits? and so forth. Of course, we must always take the answers with a healthy skepticism. Our physical world is simply

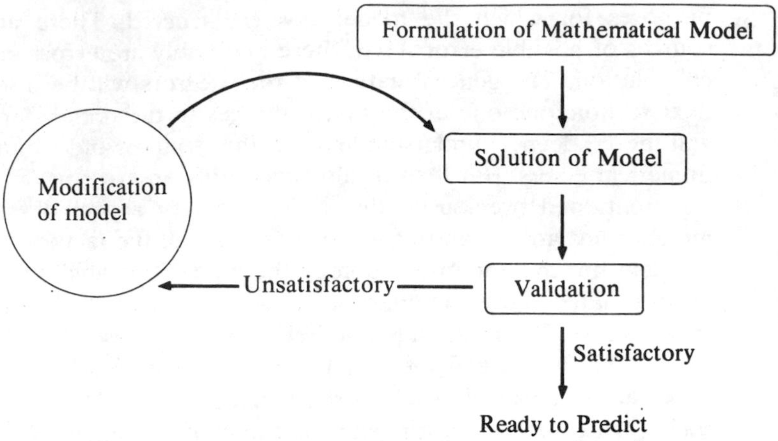

FIGURE 1.2 *The Mathematical Modeling and Solution Process.*

too complicated and our knowledge of it too meager for us to be able to predict the future perfectly. Nevertheless, we hope that our computer solutions will give us increased insight into the problem being studied, be it a physical phenomenon or an engineering design.

1.3 The Process of Numerical Solution

We will discuss in this section the general considerations that arise in the computer solution of a mathematical model, and in the remainder of the book these matters will be made more specific.

Once the mathematical model is given, our first thought usually is to try to obtain an explicit closed-form solution, but such a solution will usually only be possible for certain (perhaps drastic) simplifications of the problem. These simplified problems with known solutions may be of great utility in providing "check cases" for the more general problem.

After realizing that explicit solutions are not possible, we then turn to the task of developing a numerical method for the solution. Implicit in our thinking at the outset—and increasingly explicit as the development proceeds—will be the computing equipment as well as the software environment that is at our disposal. Our approach may be quite different for a minicomputer than for a very large computer. But usually these differences in approach will be of degree rather than of kind, and certain general factors must be considered regardless of the computer to be used.

Perhaps the most important factor in scientific computing is that computers deal with a finite number of digits or characters. Because of this, we cannot, in general, do arithmetic within the real number system as we become accustomed to in pure mathematics. That is, the arithmetic done by a computer is restricted to finitely many digits whereas the numerical representation of most real numbers requires infinitely many. For example, such fundamental constants as π and e require an infinite number of digits for a numerical representation and can *never* be entered exactly in a computer. Moreover, even if we could start with numbers that have an exact numerical representation in the computer, the processes of arithmetic require that eventually we make certain errors. For example, the quotient of two four-digit numbers may require infinitely many digits for its numerical representation. And even the product of two four-digit numbers will, in general, require eight digits, so as several multiplications are performed, the number of digits required to keep the result exact quickly gets out of hand. For example, assuming four-digit decimal arithmetic, $0.8132 \times 0.6135 = 0.49889820$ will be represented by 0.4988 or 0.4989 depending on the computer. Therefore, we resign ourselves at the outset to the fact that we cannot do arithmetic exactly on a computer. We shall make small errors, called *rounding errors*, on almost all arithmetic operations, and our task is to insure that these small errors do not accumulate so badly as to invalidate the computation.

More precisely, each machine has a word length consisting of the number of binary digits contained in each memory word, and this word length determines the number of digits that can be carried in the usual arithmetic, called single-precision arithmetic, of the machine. On most scientific computers, this is the equivalent of between 7 and 14 decimal digits. *Higher-precision* arithmetic can also be carried out. On many machines, *double-precision* arithmetic, which essentially doubles the number of digits that are carried, is a part of the hardware; in this case, programs with double-precision arithmetic usually require only modest, if any, increases in execution times compared to single-precision versions, and rarely require twice as much time. Fortunately, most current large-scale computers with short word lengths have very efficient double-precision arithmetic. On the other hand, some machines implement double precision by software and require several times as much time as single precision. Precision higher than double is always carried out by means of software and becomes increasingly inefficient as the precision increases. Higher-precision arithmetic is rarely used on practical problems.

Round-off errors can affect the final computed result in different ways. First, during a sequence of millions of operations each subject to a small error, there is the danger that these small errors will accumulate so as to eliminate much of the accuracy in the computed result. If we round to the nearest digit, the individual errors will tend to cancel out, but the standard deviation of the accumulated error will tend to increase with the number of operations, leaving the possibility of a large final error. If chopping—that is, dropping the trailing digits rather than rounding—is used, there is a bias to errors in one direction, and the possibility of a large final error is increased. As an example of this phenomenon, consider the computation $0.8132 \times 0.6135 \times 0.2103 = 0.10491829$ correct to ten digits. Chopping the product of the first two numbers to four digits yields 0.4988, with an error of 0.9820×10^{-4}. Multiplying 0.4988 by 0.2103 gives 0.1048 after chopping, with an error of 0.9764×10^{-4}. The accumulated error is 0.1183×10^{-3}.

In addition to this possible accumulation of errors over a large number of operations, there is the danger of *catastrophic cancellation.* Suppose that two numbers a and b are equal to within their last digits. Then the difference $c = a - b$ will have only one significant digit of accuracy *even though no round-off error will be made in the subtraction.* Future calculations with c will then usually limit the final result to one correct digit. Whenever possible, one tries to eliminate the possibility of catastrophic cancellation by rearranging the operations.

Catastrophic cancellation is one way in which an algorithm can be *numerically unstable,* although in exact arithmetic it may be a correct algorithm. Indeed, it is possible for the results of a computation to be completely erroneous because of round-off error even though only a small number of arithmetic operations have been performed. Examples of this will be given later.

Detailed round-off error analyses have now been completed for a number of the simpler and more basic algorithms such as those that occur in the solution of linear systems of equations; some of these results will be described in more detail in Chapter 3. A particular type of analysis that has proved to be very powerful is *backward error analysis.* In this approach, the round-off errors are shown to have the same effect as that caused by perturbations to the original problem data. When this analysis is possible, it can be stated that the error in the solution caused by round off is no worse than that caused by certain errors in the original model. The question of errors in the solution is then equivalent to the study of the sensitivity of the solution to perturbations in the model.

Another way that the finiteness of computers manifests itself in causing errors in numerical computation is due to the need to replace "continuous" problems by "discrete" ones. As a simple example, the integral of a continuous function requires knowledge of the integrand along the whole interval of integration, that is, at infinitely many points, whereas a computer approximation to the integral can use values of the integrand at only finitely many points. Hence, even if the subsequent arithmetic were done exactly with no rounding errors, there would still be the error due to the discrete approximation to the integral. This type of error is usually called *discretization error* or *truncation error* and it affects, except in trivial cases, all numerical solutions of differential equations and other "continuous" problems.

There is one more general type of error which is somewhat akin to discretization error. Many numerical methods are based on the idea of an *iterative process.* In such a process, a sequence of approximations to a solution is generated with the hope that the approximations will converge to the solution; in many cases, mathematical proofs of the convergence can be given. However, only finitely many such approximations can ever be generated on a computer, and, therefore, we must necessarily stop short of mathematical convergence. The error caused by such finite termination of an iterative process is sometimes called *convergence error* although there is no generally accepted terminology here.

If we rule out trivial problems that are of no interest in scientific computing, we can summarize the situation with respect to computational errors as follows. Every calculation will be subject to rounding error. Whenever the mathematical model of the problem is a differential equation or other "continuous" problem, there also will be discretization error, and in many cases, especially when the problem is nonlinear, there will be convergence error. These types of errors and methods of analyzing and controlling them will be discussed more fully in concrete situations throughout the remainder of the book.

The other major consideration besides accuracy in the development of computer methods for the solution of mathematical models is *efficiency*. By this, we will mean the amount of effort—both human and computer—required to solve a given problem. For most problems, such as solving a system of linear algebraic equations, there are a variety of possible methods, some going back many tens or even hundreds of years. Clearly, we would like to choose a method that minimizes the computing time while at the same time retaining suitable accuracy in the approximate solution. This turns out to be a surprisingly difficult problem which involves a number of considerations. Although it is frequently possible to estimate the computing time of an algorithm by counting the required arithmetic operations, the question of how, with minimal running time and/or computations, to solve a problem to a given tolerance is still an open question except in a few cases. Even if one ignores the effects of round-off error, surprisingly little is known. In the past few years, these questions have spawned the subject of *computational complexity*. However, even if such theoretical results were known, they would still give only approximations to the actual computing time, which depends on a number of factors involving the computer system: the size and speed of the main and secondary memories, the number of references to secondary memory, and the characteristics of the operating system. And these considerations continue to change as the result of new systems and architectures. Indeed, the design and analysis of numerical algorithms should provide incentives and directions for such changes.

We give a simple example of the way a very inefficient method can arise. Many elementary textbooks on matrix theory or linear algebra present Cramer's rule for solving systems of linear equations. This rule involves quotients of certain determinants, and the definition of a determinant is usually given as the sum of all possible products of elements of the matrix, one element from each row and each column. There are $n!$ such products. Now, if we proceeded to carry out the computation of a determinant based on a straightforward implementation of this definition, it would require $(n - 1)n!$ multiplications and $n!$ additions. If we apply this method to very small matrices, say 3×3 or 4×4, nothing amiss will happen. Suppose, however, we apply it to a 20×20 matrix, a very small size in current scientific computing. If we assume that each arithmetic operation requires 1 microsecond (10^{-6} second), then the time required for this calculation—even ignoring all overhead operations in the computer program—will exceed one million years! On the other hand, the Gaussian elimination method, which will be discussed in Chapter 3, will do the arithmetic operations for the solution of a 20×20 linear system in less than 0.005 second, again assuming 1 microsecond per operation. Although this is an extreme example, it does forcefully illustrate the difficulties that can occur by naively following a mathematical prescription for solving a problem on a computer.

But even if a method is intrinsically "good," it is extremely important to implement the corresponding computer code in the best possible way, especially if other people are to use it. Some of the criteria for a good code are the following:

1. *Reliability*—the code does not have errors and can be trusted to compute what it is supposed to compute.
2. *Robustness*, which is closely related to reliability—the code has the ability to detect bad data, "singular" or other problems that it cannot be expected to handle, and other abnormal situations, and deal with them in a way that is satisfactory to the user.
3. *Portability*—the code can be transferred from one computer to another with a minimum effort and without losing reliability. Usually this means that the code has been written in a general high-level language like FORTRAN and uses no "tricks" that are dependent on the characteristics of a particular computer. Any machine characteristics, such as word length, that must be used are clearly delineated.
4. *Maintainability*—any code will necessarily need to be changed from time to time, either to make corrections or to add enhancements.

The code should be written in a clear and straightforward way so that such changes can be made easily and with a minimum likelihood of creating new errors. An important part of maintainability is that there be good *documentation* of the program so that it can be changed in an efficient way by individuals who did not write the code originally. Good documentation is also very important so that the program user will understand how to use the code, its capabilities and limitations, and so on. Finally, extensive *testing* of the program must be done to ensure that the preceding criteria have been met.

The subarea of mathematics and computer science that deals with the development of good computer programs for mathematical problems is known as *mathematical software.* There are now very high quality codes for a number of mathematical problems, in particular, the solution of linear systems of equations, computation of matrix eigenvalues, and solution of initial-value problems for ordinary differential equations.

1.4 The Impact of Computer Science on Scientific Computing

As indicated in the last section, there is usually a long road from a mathematical method to a successful computer program. In addition to the tools needed to produce good mathematical software, there are a number of other areas of computer science that play an increasingly important role in scientific computing.

Obviously, the environment of hardware and basic software is of utmost importance. Computer architecture is in the midst of a revolution, and the potential impact of low-cost microprocessors interconnected in large arrays is an exciting possibility. Already, successful use of array processors, such as the Illiac IV, and vector computers such as the CRAY-1 and CDC CYBER 200 series, has required a reexamination of numerical methods for such machines. If arrays of microprocessors should become commonplace, a drastic review of numerical methods will become necessary if they are to be efficient.

Almost all computer programming for scientific computing is done in a *high-level programming language* such as FORTRAN, ALGOL, PASCAL and so on. Of these, FORTRAN has remained the primary programming language for scientific computing since its development in the mid 1950s, and has been continually modified and extended (and some would even say improved). More recently, a number of "FORTRAN preprocessors" have been developed which allow the use of features not part of the FORTRAN language itself; programs written in these extended languages are then first "precompiled" into a FORTRAN program suitable for a standard compiler. Further developments in programming languages for scientific computing are to be expected, especially in regard to still higher level languages.

Many of the problems in scientific computing require huge amounts of data, both input and output as well as data generated during the course of the computation. The storing and retrieving of these data in an efficient manner is called *data management.* As an example of this in the area of computer-aided design, the data base containing all information relevant to a particular design application—which might be for an aircraft, an automobile, a dam, and so forth—may contain several billion characters. In an aircraft design, this information would include everything relevant about the geometry of each part of the aircraft, the material properties of each part, and so on. An engineer may use this data base simply to find all materials with a certain property. On the other hand, the data base will also be used in doing various analyses of the structural properties of the aircraft, which requires the solution of certain partial differential equations. Large data management programs for use in such business applications as inventory control have been developed over the past several years, and some of the techniques used there are now being applied to the management of large data bases for scientific computation.

In addition to the preceding areas of computer science, there are two more—computer graphics and symbolic computation—that we will discuss in more detail.

The results of a scientific computation are numbers that may represent, for example, the solution of a differential equation at certain selected points. Typically, these numbers are recorded in the form of tables, or other representations, by means of high-speed printers. However, the volume of such information may be overwhelming, and it is usually much more efficient for the engineer or scientist doing the computation to have these results presented in the form of graphs, curves, or other types of pictures whenever possible. For example, output that represents a complicated function or a physical structure such as a vehicle is most useful when viewed pictorially (see Figures 1.3 and 1.4). For many years, mechanical plotters have routinely given this type of output for certain computations. More recently, cathode ray tubes and other types of visual terminals have become increasingly available. The use of these

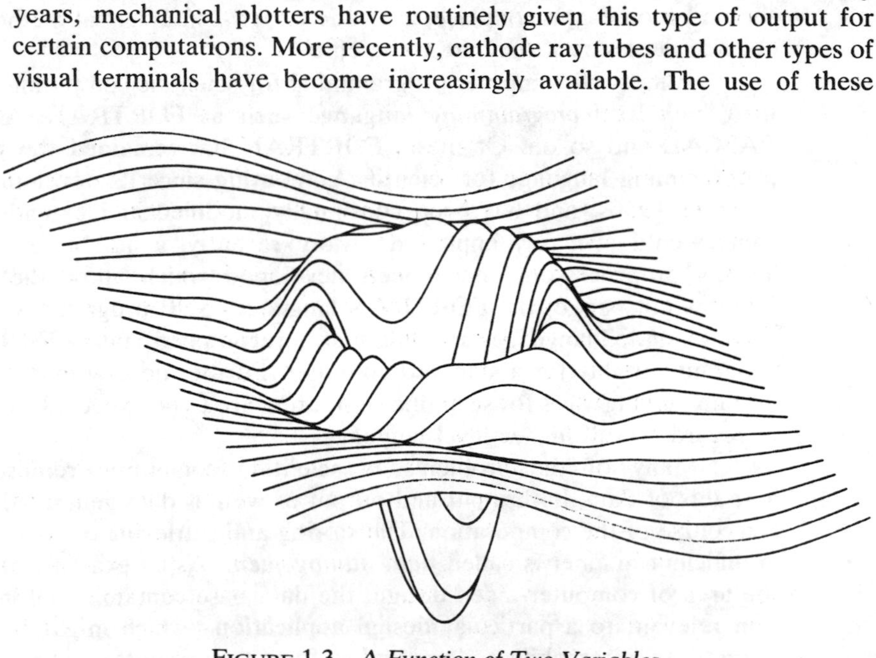

FIGURE 1.3 *A Function of Two Variables.*

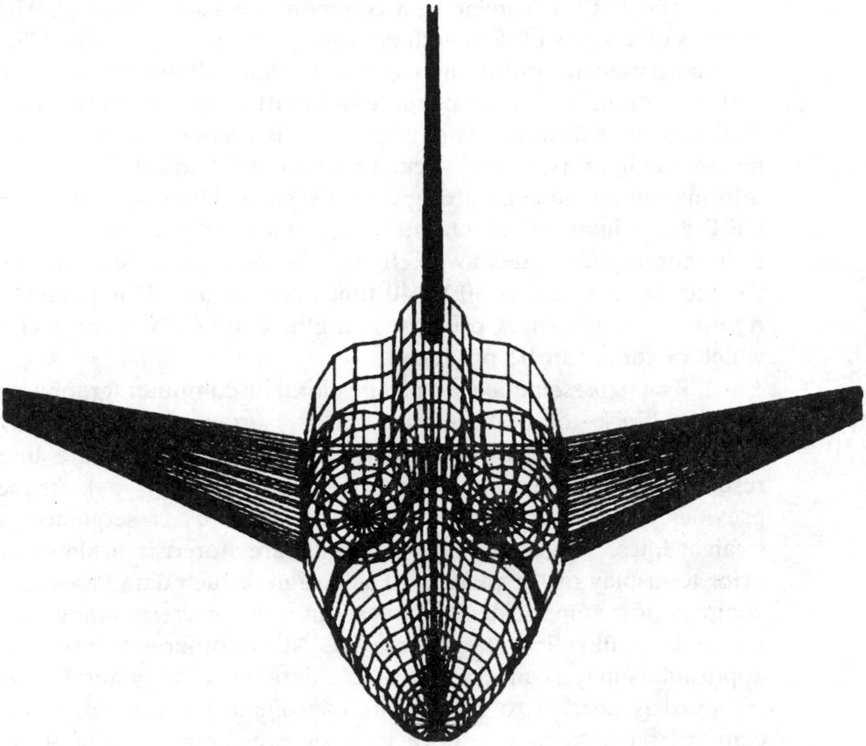

FIGURE 1.4 *A View of a Single-Stage Orbiter.*

devices for pictorial output (as well as input in certain cases) is known as *computer graphics.* An especially important development has been interactive graphics, which allows the problem solver to monitor the course of a computation and make changes or corrections on the spot, if necessary.

There are many different types of *graphical output devices,* but we will limit our discussion to two common types—the drum incremental plotter, which uses a pen and ink, and the televisionlike cathode ray tube (CRT). (Other types include the line printer, flat-bed plotter, dot matrix plotter, and plasma panels, to name a few.) The pen of the drum plotter moves up and down the paper which is on the wall of a drum or cylinder. Lengthwise motion is obtained by rolling the paper backward and forward under the pen. These basic motions are usually combined to allow eight directions of movement. Because of this limit, a curve must be represented by a sequence of several small straight lines. The minimum step length is usually between 0.001 and 0.01 inch. A plotter produces high-quality hard copy (paper). However, it is very slow compared to the CRT.

The CRT is similar to a common television monitor. The display consists of a series of dots with phosphor for lighting up. The CRT display is usually used in an interactive mode, which allows the user to interact with the computer for the purpose of inputting or modifying data, making decisions, or whatever. This interaction is carried out by the user via a keyboard, light pen, joy stick, or other mechanical device to provide information to the computer graphics system. The major weakness of the CRT is its inability to maintain a picture on the screen because the phosphor rapidly fades away. It then becomes necessary to reconstruct the picture as often as 30 to 40 times per second. This process is called *refreshing the screen.* A primary strength of the CRT is the high speed at which pictures can be produced.

The *representation of picture data* in computer graphics uses the building blocks of points, lines, curves, surfaces, and text material. A point is represented by a coordinate triple, (x, y, z), and a line is represented by a pair of end points, (x_1, y_1, z_1) and (x_2, y_2, z_2). As mentioned previously, a curve is usually approximated by a sequence of short, straight lines. The coordinates of points are stored in a file or data base prior to display of the pictures. The design of such data bases can be very complex for complicated pictures, and the corresponding access and processing will reflect the complexity. At the other extreme, very simple applications may require fairly simple data bases. In general, one computer word is needed to specify the coordinate position of a point. Very complex pictures may require tens, or even hundreds, of thousands of points, thus straining the storage capacity of modest computer systems.

There are many types of *data processing* and *manipulation* of a graphics data base. The locations of the basic elements of the data base—points—may be specified in two different ways. An absolute specification assumes that there is some fixed global coordinate system. A relative specification gives the displacement with respect to a previously referenced point. The three basic manipulative operations found in most graphics devices are moving the pen, cursor, light beam, or plotting head to a specified point; drawing a line to a specified point; and drawing a dot at a point.

Another manipulative operation occurs when the picture to be displayed is just a portion, a certain rotated view, or a smaller size of the structure represented in the data base. Thus, one often transforms the data base or part of it. The transformation may be algebraic or trigonometric in nature such as a rotation through an angle θ about the origin in counterclockwise direction, a reflection that can be interpreted as a 180° rotation about some axis, a scaling that changes the magnitude of the coordinates, or a translation in the coordinate system. And the transformations may be in two or three dimensions. Most of the transformations are implemented as matrix operations.

There are two major parts to computer graphics software systems.

One part is the data base manipulative software which performs the operations discussed previously, such as rotation and scaling. These are mathematical operations and are generally device independent. The other major part of the software system is for controlling the graphics device. This part causes information to be sent to the graphics device for moving the cursor, drawing a line, plotting points, and so on. At the lowest level, this software is device dependent because, for example, the coordinates of a point must be expressed in a form that is compatible with hardware instructions. At one level up—moving the cursor to a point, drawing a line—the software may be device independent.

The programming required by the computer graphics user is quite different from programming required for numerical methods. However, basically it has the same general goal—to give instructions to the computer for execution. A set of low-level instructions to a CRT interactive display might resemble the following:

```
.
.
.
TURN CURSOR ON
SET COORDINATE MODE TO 'ABSOLUTE'
MOVE CURSOR TO (23.1, -16.4)
TURN CURSOR OFF
.
.
.
```

Instructions for plotters usually are subroutine calls.

We turn next to the final topic of this section—*symbolic computation*—which refers to the capability to manipulate mathematical expressions in a symbolic (as opposed to numerical) way, much as one does with pencil and paper. For example, symbolic computation systems can add, multiply, and divide polynomials or rational expressions; differentiate expressions; integrate many expressions that have a "closed-form" integral; and so on. This capability has great potential as a means of relieving the drudgery of manipulations by hand of lengthy algebraic expressions, perhaps as a prelude to a subsequent numerical computation. Several symbolic computation systems are now being used throughout the scientific computing community; they are continually increasing in efficiency and capability, and an expansion of their use is expected in the future.

Perhaps the differences in numerical and symbolic computation are best understood by examining a simple calculation. The example to be used is the calculation of the *Chebyshev polynomials of the first kind.* They are defined by

$$T_n(x) = \cos(n \arccos x), \qquad -1 \leq x \leq 1$$

although a two-term recurrence relation is of more practical value:

$$T_0(x) = 1$$
$$T_1(x) = x$$
$$T_{j+1}(x) = 2xT_j(x) - T_{j-1}(x), \qquad j = 1, 2, \ldots$$

A pseudo-FORTRAN code for evaluating the first 20 Chebyshev polynomials might look like this:

```
      DIMENSION T(20)
         .
         .
         .
      INPUT X
         .
         .
         .
      T(1) = 1.
      T(2) = X
      DO 10 J = 2,19
         T(J + 1) = 2. * X * T(J) - T(J - 1)
   10 CONTINUE
         .
         .
         .
      OUTPUT T
         .
         .
         .
```

The program segment will evaluate the Chebyshev polynomials for a given value of X. If, for example, X = 0.6, the output will be

```
T(1) = 1.
T(2) = 0.6
T(3) = -0.28
T(4) = -0.936
   .
   .
   .
```

Note that the numerically oriented FORTRAN program evaluates the polynomials for a particular value of X. If the values are needed for another value of X, the program must be executed again with that new value of X.

On the other hand, a symbolic computation system is able to represent the variable X as a symbol and carry out the prescribed operations in the unknown X as the loop is executed. The output of a symbolic computation system might be

```
T(1) = 1
T(2) = X
T(3) = 2*X**2 - 1
T(4) = 4*X**3 - 3*X
  .
  .
  .
```

This example clearly demonstrates one of the primary differences between a numerical calculation using a numerically oriented language such as FORTRAN and a symbolic computation: in a symbolic system, variables and expressions have symbolic (or algebraic) values instead of numerical values. Another important difference is that the symbolic representation is exact rather than approximate.

There are several different symbolic systems now available. Those that have FORTRAN- or ALGOL-like syntax would generate the Chebyshev polynomials with a segment of code that would look very much like the FORTRAN code described. Only the output would differ, On the other hand, many symbolic systems have syntax that is quite different from that of FORTRAN. For example, one of the most widely used systems is called MACSYMA, which was developed at the Massachusetts Institute of Technology.

Commonly used symbolic computation systems offer a wide range of capabilities, and we will describe some of the more important ones for scientific applications.

In a manner analogous to FORTRAN, symbolic systems have (symbolic) *expressions* and *operations*. For example, we can define an expression by

```
EXPR: X↑2 + (Y - 6)*Z
```

and EXPR will be displayed as

$$(Y - 6)Z + X^2$$

Symbolic substitutions can be made by

```
EXPR, X = SIN(A), Y = LOG(A)
```

which yields

$$(\mathrm{LOG}(A) - 6)Z + \mathrm{SIN}^2 A$$

Symbolic matrices are available:

M: MATRIX([A, B, C], [1, 2, 3], [1.7, X, Y])

which defines the matrix row by row:

$$M = \begin{bmatrix} A & B & C \\ 1 & 2 & 3 \\ 1.7 & X & Y \end{bmatrix}$$

Also, matrix operations like M^2 and M^{-1} can be symbolically generated. Generally, M^{-1} can only be computed for small-size matrices because of the complexity of the calculation.

There are many symbolic operations that can be applied to expressions. Let us redefine EXPR as

EXPR: (X + 3) * (X + 7)↑4 − X↑3 * (X + 2)↑2

Then EXPR might appear as

$$(X + 3)(X + 7)^4 - X^3(X + 2)^2$$

EXPAND (EXPR) is an operator with an obvious function:

$$27X^4 + 374X^3 + 2254X^2 + 6517X + 7203$$

To demonstrate some of the other features of symbolic systems, let Y be

$$\frac{2}{X + 2} - \frac{1}{X + 1} - \frac{X}{(X + 1)^2}$$

A simplification command, V: SIMPLIFY (Y), might generate

$$-\frac{X}{X^3 + 4X^2 + 5X + 2}$$

A partial fraction representation, W: PARFRACT (V),

$$\frac{2}{X + 2} + \frac{-2X - 1}{(X + 1)^2}$$

can be further modified by Z: FACTOR (W):

$$-\frac{X}{(X + 1)^2(X + 2)}$$

In conjunction with FACTOR, a SOLVE function is commonly used: SOLVE (Y = 0, X) yields

$$X = 0$$

A different class of functions consists of SUM and PRODUCT. SUM(I^{-4}, I = 1, INFINITY) may be expressed as a formal sum: .

$$\sum_{I=1}^{INF} \frac{1}{I^4}$$

or one may ask that the summation actually be performed, in which case the system would output

$$\frac{(PI)^4}{90}$$

Analogously, products can be represented and performed.

Many of the operations of calculus are available in symbolic systems. For example, if Y is

$$\frac{X^{5/2}}{LOG(X + 1)TAN(X^{3/2})}$$

then LIMIT (Y, X→0) yields 1 and LIMIT (X * LOG(X), X→0^+) is 0. To demonstrate differentiation and integration, let

$$Y = \frac{X}{X^3 + 1}$$

Now Z = INTEGRATE (Y, X) will yield

$$\frac{LOG(X^2 - X + 1)}{6} + \frac{ARCTAN\left(\frac{2X - 1}{SQRT(3)}\right)}{SQRT(3)} - \frac{LOG(X + 1)}{3}$$

One could check the answer by DIFFERENTIATE (Z). This result might need to be simplified to return it to the original form.

As another example, the command

INTEGRATE (T↑2 * SIN(T)↑12 * COS(T)↑8,T,−PI,PI)

would be asking the system to find

$$\int_{-\pi}^{\pi} T^2 \, COS^8(T) SIN^{12}(T) \, dT$$

which might be returned in exact form as

$$\frac{77\ PI^3}{393216} - \frac{45261359\ PI}{23781703800}$$

and could be converted (by the system) to

$$5.4737758E - 3$$

Infinite integrals can also be handled as demonstrated by

INTEGRATE (1/(X↑2 + 5)↑(3/2),X,O,INF)

which asks for

$$\int_0^\infty \frac{1}{(X^2 + 5)^{3/2}}\, dx$$

which is 1/5. In conjunction with the INTEGRATE command, many of the manipulative operations like EXPAND, SIMPLIFY, and FACTOR are often used.

In this section, we have discussed briefly some of the areas of computer science that are having an increasing impact on scientific computing and the solution of differential equations. In the remainder of the book, we will point out in various places where these techniques can be profitably used although it will be beyond the scope of the book to pursue their application in detail.

Supplementary Discussion and References for 1.4

A good introduction to the principles of computer graphics may be found in Newman and Sproul [1979]. For additional reading, see Chasen [1978], Giloi [1978], Hirt and Cook [1975], Rogers and Adams [1976], and Walker, Gurd, and Drawneek [1976]. There are a number of different graphics systems, and the potential user should consult the local computer center to ascertain what is available in both equipment and software.

Symbolic computation systems first became available during the middle 1960s, but it was the early 1970s before several different systems were readily accessible to many users. The primary motivation for the development of the first systems was scientific (primarily physics) and mathematical applications. Considerable effort is currently being expended to improve existing systems and develop new ones. A common weakness of symbolic systems is that they are very machine dependent.

Each system usually runs on only one type of computer, and thus there is very little portability of systems from computer to computer. Another weakness is that it is difficult to connect a symbolic system directly to a more common programming language such as FORTRAN or PASCAL.

Some of the more widely known symbolic computation systems are ALTRAN (Brown [1973]), FORMAC (Tobey et al. [1969]), MACSYMA Anonymous [1977]), REDUCE (Hearn [1973]), and SCRATCHPAD (Jenks [1974]). A review of the use of symbolic computation systems in scientific computing can be found in Hearn [1976], where an example quite similar to the one in this section is given, but using Legendre rather than Chebyshev polynomials.

A collection of review articles on various aspects of the impact of computer science on scientific computing can be found in Ortega [1976].

2 Initial-Value Problems in Ordinary Differential Equations

2.1 Examples of Initial-Value Problems

In this section, we shall derive the mathematical models for two initial-value problems, one from the field of ecology and the other with aerospace applications.

A Predator–Prey Problem

Let us consider the population dynamics of two interacting species that have a predator–prey relationship. That is, the prey is able to find sufficient food but is killed by the predator whenever they encounter each other. Examples of such species interactions are wolves and rabbits, and parasites and certain hosts. What we want to investigate is how the predator and prey populations vary with time. Predator–prey relationships have received considerable attention from both ecologists and mathematicians.

Let $x = x(t)$ and $y = y(t)$ designate the number of prey and predators, respectively, at time t. To derive mathematical equations that approximate the population dynamics, we make several simplifying assumptions. First, we assume that the prey's birthrate, x_b, and natural death rate (exclusive of predator killing), x_d, are constant with $x_b > x_d$. Thus, the prey population, if left alone, increases at the rate $(x_b - x_d)x$. Second, we assume that the number of times that the predator kills the prey depends on the chance probability of the two coming together and is therefore proportional to xy. Combining these two assumptions, the prey population is governed by the ordinary differential equation

$$\frac{dx}{dt} = \alpha x + \beta xy \tag{2.1.1}$$

where $\alpha \equiv x_b - x_d > 0$ and $\beta < 0$.

In order to derive the predator equation, we assume that the number of predators would decrease by natural causes if the prey were removed, contributing a γy term. However, the number of predators increases as a result of encounters with prey, leading to

$$\frac{dy}{dt} = \gamma y + \delta xy \tag{2.1.2}$$

with $\gamma < 0$ and $\delta > 0$. In summary, we have the nonlinear system of two ordinary differential equations

$$\frac{dx}{dt} = \alpha x + \beta xy \qquad \frac{dy}{dt} = \gamma y + \delta xy \tag{2.1.3}$$

with the assumptions $\alpha > 0$, $\beta < 0$, $\gamma < 0$, and $\delta > 0$. These equations were first formulated in 1925 and are known as the *Lotka–Volterra equations.* The problem statement is not complete; we must start the process at some time (for example, $t = 0$) with given values for initial populations $x(0)$ and $y(0)$. Thus we supplement the differential equations by two *initial conditions*:

$$x(0) = x_0 \qquad y(0) = y_0 \tag{2.1.4}$$

A Trajectory Problem

Suppose that a rocket is launched at a given angle of inclination to the ground (the launch angle). How high will the rocket go? The answer depends on a number of factors: the characteristics of the rocket and its engine, the drag caused by air density, the gravitational forces, and so on.

To set up a mathematical model for this problem, we will make a number of simplifying assumptions. First, we shall consider only rockets going to a height and range of, perhaps, 100 kilometers; in this case, we can assume that the earth is flat with little loss of accuracy. Second, we shall assume that the trajectory of the rocket lies entirely in a plane; for example, we assume no wind effects, and so forth. With these two assumptions, we set up a two-dimensional coordinate system centered at the launching site, and in Figure 2.1, we depict a typical trajectory.

As shown in Figure 2.1, $x(t)$ and $y(t)$ denote the x and y coordinates of the rocket at time t where we assume that launch occurs at $t = 0$,

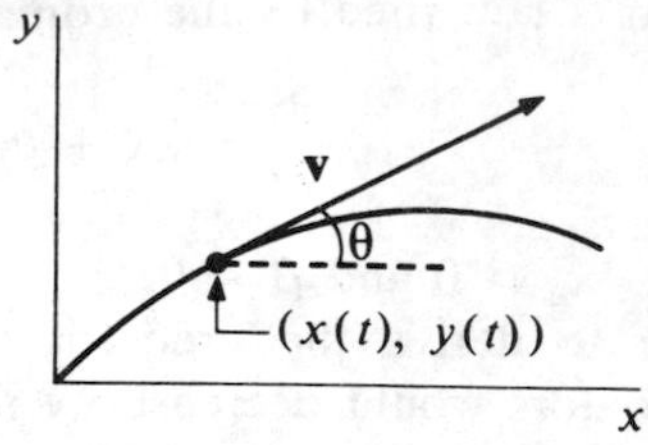

FIGURE 2.1 *A Typical Trajectory.*

and, hence,

(2.1.5) $$x(0) = y(0) = 0$$

If we denote differentiation with respect to time by $\dot{x} = dx/dt$ and $\dot{y} = dy/dt$, then the velocity vector of the rocket at time t is $\mathbf{v}(t) = (\dot{x}(t), \dot{y}(t))$. We denote the magnitude of the velocity vector by $v(t)$ and its angle from the horizontal by $\theta(t)$, as shown in Figure 2.1. These quantities are then given by

(2.1.6) $$v(t) = [(\dot{x}(t))^2 + (\dot{y}(t))^2]^{1/2} \qquad \theta(t) = \tan^{-1} \frac{\dot{y}(t)}{\dot{x}(t)}$$

The basic mathematical model of the trajectory is derived from Newton's laws of motion, which give

(2.1.7) $$\frac{d}{dt}(m\mathbf{v}) = F.$$

Here, $m(t)$ is the mass of the rocket, and F denotes the forces acting on the rocket and is composed of three terms: (1) the thrust, $T(t)$, when the rocket engine is firing; (2) the drag force

(2.1.8) $$\tfrac{1}{2}c\rho s v^2$$

where c is the coefficient of drag, ρ is air density, and s is the cross-sectional area of the rocket; and (3) the gravitational force, gm, where g is the acceleration of gravity.

To write (2.1.7) in terms of x and y, we note that the part of the force F that consists of the thrust and the drag acts along the axis of the rocket. If we call this part F_1, then

(2.1.9) $$F_1 = T - \tfrac{1}{2}c\rho s v^2$$

and (2.1.7) can be written

(2.1.10) $$\dot{m}\dot{x} + m\ddot{x} = F_1 \cos\theta \qquad \dot{m}\dot{y} + m\ddot{y} = F_1 \sin\theta - mg$$

since the gravitational force acts only in the vertical direction. Using

(2.1.9) and rearranging terms, we rewrite (2.1.10) as

(2.1.11)
$$\ddot{x} = \frac{1}{m}(T - \tfrac{1}{2}c\rho s v^2)\cos\theta - \frac{\dot{m}}{m}\dot{x}$$
$$\ddot{y} = \frac{1}{m}(T - \tfrac{1}{2}c\rho s v^2)\sin\theta - \frac{\dot{m}}{m}\dot{y} - g$$

This is a coupled system of two second-order nonlinear [recall equation (2.1.6)] differential equations. We are assuming that c and s are known constants, ρ is a known function of y (that is, height above the surface), and T and m (and hence $\dot{m}$) are known functions of t. (The change in mass is caused by the expenditure of fuel.)

The solution of (2.1.11) must satisfy (2.1.5), and this gives two of the four initial conditions that are needed. The other two are

(2.1.12)
$$v(0) = 0 \qquad \theta(0) = \theta_0$$

Thus, for a given rocket, the only "free parameter" is the launch angle θ_0, and changes in the launch angle obviously cause changes in the trajectory.

Equations (2.1.11) also serve as the mathematical model for the "projectile problem," for example, a shell being shot from a cannon or a rock launched from a slingshot. In this case, we assume that the projectile starts with a given velocity v_0, and thus (2.1.12) is changed to

(2.1.13)
$$v(0) = v_0 \qquad \theta(0) = \theta_0$$

There is now no thrust, and hence no change of mass, so (2.1.11) simplifies to

(2.1.14)
$$\ddot{x} = \frac{-c\rho s v^2}{2m}\cos\theta \qquad \ddot{y} = \frac{-c\rho s v^2}{2m}\sin\theta - g$$

which, in the context of our simplified model, shows that, given the initial velocity and launch angle, the trajectory depends only on the drag and gravitational forces.

Our task, now, is to solve the equations (2.1.11) with the initial conditions (2.1.5) and (2.1.13). [Henceforth, we shall use (2.1.13) since it includes the special case $v_0 = 0$ of (2.1.12).] In the trivial case in which there is neither thrust nor drag, the equations can be solved explicitly (exercise 2.1.3). However, for any realistic specification of the air density ρ and the thrust, this is not possible, and an approximate numerical solution is required.

For the numerical solution, it will be convenient to reformulate the two second-order equations (2.1.11) as a system of four first-order equations. By differentiating the relations

(2.1.15)
$$\dot{x} = v\cos\theta \qquad \dot{y} = v\sin\theta$$

we have

(2.1.16) $$\ddot{x} = \dot{v}\cos\theta - v\dot{\theta}\sin\theta \qquad \ddot{y} = \dot{v}\sin\theta + v\dot{\theta}\cos\theta$$

and if we substitute (2.1.15) and (2.1.16) into (2.1.11) and solve for $\dot{v}$ and $\dot{\theta}$, we obtain

(2.1.17) $$\dot{v} = \frac{1}{m}(T - \tfrac{1}{2}c\rho s v^2) - g\sin\theta - \frac{\dot{m}}{m}v$$

(2.1.18) $$\dot{\theta} = -\frac{g}{v}\cos\theta$$

Equations (2.1.17) and (2.1.18) together with (2.1.15) constitute a system of four first-order equations in the variables x, y, v, and θ. Again, the initial conditions are given by (2.1.5) and (2.1.13).

We shall return to the numerical solution of both the predator–prey problem and the trajectory problem after we have discussed the basic methods used for the solution.

Supplementary Discussion and References: 2.1

Unfortunately, there is no known analytical form for nontrivial solutions of the problem given by (2.1.3)/(2.1.4). Thus, we are led to approximation methods for this problem. The primary concern of this book is with *numerical* methods that replace the continuous problem with a discrete problem that is solved on a computer. But we will demonstrate here another approach to solving (2.1.3)/(2.1.4). These *perturbation* methods replace the original continuous problem with a slightly different and simpler continuous problem, one which can be solved analytically.

The first step is to identify *stationary* or equilibrium states, (x_s, y_s). In our case, the equations

$$x = x_s \equiv \frac{-\gamma}{\delta} \qquad y = y_s \equiv \frac{-\alpha}{\beta}$$

represent stationary states because

$$\left.\frac{dx}{dt}\right|_{(x_s,\, y_s)} = x_s(\alpha + \beta y_s) = 0 \qquad \left.\frac{dy}{dt}\right|_{(x_s,\, y_s)} = y_s(\gamma + \delta x_s) = 0$$

By expanding the right-hand sides of (2.1.3) in a Taylor series about (x_s, y_s), we get

$$x(\alpha + \beta y) = \beta x_s(y - y_s) + \cdots \qquad y(\gamma + \delta x) = \delta y_s(x - x_s) + \cdots$$

Thus, in the neighborhood of (x_s, y_s), we approximate (2.1.3) by the linear equations

(2.1.19) $$\dot{x} = \beta x_s(y - y_s) \qquad \dot{y} = \delta y_s(x - x_s)$$

Using some basic ideas for solving ordinary differential equations, it can be shown that

$$\textbf{(2.1.20)} \qquad \frac{(x - x_s)^2}{-\beta x_s} + \frac{(y - y_s)^2}{\delta y_s} = c$$

where c is some constant determined by the initial conditions. Formula (2.1.20) is the equation of an ellipse whose center is at (x_s, y_s) and different starting values of $x(0)$ and $y(0)$ determine different ellipses. The figure that follows shows a family of ellipses about (x_s, y_s), the arrows indicating the direction of increasing time. It can be seen that the populations are cyclical: after a certain time, the populations return to their original levels.

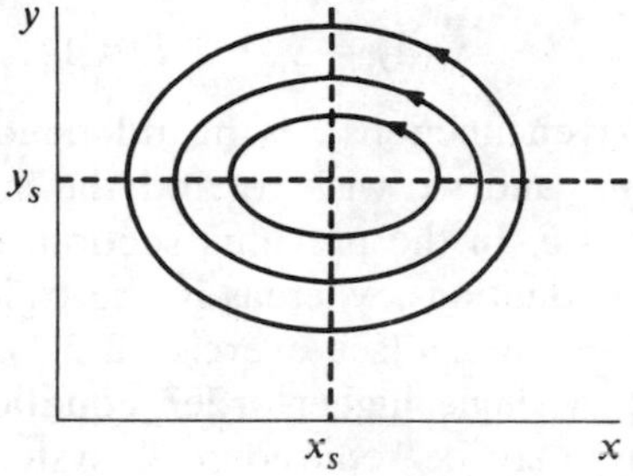

This type of perturbation analysis can provide useful information about the solution of (2.1.3) in the neighborhood of a stationary point. Because the equations (2.1.3) are approximated by equations (2.1.19), we might expect that the solutions to (2.1.3) would be close to the ellipses that solve (2.1.19). Such a relationship is verified by the numerical approximations described in the remainder of this chapter.

For further information on the predator–prey problem and other topics in mathematical biology, see Rubinow [1975], and for additional information on the theory of rocket trajectories, see, for example, Rosser, Newton, and Gross [1974].

EXERCISES 2.1

2.1.1. What relationships among the coefficients α, β, γ, and δ and the population levels x and y of (2.1.3) would guarantee stable populations for x and y (that is, $x(t + \Delta t) = x(t)$ and $y(t + \Delta t) = y(t)$ for all $\Delta t > 0$)?

2.1.2. Verify (2.1.6).

2.1.3. Show that the solution of $\ddot{x} = 0$, $\ddot{y} = -mg$, with initial conditions $x(0) = y(0) = 0$, $v(0) = v_0$, $\theta(0) = \theta_0$ is given by $x(t) = (v_0 \cos \theta_0)t$ and $y(t) = -mgt^2/2 + (v_0 \sin \theta_0)t$.

2.2 Numerical Solutions: One-Step Methods

In the previous section, we gave two examples of initial-value problems for systems of ordinary differential equations. We will now consider such problems in the general form

$$\textbf{(2.2.1)} \quad \frac{dy_i}{dx} = f_i(x, y_1(x), \ldots, y_n(x)), \qquad i = 1, \ldots, n, a \le x \le b$$

with initial conditions

$$\textbf{(2.2.2)} \qquad y_i(a) = \hat{y}_i, \qquad i = 1, \ldots, n$$

Here, the f_i are given functions, x is the independent variable, the $\hat{y}_i$ are given initial conditions, and we wish to find the solution functions y_i on the interval $a \le x \le b$. In the previous section, the predator–prey problem gave rise to two equations, whereas in the trajectory problem, there were four first-order equations (see exercise 2.2.1). More generally, as shown in Appendix 2, a single higher-order equation, or a system of higher-order equations, may be reduced to a system of first-order equations; thus, the problem (2.2.1)/(2.2.2) is very general. For simplicity in the subsequent presentation, we shall restrict our attention to a single equation

$$\textbf{(2.2.3)} \qquad \frac{dy}{dx} = f(x, y), \qquad a \le x \le b$$

in the single unknown function y, and with the initial condition

$$\textbf{(2.2.4)} \qquad y(a) = \hat{y}$$

At the end of the section, we shall then show how the methods extend easily to systems of the form (2.2.1).

Although some initial-value problems have solutions that can be obtained analytically, many problems, including most of those of practical interest, cannot be solved in this manner. The purpose of the chapter is to describe methods for approximating solutions by using numerical methods, in particular, by what are known as *finite difference methods.*

The first step in the numerical solution is to partition the interval $[a, b]$ into a finite number of subintervals by introducing the *grid points* $a = x_0 < x_1 < \cdots < x_N = b$ as shown in Figure 2.2. Although unequal spacing of the grid points presents no particular difficulties, we shall assume that the grid points are equally spaced in order to simplify the

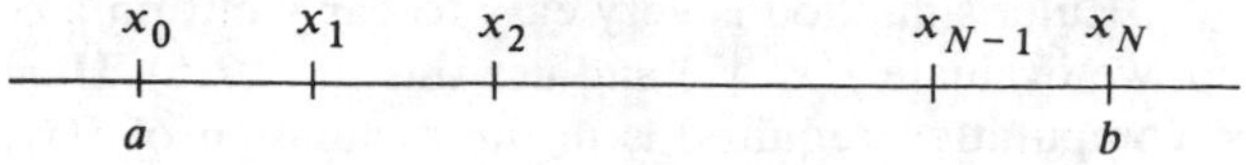

FIGURE 2.2 *Partitioned Interval* $[a, b]$.

discussion and analysis. If we let h denote the spacing, then $h = (b - a)/N$, and $x_k = a + kh$, $k = 0, 1, \ldots, N$, where N is the (integer) number of subintervals. In what follows, $y(x_k)$ will denote the value of the exact solution of (2.2.3) at the point x_k, and y_k will denote the approximation generated by the numerical method under consideration.

Perhaps the simplest numerical scheme is *Euler's method*, which is defined by

(2.2.5) $$y_0 = \hat{y} \qquad y_{k+1} = y_k + hf(x_k, y_k), \qquad k = 0, 1, \ldots, N-1$$

The derivation of Euler's method is straightforward. By the Taylor expansion (see Appendix 1) of y about x_k, we have

(2.2.6) $$\begin{aligned} y(x_{k+1}) &= y(x_k) + hy'(x_k) + \frac{h^2}{2} y''(z_k) \\ &= y(x_k) + hf(x_k, y(x_k)) + \frac{h^2}{2} y''(z_k) \end{aligned}$$

where z_k is in the interval $[x_k, x_{k+1}]$. We will always assume that all derivatives shown do exist. Now, if y'' is bounded and h is small, we may ignore the last term and have, using the notation $\doteq$ to mean "approximately equal to,"

$$y(x_{k+1}) \doteq y(x_k) + hf(x_k, y(x_k))$$

This is the basis for (2.2.5). Geometrically, Euler's method consists of approximating the solution at x_{k+1} by following the tangent to the solution curve at x_k (see Figure 2.3).

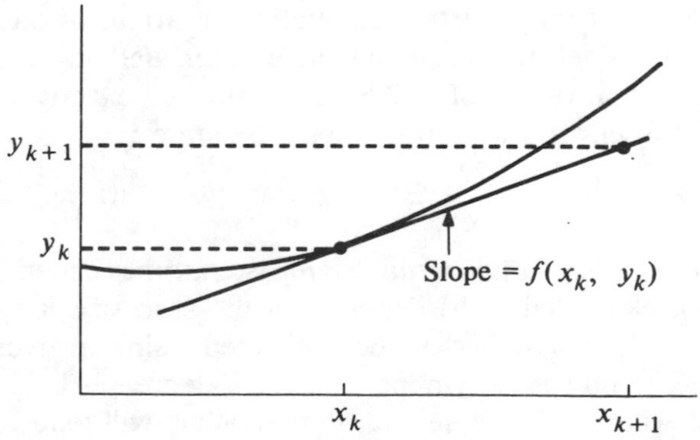

FIGURE 2.3 *One Step of Euler's Method.*

Euler's method is very easy to carry out on a computer: at the kth step, we evaluate $f(x_k, y_k)$ and use this in (2.2.5). Hence, essentially all of the computation required is in the evaluation of $f(x_k, y_k)$.

We now give a simple example of the use of the method. Consider the equation

(2.2.7) $$y'(x) = y^2(x) + 2x - x^4, \qquad y(0) = 0$$

It is easily verified that the exact solution of this equation is $y(x) = x^2$. Here, $f(x, y) = y^2 + 2x - x^4$, and therefore Euler's method for (2.2.7) becomes

(2.2.8) $$y_{k+1} = y_k + h(y_k^2 + 2kh - k^4h^4), \qquad k = 0, 1, \ldots, y_0 = 0$$

since $x_k = kh$. In Table 2.1, we give some computed values for (2.2.8) for $h = 0.1$, as well as the corresponding values of the exact solution.

TABLE 2.1 *Computed and Exact Solutions for* (2.2.7) *by Euler's Method*

x	Computed Solution	Exact Solution
0.1	0.00	0.01
0.2	0.02	0.04
0.3	0.06	0.09
0.4	0.12	0.16
0.5	0.20	0.25
0.6	0.30	0.36

As Table 2.1 shows, the computed solution is in error, as is to be expected, and a major question in the use of Euler's method, or any other numerical method, is the accuracy of the approximations y_k. In general, the error in these approximations will come from two sources: (1) the discretization error that results from the replacement of the differential equation (2.2.3) by the approximation (2.2.5); and (2) the rounding error made in carrying out the arithmetic operations of the method (2.2.5). We shall consider the rounding error later and for the moment we shall assume that the y_k of (2.2.5) are computed exactly so that the only error is the discretization error. Then we define

(2.2.9) $$E(h) = \max_{1 \le k \le N} |y_k - y(x_k)|$$

to be the *global discretization error* (sometimes called the *global truncation error*). Note that $E(h)$ depends on the step size h since the approximations y_k are assumed to be computed using a given h. Intuitively, we expect—and certainly hope—that as h decreases in size, the discretization error will also decrease and, in particular, will tend to zero as h tends to zero.

We will not give a complete analysis of the global discretization error but will content ourselves with indicating how such an analysis would proceed. First, we will assume that the exact solution y has a bounded second derivative y'' on the interval $[a, b]$; that is

(2.2.10) $$\max_{a \le x \le b} |y''(x)| = M$$

We then consider the expression

(2.2.11) $$L(x, h) = \frac{1}{h}[y(x + h) - y(x)] - f(x, y(x))$$

which is called the *local discretization error for Euler's method at point x* and is a measure of how much the difference quotient for $y'(x)$ differs from $f(x, y(x))$. Now, suppose that y_k equals the exact solution $y(x_k)$. Then, the difference between the Euler approximation y_{k+1} and the exact solution $y(x_{k+1})$ is simply

(2.2.12) $$y(x_{k+1}) - y_{k+1} = y(x_{k+1}) - y(x_k) - hf(x_k, y(x_k)) = hL(x_k, h)$$

That is, h times the local discretization error is the error produced in a single step of Euler's method starting from the exact solution.

We shall be interested in the maximum size of $L(x, h)$ for any value of x, and we define the local discretization error for Euler's method by

(2.2.13) $$L(h) = \max_{a \le x \le b-h} |L(x, h)|$$

Note that $L(h)$ depends on the step length, h, as well as on the function f of the differential equation and the interval $[a, b]$. The only dependence we have explicitly delineated, however, is that on h since under the assumption (2.2.10) and using a Taylor expansion analogous to (2.2.6), we obtain the bound

(2.2.14) $$L(h) \le \frac{h}{2} M = 0(h)$$

Here, we have used the standard notation $0(h)$ to denote a quantity that goes to zero as rapidly as h goes to zero. More generally, we will say that a function g of h is $0(h^p)$ if $g(h)/h^p$ is bounded as $h \to 0$ but $g(h)/h^q$ is unbounded if $q > p$.

The problem now is to relate the local discretization error to the global discretization error. If we denote the error $y(x_k) - y_k$ by e_k, then we have, by using (2.2.5) and (2.2.11),

(2.2.15) $$\begin{aligned} e_{k+1} = y(x_{k+1}) - y_{k+1} &= y(x_k) + hf(x_k, y(x_k)) + hL(x_k, h) \\ &\quad - y_k - hf(x_k, y_k) \\ &= e_k + h[f(x_k, y(x_k)) - f(x_k, y_k)] + hL(x_k, h) \end{aligned}$$

Now, assume that the function f has a bounded partial derivative with respect to its second variable; that is,

$$\left|\frac{\partial f}{\partial y}(x, y)\right| \leq M_1, \qquad a \leq x \leq b, \qquad |y| < \infty \tag{2.2.16}$$

Then, by the mean-value theorem, we have for some $0 < \theta < 1$,

$$\begin{aligned} |f(x_k, y(x_k)) - f(x_k, y_k)| &= \left|\frac{\partial f}{\partial y}(x_k, \theta y(x_k) + (1 - \theta)y_k)(y(x_k) - y_k)\right| \\ &\leq M_1 e_k \end{aligned}$$

Putting this in (2.2.15) and bounding $L(x_k, h)$ by $L(h)$ gives

$$|e_{k+1}| \leq (1 + hM_1)\,|e_k| + h\,|L(h)| \tag{2.2.17}$$

If we set $c = 1 + hM_1$ and expand out the sequence in (2.2.17), we obtain

$$\begin{aligned} |e_{k+1}| &\leq c\,|e_k| + h\,|L(h)| \leq c^2\,|e_{k-1}| + ch\,|L(h)| + h\,|L(h)| \\ &\leq \cdots \leq c^k\,|e_1| + c^{k-1}h\,|L(h)| + \cdots + ch\,|L(h)| + h\,|L(h)| \end{aligned} \tag{2.2.18}$$

In particular, the bound (2.2.18) for the final error e_N will contain a summation of the N terms $c^k hL(h)$, all of which are $0(h^2)$. Since $N = (b - a)/h$, the summation will be $0(h)$. Thus, we expect that the best result will be the following:

THEOREM 2.2.1 (Euler Discretization Error) *If the function f has a bounded partial derivative with respect to its second variable and if the solution of* (2.2.3)/(2.2.4) *has a bounded second derivative, then the global discretization error of Euler's method satisfies $E(h) = 0(h)$.*

To complete the proof of this theorem, we need to show that $c^N = (1 + hM_1)^N$ is bounded as $h \to 0$, and this is omitted.

The preceding analysis shows that the global discretization error is $0(h)$. This is usually expressed by saying that Euler's method is *first order.* The practical consequence of this is that as we decrease h, we expect that the approximate solution will become more accurate—and converge to the exact solution as h tends to zero—and at a linear rate in h; that is, if we halve the step size, h, we expect that the error will decrease by about a factor of 2. This error behavior is shown in the following example.

Consider the equation $y' = y$, $y(0) = 1$ for which the exact solution is $y(x) = e^x$. We compute the solution at $x = 1$ by Euler's method using various values of h (see Table 2.2). The exact solution at $x = 1$ is $e = 2.718\ldots$; the errors for the different step sizes are given in the middle column. The ratios of the errors for successive halvings of h are given in the right-hand column, and it is seen that these ratios are tending to $\frac{1}{2}$, as expected.

TABLE 2.2

h	Computed Value	Error	Error Ratio
1	2.000	0.718	
1/2	2.250	0.468	0.65
1/4	2.441	0.277	0.59
1/8	2.566	0.152	0.55
1/16	2.638	0.080	0.53

The very slow rate of convergence shown in Table 2.2 as h decreases is typical of first-order methods and militates against their use. Much of the rest of this chapter will be devoted to studying other methods for which the error tends to zero at a faster rate as h tends to zero. As an example of one of the approaches to such methods, we next discuss the *Heun method,* which is given by

(2.2.19) $$y_{k+1} = y_k + \frac{h}{2}[f(x_k, y_k) + f(x_{k+1}, y_k + hf(x_k, y_k))]$$

Note that we have just replaced $f(x_k, y_k)$ in Euler's method by an average of f evaluated at two different places. This is illustrated in Figure 2.4. The Heun method is also known as a second-order *Runge–Kutta method* and has a local discretization error that is $0(h^2)$, as we will show shortly. The most famous of the Runge–Kutta methods is the classical fourth-order method, given by

(2.2.20) $$y_{k+1} = y_k + \frac{h}{6}(F_1 + 2F_2 + 2F_3 + F_4)$$

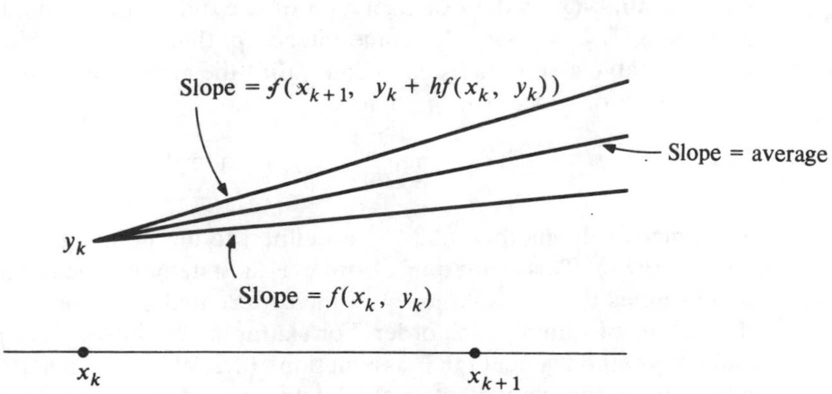

FIGURE 2.4 *The Heun Method.*

where

$$F_1 = f(x_k, y_k) \qquad F_2 = f\left(x_k + \frac{h}{2}, y_k + \frac{h}{2}F_1\right)$$

$$F_3 = f\left(x_k + \frac{h}{2}, y_k + \frac{h}{2}F_2\right) \qquad F_4 = (x_{k+1}, y_k + hF_3)$$

Here, the $f(x_k, y_k)$ in Euler's method has been replaced by a weighted average of f evaluated at four different points. It is instructive to draw for this the figure corresponding to Figure 2.4; this is left to exercise 2.2.9.

In Section 2.4, we will consider methods based on using information from prior steps; that is, y_{k+1} will be a function not only of y_k but also of y_{k-1}, y_{k-2}, and so on. The present section deals with methods that depend only on y_k and no prior values. Such methods are called *one-step methods* and can be written in the general form

(2.2.21) $$y_{k+1} = y_k + h\phi(x_k, y_k)$$

for some suitable function ϕ. In the case of Euler's method, ϕ is just f itself, whereas for the Heun method,

(2.2.22) $$\phi(x, y) = \tfrac{1}{2}[f(x, y) + f(x + h, y + hf(x, y))]$$

The fourth-order Runge–Kutta method (2.2.20) is also a one-step method, and the corresponding function ϕ can be written down in a manner similar to (2.2.22) (see exercise 2.2.5).

For any one-step method (2.2.21), we define the local discretization error in a manner analogous to that for Euler's method by

(2.2.23)

$$L(h) = \max_{a \le x \le b-h} |L(x, h)|, \; L(x, h) = \frac{1}{h}[y(x + h) - y(x)] - \phi(x, y(x))$$

when, again, $y(x)$ is the exact solution of the differential equation. If, for a given ϕ, $L(h) = 0(h^p)$ for some integer p, then it is possible to show, under suitable assumptions on ϕ and f, that the global discretization error will also be of order p in h; that is,

(2.2.24) $$E(h) \equiv \max_{1 \le k \le N} |y(x_k) - y_k| = 0(h^p)$$

The *order* of the method (2.2.21) is defined to be the integer p for which $L(h) = 0(h^p)$. This definition of order is a statement about the method and assumes that the solution y of the differential equation has bounded derivatives of suitably high order. For example, we showed that $p = 1$ for Euler's method under the assumption (2.2.10). For other methods, higher-order derivatives of the solution and of the function f may be required to be bounded, as will be illustrated later.

It is a relatively simple matter to show that the local discretization error for Heun's method is $0(h^2)$, but this will be a consequence of the following, more general analysis which is the basis for the Runge–Kutta methods. Let us consider a function ϕ defined by

$$\phi(x, y) = c_2 f(x, y) + c_3 f(x + c_1 h, y + c_1 h f(x, y))$$

where we wish to determine the constants c_1, c_2, and c_3 so as to maximize the order of the one-step method (2.2.21); that is, we wish the best linear combination, as determined by c_2 and c_3, of two values of f, and how far along the interval the second evaluation of f should be done, as determined by c_1.

We expand ϕ in a Taylor series in two variables about the point (x, y). First, in the x variable, we have

$$\begin{aligned}\phi = c_2 f + c_3[&f(x, y + c_1 hf) + c_1 h f_x(x, y + c_1 hf)\\ &+ \frac{c_1^2 h^2}{2} f_{xx}(x, y + c_1 hf) + 0(h^3)]\end{aligned}$$

where we have denoted $f(x, y)$ simply by f and the partial derivatives of f with respect to x by f_x and f_{xx}. Next, expand in y where all partial derivatives shown are evaluated at (x, y):

$$\begin{aligned}\textbf{(2.2.25)}\qquad \phi &= c_2 f + c_3\{f + c_1 h f f_y + \tfrac{1}{2}c_1^2 h^2 f^2 f_{yy} + 0(h^3)\\ &\quad + c_1 h[f_x + c_1 h f f_{xy} + 0(h^2)] + \tfrac{1}{2}c_1^2 h^2 f_{xx} + 0(h^3)\}\\ &= (c_2 + c_3)f + c_1 c_3 h(f f_y + f_x)\\ &\quad + \tfrac{1}{2}c_1^2 c_3 h^2(f^2 f_{yy} + 2f f_{xy} + f_{xx}) + 0(h^3)\end{aligned}$$

On the other hand, the exact solution $y(x)$ of the differential equation satisfies

$$\begin{aligned}\textbf{(2.2.26)}\quad \frac{1}{h}[y(x + h) - y(x)] &= y'(x) + \tfrac{1}{2}y''(x)h + \tfrac{1}{6}y'''(x)h^2 + 0(h^3)\\ &= f + \tfrac{1}{2}h\frac{df}{dx} + \tfrac{1}{6}h^2\frac{d^2 f}{dx^2} + 0(h^3)\\ &= f + \tfrac{1}{2}h(f f_y + f_x)\\ &\quad + \frac{h^2}{6}(f^2 f_{yy} + 2f f_{xy} + f_{xx} + f_x f_y + f f_y^2)\\ &\quad + 0(h^3)\end{aligned}$$

Therefore, (2.2.25) and (2.2.26) combine to yield

$$\begin{aligned}\textbf{(2.2.27)}\quad &\frac{1}{h}[y(x + h) - y(x)] - \phi(x, y(x))\\ &= (1 - c_2 - c_3)f + h(\tfrac{1}{2} - c_1 c_3)(f f_y + f_x)\\ &\quad + \frac{h^2}{2}(\tfrac{1}{3} - c_1^2 c_3)(f^2 f_{yy} + 2f f_{xy} + f_{xx}) + \frac{h^2}{6}(f_x f_y + f f_y^2) + 0(h^3)\end{aligned}$$

If we require that

(2.2.28) $$c_2 + c_3 = 1 \qquad c_1c_3 = \tfrac{1}{2}$$

then the first two terms of (2.2.27) vanish for any f. However, $f_xf_y + ff_y^2$ will not in general be identically zero; hence, regardless of the choice of the constants, we can have, at most,

(2.2.29) $$\frac{1}{h}[y(x+h) - y(x)] - \phi(x, y(x)) = 0(h^2)$$

which will hold whenever (2.2.28) is satisfied and the various derivatives we have used are bounded. Therefore, $L(h) = 0(h^2)$, and the methods delineated by (2.2.28) are all second order.

If we set $c_1 = \gamma/2$ and solve the two equations of (2.2.23) in terms of γ, we obtain a function that will always satisfy (2.2.28). Therefore, the method

$$y_{k+1} = y_k + h\left[\left(1 - \frac{1}{\gamma}\right)f(x_k, y_k) + \frac{1}{\gamma}f\left(x_k + \frac{\gamma}{2}h, y_k + \frac{\gamma h}{2}f(x_k, y_k)\right)\right]$$

is second-order accurate for any $\gamma \neq 0$. The special choice $\gamma = 2$ gives the second-order Runge–Kutta method (2.2.19). The derivation of higher-order Runge–Kutta methods, and in particular the fourth-order method (2.2.20), can proceed in an analogous, but more complicated manner.

We next indicate how the methods that have been discussed are used for systems of equations. Consider the system (2.2.1), which we will write in the vector form

(2.2.30) $$\mathbf{y}'(x) = \mathbf{f}(x, \mathbf{y}(x))$$

Here, $\mathbf{y}(x)$ denotes the vector with components $y_1(x), \ldots, y_n(x)$, and $\mathbf{f}$ is the vector with components $f_1, \ldots, f_n$. The vector $\hat{\mathbf{y}}$ will denote the initial values (2.2.2). Then, Euler's method (2.2.5) can be written for the system (2.2.30) as

(2.2.31) $$\mathbf{y}_0 = \hat{\mathbf{y}} \qquad \mathbf{y}_{k+1} = \mathbf{y}_k + h\mathbf{f}(x_k, \mathbf{y}_k), \qquad k = 0, 1, \ldots$$

where $\mathbf{y}_1, \mathbf{y}_2, \ldots$ are the vector approximations to the solution $\mathbf{y}$. We could, of course, write out (2.2.31) in component form; for $n = 2$, this would be

$$\begin{aligned} y_{1,0} &= \hat{y}_1 \qquad y_{2,0} = \hat{y}_2 \\ \left.\begin{aligned} y_{1,k+1} &= y_{1,k} + hf_1(x_k, y_{1,k}, y_{2,k}), \\ y_{2,k+1} &= y_{2,k} + hf_2(x_k, y_{1,k}, y_{2,k}) \end{aligned}\right\}&, \qquad k = 0, 1, \ldots \end{aligned}$$

Clearly, the succinct vector notation of (2.2.31) is advantageous.

Similarly, Heun's method (2.2.19) can be written in vector form for (2.2.30) by

(2.2.32) $$\mathbf{y}_{k+1} = \mathbf{y}_k + \frac{h}{2}[\mathbf{f}(x_k, \mathbf{y}_k) + \mathbf{f}(x_{k+1}, \mathbf{y}_k + h\mathbf{f}(x_k, \mathbf{y}_k))]$$

It is left to exercise 2.2.7 to write the fourth-order Runge–Kutta method (2.2.20) in vector form.

We now turn to a brief discussion of the rounding error that will occur in carrying out the methods of this section on a computer. Consider, first, Euler's method. There are two sources of rounding error. The first is the error that occurs in the evaluation of $f(x_k, y_k)$; we will denote this error by ε_k. The second error, η_k, is the error made in carrying out the Euler formula. Thus, the computed approximations y_k satisfy

$$\textbf{(2.2.33)} \qquad y_{k+1} = y_k + h[f(x_k, y_k) + \varepsilon_k] + \eta_k, \qquad k = 0, 1, \ldots$$

It is possible to bound the effects of these errors in terms of bounds on the ε_k and η_k. However, rather than do this, we will content ourselves with the following intuitive discussion. As we have seen, the global discretization error in Euler's method goes to zero as h goes to zero. Hence, we can make the discretization error as small as we like by making h sufficiently small. However, the smaller h is, the more steps of Euler's method that will be required and, in general, the larger the effect of the rounding error on the computed solution. In practice, for a fixed word length in the computer arithmetic, there will be a size of h below which the rounding error will become the dominant contribution to the overall error. The situation is depicted schematically in Figure 2.5, in which the step size h_0 is the practical minimum that can be used. This minimum step size is very difficult to ascertain in advance, but for problems for which only a moderate accuracy is required, the step size used will be far larger than this minimum, and the discretization error will be the dominant contributor to the error. The same general behavior occurs in all the methods, although the minimum step size, h_0, will vary from method to method and problem to problem.

We complete this section with some simple calculations for the predator–prey equations introduced in Section 2.1. Recall that these

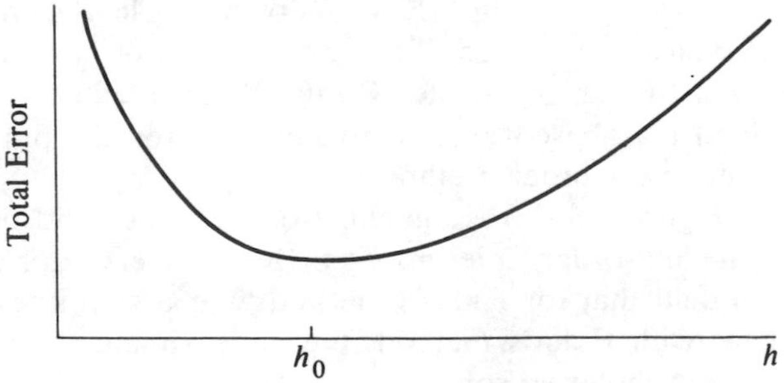

FIGURE 2.5 *Error in Euler's and Other Methods.*

equations are

$$\frac{dx}{dt} = \alpha x + \beta xy \qquad \frac{dy}{dt} = \gamma y + \delta xy, \qquad t > 0 \tag{2.2.34}$$

with the initial conditions

$$x(0) = x_0 \qquad y(0) = y_0 \tag{2.2.35}$$

The Supplementary Discussion of Section 2.1 showed that

$$x_s = \frac{-\gamma}{\delta} \qquad y_s = \frac{-\alpha}{\beta}$$

is a stationary point of (2.2.34), and, in the neighborhood of (x_s, y_s), the path traced out by $(x(t), y(t))$ for $t > 0$ is approximately an ellipse. For illustration purposes, we have chosen initial values x_0 and y_0 that are near stationary points. We have used the following values for the parameters: $\alpha = 0.25$, $\beta = -0.01$, $\gamma = -1.00$, and $\delta = 0.01$. For these parameter values, there is a stationary point at $(x_s, y_s) = (100, 25)$. Initial values of $x_0 = 80$ and $y_0 = 30$ were used in all cases.

Figures 2.6–2.8 are the plotted approximations to solutions of (2.2.34)/(2.2.35) generated by several of the numerical methods in this chapter. In all cases, we have plotted x (the prey) versus y (the predator), both as functions of time, t. The motion is in a clockwise direction as t increases. Figure 2.6 demonstrates three options that are usually available to graphics users. Part (a) plots just the discrete values (x_i, y_i), $i = 0, 1, \ldots$, generated by the numerical method, emphasizing the discrete nature of the methods. In part (b), the points are connected by straight lines, giving a polygonal shape to the approximation. This is usually a trivial option for the plotter to perform. Part (c) shows the dots connected by smooth curves. This option requires some special software based on approximation methods like those discussed in Section 5.2.

Figure 2.7 demonstrates the dependency of the approximate solution on the value of the step size, h. The numerical method used for this figure is Euler's method defined by (2.2.5). The values of h are 1, 0.5, and 0.25. One sees that, as the step size is halved, the error is roughly halved also, suggesting $0(h)$ convergence. Clearly, the errors are rather large even for $h = 0.25$. The "exact" solution used for comparison was obtained by a higher-order Runge–Kutta method, and the solution so obtained may be considered to be exact for the purpose of comparing with the lower-order methods.

Figure 2.8 shows the effect of using a second-order method rather than the first-order Euler method. Here, the error for a step size of $h = 1$ is less than that for Euler's method with a step size of $h = 0.25$. Note that, as with Euler's method, the approximate solution is spiraling out away from the exact solution.

A few interpretive remarks are perhaps in order. It is, of course,

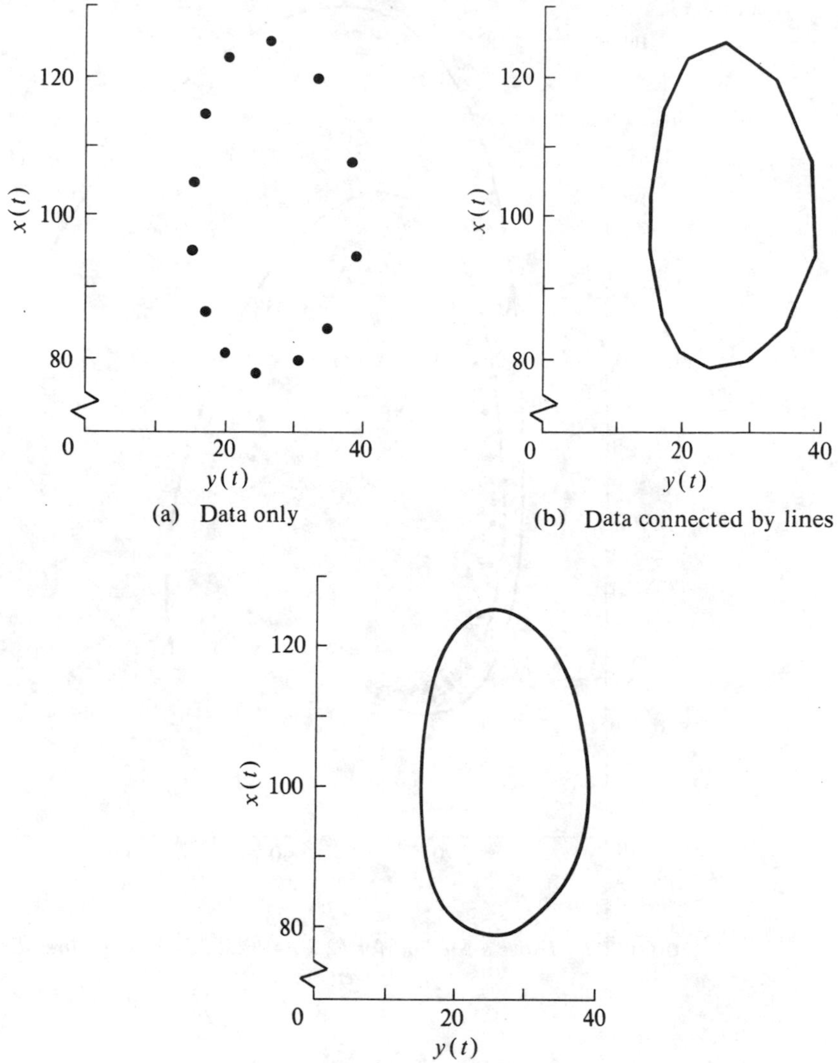

(a) Data only

(b) Data connected by lines

(c) Data interpolated by a function

FIGURE 2.6 *Options for Displaying Graphical Output. Solution to Equations* (2.2.34)/(2.2.35).

the case that equations (2.2.34)/(2.2.35) do not model the physical situation exactly. There are many considerations ignored, for example, a finite food supply for the prey, outside interference by other predators, weather effects, and so forth. This model is necessarily a simplified one for purposes of exposition in this chapter. The real test of a model comes when its results are compared with the physical situation. The computed

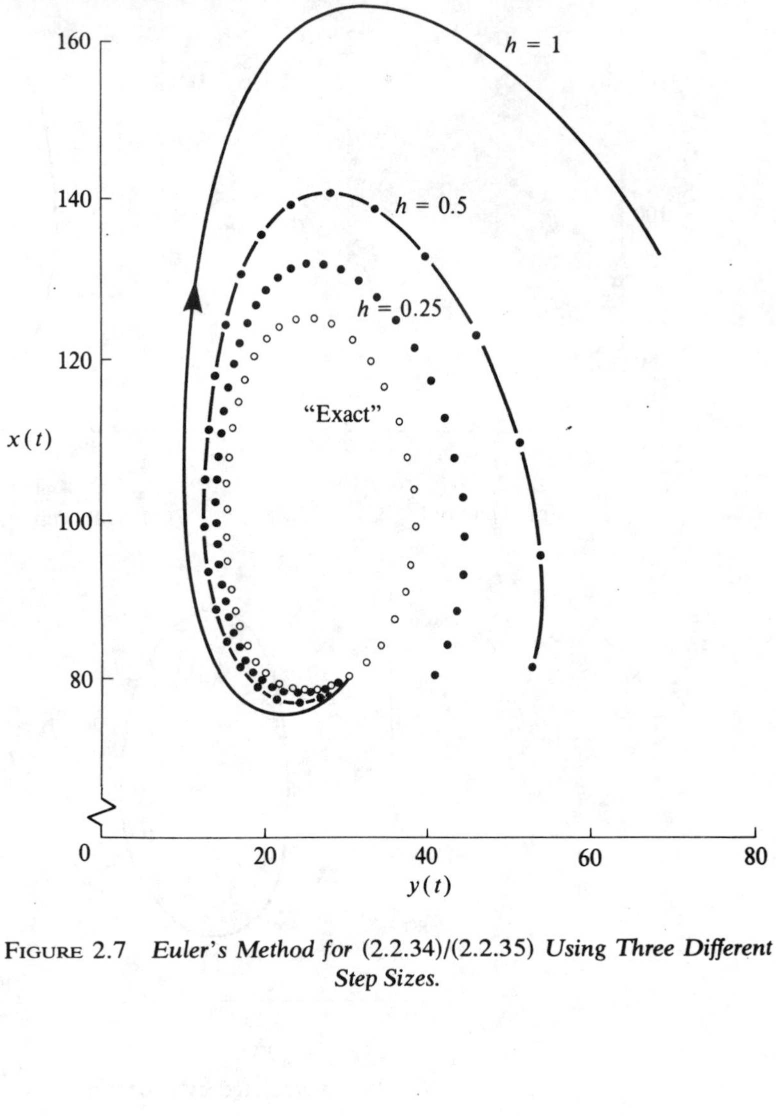

FIGURE 2.7 *Euler's Method for (2.2.34)/(2.2.35) Using Three Different Step Sizes.*

solutions to (2.2.34)/(2.2.35) have been compared to actual data of species populations, and the shape of the curve, as given in Figure 2.6(c), does a very creditable job of approximating the real data, although, as should be expected, the computed results are much smoother. As is the case in the real situation, the predator does not eliminate the prey, but, after the number of prey is reduced, the predator population decreases also, and thus the prey have a better chance of surviving since there are fewer predators. The predator population behavior continues to follow that of the prey as the cycle repeats.

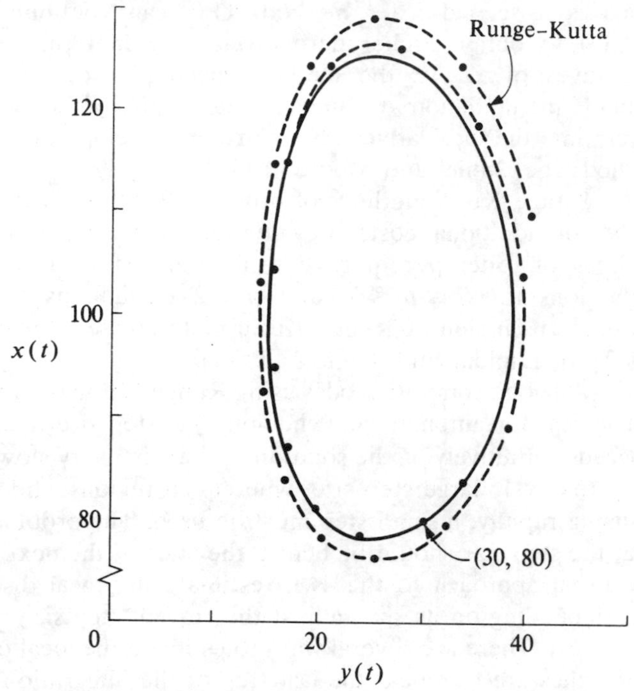

FIGURE 2.8 *Second-Order Runge–Kutta (Spiraling Outward) with Step Size h = 1, Compared to the "Exact" Solution of* (2.2.34)/(2.2.35).

Supplementary Discussion and References: 2.2

Perhaps the most conceptually simple approach to higher-order one-step methods is Taylor-series expansion of the solution. Consider the "method"

$$y_{k+1} = y_k + hy'(x_k) + \tfrac{1}{2}h^2y''(x_k) + \cdots + \frac{h^p}{p!}y^{(p)}(x_k) \tag{2.2.36}$$

where y is the exact solution. It is easy to see that the order of this is p. The higher derivatives of the solution can be obtained in principle from the differential equation itself. Thus, $y'(x) = f(x, y(x))$, and

$$y''(x) = \frac{d}{dx}f(x, y(x)) = f_x(x, y(x)) + f_y(x, y(x))y'(x) \tag{2.2.37}$$

We then approximate $y'(x_k)$ by $f(x_k, y_k)$, and similarly for higher derivatives. Thus, the method for $p = 1$ is simply Euler's method, whereas for $p = 2$, it becomes

$$y_{k+1} = y_k + hf(x_k, y_k) + \frac{h^2}{2}[f_x(x_k, y_k) + f_y(x_k, y_k)f(x_k, y_k)]$$

which is a second-order method. One can continue to differentiate (2.2.37) to obtain higher derivatives of y in terms of higher partial derivatives of x, but the methods become exceedingly cumbersome. Symbol manipulation techniques have proved somewhat useful in generating the derivatives. For further development of Taylor-series methods see Daniel and Moore [1970].

Runge–Kutta methods of order higher than four may be obtained but at still additional costs in evaluations of the function f. Runge–Kutta methods of order p require p evaluations of f for $2 \leq p \leq 4$, $p + 1$ evaluations for $5 \leq p \leq 7$, and $p + 2$ evaluations for $p \geq 8$. For a thorough discussion of Runge–Kutta methods, see, for example, Henrici [1962], or Lapidus and Seinfeld [1971].

All good computer codes using Runge–Kutta methods employ some mechanism for automatically changing the step size h as the integration proceeds. Intuitively, if the solution is changing very slowly, then one can use a relatively large step size, whereas in regions where the solution is changing rapidly, a small step must be used. The problem is to ascertain what the step size should be before the start of the next integration step. The usual approach to this is to estimate the local discretization error and, depending on its size, adjust the current step size either upward or downward. There are several ways to estimate the local error; two simple approaches are to repeat the last step of the integration with a step size half as large and then compare the two results, or to use two different Runge–Kutta formulas of different order. Both of these ways are costly in evaluations of f, and perhaps the current best approach is by means of the Runge–Kutta–Fehlberg formulas. Here, one can use, for example, a Runge–Kutta method of order five to estimate the error in a fourth-order Runge–Kutta method in such a way that a total of only six evaluations of f are needed as opposed to ten if the usual Runge–Kutta formulas were used.

EXERCISES 2.2

2.2.1. Rewrite the predator–prey equations (2.1.3) in the form (2.2.1); that is, give the functions f_1 and f_2. Do the same for the trajectory equations (2.1.15), (2.1.17), and (2.1.18).

2.2.2. Apply Euler's method (2.2.5) to the initial-value problem $y' = -y$, $0 \leq x \leq 1$, $y(0) = 1$, with $h = 0.25$. Compare your answers to the exact solution $y(x) = e^{-x}$. Repeat for smaller h.

2.2.3. Verify the calculations of Tables 2.1 and 2.2.

2.2.4. Apply the Heun method to the problem of exercise 2.2.2. Discuss your results as compared with Euler's method.

2.2.5. Write down the function ϕ of (2.2.21) for the fourth-order Runge–Kutta method (2.2.20).

2.2.6. The method $y_{k+1} = y_k + hf(x_k + (h/2), y_k + (h/2)f(x_k, y_k))$ is known as the *midpoint rule*. Show that it is second-order accurate.

2.2.7. Write the fourth-order Runge–Kutta method (2.2.20) in vector form for the system (2.2.30).

2.2.8. Apply Euler's method and the Heun method to the problem $y'(x) = x^2 + [y(x)]^2$, $y(0) = 1$, $x \geq 0$, and compute y_2 for $h = 0.1$.

2.2.9. For the fourth-order Runge–Kutta method (2.2.20), draw the figure corresponding to Figure 2.4.

2.2.10. Repeat the calculations of Figure 2.7 using Euler's method with step sizes 0.5, and 0.25. How small a step size do you have to use in order that the graph of the solution closes back on itself to visual accuracy?

2.2.11. Test the stability of the solution of predator–prey equations (2.2.34) with respect to changes in the initial conditions by changing the initial conditions $x_0 = 80$, $y_0 = 30$ by a unit amount in each direction (four different cases) and repeating the calculation using the second-order Runge–Kutta method.

2.3 Polynomial Interpolation

The methods described in Section 2.2 were all one-step methods—methods that estimate y at x_{k+1} using information only at the previous point, x_k. In Section 2.4, methods that use information at several previous points will be described. But, in order to develop such methods, we must first describe polynomial interpolation, the subject of this section.

Suppose that one is given a set of points, or nodes, $x_0, x_1, \ldots, x_n$ and a set of corresponding numbers $y_0, y_1, \ldots, y_n$. The *interpolation problem* is to find a function g that satisfies

$$g(x_i) = y_i, \qquad i = 0, 1, \ldots, n \tag{2.3.1}$$

There are many types of approximating functions, but the functions of interest in this section will be polynomials.

It is not immediately clear that polynomials can interpolate data at the given nodes. For example, if data are given at three distinct nodes, no polynomial of degree 1 (a linear function) can interpolate the data unless the data lie in a straight line. On the other hand, there is a polynomial of degree 2, and many polynomials of degree 3, that will interpolate the data. The basic result for polynomial interpolation is given in the following theorem.

THEOREM 2.3.1 (Existence and Uniqueness for Polynomial Interpolation) *If* $x_0, x_1, \ldots, x_n$ *are distinct nodes, then for any* $y_0, y_1, \ldots, y_n$, *there exists a unique polynomial* $p(x)$ *of degree* n *or less,* *such that*

$$p(x_i) = y_i, \qquad i = 0, 1, \ldots, n \tag{2.3.2}$$

Proof: The existence can be proved by constructing the *Lagrange polynomials* defined by

$$\ell_j(x) = \frac{(x - x_0)(x - x_1)\cdots(x - x_{j-1})(x - x_{j+1})\cdots(x - x_n)}{(x_j - x_0)(x_j - x_1)\cdots(x_j - x_{j-1})(x_j - x_{j+1})\cdots(x_j - x_n)} = \prod_{\substack{k=0 \\ k\neq j}}^{n} \left(\frac{x - x_k}{x_j - x_k}\right), \qquad j = 0, 1, \ldots, n \tag{2.3.3}$$

It is easy to verify that these polynomials, which are all of degree n, satisfy

$$\ell_j(x_i) = \begin{cases} 1 & \text{if } i = j \\ 0 & \text{if otherwise} \end{cases} \tag{2.3.4}$$

Therefore, $\ell_j(x)y_j$ has the value 0 at all nodes x_i, $i = 0, 1, \ldots, n$, except for x_j, where $\ell_j(x_j)y_j = y_j$. Thus, by defining

$$p(x) = \sum_{j=0}^{n} \ell_j(x)y_j \tag{2.3.5}$$

we have a polynomial of degree n or less that interpolates the data.

To prove uniqueness, suppose, on the contrary, that there is another interpolating polynomial of degree n or less, say $q(x)$. By defining

$$r(x) = p(x) - q(x)$$

we obtain a polynomial, r, of degree n or less that is equal to zero at the $n + 1$ distinct values $x_0, x_1, \ldots, x_n$. By the fundamental theorem of algebra, such a polynomial must be identically equal to zero, and it follows that $p(x) = q(x)$. Thus, uniqueness is proved.

As an example of polynomial interpolation, let us determine the polynomial $p(x)$ of degree 2 or less that satisfies $p(-1) = 4$, $p(0) = 1$, and $p(1) = 0$. The interpolating polynomial (2.3.5) is

$$p(x) = \frac{(x - 0)(x - 1)}{(-1 - 0)(-1 - 1)}4 + \frac{(x - (-1))(x - 1)}{(0 - (-1))(0 - 1)}1 + \frac{(x - (-1))(x - 0)}{(1 - (-1))(1 - 0)}0$$
$$= 2x^2 - 2x + 1 - x^2 + 0 = x^2 - 2x + 1$$

One can easily verify that this $p(x)$ does interpolate the given data.

The question of accuracy for polynomial interpolation arises naturally. But we must first describe what we mean by accuracy in this context. After all, if one is given data at only $n + 1$ points and the interpolating polynomial agrees exactly with the data at those points, what more can be asked?

In the usual context of interpolation, the scientist believes that there is some function f defined over the entire interval of interest even though values are known only at discrete points. Thus, it is of interest to discuss the discrepancy between $p(x)$ and $f(x)$ for values of x that lie between the nodes. The following theorem gives an expression for the error in terms of higher derivatives of f:

THEOREM 2.3.2 (Polynomial Interpolation Error) *Let $f(x)$ be a function with $n + 1$ continuous derivatives on an interval containing the interval $[x_0, x_n]$ where $x_0 < x_1 < \cdots < x_n$ are distinct nodes. If $p(x)$ is the unique polynomial of degree n or less satisfying*

$$p(x_i) = f(x_i), \qquad i = 0, 1, \ldots, n$$

then for any $x \in [x_0, x_n]$,

$$\textbf{(2.3.6)} \qquad f(x) - p(x) = \frac{(x - x_0)(x - x_1)\cdots(x - x_n)}{(n + 1)!} f^{(n+1)}(z)$$

for some z in the interval spanned by x_0, x_n, and x.

We indicate a proof of this theorem in the Supplementary Discussion to this section; here, we only discuss some of its ramifications. First of all, if n is at all large (even 4 or 5), it will probably be difficult, if not impossible, to compute the $(n + 1)$th derivative of f. Even if n is only 1 (linear interpolation) and only the second derivative of f is needed, this also may be impossible if f is an unknown function for which only its values at some discrete points are known; at best, we might be able to estimate some bound for the second derivative on the basis of our assumed knowledge of f. In any case, it will almost always never be the case that (2.3.6) can be used to give a very precise bound on the error. It can, however, be useful in giving various insights into the errors that are produced. As an example of this, suppose that the points x_i are equally spaced with spacing h. Then, it is easy to see that

$$|(x - x_0)(x - x_1)\cdots(x - x_n)| \le (n + 1)!h^{n+1}$$

for any x in the interval $[x_0, x_n]$, and (2.3.6) can be bounded by

$$\textbf{(2.3.7)} \qquad |f(x) - p(x)| \le Mh^{n+1}$$

where

$$M = \max_{x_0 \le z \le x_n} |f^{(n+1)}(z)|$$

The bound (2.3.7) is, of course, still difficult to compute because of the quantity M. But it is useful in the following way. Suppose that we wish to approximate the function f over a given interval $[a, b]$ by means of *piecewise polynomials*, that is, functions that are polynomials on given subintervals of $[a, b]$. For example, if $a = \gamma_0 < \gamma_1 < \cdots < \gamma_p < \gamma_{p+1} = b$ is a partitioning of the interval $[a, b]$ and g is a function that is continuous on $[a, b]$ and is a polynomial on each of the intervals (γ_i, γ_{i+1}), $i = 0, 1, \ldots, p$, then g is called a piecewise polynomial function on $[a, b]$.

As an example of a piecewise quadratic function, suppose that the values of the function f on the interval $[0, 1]$ are given by

x	0	1/6	1/3	1/2	2/3	5/6	1
f	1	3	2	1	0	2	1

Then, the function g defined by

$$\begin{aligned} g(x) &= -54x^2 + 21x + 1, & 0 \le x \le \tfrac{1}{3} \\ &= -6x + 4, & \tfrac{1}{3} \le x \le \tfrac{2}{3} \\ &= -54x^2 + 93x - 38, & \tfrac{2}{3} \le x \le 1 \end{aligned} \tag{2.3.8}$$

is the piecewise quadratic function on $[0, 1]$ that agrees with f at the given nodes, is continuous on the whole interval, and is a quadratic on each of the subintervals $[0, \frac{1}{3}]$, $[\frac{1}{3}, \frac{2}{3}]$, $[\frac{2}{3}, 1]$. This function is shown in Figure 2.9.

Consider now the error in approximating the function f by the function g of (2.3.8). Suppose that M is a bound for the third derivative of f on the entire interval $[0, 1]$. Then, on each of the intervals $[0, \frac{1}{3}]$, $[\frac{1}{3}, \frac{2}{3}]$, and $[\frac{2}{3}, 1]$, the error bound (2.3.7) can be applied; here, $h = \frac{1}{6}$, and $n = 2$. Therefore,

$$|f(x) - g(x)| \le h^3 M \le \frac{M}{6^3}, \qquad 0 \le x \le 1 \tag{2.3.9}$$

Without further information on M, this estimate does not do much as far as a quantitative bound is concerned. It does, however, show how the spacing h between the points enters the error estimate. In fact, suppose that instead of three subintervals, there are six and g is a piecewise quadratic function composed of quadratics on these six subintervals. Then

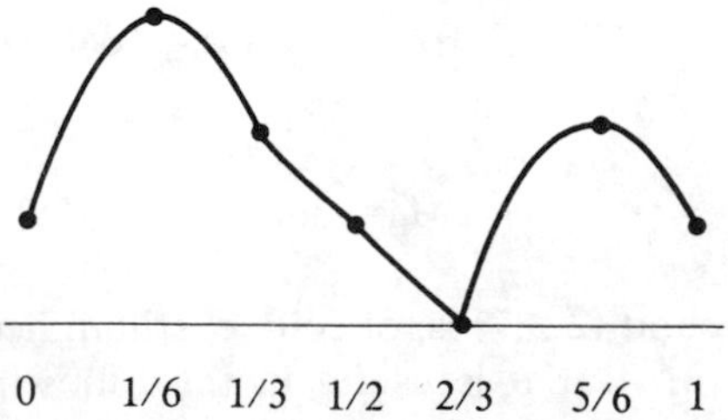

FIGURE 2.9 *A Piecewise Quadratic Function.*

h would be halved to $\frac{1}{12}$, and the estimate (2.3.9) would become

$$|f(x) - g(x)| \leq \frac{M}{12^3}$$

so the bound is one-eighth the size of that for three quadratics. Of course, this does not mean that the actual error will differ by a factor of 8. Similar considerations apply in using cubic or higher-degree polynomials.

Even though the interpolating polynomial is unique, as shown by theorem 2.3.1, there are several alternative approaches to obtaining or representing the polynomial, other than by the Lagrange polynomials. Perhaps the most basic approach is the following. Suppose that the interpolation polynomial p is

$$p(x) = a_0 + a_1x + \cdots + a_nx^n$$

Then, we want

(2.3.10) $$a_0 + a_1x_i + \cdots + a_nx_i^n = y_i, \qquad i = 0, 1, \ldots, n$$

Since the x_i's and the y_i's are known, this is simply a system of $n + 1$ linear equations in the $n + 1$ unknowns $a_0, a_1, \ldots, a_n$. We write this system in the matrix-vector form:

(2.3.11) $$\begin{bmatrix} 1 & x_0 & x_0^2 & \cdots & x_0^n \\ 1 & x_1 & x_1^2 & \cdots & x_1^n \\ \cdot & \cdot & \cdot & & \\ \cdot & \cdot & \cdot & & \\ \cdot & \cdot & \cdot & & \\ 1 & x_n & x_n^2 & \cdots & x_n^n \end{bmatrix} \begin{bmatrix} a_0 \\ a_1 \\ \cdot \\ \cdot \\ \cdot \\ a_n \end{bmatrix} = \begin{bmatrix} y_0 \\ y_1 \\ \cdot \\ \cdot \\ \cdot \\ y_n \end{bmatrix}$$

The coefficient matrix of (2.3.11), which we denote by V, is called the *Vandermonde matrix* and is nonsingular if the x_i's are distinct. (This statement can be proved directly rather easily, but note that we already have proved it indirectly by means of theorem 2.3.1, which showed the existence and uniqueness of the interpolating polynomial. For if V were singular, this would imply that either no interpolating polynomial exists for the given data or infinitely many exist.)

The Vandermonde matrix approach is sometimes useful for theoretical purposes, but not so much for computation of the polynomial. For the latter, the Lagrange polynomials are usually better, but they are not convenient if a node is added or dropped from the data. For example, if (x_{n+1}, y_{n+1}) were added to the set of data (x_i, y_i), $i = 0, 1, \ldots, n$, and we wished to compute the polynomial of degree $n + 1$ that interpolated this data, then the Lagrange polynomials would all have to be recomputed. There is another representation of the interpolating polynomial that is very useful in this context; this is the *Newton representation*, which we now describe.

We assume now that the points x_i are equally spaced with spacing h. We define differences of the data y_i by means of $\Delta y_i = y_{i+1} - y_i$, and higher differences by means of repeated application of this:

$$\Delta^2 y_0 = \Delta y_1 - \Delta y_0 = y_2 - 2y_1 + y_0$$
$$\Delta^3 y_0 = \Delta^2 y_1 - \Delta^2 y_0 = y_3 - 3y_2 + 3y_1 - y_0$$

(2.3.12)
$$\vdots$$
$$\Delta^n y_0 = y_n - \binom{n}{1} y_{n-1} + \binom{n}{2} y_{n-2} - \cdots + (-1)^n y_0$$

where, as usual, the binomial coefficients $\binom{n}{i}$ are given by

$$\binom{n}{i} = \frac{n(n-1)\cdots(n-i+1)}{i!}$$

In terms of the differences (2.3.12), we define the polynomial of degree n by

(2.3.13)
$$p_n(x) = y_0 + \frac{(x-x_0)}{h}\Delta y_0 + \frac{(x-x_0)(x-x_1)}{2h^2}\Delta^2 y_0 + \cdots + \frac{(x-x_0)(x-x_1)\cdots(x-x_{n-1})}{n!h^n}\Delta^n y_0$$

Clearly, $p_n(x_0) = y_0$ since all remaining terms in (2.3.13) vanish. Similarly,

$$p_n(x_1) = y_0 + \frac{(x_1-x_0)}{h}(y_1 - y_0) = y_1$$

and

$$p_n(x_2) = y_0 + \frac{(x_2-x_0)}{h}(y_1-y_0) + \frac{(x_2-x_0)(x_2-x_1)}{2h^2}(y_2 - 2y_1 + y_0)$$
$$= y_0 + 2(y_1 - y_0) + (y_2 - 2y_1 + y_0) = y_2$$

It is easy to verify in an analogous way that $p_n(x_i) = y_i$, $i = 3, \ldots, n$, although the computations become increasingly tedious.

It is of interest to note that the polynomial p_n of (2.3.13) is analogous to the first $n+1$ terms of a Taylor expansion about x_0.

Now, suppose that we add (x_{n+1}, y_{n+1}) to the data set. Then, the polynomial p_{n+1} that satisfies $p_{n+1}(x_i) = y_i$, $i = 0, 1, \ldots, n+1$, is given by

$$p_{n+1}(x) = p_n(x) + \frac{(x-x_0)(x-x_1)\cdots(x-x_n)}{(n+1)!h^{n+1}}\Delta^{n+1} y_0$$

and it is this feature of the Newton form of the interpolating polynomial that is sometimes useful in practice.

In the next section, we will use interpolating polynomials to derive other methods for the solution of differential equations. They will also play useful roles in other parts of the book.

Supplementary Discussion and References: 2.3

We will indicate the proof of the basic error theorem 2.3.2. Assume that $x \neq x_j$, $j = 0, 1, \ldots, n$; otherwise, both sides of (2.3.6) are zero, and the result is trivially true. Now, for x held fixed, define the function

$$\phi(s) = f(s) - p(s) - q(x)\psi(s)$$

where

$$\psi(s) = (s - x_0)(s - x_1)\cdots(s - x_n) \qquad q(x) = \frac{f(x) - p(x)}{\psi(x)}$$

It is clear that $\phi(x_i) = 0$, $i = 0, 1, \ldots, n$, and $\phi(x) = 0$; hence, ϕ has at least $n + 2$ distinct roots $x_0, x_1, \ldots, x_n, x$. Then, it follows by repeated application of Rolle's theorem that ϕ' has at least $n + 1$ distinct roots, ϕ'' has at least n distinct roots, and so on. In particular, $\phi^{(n+1)}$ has at least one root z in the interval spanned by $x_0, x_1, \ldots, x_n, x$. But

$$\begin{aligned} \phi(s)^{(n+1)} = f(s)^{(n+1)} - p(s)^{(n+1)} - q(x)\psi(s)^{(n+1)} \\ = f(s)^{(n+1)} - (n + 1)!q(x) \end{aligned}$$

since p is a polynomial of degree n and ψ is a polynomial of degree $n + 1$. Thus,

$$0 = \phi(z)^{(n+1)} = f(z)^{(n+1)} - (n + 1)!q(x)$$

and solving for $q(x)$ gives (2.3.6).

For further discussions of interpolation, see, for example, Young and Gregory [1972] and Shampine and Allen [1973].

EXERCISES 2.3

2.3.1. Compute the polynomial p of degree 2 that satisfies $p(0) = 0$, $p(1) = 1$, $p(2) = 0$ by all three methods, that is, by using Lagrange polynomials, the Vandermonde matrix, and the Newton representation. Conclude that the polynomial is the same in all three cases.

2.3.2. Let $f(x) = \sin \pi x/2$, and let p be the polynomial of exercise 2.3.1 that agrees with f at the points $x = 0, 1, 2$. Use (2.3.7) to compute a bound for $|f(x) - p(x)|$ on the interval $[0, 2]$. Compare this bound with the actual error at selected points in the interval, and in particular at $x = \frac{1}{4}$ and $\frac{3}{4}$.

2.3.3. Find the piecewise linear and quadratic functions that agree with the following data:

x	0	1/6	1/3	1/2	2/3	5/6	1
f	1	4	1	−1	2	4	0

Compute error bounds for these functions on the interval [0, 1], assuming that the function f satisfies $|f''(z)| \le 4$, $|f'''(z)| \le 10$, $0 \le z \le 1$.

2.3.4. Let $f(x) = \sin x$ and let p and q be two polynomials of degree 3 that satisfy $p(k/3) = q(k/3) = f(k/3)$, $k = 0, 1, 2, 3$. Compute a bound for $|p(x) - q(x)|$ that holds on the whole interval [0, 1].

2.4 Numerical Solutions: Multistep Methods

We return now to the initial-value problem

(2.4.1) $$y' = f(x, y), \qquad a \le x \le b,\ y(a) = \hat{y}$$

In the methods of Section 2.2, the value of y_{k+1} depended only on information at the previous point, x_k. It seems plausible that more accuracy might be gained if information at several previous points, $x_k, x_{k-1}, \ldots$ was used. Multistep methods do just that.

A large and important class of multistep methods arises from the following approach. If we integrate (2.4.1) for the exact solution $y(x)$ over the interval $[x_k, x_{k+1}]$, we have

(2.4.2) $$y(x_{k+1}) - y(x_k) = \int_{x_k}^{x_{k+1}} y'(x)\,dx = \int_{x_k}^{x_{k+1}} f(x, y(x))\,dx$$

$$\doteq \int_{x_k}^{x_{k+1}} p(x)\,dx$$

where in the last term we assume that $p(x)$ is a polynomial that approximates $f(x, y(x))$. To obtain this polynomial, suppose that, as usual, $y_k, y_{k-1}, \ldots, y_{k-N}$ are approximations to the solution at $x_k, x_{k-1}, \ldots, x_{k-N}$, where we assume as before that the x_i are equally spaced with spacing h. Then, $f_i \equiv f(x_i, y_i)$, $i = k, k-1, \ldots, k-N$, are approximations to $f(x, y(x))$ at $x_k, x_{k-1}, \ldots, x_{k-N}$, and we take p to be the interpolating polynomial for the data set (x_i, f_i), $i = k, k-1, \ldots, k-N$. Thus, p is the polynomial of degree N that satisfies $p(x_i) = f_i$, $i = k, k-1, \ldots, k-N$. In principle, we can integrate this polynomial explicitly to give rise to the method

(2.4.3) $$y_{k+1} = y_k + \int_{x_k}^{x_{k+1}} p(x)\,dx$$

As the simplest example, if $N = 0$, then p is the constant f_k and (2.4.3) is simply Euler's method. If $N = 1$, then p is the linear function that interpolates (x_{k-1}, f_{k-1}) and (x_k, f_k); that is,

$$p(x) = -\frac{(x - x_k)}{h} f_{k-1} + \frac{(x - x_{k-1})}{h} f_k$$

If we integrate this from x_k to x_{k+1}, we obtain the method

$$y_{k+1} = y_k + \frac{h}{2}(3f_k - f_{k-1}) \tag{2.4.4}$$

which is a two-step method since it uses information at the two points x_k and x_{k-1}. Similarly, if $N = 2$, then p is the interpolating quadratic polynomial for (x_{k-2}, f_{k-2}), (x_{k-1}, f_{k-1}), and (x_k, f_k), and the corresponding method is

$$y_{k+1} = y_k + \frac{h}{12}(23f_k - 16f_{k-1} + 5f_{k-2}) \tag{2.4.5}$$

If $N = 3$, the interpolating polynomial is a cubic, and the method is

$$y_{k+1} = y_k + \frac{h}{24}(55f_k - 59f_{k-1} + 37f_{k-2} - 9f_{k-3}) \tag{2.4.6}$$

Note that (2.4.5) is a three-step method whereas (2.4.6) is a four-step method.

The formulas (2.4.4)–(2.4.6) are known as *Adams–Bashforth methods.* As we shall see later, (2.4.4) is second-order accurate and hence is known as the *second-order Adams–Bashforth method.* Similarly, (2.4.5) and (2.4.6) are the *third-* and *fourth-order Adams–Bashforth methods,* respectively. We can, in principle, continue the preceding process to obtain Adams–Bashforth methods of arbitrarily high order by increasing the number of prior points used and, hence, the degree of the interpolating polynomial p. The formulas become increasingly complex as N increases, but the principle is still the same.

Multistep methods suffer from a problem not encountered with one-step methods. The problem is easily seen if we consider the fourth-order Adams–Bashforth method of (2.4.6). The initial value y_0 is given to us; but for $k = 0$ in (2.4.6), information is needed at x_{-1}, x_{-2}, and x_{-3}, which, of course, doesn't exist. The problem is that multistep methods need "help" getting started. We cannot use (2.4.6) until $k \geq 3$, nor can we use (2.4.5) until $k \geq 2$. The usual solution is to use a one-step method, such as Runge–Kutta, of the same order of accuracy until enough values have been computed so that the multistep method is usable. Alternatively, one may use a one-step method at the first step, a two-step method at the second, and so on until enough starting values have been built up. However, it is important that the starting values obtained in this fashion are as accurate as those to be produced by the final method, and since the starting methods are of lower order, this will necessitate using a smaller step size and generating more intermediate points at the outset.

The Adams–Bashforth methods were obtained by using information already computed at x_k and prior points. In principle, we can also form the interpolating polynomial by using x_{k+1}, x_{k+2}, and so on. The simplest situation is to use the points $x_{k+1}, x_k, \ldots, x_{k-N}$ and form the interpolating polynomial of degree $N + 1$ that satisfies $p(x_i) = f_i$, $i = k + 1, k, \ldots, k - N$. This generates a class of methods known as *Adams–Moulton methods.* If $N = 0$, then p is the linear function that interpolates (x_k, f_k) and (x_{k+1}, f_{k+1}), and the corresponding method is

$$y_{k+1} = y_k + \frac{h}{2}(f_{k+1} + f_k) \tag{2.4.7}$$

which is the *second-order Adams–Moulton method.* If $N = 2$, then p is the cubic polynomial that interpolates (x_{k+1}, f_{k+1}), (x_k, f_k), (x_{k-1}, f_{k-1}), and (x_{k-2}, f_{k-2}); in this case, the corresponding method is

$$y_{k+1} = y_k + \frac{h}{24}(9f_{k+1} + 19f_k - 5f_{k-1} + f_{k-2}) \tag{2.4.8}$$

which is the *fourth-order Adams–Moulton method.*

Now, note that in the formulas (2.4.7) and (2.4.8), f_{k+1} is not known since we need y_{k+1} to evaluate $f(x_{k+1}, y_{k+1}) = f_{k+1}$, but y_{k+1} is not yet known either. Hence, the Adams–Moulton methods define y_{k+1} only implicitly. For example, (2.4.7) is really an equation

$$y_{k+1} = y_k + \frac{h}{2}[f(x_{k+1}, y_{k+1}) + f_k] \tag{2.4.9}$$

for the unknown value y_{k+1}, and similarly for (2.4.8). Thus, the Adams–Moulton methods are called *implicit* whereas the Adams–Bashforth methods are called *explicit* since no equation needs to be solved in order to obtain y_{k+1}.

In practice, we do not actually solve (2.4.9) but rather combine an explicit formula with an implicit one to form a *predictor-corrector method.* A commonly used predictor-corrector method is the combination of the fourth-order Adams methods (2.4.6) and (2.4.8):

$$\begin{aligned} y_{k+1}^{(p)} &= y_k + \frac{h}{24}(55f_k - 59f_{k-1} + 37f_{k-2} - 9f_{k-3}) \\ f_{k+1}^{(p)} &= f(x_{k+1}, y_{k+1}^{(p)}) \\ y_{k+1} &= y_k + \frac{h}{24}(9f_{k+1}^{(p)} + 19f_k - 5f_{k-1} + f_{k-2}) \end{aligned} \tag{2.4.10}$$

Note that this method is entirely explicit; first, a "predicted" value $y_{k+1}^{(p)}$ of y_{k+1} is computed by the Adams–Bashforth formula, then $y_{k+1}^{(p)}$ is used to give an approximate value of f_{k+1}, which is used in the Adams–Moulton formula. The Adams–Moulton formula "corrects" the approximation given by the Adams–Bashforth formula.

We turn now to the question of the discretization error and for simplicity, we will consider in detail only the Adams–Bashforth method (2.4.4). In a manner analogous to (2.2.23) for one-step methods, we define the local discretization error at x by

(2.4.11)
$$L(x, h) = \frac{1}{h}\left\{y(x+h) - y(x) - \frac{h}{2}[3f(x, y(x)) - f(x-h, y(x-h))]\right\}$$

where $y(x)$ is the exact solution of the differential equation. Since $y'(x) = f(x, y(x))$, we can rewrite (2.4.11) in terms of y and y' and then expand y and y' in a Taylor series about x. This gives

(2.4.12)
$$\begin{aligned} L(x, h) &= \frac{1}{h}\left\{y(x+h) - y(x) - \frac{h}{2}[3y'(x) - y'(x-h)]\right\} \\ &= \frac{1}{h}\left\{hy'(x) + \frac{h^2}{2}y''(x) + \frac{h^3}{6}y'''(x) + \frac{h^4}{24}y^{(4)}(z_1)\right. \\ &\qquad \left. - \frac{h}{2}[3y'(x) - y'(x) + hy''(x) - \frac{h^2}{2}y'''(x) + \frac{h^3}{6}y^{(4)}(z_2)]\right\} \\ &= \frac{5}{12}h^2y'''(x) + \frac{h^3}{24}y^{(4)}(z_1) - \frac{h^4}{12}y^{(4)}(z_2) \end{aligned}$$

where the points z_1 and z_2 are the intermediate points for the remainder terms in the Taylor expansion. Therefore, assuming that the fourth derivative of the solution is bounded (and, hence, the second derivative also), we have that the local discretization error $L(h)$ satisfies

(2.4.13)
$$L(h) = \max_{a \leq x \leq b-h} |L(x, h)| = 0(h^2)$$

which shows that the method is second order.

We could define the local discretization error separately for each of the other methods of this section. However, all of these methods are special cases of what are called *linear multistep* methods which are of the form

(2.4.14)
$$y_{k+1} = \sum_{i=1}^{m} \alpha_i y_{k+1-i} + h \sum_{i=0}^{m} \beta_i f_{k+1-i}$$

where, as usual, $f_j = f(x_j, y_j)$, and m is some fixed integer. The method (2.4.14) is called linear since y_{k+1} is a linear combination of the y_i and f_i. If $\beta_0 = 0$, the method is explicit, and if $\beta_0 \neq 0$, then the method is implicit. In all of the Adams methods, $\alpha_1 = 1$ and $\alpha_i = 0$, $i > 1$; in the Adams–Bashforth methods, $\beta_0 = 0$; for Adams–Moulton, $\beta_0 \neq 0$.

For the general linear multistep method (2.4.14), we define the local discretization error at x by

(2.4.15)

$$L(x, h) = \frac{1}{h}[y(x + h) - \sum_{i=1}^{m} \alpha_i y(x - (i - 1)h)] - \sum_{i=0}^{m} \beta_i f(x, y(x - (i - 1)h))$$
$$= \frac{1}{h}[y(x + h) - \sum_{i=1}^{m} \alpha_i y(x - (i - 1)h)] - \sum_{i=0}^{m} \beta_i y'(x - (i - 1)h)$$

and the local discretization error by

(2.4.16) $$L(h) = \max_{a \leq x \leq b-h} |L(x, h)|$$

For any given method, that is, for any given choice of m and the constants α_i and β_i, one can compute the local discretization error by expansion of y and y' in Taylor series about x. In particular, under suitable assumptions on the differentiability of the solution, one can show that the Adams–Bashforth methods (2.4.5) and (2.4.6) are third and fourth order, respectively, whereas the Adams–Moulton methods (2.4.7) and (2.4.8) are second and fourth order. The verification of these statements is left to exercise 2.4.6.

Once the local discretization error is known, there remains the problem of bounding the global discretization error, which is defined—as for one-step methods—by $E(h) = \max_{1 \leq k \leq N} |y(x_k) - y_k|$. In general, this is a difficult problem, but under suitable assumptions on f and the solution y, it can be shown for all of the methods of this section that $E(h) = 0(h^p)$ when $L(h) = 0(h^p)$.

The methods of this section constitute an attractive alternative to the one-step methods of Section 2.2. High-order methods can be constructed that require only one evaluation of f at each step but at the price that the methods are not self-starting. Indeed, high-order Adams methods are the basis of the most efficient computer codes available today. (See the Supplementary Discussion at the end of this section.)

We conclude this section by returning to the sample problems of Section 2.1. In Section 2.2, Figure 2.8, we gave an approximate solution of the predator–prey equations (2.2.34)/(2.2.35) obtained by the second-order Runge–Kutta method. In Figure 2.10, we superimpose on Figure 2.8 an approximate solution obtained by a second-order Adams–Bashforth/Adams–Moulton predictor-corrector method, which is based on (2.4.4) and (2.4.7) and given explicitly in exercise 2.4.5. Note that these two second-order methods are in error by a comparable amount

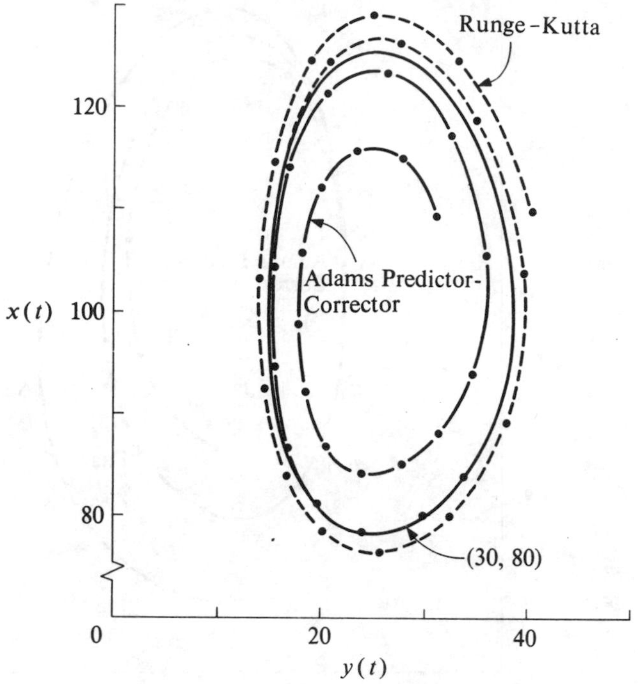

FIGURE 2.10 *Second-Order Runge–Kutta (Spiraling Outward) and Second-Order Adams Predictor-Corrector (Spiraling Inward), with Step Size $h = 1$ for Both, Compared to the "Exact" Solution of* (2.2.34)/(2.2.35).

although one approximate solution spirals in whereas the other spirals out. The step size used for both methods was $h = 1$.

Figure 2.11 compares the second-order predictor-corrector method of Figure 2.10 with the second-order Adams–Bashforth method. Note the strong effect that the correction step has on the Adams–Bashforth method; the accuracy is improved somewhat but, more noticeably, the approximate solution now spirals in rather than out. Again, the step size for both methods was $h = 1$.

We turn now to the trajectory problem discussed in Section 2.1. The system of ordinary differential equations used for the projectile problem is given by (2.1.15), (2.1.17), and (2.1.18) with $T = 0$ and $\dot{m} = 0$:

(2.4.17)
$$\dot{x} = v\cos\theta \qquad \dot{y} = v\sin\theta$$
$$\dot{v} = -\frac{1}{2m}c\rho s v^2 - g\sin\theta \qquad \dot{\theta} = -\frac{g}{v}\cos\theta$$

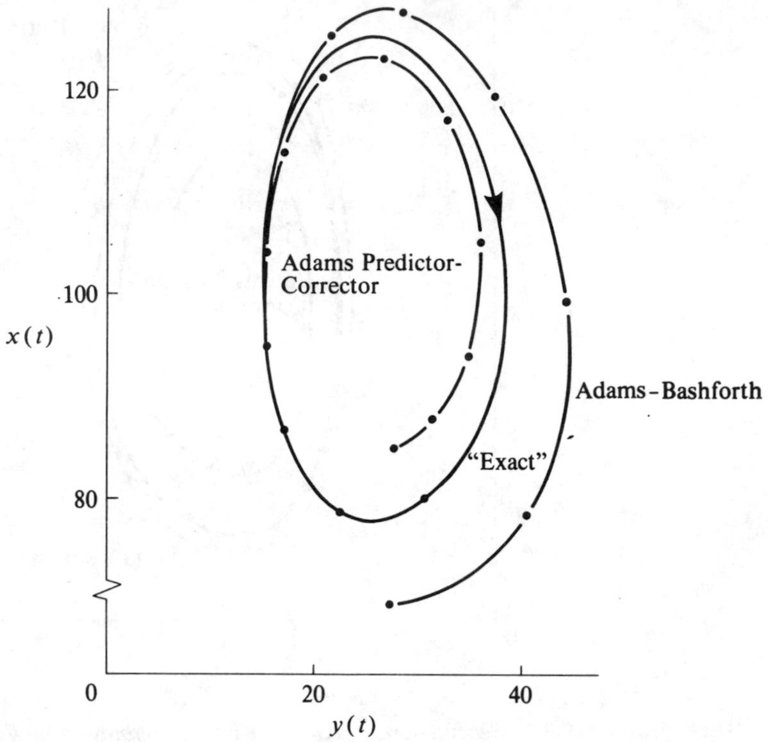

FIGURE 2.11 *Second-Order Adams–Bashforth and Adams Predictor-Corrector Compared to the "Exact" Solution of* (2.2.34)/(2.2.35).

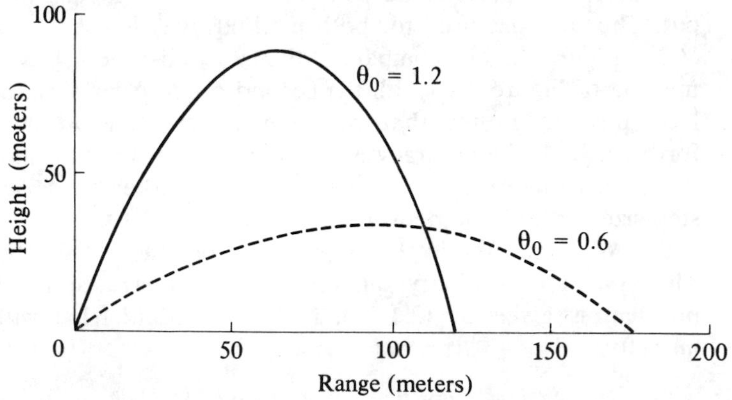

FIGURE 2.12 *Second-Order Adams Predictor-Corrector Applied to the Trajectory Problem* (2.4.17)/(2.4.18) *Using Two Different Initial Angles.*

with initial conditions

(2.4.18) $x(0) = 0 \qquad y(0) = 0 \qquad v(0) = v_0 \qquad \theta(0) = \theta_0$

Values for the parameters in (2.4.17) are $m = 15$ kg, $c = 0.2$, $\rho = 1.29$ kg/m, $s = 0.25$ m^2, and $g = 9.81$ m/s^2. The initial value for v is $v_0 = 50$ m/s. Two different initial angles were used: $\theta_0 = 0.6$ and 1.2 radians. Figure 2.12 is a plot of the height versus range of the projectile.

Supplementary Discussion and References: 2.4

The Adams methods form the basis for a number of highly sophisticated computer codes. In these codes, the Adams methods are implemented with the capability of changing not only the step size—as we discussed with the Runge–Kutta methods—but also the order of the method: the order is allowed to go as high as thirteen in current codes. For more discussion of the theory and practice of Adams methods see, for example, Gear [1971], Lambert [1973], and Lapidus and Seinfeld [1971]. For an excellent account of the state of computer codes for both Runge–Kutta and multistep methods as of the mid 1970s, see Shampine, Watts, and Davenport [1976]; this article makes the important point that the difference in the way a given method is implemented on a computer can be more important than the intrinsic difference between methods.

Another approach to the derivation of multistep methods starts with the general linear method (2.4.14) and requires that it be exact when the solution y of the differential equation is a polynomial of degree q. This then implies that the method is order q. For example, if $q = 1$, then (2.4.14) must be exact whenever the solution is a constant; in this case, the f_i all vanish [since $f(x, y(x)) = y'(x) = 0$], and we are left with the condition

(2.4.19) $$1 = \sum_{i=1}^{m} \alpha_i$$

Similarly, the requirement that (2.4.14) be exact whenever the solution is $y(x) = x$ leads to the condition

(2.4.20) $$m + 1 = \alpha_1 m + \alpha_2(m - 1) + \cdots + \alpha_m + \sum_{i=0}^{m} \beta_i$$

The relations (2.4.19) and (2.4.20) for the coefficients α_i and β_i are known as the *consistency conditions* for the multistep method and are necessary and sufficient conditions that the method be first order. One can continue this process to obtain relations on the α_i and β_i that are necessary and sufficient that the method be of any given order. For further discussions of multistep methods, see, for example, Henrici [1962] and Lambert [1973].

We can combine the one-step methods of Section 2.2 with the multistep methods of this section into the same general formulation:

(2.4.21)

$$y_{k+1} = \sum_{i=1}^{m} \alpha_i y_{k+1-i} + h\phi(x_{k+1}, x_k, \ldots, x_{k+1-m}; y_{k+1}, y_k, \ldots, y_{k+1-m})$$

For one-step methods, $m = 1$, and if $\alpha_1 = 1$ and ϕ is independent of x_{k+1} and y_{k+1}, then (2.4.21) reduces to the one-step method (2.2.21). On the other hand, if ϕ is the function

$$\phi = \sum_{i=0}^{m} \beta_i f(x_{k+1-i}, y_{k+1-i})$$

then (2.4.21) reduces to the linear multistep method (2.4.4). The formulation (2.4.21) contains virtually all methods in current use.

EXERCISES 2.4

2.4.1. Write down the interpolating polynomial of degree 2 for the data set (x_{k-2}, f_{k-2}), (x_{k-1}, f_{k-1}), (x_k, f_k) and then integrate this polynomial in (2.4.3) to obtain (2.4.5). Derive the formula (2.4.6) in a similar manner by integrating the third-degree polynomial obtained by adding (x_{k-3}, f_{k-3}) to the data set.

2.4.2. Write a computer program to carry out the second-order Adams–Bashforth method (2.4.4). Use the second-order Runge–Kutta method to supply the missing starting value y_1. Apply your program to the problems of exercises 2.2.2 and 2.2.4 and compare your results with the Euler and Heun methods.

2.4.3. Repeat exercise 2.4.2 using the fourth-order Adams–Bashforth method (2.4.6).

2.4.4. Carry out in detail the derivation of the Adams–Moulton method (2.4.7). Do the same for the method (2.4.8).

2.4.5. Use as much of your program of exercise 2.4.2 as possible to write a computer program to carry out the predictor-corrector method $y_{k+1}^{(p)} = y_k + (h/2)(3f_k - f_{k-1})$, $f_{k+1}^{(p)} = f(x_{k+1}, y_{k+1}^{(p)})$, $y_{k+1} = y_k + (h/2)(f_{k+1}^{(p)} + f_k)$. Apply this to the same problem $y' = -y$, $y(0) = 1$ and compare your results with the method of exercise 2.4.2. Similarly, write a program to carry out (2.4.10).

2.4.6. Compute the local discretization errors for the Adams–Bashforth methods (2.4.5) and (2.4.6) and show that they are third and fourth order, respectively. (Assume that the solution is sufficiently differentiable.) Do the same for the Adams–Moulton methods (2.4.7) and (2.4.8) and verify that they are second and fourth order, respectively.

2.4.7. Write down the coefficients α_i and β_i in the linear multistep formulation (2.4.14) for the Adams–Bashforth and Adams–Moulton methods of second, third, and fourth order.

2.4.8. Consider the method $y_{k+1} = y_{k-1} + (h/2)(f_{k+1} + 2f_k + f_{k-1})$ for solving the initial-value problem $y'(x) = f(x, y(x))$, $y(0) = \alpha$.

a. Find the order of the method.

b. Discuss how to apply this method to the *system* of equations $\mathbf{y}' = \mathbf{f}(x, \mathbf{y})$, $\mathbf{y}(0) = \boldsymbol{\alpha}$, what difficulties you expect to encounter in carrying out the method, and so on.

2.4.9. Repeat the calculations of Figure 2.11 using the second-order Adams–Bashforth method and the predictor-corrector method of exercise 2.4.5.

2.4.10. Repeat the calculations of Figure 2.12. Find the value of θ_0 such that the range of the rocket is 150 m.

2.5 Stability, Instability, and Stiff Equations

One of the pervading concerns of scientific computing is that of *stability*, a much overused word that tends to have somewhat different meanings depending on the context. In this section, we will discuss several aspects of stability as it pertains to the numerical solution of ordinary differential equations.

Consider the second-order differential equation

(2.5.1)
$$y'' - 10y' - 11y = 0$$

with the initial conditions

(2.5.2)
$$y(0) = 1 \qquad y'(0) = -1$$

The solution of (2.5.1)/(2.5.2) is $y(x) = e^{-x}$, as is easily verified. Now, suppose we change the first initial condition by a small quantity ε so that the initial conditions are

(2.5.3)
$$y(0) = 1 + \varepsilon \qquad y'(0) = -1$$

Then, as is again easily verified by direct calculation, the solution of (2.5.1) with the initial conditions (2.5.3) is

(2.5.4)
$$y(x) = (1 + \tfrac{11}{12}\varepsilon)e^{-x} + \frac{\varepsilon}{12}e^{11x}$$

Therefore, for any $\varepsilon > 0$, no matter how small, the second term in (2.5.4) causes the solution to tend to infinity as $x \to \infty$. The two solutions are shown in Figure 2.13. We say that the solution $y(x) = e^{-x}$ of the problem (2.5.1)/(2.5.2) is *unstable*; that is, arbitrarily small changes in the initial conditions can produce arbitrarily large changes in the solution as $x \to \infty$. In the parlance of numerical analysis, one would also say that this

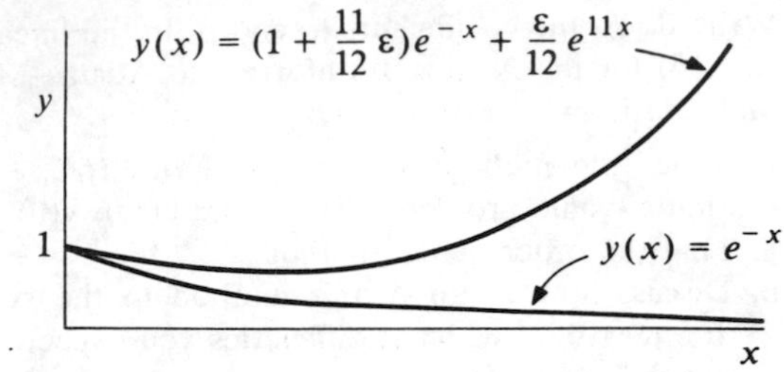

FIGURE 2.13 *Solutions of Slightly Different Problems.*

problem is *ill-conditioned*; it is extremely difficult to obtain the solution numerically because rounding and truncation error will cause the same effect as changing the initial conditions and the approximate solution will tend to diverge to infinity (see exercise 2.5.1).

Even more pronounced instabilities can occur with nonlinear equations. For example, the problem

(2.5.5) $$y' = xy(y-2), \qquad y(0) = 2$$

has the solution $y(x) \equiv 2$, which is unstable. To see this, note that for the initial condition $y(0) = y_0$, the solution is

$$y(x) = \frac{2y_0}{y_0 + (2 - y_0)e^{x^2}}$$

so, if $y_0 < 2$, then $y(x) \to 0$ as $x \to \infty$, and if $y_0 > 2$, the solution increases and has a singularity when $y_0 + (2 - y_0)e^{x^2} = 0$. Typical solutions are shown in Figure 2.14.

The two previous examples illustrated instabilities of solutions of the differential equation itself. We now turn to possible instabilities in the numerical method. Let us consider the method

(2.5.6) $$y_{n+1} = y_{n-1} + 2hf_n$$

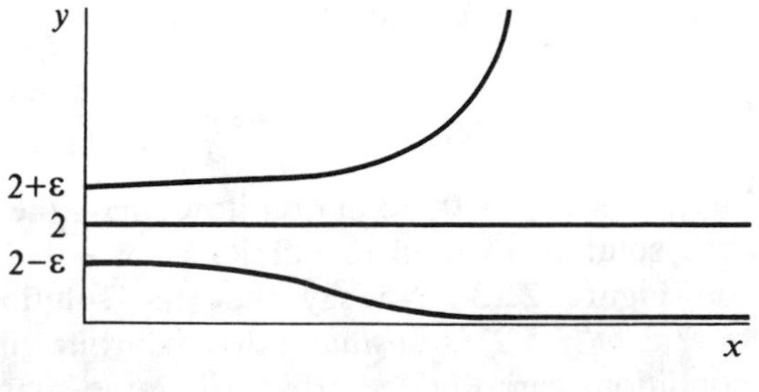

FIGURE 2.14 *Solutions to Three Slightly Different Problems.*

which is a multistep method similar to Euler's method but which is second-order accurate, as is easy to verify (see exercise 2.5.3).

We now apply (2.5.6) to the problem

(2.5.7) $$y' = -2y + 1, \qquad y(0) = 1$$

whose exact solution is

(2.5.8) $$y(x) = \tfrac{1}{2}e^{-2x} + \tfrac{1}{2}$$

This solution is stable since, if the initial condition is changed to $y(0) = 1 + \varepsilon$, the solution becomes

$$y(x) = (\tfrac{1}{2} + \varepsilon)e^{-2x} + \tfrac{1}{2}$$

so the change in the solution is only εe^{-2x}.

The method (2.5.6) applied to (2.5.7) is

(2.5.9) $$y_{n+1} = y_{n-1} + 2h(-2y_n + 1), \qquad y_0 = 1$$

with y_0 taken as the initial condition. However, since (2.5.6) is a two-step method, we need to supply y_1 also in order to start the process, and we will take y_1 to be the exact solution (2.5.8) at $x = h$; that is,

(2.5.10) $$y_1 = \tfrac{1}{2}e^{-2h} + \tfrac{1}{2}$$

It is relatively easy to analyze the behavior of the sequence $\{y_n\}$ generated by (2.5.9). To do this, we shall view (2.5.9) as a *difference equation.* The theory of difference equations parallels that of differential equations, and we will sketch the basic parts of this theory in the case of *linear difference equations of order m with constant coefficients*; such an equation is of the form

(2.5.11)

$$y_{n+1} = a_m y_n + \cdots + a_1 y_{n-m+1} + a_0, \qquad n = m - 1, m, m + 1, \ldots$$

with given constants $a_0, a_1, \ldots, a_m$. The *homogeneous part* of (2.5.11) is

(2.15.12) $$y_{n+1} = a_m y_n + \cdots + a_1 y_{n-m+1}$$

In analogy with differential equations, we attempt to find an exponential type solution of (2.5.12), only now the exponential takes the form $y_k = \lambda^k$ for some unknown constant λ. We see that $y_k = \lambda^k$ indeed is a solution of (2.5.12) provided that λ satisfies

(2.5.13) $$\lambda^m - a_m\lambda^{m-1} - \cdots - a_1 = 0$$

which is the *characteristic equation* of (2.5.12). If we assume that the m roots $\lambda_1, \ldots, \lambda_m$ of (2.5.13) are distinct, then the fundamental solutions of (2.5.12) are $\lambda_1^k, \ldots, \lambda_m^k$, and the general solution of (2.5.12) is

(2.5.14) $$y_k = \sum_{i=1}^{m} c_i\lambda_i^k, \qquad k = 0, 1, \ldots$$

where the c_i are arbitrary constants. Provided that $1 - a_m - a_{m-1} - \cdots - a_1 \neq 0$, a *particular solution* of (2.5.11) is given by

(2.5.15) $$y_k = \frac{a_0}{1 - a_1 - \cdots - a_m}$$

as is easily verified. Therefore, the general solution of (2.5.11) is the sum of (2.5.14) and (2.5.15):

(2.5.16) $$y_k = \sum_{i=1}^{m} c_i \lambda_i^k + \frac{a_0}{1 - a_1 - \cdots - a_m}, \qquad k = 0, 1, \ldots$$

The arbitrary constants in (2.5.16) can be determined—just as for differential equations—by imposing additional conditions on the solution. In particular, suppose we are given the initial conditions

(2.5.17) $$y_0, y_1, \ldots, y_{m-1}$$

Then, (2.5.16) gives the conditions

(2.5.18) $$\sum_{i=1}^{m} c_i \lambda_i^k + \frac{a_0}{1 - a_1 - \cdots - a_m} = y_k, \qquad k = 0, 1, \ldots, m - 1$$

which is a system of m linear equations in the m unknowns $c_1, \ldots, c_m$, and can be used to determine the c_i.

We now apply this theory to the difference equation (2.5.9), which we write in the form

(2.5.19) $$y_{n+1} = -4hy_n + y_{n-1} + 2h, \qquad y_0 = 1, y_1 = \tfrac{1}{2}e^{-2h} + \tfrac{1}{2}$$

The characteristic equation (2.5.13) is $\lambda^2 + 4h\lambda - 1 = 0$ with roots

(2.5.20) $$\lambda_1 = -2h + \sqrt{1 + 4h^2} \qquad \lambda_2 = -2h - \sqrt{1 + 4h^2}$$

The conditions (2.5.18) then become

$$c_1 + c_2 + \tfrac{1}{2} = y_0 = 1 \qquad c_1\lambda_1 + c_2\lambda_2 + \tfrac{1}{2} = y_1 = \tfrac{1}{2}e^{-2h} + \tfrac{1}{2}$$

which can be solved for c_1 and c_2 to give

(2.5.21) $$c_1 = \tfrac{1}{4} + \frac{y_1 - \frac{1}{2} + h}{2\sqrt{1 + 4h^2}} \qquad c_2 = \tfrac{1}{4} - \frac{(y_1 - \frac{1}{2} + h)}{2\sqrt{1 + 4h^2}}$$

Thus, the solution of (2.5.19) is

(2.5.22) $$y_n = c_1(-2h + \sqrt{1 + 4h^2})^n + c_2(-2h - \sqrt{1 + 4h^2})^n + \tfrac{1}{2}$$

Although this representation of the solution is perhaps a little formidable, it allows us to see very easily the behavior of y_n as $n \to \infty$. In particular, for any fixed step size $h > 0$, it is evident that

$$0 < -2h + \sqrt{1 + 4h^2} < 1 \qquad 2h + \sqrt{1 + 4h^2} > 1$$

Therefore, the first term in (2.5.22) tends to zero while the second tends to infinity, in an oscillatory way, as n tends to infinity. Since the exact solution (2.5.8) of the differential equation tends to 1/2 as x tends to infinity, we see that the error in the approximate solution $\{y_n\}$ diverges to infinity, and the method (2.5.9) is unstable applied to the problem (2.5.7). Note that this divergence of the error has nothing to do with rounding error; (2.5.22) is the exact mathematical representation of y_n, and if the sequence (2.5.19) were computed in exact arithmetic, it would correspond precisely with that given by (2.5.22).

From the preceding example, it is clear that an important property of a method is that it be stable in some sense. The most basic definition of stability may be given in terms of the general method (2.4.21), that is,

(2.5.23) $$y_{n+1} = \sum_{i=1}^{m} \alpha_i y_{n+1-i} + h\phi(x_{n+1}, \ldots, x_{n+1-m}, y_{n+1}, \ldots, y_{n+1-m})$$

The method (2.5.23) is *stable* provided that all roots λ_i of the polynomial

(2.5.24) $$\rho(\lambda) \equiv \lambda^m - \alpha_1\lambda^{m-1} - \cdots - \alpha_m$$

satisfy $|\lambda_i| \leq 1$ and that any root for which $|\lambda_i| = 1$ is simple. The method is *strongly stable* if, in addition, $m - 1$ roots of (2.5.24) satisfy $|\lambda_i| < 1$.

Any method that is at least first-order accurate must satisfy the condition $\sum_{i=1}^{m} \alpha_i = 1$; that is, 1 is a root of (2.5.24). In this case, a strongly stable method will then have one root of (2.5.24) equal to 1 and all the rest strictly less than 1 in absolute value. For Runge–Kutta methods, $\rho(\lambda) = \lambda - 1$ since the method is one-step; hence, there are no roots of (2.5.24) besides the root $\lambda = 1$, and these methods are always strongly stable. For an m-step Adams method, $\rho(\lambda) = \lambda^m - \lambda^{m-1}$, so the other $m - 1$ roots of (2.5.24) are zero, and these methods also are strongly stable.

For the method (2.5.19), the polynomial (2.5.24) is $\rho(\lambda) = \lambda^2 - 1$ with roots ± 1; hence, this method is stable but not strongly stable, and it is this lack of strong stability that gives rise to the unstable behavior of the sequence $\{y_k\}$ defined by (2.5.19). The reason for this is as follows. The difference equation (2.5.19) is second order (since y_{n+1}, y_n, and y_{n-1} appear in the equation) and has two fundamental solutions, λ_1^n and λ_2^n, where λ_1 and λ_2 are the roots (2.5.20). Now, the sequence $\{y_k\}$ generated by (2.5.19) is meant to approximate the solution of the differential equation (2.5.7), which is a first-order equation with only one fundamental solution. This fundamental solution is approximated by λ_1^n; λ_2^n is spurious and should rapidly go to zero. However, for any $h > 0$, $|\lambda_2| > 1$, and hence λ_2^n tends to infinity and not zero; it is this that causes the instability. Now, note that λ_1 and λ_2 converge to the roots of the stability polynomial (2.5.24) as $h \to 0$; indeed, this polynomial is just the limit, as $h \to 0$, of the characteristic polynomial $\lambda^2 + 4h\lambda - 1$ of (2.5.19). The idea of strong stability now becomes more evident. If all the roots except one of the stability polynomial are less than 1 in magnitude, then all but one of the roots of the characteristic equation of the method must be less than 1 for sufficiently small h, and hence powers of these roots—the spurious fundamental solutions of the difference equation—tend to zero and cause no instability.

The stability theory that we have just discussed is essentially stability in the limit as $h \to 0$, and the example of instability that we gave shows what can happen for arbitrarily small h if the method is stable but not strongly stable. But even strongly stable methods can exhibit unstable behavior if h is too large, and although, in principle, h can be taken sufficiently small to overcome this difficulty, it may be that the computing time then becomes prohibitive. This is the situation with differential equations that are known as *stiff*, and we shall conclude this section with a short discussion of such problems.

Consider the equation

(2.5.25) $$y' = -100y + 100, \qquad y(0) = y_0$$

The exact solution of this problem is

(2.5.26) $$y(x) = (y_0 - 1)e^{-100x} + 1$$

It is clear that the solution is stable since, if we change the initial condition to $y_0 + \varepsilon$, then the solution changes by εe^{-100x}. Euler's method applied to (2.5.25) is

(2.5.27) $$y_{n+1} = y_n + h(-100y_n + 100) = (1 - 100h)y_n + 100h$$

and the exact solution of this first-order difference equation is

(2.5.28) $$y_n = (y_0 - 1)(1 - 100h)^n + 1$$

For concreteness, suppose that $y_0 = 2$ so that the exact solutions (2.5.26) and (2.5.28) become

(2.5.29) $$y(x) = e^{-100x} + 1$$

(2.5.30) $$y_n = (1 - 100h)^n + 1$$

Now, $y(x)$ decreases very rapidly from $y_0 = 2$ to its limiting value of 1; for example, $y(0.1) \doteq 1 + (5)(10)^{-5}$. Initially, therefore, we expect to require a small step size h to compute the solution accurately. However, beyond, say, $x = 0.1$, the solution varies slowly and is essentially equal to 1, so intuitively, we would expect to obtain sufficient accuracy with Euler's method using a relatively large h. However, we see from (2.5.30) that if $h > 0.02$, then $|1 - 100h| > 1$ and the approximation y_n grows rapidly at each step and shows an unstable behavior. If we compare the exact solutions (2.5.29) and (2.5.30), we see that the particular solutions of (2.5.25) and (2.5.27) are identical (and equal to 1). The quantity $(1 - 100h)^n$ is an approximation to the exponential term e^{-100x} and is, indeed, a good approximation for small h but rapidly becomes a poor approximation as h becomes as large as 0.02. Even though this exponential term contributes virtually nothing to the solution after $x = 0.1$, Euler's method still requires that we approximate it sufficiently accurately to maintain stability. This is the typical problem with stiff equations: the solution contains a component that contributes very little to the solution, but the usual methods require that it be approximated accurately in order to maintain stability.

This problem occurs very frequently in systems of equations. For example, consider the second-order equation

(2.5.31) $$y'' + 101y' + 100y = 0$$

As discussed in Appendix 2, we can convert (2.5.31) to an equivalent system of two first-order equations, but it is sufficient for our purposes to treat it in its second-order form. The general solution of (2.5.31) is

$$y(x) = c_1e^{-100x} + c_2e^{-x}$$

and if we impose the initial conditions

$$y(0) = 1.01 \qquad y'(0) = -2$$

the solution is

(2.5.32) $$y(x) = \tfrac{1}{100}e^{-100x} + e^{-x}$$

Clearly, the first term of this solution contributes very little after x reaches a value such as $x = 0.1$. Yet, we will have the same problem as in the previous example if we apply Euler's method to the first-order system corresponding to (2.5.31); that is, we will need to make the step size sufficiently small to approximate e^{-100x} accurately even though this term contributes very little to the solution.

The preceding example illustrates the essence of the problem of stiffness in systems of equations. Usually, the independent variable in such problems is time and the physical problem that is being modeled has transients that decay to zero very rapidly but with which the numerical scheme must cope even after they no longer contribute to the solution.

The general approach to the problem of stiffness is to use implicit methods. It is beyond the scope of this book to discuss these in detail, and we will only give an indication of the value of implicit methods in this context by applying one of the simplest such methods to the problem (2.5.25).

For the general equation $y' = f(x, y)$, the method

(2.5.33) $$y_{n+1} = y_n + hf(x_{n+1}, y_{n+1})$$

is known as the *backward Euler method*. It is of the same form as Euler's method except that f is evaluated at (x_{n+1}, y_{n+1}) rather than at (x_n, y_n); hence, the method is implicit. If we apply (2.5.33) to (2.5.25), we obtain

(2.5.34) $$y_{n+1} = y_n + h(-100y_{n+1} + 100)$$

which is easily put in the form

(2.5.35) $$y_{n+1} = (1 + 100h)^{-1}(y_n + 100h)$$

The exact solution of (2.5.35) is

(2.5.36) $$y_n = (y_0 - 1)(1 + 100h)^{-n} + 1$$

as is easily verified (exercise 2.5.10). In particular, for the initial condition $y_0 = 2$, which was treated previously, (2.5.36) becomes

(2.5.37) $$y_n = \frac{1}{(1 + 100h)^n} + 1$$

and we see that there is no unstable behavior regardless of the size of h.

The backward Euler method, like Euler's method itself, is only first-order accurate, and a better choice would be the second-order Adams–Moulton method (2.4.7),

(2.5.38) $$y_{n+1} = y_n + \frac{h}{2}[f_n + f(x_{n+1}, y_{n+1})]$$

which is also known as the *trapezoid rule*. The application of this method to (2.5.25) is left to exercise 2.5.14.

The application of an implicit method to (2.5.25) was deceptively simple since the differential equation is linear, and hence we could easily solve for y_{n+1} in (2.5.34). If the differential equation had been nonlinear, however, the method would have required the solution of a nonlinear equation for y_{n+1} at each step. More generally, for a system of differential equations, the solution of a system of equations (linear or nonlinear, depending on the differential equations) would be needed at each step. This is costly in computer time, but the effective handling of stiff equations requires that some kind of implicitness be brought into the numerical method.

Supplementary Discussion and References: 2.5

There is a vast literature on the theory of stability of solutions of differential equations. For a readable introduction, see LaSalle and Lefschetz [1961].

We have given the basic result for linear difference equations with constant coefficients only for the case where the roots of the characteristic equation are distinct. If there are multiple roots, then polynomial terms in n enter the solution in a manner entirely analogous to that for differential equations. For more discussion of the theory of linear difference equations, see, for example, Henrici [1962].

The method (2.5.6) arises in a natural way by differentiation of an interpolating polynomial; for the derivation, see Henrici [1962, p. 219].

The main results of the theory of stability of multistep methods were developed by G. Dahlquist in the 1950s; for a detailed treatment of this theory, see Henrici [1962]. Since then, there have been a number of refined definitions of stability; in particular, the terms stiffly stable and A stable deal with types of stability needed for methods to handle stiff equations. For more on different definitions of stability, see, for example, Gear [1971] and Lambert [1973].

The most effective way of handling systems of stiff equations is still an open problem, although a number of methods have been proposed and are in use. For a discussion of many of these methods and further considerations on stiff equations, see the books by Gear [1971], Lambert [1973], and Lapidus and Seinfeld [1971], and the review article by Shampine and Gear [1979].

EXERCISES 2.5

2.5.1. By letting $z = y'$, show that the problem (2.5.1)/(2.5.2) is equivalent to the first-order system $y' = z$, $z' = 10z + 11y$, with initial conditions $y(0) = 1$ and $z(0) = -1$. Attempt to solve this system numerically by any of the methods of this chapter and discuss your results.

2.5.2. Attempt to solve the problem (2.5.5) numerically by any of the methods of Sections 2.2 or 2.4 and discuss your results.

2.5.3. Verify that the method (2.5.6) is second-order accurate.

2.5.4. Carry out the algorithm (2.5.9)/(2.5.10) numerically for various values of h. Discuss your results.

2.5.5. Solve the difference equation $y_{n+1} = \frac{5}{2}y_n + y_{n-1}$, $y_0 = y_1 = 1$, in terms of the roots of its characteristic equation. Discuss the behavior of the sequence $\{y_n\}$ as $n \to \infty$.

2.5.6. Find a value of y_1 such that the resulting solution of (2.5.9) with $y_0 = 1$ tends to zero as n tends to infinity. Write a program to carry out (2.5.9) with y_1 given in this way as well as by (2.5.10). Discuss your results.

2.5.7. Consider the method $y_{n+1} = y_{n-3} + (4h/3)(2f_n - f_{n-1} + 2f_{n-2})$, which is known as *Milne's method.* Ascertain whether this method is stable and strongly stable.

2.5.8. Write a program to carry out Euler's method (2.5.27) for different values of h both less than and greater than 0.02. Discuss your results.

2.5.9. The system $y' = z$, $z' = -100y - 101z$ is the first-order system equivalent to the second-order equation (2.5.31). Using the initial conditions $y(0) = 2$ and $z(0) = -2$, apply Euler's method to this system and determine experimentally how small the step size h must be to maintain stability. Attempt to verify analytically your conclusion about the size of h.

2.5.10. Find the solution of the difference equation $y_{n+1} = cy_n + d$ as a function of the initial condition y_0. Apply your result to verify that (2.5.36) is the solution of (2.5.35).

2.5.11. The function $y(x) = e^{-x}$ is the solution of the problem $y'' = y$, $y(0) = 1$, $y'(0) = -1$. Is this solution stable? Prove your assertion.

2.5.12. Ascertain which of the following methods are stable and which are strongly stable:

a. $y_{k+1} = y_k + \dfrac{h}{6}(6f_k - 3f_{k-1} + 3f_{k-2})$

b. $y_{k+1} = y_{k-1} + \dfrac{h}{2}(f_{k+1} + 2f_k + f_{k-1})$

c. $y_{k+1} = 3y_k - 2y_{k-1} + \dfrac{h}{2}(f_{k+1} + 2f_k + f_{k-1})$

2.5.13. Consider the multistep method $y_{k+1} = (1/2)(y_k + y_{k-1}) + (3h/4)(3f_k - f_{k-1})$. Is this method stable? Strongly stable? What is its order?

2.5.14. Apply the trapezoid rule (2.5.38) to the equation (2.5.25).

3 Pinning It Down on Both Ends: Two-Point Boundary-Value Problems

3.1 A Diffusion Problem

Many problems in scientific computing are governed by nonlinear partial differential equations of the form

$$u_t = (pu_x)_x + g(x, u) \tag{3.1.1}$$

with appropriate initial and boundary conditions such as

$$\begin{aligned} &u(0, x) = q(x), \qquad 0 \le x \le 1 && \textit{(initial condition)} \\ &u(t, 0) = \alpha \qquad u(1, t) = \beta, \qquad t \ge 0 && \textit{(boundary conditions)} \end{aligned} \tag{3.1.2}$$

Here p and q are given functions of x, g is a given function of two variables, α and β are given constants, u is the solution to be determined, and u_t denotes the partial derivative $\partial u/\partial t$.

In Chapter 7 we shall return to the study of time-dependent partial differential equations such as (3.1.1). Our concern in this and the following two chapters will be the corresponding *steady-state* problem. In many situations governed by an equation such as (3.1.1) involving both space and time as independent variables, one is interested primarily in the behavior of the solution as $t \to \infty$. If the solution reaches a limiting value as $t \to \infty$, that is,

$$u(t, x) \to v(x) \text{ as } t \to \infty, \qquad x \in [0, 1] \tag{3.1.3}$$

the function v is said to be a steady-state solution. One approach to obtaining this steady-state solution is by computing the time-dependent solution $u(t, x)$, as will be discussed in Chapter 7; this approach is, of course, necessary if one is also interested in the solution as a function of t before a steady state is reached.

Another approach is to argue that the steady-state solution must satisfy the equation (3.1.1) with the time derivative set to zero; that is,

(3.1.4) $$(pv_x)_x + g(x, v) = 0$$

with the boundary conditions

(3.1.5) $$v(0) = \alpha \qquad v(1) = \beta$$

Since v is a function of only the variable x, (3.1.4) is now an ordinary differential equation, which we rewrite as

(3.1.6) $$(pv')' + g(x, v) = 0$$

The equation (3.1.6) together with the boundary conditions (3.1.5) is called a *two-point boundary-value problem* since the boundary conditions, (3.1.5), are given at both end points of the interval. It is the numerical solution of such problems—which are discussed in more detail in Appendix 2—that will be the subject of this and the following two chapters.

We note that we have chosen the interval [0, 1] for convenience, but it is not as special as might seem. If the equation (3.1.6) is defined on an arbitrary finite interval, the problem can be reduced to one on the interval [0, 1]; see exercise 3.1.1.

As an example of an equation such as (3.1.6), we will consider the following problem from biophysics. Consider the cell shown in Figure 3.1, where we make the idealization that the cell is perfectly spherical. Assume that some element, such as oxygen, reacts with other substances within the cell and thus disappears as free oxygen. Next, suppose that the cell is immersed in a medium in which free oxygen molecules exist; we assume that these molecules can penetrate the boundary of the cell and then possibly undergo the reaction mentioned previously. Given the concentration of oxygen in the surrounding medium and the rate at which oxygen molecules react within the cell to form other compounds, we wish

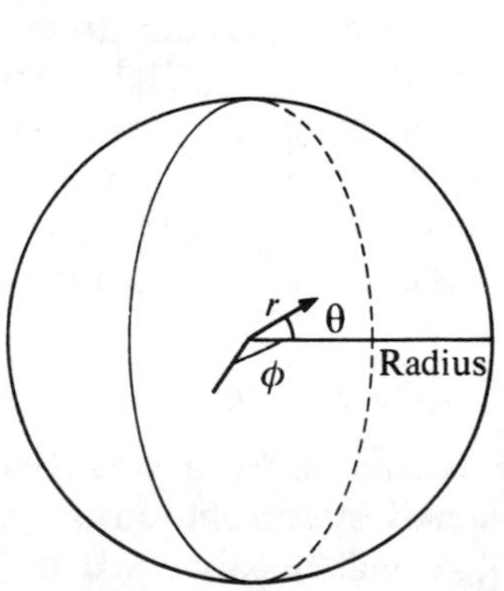

FIGURE 3.1 *A Spherical Cell.*

to discover what will be the concentration of oxygen within the cell at any given time and, in particular, what will be the steady-state concentration.

If we denote by u the concentration of oxygen within the cell as a function of time and three space variables, then it can be shown that u will satisfy the equation

$$u_t = \Delta u + g(u) \tag{3.1.7}$$

where Δ is the Laplacian operator in three space dimensions, that is, $\Delta u = u_{xx} + u_{yy} + u_{zz}$. Here, the first term models the diffusion of oxygen through the cell (the diffusion coefficient has been assumed constant and normalized to be 1), while the second term is of the form

$$g(u) = -c\frac{u}{u + d} \tag{3.1.8}$$

where c and d are constants that depend on such things as the reaction rate, number of bacteria present, concentrations of substances within the cell, and so on.

In order to be able to handle equation (3.1.7), we make some further simplifying assumptions. In addition to the cell being spherical, we assume that the cell, the diffusion, and the reactions are all spherically symmetrical; that is, in terms of the spherical coordinates r, ϕ, and θ of Figure 3.1, we assume that the reaction rate and resulting concentration depend only on r. In this case, the Laplacian operator Δ in spherical coordinates reduces to simply

$$\Delta u = \frac{1}{r^2}\frac{\partial}{\partial r}\left(r^2\frac{\partial u}{\partial r}\right)$$

(see exercise 3.1.2). If we now set $u_t = 0$ in (3.1.7) to obtain the steady-state equation, we have

$$\frac{1}{r^2}(r^2v')' + g(v) = 0$$

or

$$(r^2v')' + r^2g(v) = 0 \tag{3.1.9}$$

where $v = v(r)$ is the steady-state concentration of oxygen within the cell.

We assume that the concentration of oxygen outside the cell is some constant β and that the cell membrane has infinite permeability. This gives us the boundary condition

$$v(1) = \beta \tag{3.1.10}$$

where we have normalized the radius of the cell to be of length 1. To obtain another boundary condition at $r = 0$, we observe that the assumption of spherical symmetry implies that

$$v'(0) = 0 \tag{3.1.11}$$

Note that (3.1.11) is a different condition from (3.1.5), where the value of the function was specified at both end points. We could, at the outset, have replaced (3.1.5) by the more general condition

$$\textbf{(3.1.12)} \qquad \eta_1 v(0) + \eta_2 v'(0) = \alpha \qquad \gamma_1 v(1) + \gamma_2 v'(1) = \beta$$

in which a linear combination of the function value and its derivative is specified at each end point. Then, (3.1.10) and (3.1.11) are the special case of (3.1.12) in which $\eta_1 = 0$, $\eta_2 = 1$, $\gamma_1 = 1$, and $\gamma_2 = 0$.

The problem represented by (3.1.9), together with the boundary conditions (3.1.10) and (3.1.11), is a two-point boundary-value problem. Such problems are extremely important in scientific computing, both in their own right and also as models for boundary-value problems in more than one variable. Equation (3.1.9) is nonlinear because the function g of (3.1.8) is a nonlinear function, and it is the case that almost all two-point boundary-value problems occurring in applications are nonlinear. However, in the remainder of this chapter we will develop an important method for solving linear two-point boundary-value problems, and then we will return to nonlinear problems in the next chapter.

Supplementary Discussion and References: 3.1

The mathematical theory of two-point boundary-value problems for ordinary differential equations, as well as several examples of such problems, is discussed in Bailey, Shampine, and Waltman [1968]. Particularly important questions concern the existence and uniqueness of solutions, especially when the problem is nonlinear. One type of condition that is sufficient for both existence and uniqueness of a solution for the simple equation $v'' = f(v)$, with $v(0) = \alpha$ and $v(1) = \beta$, is that the function f be continuously differentiable, and $f'(v) \geq 0$ for $|v| < \infty$. Various other conditions and extensions to more general equations are given in the cited reference as well as, for example, Keller [1968].

We have considered in the text only second-order equations in a single variable. For higher-order equations such as

$$a_0(x)v^{(n)} + a_1(x)v^{(n-1)} + \cdots + a_{n-1}(x)v'(x) + a_n(x)v(x) = d(x)$$

n conditions on v and some of its first $n - 1$ derivatives must be specified at the two end points 0 and 1. Alternatively, as in Chapter 2, higher-order equations can be reduced to a system

$$\mathrm{A}(x)\mathbf{w}' = \mathbf{f}(x)$$

where $\mathbf{w}$ and $\mathbf{f}$ are n vectors and $\mathrm{A}(x)$ is an $n \times n$ matrix. Here, n conditions at 0 and 1 are now given on some of the components of $\mathbf{w}$. For further discussion of two-point boundary-value problems for systems of equations, see Section 4.1 and Keller [1968].

The presentation of the biophysics problem in this section generally follows that of Keller [1968]; see also Murray [1968] and Laidler [1958]. The resulting two-point boundary-value problem (3.1.9) is called *singular* because the coefficient of v'' vanishes at the origin. The singular nature of the problem is seen more clearly by carrying out the differentiation in (3.1.9) and dividing by r^2 to give the equivalent differential equation

$$v'' + \frac{2}{r}v' + g(v) = 0 \tag{3.1.13}$$

In this form, the coefficient of v' becomes infinite at $r = 0$. For the theory of ordinary differential equations with singularities, see, for example, Coddington and Levinson [1955]. For recent work on the numerical solution of second-order, two-point boundary-value problems with singularities of the first kind, see Russell and Shampine [1975].

In addition to the singularity at $r = 0$, the coefficient c in the nonlinear function g of (3.1.8) may be very large. Alternatively, if we divide equation (3.1.13) through by c and set $\varepsilon = c^{-1}$, then it takes the form

$$\varepsilon\left(v'' + \frac{2}{r}v'\right) = \frac{v}{v + d}$$

Differential equations where the highest-order derivative is multiplied by a small constant are known as *singular perturbation* problems. For further discussion of problems of this type, see, for example, Cole [1968].

EXERCISES 3.1

3.1.1. Let u be the solution of the boundary-value problem on the interval $[a, b]$:

$$(p(x)u')' + q(x)u = g(u), \qquad u(a) = \alpha, \qquad u(b) = \beta$$

Show that u can be obtained by solving the boundary-value problem on the interval $[0, 1]$:

$$\frac{d}{dy}\left(\hat{p}(y)\frac{dv}{dy}\right) + \hat{q}(y)v = \hat{g}(v), \qquad v(0) = \alpha, \qquad v(1) = \beta$$

where

$$\hat{p}(y) = p(a + (b - a)y), \qquad \hat{q}(y) = q(a + (b - a)y)(b - a)^2$$

and

$$\hat{g}(v) = (b - a)^2 g(u)$$

by setting

$$u(x) = v\left(\frac{x - a}{b - a}\right)$$

3.1.2. The Laplacian Δ in spherical coordinates r, θ, and ϕ is

$$\Delta u(r, \theta, \phi) = \frac{1}{r^2}\frac{\partial}{\partial r}\left(r^2 \frac{\partial u}{\partial r}\right) + \frac{1}{r^2 \sin\theta}\frac{\partial}{\partial \theta}\left(\sin\theta \frac{\partial u}{\partial \theta}\right) + \frac{1}{r^2 \sin^2\theta}\frac{\partial^2 u}{\partial \phi^2}$$

Conclude that if u is spherically symmetric, that is, if u is a function only of r, then

$$\Delta u = \frac{1}{r^2}\frac{\partial}{\partial r}\left(r^2 \frac{\partial u}{\partial r}\right)$$

3.1.3. Find the solution explicitly for the two-point boundary-value problem $v'' + v' = 2e^x$, $v(0) = 1$, $v(1) = e$.

3.2 The Finite Difference Method for Linear Problems

We consider in this section what is probably the most common approach to the solution of boundary-value problems: the *finite difference method.* We will restrict our attention now to linear equations of the form

(3.2.1) $$a(x)v'' + b(x)v' + c(x)v = d(x), \qquad 0 \le x \le 1$$

where a, b, c, and d are given functions of x. The boundary conditions that we consider first will be

(3.2.2) $$v(0) = \alpha \qquad v(1) = \beta$$

Later, we shall treat more general boundary conditions involving derivations of v at the end points, such as given by (3.1.12). A particularly simple special case of (3.2.1) and (3.2.2) is

(3.2.3) $$v'' = d(x), \qquad v(0) = 0, \qquad v(1) = 0$$

which will be useful for certain discussions later.

Equations (3.2.1) and (3.2.2) define a linear two-point boundary-value problem for the unknown function v, and our task is to develop procedures to approximate the solution on a computer. We will assume that the problem has a unique solution that is at least two times continuously differentiable.

If x, $x + h$, and $x - h$ are three points in the interval [0, 1], then

(3.2.4) $$v'(x) \doteq \frac{v(x + h) - v(x)}{h}$$

and

(3.2.5) $$v''(x) \doteq \frac{v(x + h) - 2v(x) + v(x - h)}{h^2}$$

are called *finite difference approximations* to the derivatives. To see how well the expressions on the right-hand sides approximate the derivatives, we use the Taylor expansion

$$v(x + h) = v(x) + v'(x)h + \tfrac{1}{2}v''(x)h^2 + 0(h^3) \tag{3.2.6}$$

where the symbol $0(h^3)$ denotes, as before, that the remainder term in the expansion goes to zero as h^3, as h tends to zero. From (3.2.6), we obtain immediately

$$v'(x) - \left[\frac{v(x + h) - v(x)}{h}\right] = -\tfrac{1}{2}v''(x)h + 0(h^2) \tag{3.2.7}$$

which shows that for small h, the error in the approximation (3.2.4) is proportional to h as well as to $v''(x)$. In order to obtain the error in the approximation (3.2.5), we need to carry the expansion in (3.2.6) to two more terms, assuming now that v is four times differentiable, and then use the corresponding expansion for $v(x - h)$. If we do this, then after a little algebra (the details of which are left to exercise 3.2.1), we obtain

$$v''(x) - \frac{[v(x + h) - 2v(x) + v(x - h)]}{h^2} = -\tfrac{1}{12}v^{(4)}(x)h^2 + 0(h^4) \tag{3.2.8}$$

which shows that the error in the approximation (3.2.5) is proportional to h^2, for small h, as well as to the fourth derivative.

The purpose of (3.2.7) and (3.2.8) is to show that (3.2.4) and (3.2.5) are indeed reasonable approximations to the derivatives. The dependence of the error on h will be of importance later when we discuss the error in our approximate solution of (3.2.1). We note here that the difference in the error dependence on h between (3.2.4) and (3.2.5) is typical of *one-sided* as opposed to *centered* difference approximations. If we used instead of (3.2.4) the centered approximation

$$v'(x) \doteq \frac{v(x + h) - v(x - h)}{2h} \tag{3.2.9}$$

then it is easy to see (exercise 3.2.2) that the error would also be proportional to h^2.

We now divide the interval [0, 1] into a number of equal subintervals of length h. As in Chapter 2, the points x_i are called the grid points, or nodes, and h is the grid spacing; x_0 and x_{n+1} are called the *boundary* grid points, and $x_1, \ldots, x_n$ are called the *interior* grid points. At each of the interior grid points, we approximate the derivatives of the solution v

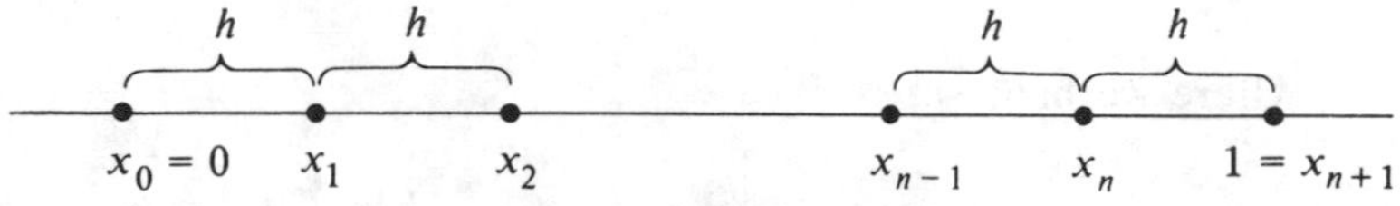

FIGURE 3.2 *Grid Points.*

by (3.2.9) and (3.2.5):

$$\textbf{(3.2.10)}\qquad \begin{aligned} v'(x_i) &\doteq \frac{v(x_{i+1}) - v(x_{i-1})}{2h} \\ v''(x_i) &\doteq \frac{v(x_{i+1}) - 2v(x_i) + v(x_{i-1})}{h^2} \end{aligned}$$

If we now put these approximations into equation (3.2.1) and denote the functions a, b, c, and d evaluated at x_i by a_i, b_i, c_i, and d_i, we obtain

$$\textbf{(3.2.11)}\qquad a_i \frac{[v(x_{i+1}) - 2v(x_i) + v(x_{i-1})]}{h^2} + b_i \frac{[v(x_{i+1}) - v(x_{i-1})]}{2h} + c_i v(x_i) \doteq d_i$$

What we have shown so far is that if we replace the first and second derivatives of the solution v by finite difference approximations and put these approximations into the differential equation, then we obtain the approximate relations (3.2.11) that the solution must satisfy. We now turn this procedure around. Suppose that we can find numbers $v_1, \ldots, v_n$ that satisfy exactly the relations (3.2.11), that is, that satisfy the equations

$$\textbf{(3.2.12)}\qquad \frac{a_i}{h^2}(v_{i+1} - 2v_i + v_{i-1}) + \frac{b_i}{2h}(v_{i+1} - v_{i-1}) + c_i v_i = d_i, \qquad i = 1, \ldots, n$$

with $v_0 = \alpha$ and $v_{n+1} = \beta$. Then, we can consider $v_0, v_1, \ldots, v_{n+1}$ to be approximations, at the grid points $x_0, x_1, \ldots, x_{n+1}$, to the solution v of the boundary-value problem (3.2.1)/(3.2.2). We shall return shortly to the question of how good the approximations are.

The equations (3.2.12) form a system of n linear equations in the n unknowns $v_1, \ldots, v_n$. If we collect coefficients of the v_i, we can rewrite (3.2.12) as

$$\left(-a_i + \frac{b_i h}{2}\right)v_{i-1} + (2a_i - c_i h^2)v_i + \left(-a_i - \frac{b_i h}{2}\right)v_{i+1} = -h^2 d_i, \qquad i = 1, \ldots, n$$

or

$$r_i v_{i-1} + p_i v_i + q_i v_{i+1} = -h^2 d_i, \qquad i = 1, \ldots, n$$

where we have set

$$\textbf{(3.2.13)}\qquad p_i = 2a_i - c_i h^2 \qquad q_i = -a_i - \frac{b_i h}{2} \qquad r_i = -a_i + \frac{b_i h}{2}$$

Then we can write these equations in matrix form as

$$\text{(3.2.14)}\qquad \begin{bmatrix} p_1 & q_1 & & & \bigcirc \\ r_2 & p_2 & q_2 & & \\ & \cdot & \cdot & \cdot & \\ & & \cdot & \cdot & \cdot \\ & & \cdot & \cdot & \cdot \\ & \bigcirc & & & q_{n-1} \\ & & & r_n & p_n \end{bmatrix} \begin{bmatrix} v_1 \\ \cdot \\ \cdot \\ \cdot \\ \cdot \\ \cdot \\ v_n \end{bmatrix} = -h^2 \begin{bmatrix} d_1 + r_1\alpha/h^2 \\ d_2 \\ \cdot \\ \cdot \\ \cdot \\ d_{n-1} \\ d_n + q_n\beta/h^2 \end{bmatrix}$$

Thus, our task is to solve this system of linear equations, and techniques for this will be discussed in subsequent sections of this chapter.

In the special case of the very simple problem (3.2.3), we have $a_i = 1$, $b_i = 0$, and $c_i = 0$, so $p_i = 2$, and $r_i = q_i = -1$, and the coefficient matrix of (3.2.14) becomes simply

$$\text{(3.2.15)}\qquad \begin{bmatrix} 2 & -1 & & & \\ -1 & 2 & \cdot & & \\ & \cdot & \cdot & \cdot & \\ & & \cdot & \cdot & \cdot \\ & & & \cdot & \cdot & -1 \\ & & & & -1 & 2 \end{bmatrix}$$

As a slightly more complicated example, consider the equation

$$(x^2 + 1)v''(x) + 2xv'(x) + \sin xv(x) = \cos x, \qquad 0 \le x \le 1$$

with the boundary conditions $v(0) = 0$ and $v(1) = 1$. Here, $a(x) = x^2 + 1$, $b(x) = 2x$, $c(x) = \sin x$, and $d(x) = \cos x$, so

$$a_j = (jh)^2 + 1 \qquad b_j = 2jh \qquad c_j = \sin jh \qquad d_j = \cos jh \qquad j = 1, \ldots, n$$

Hence, the quantities of (3.2.13) are

$$p_j = 2(jh)^2 - h^2 \sin jh + 2 \qquad q_j = -(jh)^2 - jh^2 - 2$$
$$r_j = -(jh)^2 + jh^2 - 2$$

and the jth equation of the system (3.2.14) is

$$[-(jh)^2 + jh^2 - 2]v_{j-1} + [2(jh)^2 - h^2 \sin jh + 2]v_j$$
$$+ [-(jh)^2 - jh^2 - 2]v_{j+1} = -h^2 \cos jh$$

for $2 \le j \le n - 1$, and the first and last equations, which contain the boundary values, are

$$(2h^2 - h^2 \sin h + 2)v_1 - (2h^2 + 2)v_2 = -h^2 \cos h$$

and

$$[-(nh)^2 + nh^2 - 2]v_{n-1} + [2(nh)^2 - h^2 \sin nh + 2]v_n$$
$$= -h^2 \cos nh + [(nh)^2 + nh^2 + 2]$$

We return to the important question of the error in the approximations $v_1, \ldots, v_n$. Since the linear system (3.2.14) which determines these quantities will be solved numerically, the computed v_i will be in error because of rounding; this will be discussed in more detail in the next two sections. For the present, let us assume that the v_i are computed with no rounding error—that is, $v_1, \ldots, v_n$ is the exact solution of the system (3.2.14)—and let $v(x_i)$ be again the exact solution of the boundary-value problem at x_i. Then, analogous to the definition for initial-value problems in Chapter 2,

$$\max_{1 \le i \le n} |v_i - v(x_i)| \qquad \textbf{(3.2.16)}$$

is called the *global discretization error*; that is, it is the error caused by replacing the continuous boundary-value problem by the discrete analog represented by (3.2.14).

It is beyond the scope of this book to give a detailed and rigorous analysis of the discretization error, but we can indicate how such an analysis would proceed. Since the error estimates (3.2.7) and (3.2.8) show that the smaller the h, the closer the difference quotients approximate the derivatives, we would expect, intuitively, that the same would be true of the discretization error itself. The problem is to relate the errors in the derivatives to (3.2.16), and we will indicate how this can be done in the case of the very simple problem (3.2.3). In this case, the difference equations (3.2.12) reduce to

$$\frac{1}{h^2}(v_{i+1} - 2v_i + v_{i-1}) = d_i, \qquad i = 1, \ldots, n$$

with $v_0 = \alpha$ and $v_{n+1} = \beta$.

We first define the *local discretization error*, in a manner analogous to that for initial-value problems, by

$$L(x, h) = \frac{1}{h^2}[v(x+h) - 2v(x) + v(x-h)] - d(x) \qquad \textbf{(3.2.17)}$$

where v is the exact solution of the differential equation. Since $d(x) = v''(x)$, we can make this substitution in (3.2.17) and then use (3.2.8), provided that v is sufficiently differentiable, to conclude that

$$L(x, h) = \frac{1}{h^2}[v(x+h) - 2v(x) - v(x-h)] - v''(x) = 0(h^2)$$

We next evaluate (3.2.17) at the grid points and use the fact that $h^2 d_i = v_{i+1} - 2v_i + v_{i-1}$; thus, with $\sigma_i = L(x_i, h)$,

$$[v(x_{i+1}) - 2v(x_i) + v(x_{i-1})] - (v_{i+1} - 2v_i + v_{i-1}) = h^2\sigma_i, \qquad i = 1, \ldots, n$$

and, if we set $e_i = v(x_i) - v_i$, we can rewrite this as simply

$$e_{i+1} - 2e_i + e_{i-1} = h^2\sigma_i, \qquad i = 1, \ldots, n \tag{3.2.18}$$

where $e_0 = e_{n+1} = 0$. If A is the matrix of (3.2.15) and $\mathbf{e}$ and $\boldsymbol{\sigma}$ are the vectors with components $e_1, \ldots, e_n$ and $\sigma_1, \ldots, \sigma_n$, we can write (3.2.18) as

$$\mathrm{A}\mathbf{e} = -h^2\boldsymbol{\sigma} \tag{3.2.19}$$

or, assuming that A^{-1} exists,

$$\mathbf{e} = -h^2\mathrm{A}^{-1}\boldsymbol{\sigma} \tag{3.2.20}$$

which is the basic relationship between the global and local discretization errors.

The technical problem—which is beyond the scope of this book—is to study the behavior of A^{-1} as $h \to 0$. This is made more difficult by the fact that n, the order of A, is proportional to $1/h$, so that $n \to \infty$ as $h \to 0$. It can be shown, however, that as h tends to zero, the discretization errors e_i also tend to zero—an essentially necessary property for a good approximation scheme. Moreover, under very mild assumptions about the solution, the e_i tend to zero as $0(h^2)$, which gives an indication of the rate of convergence.

The same general approach to the analysis of the discretization error holds for the more general problem (3.2.1) under suitable assumptions on the coefficients a, b, c, and d.

There are a number of other possible difference approximations that can be used for (3.2.1), and we will consider two of them that are sometimes quite important in practice.

One desirable property of the coefficient matrix of (3.2.14) is *diagonal dominance*, as we shall see in Section 3.4. A general $n \times n$ matrix $\mathrm{A} = (a_{ij})$ is (row) *diagonally dominant* if

$$|a_{ii}| \geq \sum_{j \neq i} |a_{ij}|, \qquad i = 1, \ldots, n \tag{3.2.21}$$

that is, the diagonal element of each row is at least as large as the sum of the absolute values of all the off-diagonal elements in that row.

Let us see if the matrix of (3.2.14) is diagonally dominant. We need that

$$|p_i| \geq |r_i| + |q_i|$$

or, using (3.2.13),

$$|2a_i - c_ih^2| \geq \left|a_i - \frac{b_ih}{2}\right| + \left|a_i + \frac{b_ih}{2}\right| \tag{3.2.22}$$

If we assume that $a_i > 0$ and $c_i \leq 0$ (these conditions on the coefficients a and c are quite natural, as we shall see later), then (3.2.22) certainly holds if h is sufficiently small, in particular, if

(3.2.23) $$|b_i|\, h \leq 2a_i$$

This condition on h is a rather stringent one and can be avoided by using one-sided differences in place of the central difference (3.2.9) to approximate the first derivative. More precisely, we use the approximations

(3.2.24) $$v'(x_i) \doteq \begin{cases} \frac{1}{h}(v_{i+1} - v_i) & \text{if} \quad b_i \geq 0 \\ \frac{1}{h}(v_i - v_{i-1}) & \text{if} \quad b_i < 0 \end{cases}$$

so the direction of the one-sided difference is determined by the sign of b_i. Such differences are quite commonly used in fluid dynamics problems and in that context are called *upwind* (or *upstream*) differences. With (3.2.24), the ith row of the coefficient matrix (3.2.14) becomes

(3.2.25) $$\begin{array}{llll} -a_i, & 2a_i - c_ih^2 + b_ih, & -(a_i + b_ih), & b_i \geq 0 \\ -(a_i - b_ih), & 2a_i - c_ih^2 - b_ih, & -a_i, & b_i < 0 \end{array}$$

and it is easy to verify that diagonal dominance holds, independent of the size of h, assuming again that $a_i > 0$ and $c_i \leq 0$. We note, however, that although the centered difference approximation (3.2.9) is second-order accurate, the one-sided approximations (3.2.24) are only first-order accurate, and this increase in the discretization error must be weighed against the better properties of the coefficient matrix.

Another desirable property of the coefficient matrix of (3.2.14) is symmetry. A matrix $A = (a_{ij})$ is symmetric if

(3.2.26) $$a_{ij} = a_{ji}, \qquad i, j = 1, \ldots, n$$

or, in matrix terms, if $A = A^T$, where A^T denotes the transpose matrix (a_{ji}). In order that the matrix of (3.2.14) be symmetric, we need that $q_i = r_{i+1}$, or, using (3.2.13),

$$-a_i - \tfrac{1}{2}b_ih = -a_{i+1} + \tfrac{1}{2}b_{i+1}h, \qquad i = 1, \ldots, n-1$$

Clearly, these relations will not usually hold. In many situations, however, the differential equation (3.2.1) is of the form

(3.2.27) $$[a(x)v']' = d(x)$$

[Recall that this was the case for the sample problem of the previous section except for the nonlinear term; see (3.1.6).] In this case, we can obtain a symmetric coefficient matrix by differencing as follows. First, introduce auxiliary grid points $x_{i\pm1/2}$ midway between the grid points x_{i-1}, x_i, and x_{i+1} as shown in Figure 3.3. Using these auxiliary grid points, we

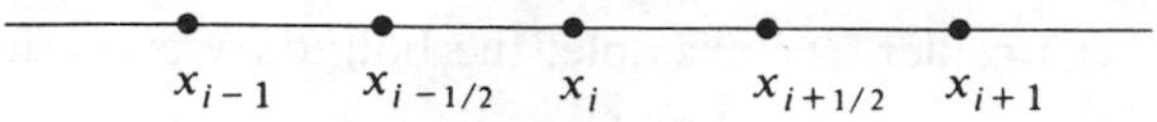

FIGURE 3.3

approximate the outermost derivative of $(av')'$ at x_i by

$$\textbf{(3.2.28)}\qquad [a(x)v'(x)]_i' \doteq \frac{1}{h}(a_{i+1/2}v_{i+1/2}' - a_{i-1/2}v_{i-1/2}')$$

where the subscripts indicate the grid point at which the evaluation is done. Next, we approximate the first derivatives by the centered differences

$$v_{i+1/2}' \doteq \frac{1}{h}(v_{i+1} - v_i) \qquad v_{i-1/2}' \doteq \frac{1}{h}(v_i - v_{i-1})$$

and use these in (3.2.28) to obtain

$$\textbf{(3.2.29)}\quad [a(x)v'(x)]_i' \doteq \frac{1}{h^2}[a_{i+1/2}(v_{i+1} - v_i) - a_{i-1/2}(v_i - v_{i-1})]$$

$$= \frac{1}{h^2}[a_{i-1/2}v_{i-1} - (a_{i+1/2} + a_{i-1/2})v_i + a_{i+1/2}v_{i+1}]$$

Therefore, the system of difference equations corresponding to (3.2.14) is of the form

$$\mathbf{Av} = \mathbf{q}$$

where

$$\textbf{(3.2.30)}\quad A = \begin{bmatrix} a_{3/2} + a_{1/2} & -a_{3/2} & & & \\ -a_{3/2} & a_{5/2} + a_{3/2} & -a_{5/2} & & \\ & \ddots & \ddots & \ddots & \\ & & \ddots & \ddots & -a_{n-1/2} \\ & & & -a_{n-1/2} & a_{n+1/2} + a_{n-1/2} \end{bmatrix}$$

Clearly, this matrix is both symmetric and diagonally dominant. Note also that if $a(x) \equiv 1$, (3.2.30) reduces to the 2, -1 matrix (3.2.15). If a term $c(x)v$ is also present in (3.2.27), this will just subtract c_ih^2 from the ith diagonal element of (3.2.30).

The previous discussion has all been for the boundary conditions (3.2.2). We saw in the previous section, however, that boundary conditions on the derivative rather than the function itself may arise, and we now consider the modifications that this situation requires.

Consider, for example, the boundary conditions

(3.2.31) $$v'(0) = \alpha \qquad v(1) = \beta$$

in place of (3.2.2); that is, we specify $v'(0)$ rather than $v(0)$. Assume that we again approximate the derivatives in (3.2.1) by (3.2.10), which then gives the difference equations (3.2.12). In the first of these equations, that is, for $i = 1$, the value of v_0 is no longer known from the boundary condition at $x = 0$. Instead, we approximate the first condition of (3.2.31) by the one-sided difference approximation (3.2.4) at $x = 0$; that is,

(3.2.32) $$v'(0) \doteq \frac{v_1 - v_0}{h} = \alpha$$

This adds another equation, $v_1 - v_0 = \alpha h$, to the n equations (3.2.12), so there are now $n + 1$ equations in the $n + 1$ unknowns $v_0, v_1, \ldots, v_n$. If the derivative boundary condition were given at the right end point, we would use the one-sided approximation

$$v'(1) \doteq \frac{v_{n+1} - v_n}{h} = \beta$$

More generally, boundary conditions may be given as linear combinations of both function and derivative values at both end points as given in (3.1.12); that is,

(3.2.33) $$\eta_1 v(0) + \eta_2 v'(0) = \alpha \qquad \gamma_1 v(1) + \gamma_2 v'(1) = \beta$$

In this case, the approximations analogous to those discussed previously would be

(3.2.34) $$\eta_1 v_0 + \eta_2 \frac{(v_1 - v_0)}{h} = \alpha \qquad \gamma_1 v_{n+1} + \gamma_2 \frac{(v_{n+1} - v_n)}{h} = \beta$$

and there would now be the $n + 2$ equations (3.2.14) plus (3.2.34) in the $n + 2$ unknowns $v_0, v_1, \ldots, v_{n+1}$. The matrix form of this system would be

(3.2.35)

$$\begin{bmatrix} h\eta_1 - \eta_2 & \eta_2 & & & & \\ r_1 & p_1 & q_1 & & & \\ & r_2 & p_2 & q_2 & & \\ & & \ddots & \ddots & q_{n-1} & \\ & & & r_n & p_n & q_n \\ & & & & -\gamma_2 & h\gamma_1 + \gamma_2 \end{bmatrix} \begin{bmatrix} v_0 \\ v_1 \\ \cdot \\ \cdot \\ \cdot \\ v_n \\ v_{n+1} \end{bmatrix} = h^2 \begin{bmatrix} \alpha/h \\ -d_1 \\ \cdot \\ \cdot \\ \cdot \\ -d_n \\ \beta/h \end{bmatrix}$$

Whatever difference approximations or boundary conditions are involved, the basic computational problem is to solve the resulting system of linear equations, and we will address ourselves to this question in the remainder of this chapter.

Supplementary Discussion and References: 3.2

We have discussed in the text only the simplest differencing procedures for rather simple problems. As we saw, the central difference approximations (3.2.10) give rise to second-order errors, that is, errors proportional to h^2. To obtain more accuracy, in principle one can use higher-order approximations; for example,

$$\textbf{(3.2.36)} \quad v''(x_i) \doteq \frac{1}{12h^2}(-v_{i-2} + 16v_{i-1} - 30v_i + 16v_{i+1} - v_{i+2})$$

is a fourth-order approximation (the error is proportional to h^4) provided that v is sufficiently differentiable. One difficulty with applying approximations of this type to two-point boundary-value problems occurs near the boundary. For example, if we apply the approximation at the first interior grid point x_1, it requires values of v not only at x_0 but also at x_{-1}, which is outside the interval.

Another approach to obtaining higher-order approximations to the solution while using only second-order approximations to the derivatives is known as *extrapolation to the limit* (or *Richardson extrapolation*). This is a very general technique that can be applied not only to boundary-value problems but also to numerical integration and differentiation, initial-value problems, and so forth. It is based on the following principle. Suppose a is a quantity to be approximated and $\hat{a}(h)$ is an approximation that depends on a parameter h (which may be the distance between grid points in many applications). Suppose, also, that the error is of the form

$$\textbf{(3.2.37)} \qquad a - \hat{a}(h) = c_1h^2 + c_2h^3 + \cdots$$

If we have two approximations for h and $h/2$, we can combine them by

$$\textbf{(3.2.38)} \qquad b(h) = \frac{4\hat{a}\left(\frac{h}{2}\right) - \hat{a}(h)}{3}$$

and this new approximation satisfies

$$a - b(h) = \frac{-c_2h^3}{6} + \cdots = 0(h^3)$$

as is easily verified.

This principle of extrapolation can be applied to two-point boundary-value problems by solving the problem twice with grid spacings

h and $h/2$ and combining these approximations at each point of the coarser grid in the manner given by (3.2.38). In certain cases, such as when the first derivative is absent in (3.2.1), the error expansion (3.2.37) may contain only even powers of h, and one application of the extrapolation principle will then give fourth-order accuracy and is particularly effective. For a discussion of extrapolation applied to numerical integration (called *Romberg integration*), see the Supplementary Discussion of Section 5.3.

For a thorough discussion of the topics of this section, see Keller [1968], and for recent work, refer to Keller [1975] and Stetter and Aktas [1977].

EXERCISES 3.2

3.2.1. Assume that the function $v(x)$ is six times differentiable. By expanding $v(x + h)$ and $v(x - h)$ in Taylor series, verify that (3.2.8) holds.

3.2.2. Assume that the function $v(x)$ is twice differentiable. Show that the error in the centered difference approximation (3.2.9) is proportional to h^2.

3.2.3. Consider the two-point boundary-value problem $(1 + x^2)v'' + 2xv' - v = x^2$, $v(0) = 1$, $v(1) = 0$.

a. Let $h = \frac{1}{4}$ and write out explicitly the difference equations (3.2.12).

b. Rewrite the equations of part a in the matrix form (3.2.14). Ascertain whether the coefficient matrix is symmetric and/or diagonally dominant.

c. Repeat parts a and b using the one-sided approximations (3.2.24) for v'.

d. Repeat parts a and b for the equation written in the form $[(1 + x^2)v']' - v = x^2$ using the differencing scheme (3.2.29).

e. Repeat parts a and b for the boundary conditions $v'(0) = 1$, $v(1) = 0$, and then $v'(0) + v(0) = 1$, $v'(1) + \frac{1}{2}v(1) = 0$.

3.3 Solution of Systems of Linear Equations

One of the most commonly occurring problems in scientific computing is to find the solution to a system of linear equations (for example, see the previous section and Sections 4.3, 5.2, and 8.2). In this section, we will restrict our attention to systems where the number of equations is equal to the number of unknowns, and we will denote such systems by

$$\mathrm{A}\mathbf{x} = \mathbf{b} \tag{3.3.1}$$

where A is a given $n \times n$ matrix, $\mathbf{b}$ is a given column n vector, and $\mathbf{x}$ is the n vector whose values are to be determined. (The reader may wish to read Appendix 3, which reviews many of the concepts that are basic to this section.)

If A is a nonsingular matrix, then (3.3.1) is mathematically equivalent to

$$\mathbf{x} = \mathrm{A}^{-1}\mathbf{b} \tag{3.3.2}$$

where A^{-1} is the inverse of A. However, in almost all cases, the computation of the inverse is not advised since the amount of computing time is considerably more than for solving (3.3.1) directly.

In this section, we shall develop methods for the direct solution of (3.3.1) under the assumption that all of the entries in the matrix are stored in the computer's main memory. As a special case, attention will be given to "banded" matrices where only a few of the diagonal bands—those containing the nonzero entries—are stored; the simplest case of a nontrivial banded matrix is a tridiagonal matrix, such as arose in Section 3.2. Other types of sparse matrices are treated in Chapter 8.

There is one algorithm for solving (3.3.1), which, including all of its modifications, is almost always used for solving small to moderately large ($n = 200$, say) linear systems that are dense (that is, almost all coefficients are nonzero). This algorithm is called *Gaussian elimination.* We will first demonstrate the algorithm using the following 3×3 example:

$$\begin{aligned} 4x_1 - 9x_2 + 2x_3 &= 2 \\ 2x_1 - 4x_2 + 4x_3 &= 3 \\ -x_1 + 2x_2 + 2x_3 &= 1 \end{aligned} \tag{3.3.3}$$

which, in matrix notation, is

$$\begin{bmatrix} 4 & -9 & 2 \\ 2 & -4 & 4 \\ -1 & 2 & 2 \end{bmatrix} \begin{bmatrix} x_1 \\ x_2 \\ x_3 \end{bmatrix} = \begin{bmatrix} 2 \\ 3 \\ 1 \end{bmatrix} \tag{3.3.4}$$

The first major step of Gaussian elimination is to eliminate the first variable, x_1, from the second and third equations. If we subtract 0.5 times the first equation from the second and -0.25 times the first from the third, we obtain the equivalent system of equations:

$$\begin{bmatrix} 4 & -9 & 2 \\ 0 & 0.5 & 3 \\ 0 & -0.25 & 2.5 \end{bmatrix} \begin{bmatrix} x_1 \\ x_2 \\ x_3 \end{bmatrix} = \begin{bmatrix} 2 \\ 2 \\ 1.5 \end{bmatrix} \tag{3.3.5}$$

The second major step eliminates x_2 from the third equation. This is accomplished by subtracting -0.5 times the second equation from the third, leading to

$$\begin{bmatrix} 4 & -9 & 2 \\ 0 & 0.5 & 3 \\ 0 & 0 & 4 \end{bmatrix} \begin{bmatrix} x_1 \\ x_2 \\ x_3 \end{bmatrix} = \begin{bmatrix} 2 \\ 2 \\ 2.5 \end{bmatrix} \tag{3.3.6}$$

This algorithm is based on the fact (usually established in an introductory linear algebra course) that replacing any equation by a linear combination of itself and another equation does not change the solution. Such operations are called *elementary row operations.* At this point, we have completed the *forward elimination* or *reduction* part of Gaussian elimination. This point is reached when the last row [see (3.3.6)] has only zeros except for the final entry.

The second part of the algorithm consists of solving the remaining *upper-triangular* system of linear equations (3.3.6). This is easily accomplished by the process of *back substitution*: the last equation of (3.3.6) is

$$4x_3 = 2.5$$

Therefore, $x_3 = 0.625$. This value now is substituted into the second equation:

$$0.5x_2 + (3)(0.625) = 2$$

Hence, $x_2 = 0.25$. Substitution of these values for x_2 and x_3 into the first equation yields

$$4x_1 - (9)(0.25) + (2)(0.625) = 2$$

or $x_1 = 0.75$. To check this computed solution, we multiply

$$\begin{bmatrix} 4 & -9 & 2 \\ 2 & -4 & 4 \\ -1 & 2 & 2 \end{bmatrix} \begin{bmatrix} 0.75 \\ 0.25 \\ 0.625 \end{bmatrix}$$

which agrees with the right-hand side of (3.3.3).

For a general $n \times n$ system, Gaussian elimination follows the same steps as for the 3×3 example. If the system is written in the form

$$\begin{aligned} a_{11}x_1 + \cdots + a_{1n}x_n &= b_1 \\ a_{21}x_1 + \cdots + a_{2n}x_n &= b_2 \\ &\vdots \\ a_{n1}x_1 + \cdots + a_{nn}x_n &= b_n \end{aligned} \tag{3.3.7}$$

the first stage eliminates the coefficients of x_1 in the last $n - 1$ equations by subtracting a_{21}/a_{11} times the first equation from the second equation, a_{31}/a_{11} times the first equation from the third equation, and so on. This gives the reduced system of equations

$$\begin{aligned} a_{11}x_1 + a_{12}x_2 + \cdots + a_{1n}x_n &= b_1 \\ a_{22}^{(1)}x_2 + \cdots + a_{2n}^{(1)}x_n &= b_2^{(1)} \\ &\vdots \\ a_{n2}^{(1)}x_2 + \cdots + a_{nn}^{(1)}x_n &= b_n^{(1)} \end{aligned} \tag{3.3.8}$$

where

$$a_{ij}^{(1)} = a_{ij} - a_{1j}\frac{a_{i1}}{a_{11}} \qquad b_j^{(1)} = b_i - b_1\frac{a_{i1}}{a_{11}}, \qquad i, j = 2, \ldots, n$$

Precisely the same process is now applied to the last $n - 1$ equations of the system (3.3.8) to eliminate the coefficients of x_2 in the last $n - 2$ equations, and so on, until the entire system has been reduced to the *triangular form*

(3.3.9)
$$\begin{bmatrix} a_{11} & a_{12} & \cdots & a_{1n} \\ & a_{22}^{(1)} & \cdots & a_{2n}^{(1)} \\ & & \ddots & \vdots \\ \bigcirc & & & a_{nn}^{(n-1)} \end{bmatrix} \begin{bmatrix} x_1 \\ x_2 \\ \vdots \\ x_n \end{bmatrix} = \begin{bmatrix} b_1 \\ b_2^{(1)} \\ \vdots \\ b_n^{(n-1)} \end{bmatrix}$$

where the superscripts indicate the number of times the elements have, in general, been changed. This completes the *forward reduction* (or *forward elimination* or *triangular reduction*) phase of the Gaussian elimination algorithm. The solution of the triangular system (3.3.9) is now easily obtained by the *back substitution* phase of the process, in which the equations in (3.3.9) are solved in reverse order:

(3.3.10)
$$\begin{aligned} x_n &= \frac{b_n^{(n-1)}}{a_{nn}^{(n-1)}} \\ x_{n-1} &= \frac{b_{n-1}^{(n-2)} - a_{n-1,n}^{(n-2)}x_n}{a_{n-1,n-1}^{(n-2)}} \\ &\vdots \\ x_1 &= \frac{b_1 - a_{12}x_2 - \cdots - a_{1n}x_n}{a_{11}} \end{aligned}$$

In the preceding, we have assumed that a_{11} and all of the numbers $a_{ii}^{(i)}$, $i = 1, \ldots, n - 1$, that are used as divisors are nonzero. This is not necessarily the case, and the algorithm must be modified if any of these vanish or are too small. We shall return to this point in the next section.

The Gaussian elimination process can be stated in algorithmic form in a very compact way:

Forward Reduction

(3.3.11)

$$
\begin{aligned}
&\text{For } k = 1, \ldots, n-1, \\
&\quad \text{For } i = k+1, \ldots, n: \\
&\qquad \ell_{ik} \leftarrow \frac{a_{ik}}{a_{kk}} \\
&\qquad \text{For } j = k+1, \ldots, n: \\
&\qquad\quad a_{ij} \leftarrow a_{ij} - \ell_{ik} a_{kj} \\
&\qquad b_i \leftarrow b_i - \ell_{ik} b_k
\end{aligned}
$$

Back Substitution

(3.3.12)

$$
\begin{aligned}
&\text{For } k = n, n-1, \ldots, 1: \\
&\quad x_k \leftarrow \frac{b_k - \sum_{j=k+1}^{n} a_{kj} x_j}{a_{kk}}
\end{aligned}
$$

In order to translate the preceding algorithm into a computer code, one should note that the successive $a_{ij}^{(k)}$ that are computed during the process can be overwritten on the same storage spaces occupied by the original elements a_{ij} of the matrix; this is indicated in the fifth line of the algorithm. If this is done, the original matrix will, of course, be destroyed during the process. Similarly, the new $b_i^{(k)}$ may be overwritten on the original storage spaces of the b_i. The multipliers ℓ_{ik} computed in the third line of the algorithm can be written into the corresponding storage spaces for the a_{ik}, which are no longer needed after the corresponding ℓ_{ik} is computed.

Gaussian elimation is related to a factorization of the matrix A in the following sense. Let us define a lower-triangular matrix, L, with all 1s on the diagonal (a *unit* lower-triangular matrix), by setting the sub-diagonal element ℓ_{ij} equal to the multiplier used for eliminating the jth variable from the ith equation. For the example problem (3.3.4), we have

(3.3.13)

$$
L = \begin{bmatrix} 1 & 0 & 0 \\ 0.5 & 1 & 0 \\ -0.25 & -0.5 & 1 \end{bmatrix}
$$

Next, let U denote the upper-triangular matrix that remains after the completion of the elimination stage. For our example, U is given in (3.3.6) and, in general, in (3.3.9). Then, a matrix multiplication shows that

(3.3.14)

$$
A = LU
$$

which represents the *triangular factorization of* A. This is also called the LU decomposition of A. If we next solve the triangular system.

(3.3.15)
$$\mathbf{L}\mathbf{y} = \mathbf{b}$$

for $\mathbf{y}$ using forward substitution, we will obtain the right-hand-side vector in (3.3.6). Thus, the Gaussian elimination algorithm for solving $\mathbf{A}\mathbf{x} = \mathbf{b}$ is equivalent to the three-step process

(3.3.16)

1. Factor A = LU.
2. Solve $\mathbf{L}\mathbf{y} = \mathbf{b}$.
3. Solve $\mathbf{U}\mathbf{x} = \mathbf{y}$.

This matrix-theoretic view of Gaussian elimination is very useful for theoretical purposes and also forms the basis for some computational variants of the elimination process.

An important question is how efficient the Gaussian elimination algorithm is. To answer this, at least partially, we next estimate the number of arithmetic operations needed to compute the solution vector $\mathbf{x}$. The major part of the work is spent in executing the last line of algorithm (3.3.11)—the innermost loop. That line has one addition (additions and subtractions will be assumed to be equivalent) and one multiplication. In order to count the number of operations, we simply mimic the loop structure of the algorithm:

(3.3.17)
$$\begin{aligned}\text{Number of additions} &= \sum_{k=1}^{n-1}\sum_{i=k+1}^{n}\sum_{j=k+1}^{n} 1 = \sum_{k=1}^{n-1}\sum_{i=k+1}^{n}(n-k)\\ &= \sum_{k=1}^{n-1}(n-k)^2 = \sum_{k=1}^{n-1}k^2\\ &= \frac{(n-1)(n)(2n-1)}{6} \doteq \frac{n^3}{3}\end{aligned}$$

and the same count holds for the number of multiplications. These counts are only for the arithmetic needed to reduce the original matrix to triangular form. We also need the work involved in modifying the right-hand-side $\mathbf{b}$, in computing the multipliers ℓ_{ik}, and in the back substitution. All of these involve no more than order n^2 operations (see exercise 3.3.3). Hence, for sufficiently large n, the work involved in the triangular factorization makes the dominant contribution to the computing time and is proportional to n^3.

In order to obtain an understanding of the amount of time that Gaussian elimination might require on a moderate-size problem, suppose that $n = 100$ and the addition and multiplication times are 1 μs and 2 μs, respectively (μs = microsecond = 10^{-6} second). Then, the time for the additions and multiplications in the factorization is approximately

$$\frac{100^3}{3}(3\ \mu\text{s}) = 10^6\ \mu\text{s} = 1\text{ s}$$

There will also be the time required for the other arithmetical operations of the complete elimination process, but this will be much less than 1 s. More importantly, there will be the various "overhead" costs of moving data back and forth from storage, and so forth. This could easily double or triple the total computing time, but, in any case, on a computer this fast, only a few seconds would be required to solve a 100×100 system.

The previous discussion has assumed that the matrix of the system is "full," that is, it has few zero elements. Many matrices that arise in practice, and particularly in the solution of differential equations, have the property that the elements of the matrix are primarily zero. Perhaps the simplest nontrivial examples of this are the tridiagonal matrices discussed in Section 3.2; here, there are, at most, three nonzero elements in each row regardless of the size of n.

Tridiagonal matrices are special cases of so-called *banded* matrices in which the nonzero elements are all contained in a relatively few number of diagonals about the main diagonal, as illustrated in Figure 3.4. A matrix $A = (a_{ij})$ is a band matrix of *bandwidth* $p + q + 1$ if $a_{ij} = 0$ for all i, j such that $i - j > p$ or $j - i > q$. Such a matrix has all of its nonzero elements on the main diagonal, the closest p subdiagonals, and q superdiagonals.

If $p = q = 1$, so that there are only three nonzero diagonals, the matrix is tridiagonal. In Section 3.2, three different tridiagonal matrices arose in the finite difference solution of linear two-point boundary-value problems. When derivatives are approximated by higher-order difference approximations, the matrices will have larger bandwidths. For example, the fourth-order approximation given by (3.2.36) leads to a matrix with bandwidth 5 ($p = q = 2$). Matrices with larger bandwidths will be discussed in Chapter 8 in connection with the numerical solution of partial differential equations.

Let us consider Gaussian elimination for a tridiagonal system of

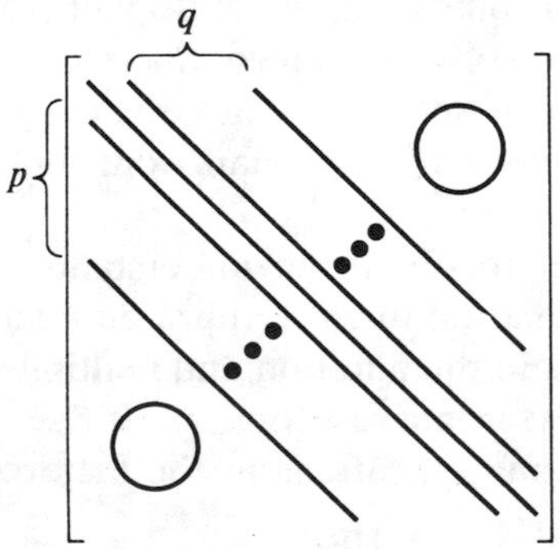

FIGURE 3.4 *Matrix with Bandwidth* $p + q + 1$.

equations:

$$
\begin{aligned}
&a_{11}x_1 + a_{12}x_2 && = b_1 \\
&a_{21}x_1 + a_{22}x_2 + a_{23}x_3 && = b_2 \\
&\qquad a_{32}x_2 + a_{33}x_3 + a_{34}x_4 && = b_3 \\
&\qquad\qquad \ddots \quad \ddots \quad \ddots && \vdots \\
&\qquad\qquad\qquad a_{nn-1}x_{n-1} + a_{nn}x_n && = b_n
\end{aligned}
\tag{3.3.18}
$$

Assuming as before that a_{11} and all subsequent divisors are nonzero, it is clear that Gaussian elimination is particularly simple for tridiagonal systems. Only one element—a_{21}—needs to be eliminated in the first column, and this elimination affects only a_{22} and b_2, and no other element in the system. The first reduced system of equations is again tridiagonal—

$$
\begin{aligned}
&a_{22}^{(1)}x_2 + a_{23}x_3 && = b_2^{(1)} \\
&a_{32}x_2 + a_{33}x_3 + a_{34}x_4 && = b_3 \\
&\quad \ddots \quad \ddots \quad \ddots && \vdots \\
&\qquad a_{nn-1}x_{n-1} + a_{nn}x_n && = b_n
\end{aligned}
$$

and the same comments apply for the next and subsequent reduction stages. Each basic reduction step requires only two additions, two multiplications, and one division, and since there are $n - 1$ stages, the total operation count to reduce the system to triangular form is only $2(n - 1)$ additions, $2(n - 1)$ multiplications, and $n - 1$ divisions.

The back substitution is also particularly simple. Each equation contains, at most, two unknowns, the typical equations being

$$a_{ii}^{(i-1)}x_i + a_{i,i+1}x_{i+1} = b_i^{(i-1)}$$

hence, the back substitution requires only $n - 1$ additions, $n - 1$ multiplications, and n divisions. Therefore, the total operation count for Gaussian elimination is

(3.3.19) Number of operations for tridiagonal system

$$= 3(n - 1) \text{ additions} + 3(n - 1) \text{ multiplications} + (2n - 1) \text{ divisions}$$

as opposed to $0(n^3)$ operations for a full matrix. Hence, Gaussian elimination for a tridiagonal system is very efficient. If we assume, as before, that multiplication and addition times are 2 μs and μs, respectively, and division time is 5 μs, then the arithmetic time for a 100×100 system is only

$$(3)(99)(2\ \mu\text{s}) + (3)(99)(\mu\text{s}) + (199)(5\ \mu\text{s}) < 0.002\ \text{s}$$

Since the operation count increases linearly with n, the arithmetic time for even a 10,000 × 10,000 system on this computer would be less than 1 s.

The storage necessary to solve tridiagonal systems is also minimal. Clearly, we do not wish to use a two-dimensional array for the matrix since that would require setting aside n^2 storage spaces for only $3n$ elements. The nonzero elements of the matrix can be stored conveniently in one-dimensional arrays, as can the right-hand side. Thus, including another array for the solution, only $5n$ storage spaces are required.

We could have phrased the elimination process in terms of the LU factorization. In this case,

(3.3.20)
$$L = \begin{bmatrix} 1 & & & & \\ l_2 & 1 & & & \\ & \cdot & \cdot & & \\ & & \cdot & \cdot & \\ & & & \cdot & \cdot \\ & & & l_n & 1 \end{bmatrix} \quad U = \begin{bmatrix} u_1 & a_{12} & & & \\ & u_2 & a_{23} & & \\ & & \cdot & \cdot & \\ & & & \cdot & \cdot \\ & & & \cdot & \cdot \\ & & & & a_{n-1,n} \\ & & & & u_n \end{bmatrix}$$

(see exercise 3.3.6), and the algorithm for the factorization is

(3.3.21)
$$\begin{aligned} &u_1 \leftarrow a_{11} \\ &\text{For } i = 2, \ldots, n, \\ &\quad \ell_i \leftarrow \frac{a_{i,i-1}}{u_{i-1}} \\ &\quad u_i \leftarrow a_{ii} - \ell_i \cdot a_{i-1,i} \end{aligned}$$

Matrices of the form (3.2.20) are sometimes called *bidiagonal.*

Many of the considerations for tridiagonal systems also apply to general banded systems. Let A be a banded matrix of the form shown in Figure 3.4, where for simplicity we will assume that $q = p$. There are p coefficients to be eliminated in the first column, and this elimination will alter only the elements in the second through pth rows and columns of A. The number of operations required will be p^2 additions, p^2 multiplications, and p divisions (not counting operations on the right-hand side of the system). The first reduced matrix will be a band matrix with the same bandwidth, and hence the same count applies. After $n - p - 1$ of these reductions, there will remain a $(p + 1) \times (p + 1)$ matrix to be reduced. Hence, the number of additions (or multiplications) required in the triangular reduction is

$$(n - p - 1)p^2 + (\tfrac{1}{6}p)(p + 1)(2p + 1) \doteq np^2 - \tfrac{2}{3}p^3$$

The storage for a banded matrix may be handled by means of $p + q + 1$ one-dimensional arrays, as was done for a tridiagonal matrix.

$$\begin{bmatrix} 0 & a_{11} & a_{12} & a_{13} \\ a_{21} & a_{22} & a_{23} & a_{24} \\ a_{32} & a_{33} & a_{34} & a_{35} \\ a_{43} & a_{44} & a_{45} & 0 \\ a_{54} & a_{55} & 0 & 0 \end{bmatrix}$$

FIGURE 3.5 *Storage for a Banded Matrix.*

However, if p is at all large, it is probably better to store the diagonals of A as columns in a $(p + q + 1) \times n$ two-dimensional array, as illustrated in Figure 3.5 for $n = 5$, $p = 1$, and $q = 2$.

We return now to general matrices (not necessarily banded). We note first that the determinant of the coefficient matrix A, denoted by det A, is an easy by-product of the elimination process. By the LU decomposition of A, we have—using the facts that the determinant of a product of two matrices is the product of the determinants and that the determinant of a triangular matrix is the product of its diagonal elements—

(3.3.22) $$\det A = \det LU = \det L \det U = u_{11}u_{22} \cdots u_{nn}$$

Thus, the determinant is just the product of the diagonal elements of the reduced triangular system and is computed by an additional $n - 1$ multiplications. Even if only the determinant of the matrix is desired—and not the solution of a linear system—the Gaussian elimination reduction to triangular form is still the best general method for its computation.

The Gaussian elimination process is also the best way to compute the inverse of A, if that is needed. Let $\mathbf{e}_i$ be the vector with 1 in the ith position and zeros elsewhere. Then $\mathbf{e}_i$ is the ith column of the identity matrix I, and from the basic relation $AA^{-1} = I$, it follows that the ith column of A^{-1} is the solution of the linear system of equations $A\mathbf{x} = \mathbf{e}_i$. Hence, we can obtain A^{-1} by solving the n systems of equations

(3.3.23) $$A\mathbf{x}_i = \mathbf{e}_i, \qquad i = 1, \ldots, n$$

where the solution vectors $\mathbf{x}_1, \ldots, \mathbf{x}_n$ will be the columns of A^{-1}.

More generally, consider the problem of solving several systems with the same coefficient matrix:

(3.3.24) $$A\mathbf{x}_i = \mathbf{b}_i, \qquad i = 1, \ldots, m$$

In terms of the LU decomposition of A, this computation can be carried out efficiently by the following modification of (3.3.16):

(3.3.25)
1. Factor A = LU.
2. Solve $L\mathbf{y}_i = \mathbf{b}_i \quad i = 1, \ldots, m.$
3. Solve $U\mathbf{x}_i = \mathbf{y}_i, \quad i = 1, \ldots, m.$

Note that the matrix A is factored only once, regardless of the number of right-hand sides. Hence, the operation count is $0(n^3) + 0(mn^2)$, the latter term representing items 2 and 3 in (3.3.25). Only when m becomes nearly as large as n does the amount of work in 2 and 3 approach that of the factorization, at least for full matrices. In the case of computing A^{-1}, $m = n$, but the total operation count is still $0(n^3)$.

To carry out the intent of (3.3.25) in terms of the elimination process, we note that we can either do 1 and 2 simultaneously, modifying the right-hand sides as the elimination proceeds, or we can first complete the factorization and save the multipliers ℓ_{ij} to do 2 at the subsequent step.

The various algorithms in this section have all been predicated on the assumption that a_{11} and the subsequent diagonal elements of the reduced matrix do not vanish. In practice, it is not sufficient that these divisors be nonzero; they must also be large enough in some sense or severe rounding error problems may occur. In Section 3.4 we will consider these problems and the modifications that are necessary for the elimination process to be a viable procedure.

Supplementary Discussion and References: 3.3

There are now a large number of books devoted to numerical linear algebra, and all of these discuss the problem of solving systems of linear equations; see, for example, Forsythe and Moler [1967] and Stewart [1973], and for a more advanced treatment, Householder [1964] and Wilkinson [1965]. A discussion of mathematical software for linear equations can be found in the Supplementary Discussion of Section 3.5.

Although the Gaussian elimination method is very efficient, there are algorithms that have a lower operation count as a function of n. In particular, the number of multiplications required to solve a linear system of size n by a method due to Strassen [1969] is $0(n^{2.8\ldots})$. The constant multiplying the high-order term is much larger than for Gaussian elimination, however, and the method is very complicated; consequently, it has not become a serious competitor to Gaussian elimination for practical computation.

EXERCISES 3.3

3.3.1. By hand calculation, solve the system

$$\begin{aligned} 3x_1 + x_2 + 2x_3 &= 1 \\ 4x_1 + 3x_2 + 2x_3 &= 2 \\ x_1 + 4x_2 + 2x_3 &= 4 \end{aligned}$$

3.3.2. Write down explicitly the matrices L and U of the factorization of the matrix A of exercise 3.3.1. Recalculate the solution using L and U.

3.3.3. Show that the following operation counts are correct for Gaussian elimination:

a. Number of additions (multiplications) to compute new right side = $n(n-1)/2$.

b. Number of divisions to compute the multipliers $\ell_{ik} = n(n-1)/2$.

c. Number of divisions in back substitution = n.

d. Number of additions (multiplications) in back substitution = $n(n-1)/2$.

3.3.4. Show that the elimination step that sets to zero the elements in the second through nth rows of the first column of the matrix A is equivalent to multiplying A by the matrix

$$L_1 = \begin{bmatrix} 1 & & & & \bigcirc \\ -\ell_{21} & 1 & & & \\ \cdot & & \cdot & & \\ \cdot & & \bigcirc & \cdot & \\ \cdot & & & & \cdot \\ -\ell_{n1} & & & & 1 \end{bmatrix}$$

More generally, show that $L_{n-1} \cdots L_2 L_1 A = U$, where

$$L_i = \begin{bmatrix} 1 & & & & & \\ & \cdot & & & \bigcirc & \\ & & \cdot & & & \\ & & & 1 & & \\ & & & -\ell_{i+1,i} & & \\ & & & \cdot & \cdot & \\ & & & \cdot & & \cdot \\ & & & -\ell_{n,i} & & 1 \end{bmatrix}$$

3.3.5. Verify that the product of L and U of (3.3.20) is tridiagonal.

3.3.6. Write a computer program to implement Gaussian elimination for tridiagonal systems. Use one-dimensional arrays to store the matrix.

3.3.7. Write a computer program to implement Gaussian elimination for a banded matrix with p subdiagonals and q superdiagonals. Use the storage pattern of Figure 3.5.

3.3.8. Prove the following statements about determinants:

a. The determinant of a triangular matrix is the product of its diagonal elements.

b. The determinant of a product of two matrices is the product of its determinants.

3.4 Interchanges

In our discussion of the Gaussian elimination process in the previous section, we assumed that a_{11} and all subsequent divisors were nonzero. However, we do not need to make such an assumption provided that we revise the algorithm so as to interchange equations if necessary, as we shall now describe.

We assume, as usual, that the coefficient matrix A is nonsingular. Suppose that $a_{11} = 0$. Then, some other element in the first column of A must be nonzero or else A is singular (see exercise 3.4.1). If, say, $a_{k1} \neq 0$, then we interchange the first equation in the system with the kth; clearly, this does not change the solution. In the new system, the (1,1) coefficient is now nonzero, and the elimination process can proceed. Similarly, an interchange can be done if any computed diagonal element that is to become a divisor in the next stage should vanish. Suppose, for example, that the elimination has progressed to the point

$$\begin{array}{ccccc} a_{11} & & & & \\ & \ddots & & & \\ & & a_{ii}^{(i-1)} & \cdots & a_{in}^{(i-1)} \\ & \bigcirc & \vdots & & \vdots \\ & & a_{ni}^{(i-1)} & \cdots & a_{nn}^{(i-1)} \end{array}$$

and that $a_{ii}^{(i-1)} = 0$. If all of the remaining elements below $a_{ii}^{(i-1)}$ in the ith column are also zero, the matrix is again singular (see exercise 3.4.2). Since the operations of adding a multiple of one row to another row, which produced this reduced matrix, do not effect the determinant, and an interchange of rows only changes the sign of the determinant, it follows that the original matrix is also singular, contrary to assumption. Hence, at least one of the elements $a_{ki}^{(i-1)}$, $k = i + 1, \ldots, n$, is nonzero, and we can interchange a row that contains a nonzero element with the ith row, thus ensuring that the new i, i element is nonzero. Again, this interchange of rows does not change the solution of the system.

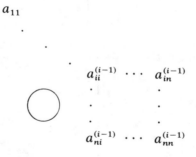

We note that an interchange of rows does change the sign of the determinant of the coefficient matrix. Hence, if the determinant is to be computed, a record must be kept of whether the number of interchanges is even or odd.

Since in exact arithmetic the Gaussian elimination process produces the solution of the linear system in a finite number of steps, and there is no discretization error associated with the process, the only thing that can affect the accuracy of our computed solution is rounding error. There are two possibilities. The first is an accumulation of rounding errors during a large number of arithmetic operations. For example, if $n =$ 1,000, the operation count of the previous section shows that on the order of $n^3 = 10^9$ operations will be required; even though the error in each individual operation may be small, the total buildup could be large. We shall see later that this potential accumulation of rounding error is not as serious as one might expect.

The second possibility is one of catastrophic rounding errors. If an algorithm has this unfortunate characteristic, it is called *numerically unstable* and is not suitable as a general method. Although the interchange process described previously ensures that Gaussian elimination can be carried out mathematically for any nonsingular system, the algorithm can give rise to catastrophic rounding errors and is numerically unstable. We shall analyze a simple 2×2 example in order to see how this can occur.

Consider the system

$$\textbf{(3.4.1)} \qquad \begin{bmatrix} -10^{-5} & 1 \\ 2 & 1 \end{bmatrix} \begin{bmatrix} x_1 \\ x_2 \end{bmatrix} = \begin{bmatrix} 1 \\ 0 \end{bmatrix}$$

whose exact solution is

$$x_1 = -0.4999975 \cdots \qquad x_2 = 0.999995$$

Now, suppose that we have a decimal computer with a word length of four digits; that is, numbers are represented in the form $0.{*}{*}{*}{*} \times 10^p$. Let us carry out Gaussian elimination on this hypothetical computer; first, we note that $a_{11} \neq 0$, and no interchange is needed. The multiplier is

$$\ell_{21} = \frac{-0.2 \times 10^1}{0.1 \times 10^{-4}} = -0.2 \times 10^6$$

which is exact, and the calculation for the new a_{22} is

$$\textbf{(3.4.2)} \quad a_{22}^{(1)} = 0.1 \times 10^1 - (-0.2 \times 10^6)(0.1 \times 10^1) = 0.1 \times 10^1 + 0.2 \times 10^6 = 0.2 \times 10^6$$

The exact sum in (3.4.2) is, of course, 0.200001×10^6, but since the computer has a word length of only four digits, this must be represented as 0.2000×10^6; this is the first rounding error in the calculation.

The new b_2 is

$$b_2^{(1)} = -(-0.2 \times 10^6)(0.1 \times 10^1) = 0.2 \times 10^6 \tag{3.4.3}$$

Note that no rounding errors occurred in this computation, nor do any occur in the back substitution:

$$x_2 = \frac{b_2^{(1)}}{a_{22}^{(1)}} = \frac{0.2 \times 10^6}{0.2 \times 10^6} = 0.1 \times 10^1$$

$$x_1 = \frac{0.1 \times 10^1 - 0.1 \times 10^1}{-0.1 \times 10^{-4}} = 0$$

The computed x_2 agrees excellently with the exact x_2, but the computed x_1 has no digits of accuracy. Note that the only error made in the calculation is in $a_{22}^{(1)}$, in which an error in the sixth decimal place was made. Every other operation was exact. How, then, can this one "small" error cause the computed x_1 to deviate so drastically from its exact value?

The answer lies in the principle of *backward error analysis*, one of the most important concepts in scientific computing. The basic idea of backward error analysis is to "ask not what the error is, but what problem have we really solved." We shall invoke this principle here in the following form. Note the quantity 0.000001×10^6 that was dropped from the computed $a_{22}^{(1)}$ in (3.4.2) is simply the original element a_{22}. Since this is the only place that a_{22} enters the calculation, the computed solution would have been the same if a_{22} were zero. Put another way, the calculation on our four-digit computer has computed the exact solution of the system

$$\begin{bmatrix} -10^{-5} & 1 \\ 2 & 0 \end{bmatrix} \begin{bmatrix} x_1 \\ x_2 \end{bmatrix} = \begin{bmatrix} 1 \\ 0 \end{bmatrix} \tag{3.4.4}$$

Intuitively, we would expect the two systems (3.4.1) and (3.4.4) to have rather different solutions, and this is, indeed, the case.

But why did this occur? The culprit is the large multiplier ℓ_{21}, which made it impossible for a_{22} to be included in the sum in (3.4.2) because of the word length of the machine. The large multiplier was due to the smallness of a_{11}, relative to a_{21}, and the remedy is, again, an interchange of the equations. Indeed, if we solve the system

$$\begin{bmatrix} 2 & 1 \\ -10^{-5} & 1 \end{bmatrix} \begin{bmatrix} x_1 \\ x_2 \end{bmatrix} = \begin{bmatrix} 0 \\ 1 \end{bmatrix} \tag{3.4.5}$$

on our hypothetical four-digit computer, we obtain

$$\ell_{21} = \frac{0.1 \times 10^{-4}}{0.2 \times 10^{1}} = -0.5 \times 10^{-5}$$

$$a_{22}^{(1)} = 0.1 \times 10^{1} - (-0.5 \times 10^{-5})(1) = 0.1 \times 10^{1}$$

$$b_2^{(1)} = 0.1 \times 10^{1} - (-0.5 \times 10^{-5})(0) = 0.1 \times 10^{1}$$

$$x_2 = \frac{0.1 \times 10^{1}}{0.1 \times 10^{1}} = 1.0$$

$$x_1 = \frac{-(0.1 \times 10^{1})(1)}{0.2 \times 10^{1}} = -0.5$$

Note that the computed solution now agrees excellently with the exact solution.

By a relatively simple strategy, we can always arrange to keep the multipliers in the elimination process less than or equal to 1 in absolute value. This is known as *partial pivoting*: at the kth stage of the elimination process, an interchange of rows is made, if necessary, to place in the main diagonal position the element of largest absolute value from the kth column below or on the main diagonal. If we include this interchange strategy in the forward reduction algorithm (3.3.11), we have

Forward Reduction with Partial Pivoting

(3.4.6)

For $k = 1, \ldots, n - 1$:
  Find $m \geq k$ such that $|a_{mk}| = \max\{|a_{ik}|: i \geq k\}$.
  If $a_{mk} = 0$, then A is singular, and stop.
    else interchange a_{kj} and a_{mj}, $j = k, k + 1, \ldots, n$.
    interchange b_k and b_m.
  For $i = k + 1, k + 2, \ldots, n$:
   $\ell_{ik} \leftarrow a_{ik}/a_{kk}$
   For $j = k + 1, k + 2, \ldots, n$:
    $a_{ij} \leftarrow a_{ij} - \ell_{ik}a_{kj}$
   $b_i \leftarrow b_i - \ell_{ik}b_k$

Gaussian elimination with partial pivoting has proved to be an extremely reliable algorithm in practice. However, there are two major cautions that should be kept in mind. First, the matrix must be properly scaled before the algorithm is used. To illustrate this point, consider the system

$$\begin{bmatrix} 10 & -10^{6} \\ 2 & 1 \end{bmatrix} \begin{bmatrix} x_1 \\ x_2 \end{bmatrix} = \begin{bmatrix} -10^{6} \\ 0 \end{bmatrix} \tag{3.4.7}$$

No interchange is called for by the partial pivoting strategy since the (1,1) element is already the largest in the first column. However, if we carry out (see exercise 3.4.5) the elimination on our hypothetical four-digit computer, we will encounter exactly the same problem that we did with the system (3.4.5). Indeed, (3.4.7) is just (3.4.1) with the first equation multiplied by -10^6.

The use of the partial pivoting strategy is predicated on the coefficient matrix being properly scaled so that the maximum element in each row and column is the same order of magnitude. This scaling is sometimes called *equilibration* of the matrix. Unfortunately, there is no known foolproof general procedure for such scaling, but usually it will be clear that some rows or columns of the matrix need scaling, and this can be done before the elimination starts. For example, if we were given the system (3.4.7), we should scale the first row so that its maximum element is approximately 1. Then, a_{11} will be small, and the partial pivoting strategy will cause an interchange of the first and second rows.

The second caution with the partial pivoting strategy is that even with an equilibrated matrix, it can be numerically unstable. Examples for which this can happen have been given, but the occurrence of such matrices in practical computations seems to be sufficiently rare that the danger can be safely ignored. (For additional remarks, see the Supplementary Discussion.)

If row interchanges are made, the Gaussian elimination process is not equivalent to a factorization of the matrix A into the product of lower- and upper-triangular matrices; the lower-triangular matrix must be modified in the following way.

A *permutation matrix*, P, is an $n \times n$ matrix that has exactly one element equal to 1 in each row and column and zeros elsewhere. A 4×4 example is

(3.4.8)
$$P = \begin{bmatrix} 1 & 0 & 0 & 0 \\ 0 & 0 & 0 & 1 \\ 0 & 0 & 1 & 0 \\ 0 & 1 & 0 & 0 \end{bmatrix}$$

Interchange of rows of a matrix can be effected by multiplication on the left by a permutation matrix. For example, multiplication of a 4×4 matrix by the permutation matrix (3.4.8) will leave the first and third rows the same and interchange the second and fourth rows (see exercise 3.4.6). Thus, the row interchanges of the coefficient matrix A that are required by the partial pivoting strategy can be represented by multiplication of A on the left by suitable permutation matrices. If P_i denotes the permutation matrix corresponding to the interchange required at the ith stage, then conceptually we are generating the triangular factorization of the matrix

(3.4.9)
$$P_{n-1}P_{n-2}\cdots P_2P_1A = PA = LU$$

rather than A itself. Thus, the factorization is $A = (P^{-1}L)U$. Since the product of permutation matrices is again a permutation matrix and the inverse of a permutation matrix is a permutation matrix (see exercises 3.4.7), the first factor is a permutation of a lower-triangular matrix, whereas the second is again upper-triangular. Note that if no interchange is required at the ith stage, the permutation matrix P_i is simply the identity matrix.

Row interchanges require additional time and, in the case of banded matrices, also slightly complicate the storage. Consider first a tridiagonal system. If an interchange is made at the first stage, the elements in the first two rows will be

$$\begin{matrix} * & * & * & 0 & \cdots \\ * & * & 0 & \cdots & \end{matrix}$$

The elimination process will then reenter a (in general) nonzero element into the (2, 3) position, and the reduced $(n-1) \times (n-1)$ matrix will again be tridiagonal. Thus, the effect of the interchanges will be to introduce possible nonzero elements into the second superdiagonal of the reduced triangular matrix; that is, the factor U in the decomposition of A will no longer be bidiagonal but will have, in general, three nonzero diagonals. Perhaps the simplest way of handling the storage is to add an additional one-dimensional array to hold these elements in the second superdiagonal.

For a banded matrix of the form shown in Figure 3.4, the same kind of problem occurs. If an interchange is made at the first stage between the first and $(p+1)$st rows, an additional p elements will be introduced into the first row, and these, in turn, will be propagated into rows 2 through $p+1$ during the elimination process. Thus, we need to provide storage for a possible additional p superdiagonals. The simplest way to handle this is to allow for an additional $n \times p$ array of storage at the outset. Of course, this requires an additional np storage locations. An alternative method is based on the observation that the amount of additional storage needed is no more than the amount of storage required for the nonzero subdiagonals. As the subdiagonals are eliminated, we no longer will need that storage, and the new superdiagonal elements can be stored in those positions. However, it is this subdiagonal space that is normally used to store the multipliers if their retention is desired; in this case, we have no alternative but to set aside additional storage.

Although for general nonsingular matrices it is necessary that the partial pivoting strategy be used, there are some types of matrices for which it is known that no interchanges are necessary. The most important of these are diagonally dominant matrices [see equation (3.2.21)], and positive-definite symmetric matrices (see Appendix 3). In both cases, it is safe to use Gaussian elimination with no interchanges at all; this will be discussed further in the next section. This is especially advantageous for banded matrices, and it is a fortunate fact that most banded matrices that arise from differential equations are either diagonally dominant or symmetric and positive-definite.

In the case of a symmetric positive-definite matrix, there is a variant of Gaussian elimination that is sometimes useful. This is *Cholesky's method*, which is based on a factorization of the form

(3.4.10)
$$A = LL^T$$

Here, L is a lower-triangular matrix but does not necessarily have 1s on the main diagonal as in the LU factorization. The symbol L^T denotes the transpose of L. The factorization (3.4.10) is unique provided that L is required to have positive diagonal elements (see exercise 3.4.8).

By equating elements on both sides of (3.4.10), we are led to a prescription for computing the elements of L in terms of A. Let ℓ_{ij} denote the elements of L, noting that $\ell_{ij} = 0$ if $j > i$. Then, the product in (3.4.10) is

(3.4.11)
$$\begin{bmatrix} a_{11} & \cdots & a_{1n} \\ \vdots & & \vdots \\ a_{i1} \cdots a_{ii} & & \vdots \\ \vdots & & \vdots \\ a_{n1} & \cdots & a_{nn} \end{bmatrix} = \begin{bmatrix} \ell_{11} & & \bigcirc \\ \vdots & \ddots & \\ \ell_{i1} \cdots \ell_{ii} & & \\ \vdots & & \ddots \\ \ell_{n1} & \cdots & \ell_{nn} \end{bmatrix} \begin{bmatrix} \ell_{11} & \cdots & \ell_{i1} & \cdots & \ell_{n1} \\ & \ddots & \vdots & & \vdots \\ & & \ell_{ii} & & \vdots \\ & \bigcirc & & \ddots & \vdots \\ & & & & \ell_{nn} \end{bmatrix}$$

By equating elements of the first columns of both sides of (3.4.11), we see that $a_{i1} = \ell_{i1}\ell_{11}$, so the first column of L is determined by

(3.4.12)
$$\ell_{11} = (a_{11})^{1/2} \qquad \ell_{i1} = \frac{a_{i1}}{\ell_{11}}, \qquad i = 2, \ldots, n$$

(3.4.13)
$$a_{ii} = \sum_{k=1}^{i} \ell_{ik}^2 \qquad a_{ij} = \sum_{k=1}^{j} \ell_{ik}\ell_{jk}, \qquad j < i$$

which forms the basis for the following algorithm for determining the columns of L in sequence:

Cholesky Decomposition

For $j = 1, \ldots, n$:

(3.4.14)
$$\ell_{jj} \leftarrow \left(a_{jj} - \sum_{k=1}^{j-1} \ell_{jk}^2\right)^{1/2}$$

For $i = j + 1, \ldots, n$:

$$l_{ij} \leftarrow \frac{a_{ij} - \sum_{k=1}^{j-1} \ell_{ik}\ell_{jk}}{\ell_{jj}}$$

Once L is computed, the solution of the linear system can proceed just as in the LU decomposition (3.3.16): solve $\mathrm{L}\mathbf{y} = \mathbf{b}$ and then solve $\mathrm{L}^T\mathbf{x} = \mathbf{y}$.

In order that the Cholesky decomposition can be carried out, it is necessary that the quantities $a_{jj} - \sum \ell_{jk}^2$ all be positive so that the square roots may be taken. If the coefficient matrix A is positive-definite, these quantities are indeed positive; moreover, the algorithm is numerically stable.

The Cholesky algorithm allows efficient storage utilization. Since A is symmetric, only its lower-triangular part need be stored, and the ℓ_{ij} can be overwritten onto the corresponding positions of A as they are computed. Furthermore, the algorithm is easily adapted to banded matrices. If p is the number of nonzero diagonals below the main diagonal of A (by symmetry, there are then p nonzero diagonals above the main diagonal), algorithm (3.4.14) becomes

Cholesky Decomposition for Banded Matrices

For $j = 1, \ldots, n$:

$$q \leftarrow \max(1, j - p)$$

$$\ell_{jj} \leftarrow \left(a_{jj} - \sum_{k=q}^{j-1} \ell_{jk}^2\right)^{1/2}$$

For $i = j + 1, \ldots, \min(j + p, n)$:

$$r \leftarrow \max(1, i - p)$$

$$\ell_{ij} \leftarrow \frac{a_{ij} - \sum_{k=q}^{j-1} \ell_{ik}\ell_{jk}}{\ell_{jj}}$$

In this section, we have discussed various questions concerning the accuracy of computed solutions of systems of linear equations. In the following section, we will consider additional questions, including the important topic of "ill-conditioning".

Supplementary Discussion and References: 3.4

The interchange of rows required by partial pivoting need not be done explicitly. Instead, the interchanges may be carried out implicitly by using a permutation vector that keeps track of which rows are interchanged; see Forsythe and Moler [1967] for a discussion. Whether one should use explicit or implicit interchanges depends on the computer's "interchange" time, time required for indexing, program clarity, and other considerations.

In those cases in which partial pivoting is not sufficient to guarantee accuracy, we can use another interchange strategy, called *complete pivoting*, in which both rows and columns are interchanged so as to bring into the diagonal divisor position the largest element in absolute value in the remaining submatrix to be processed. This strategy adds a significant amount of time to the Gaussian elimination process and is rarely incorporated into a standard program. See Wilkinson [1961] for further discussion.

EXERCISES 3.4

3.4.1. Suppose that the ith column of the matrix A consists of zero elements. Show that A is singular by the following different arguments:

a. The determinant of A is zero.

b. $A\mathbf{e}_i = 0$, where $\mathbf{e}_i$ is the vector with 1 in the ith position and zeros elsewhere.

c. A has, at most, $n - 1$ linearly independent columns.

3.4.2. Let A be a matrix of the form

$$\begin{bmatrix} a_{11} & \cdots & & & & \\ & \ddots & & & & \\ 0 & & a_{i-1,i-1} & & & \\ \vdots & \ddots & & & & \\ \vdots & & 0 & a_{ii} & & \\ \vdots & & \vdots & \vdots & \ddots & \\ & & \vdots & a_{i+1,i} & & \ddots \\ 0 & \cdots & 0 & a_{ni} & \cdots & a_{nn} \end{bmatrix}$$

If $a_{ii} = a_{i+1,i} = \cdots = a_{ni} = 0$, show that A is singular.

3.4.3. Solve the following 3×3 system by Gaussian elimination by making row interchanges where needed to avoid division by zero:

$$\begin{aligned} 2x_1 + 2x_2 + 3x_3 &= 1 \\ x_1 + x_2 + 2x_3 &= 2 \\ 2x_1 + x_2 + 2x_3 &= 3 \end{aligned}$$

3.4.4. Translate the algorithm (3.4.6) into a computer program for Gaussian elimination using partial pivoting. Include back substitution.

3.4.5. Apply Gaussian elimination to the system (3.4.7) using the four-digit decimal computer of the text. Repeat the calculation after interchanging the equations.

3.4.6. **a.** Show that multiplication of a 4×4 matrix on the left by the permutation matrix (3.4.8) interchanges the second and fourth rows and leaves the first and third rows the same.

b. Show that multiplication on the right by the permutation matrix interchanges the second and fourth columns.

c. Write down the 4×4 permutation matrix that interchanges the first and third rows and leaves the second and fourth rows the same.

3.4.7. Show that the product of two $n \times n$ permutation matrices is a permutation matrix. Show that the inverse of a permutation matrix is a permutation matrix.

3.4.8. Let $A = LL^T$ be a factorization of a symmetric positive-definite matrix A, where L is lower-triangular and has positive main diagonal elements. Show that if $\hat{L}$ is obtained from L by changing the sign of every element of the ith row, then $A = \hat{L}\hat{L}^T$. (This shows that the LL^T factorization is not unique although there is a unique L with positive main diagonal elements.)

3.5 Ill-Conditioning and Error Analysis

The Gaussian elimination algorithm with partial pivoting has proved to be an efficient and reliable method in practice. But it may, nevertheless, fail to compute accurate solutions of certain systems of equations that are "ill-conditioned". A linear system of equations is said to be *ill-conditioned* if small changes in the elements of the coefficient matrix and/or right-hand side cause large changes in the solution. In this case, no numerical method can be expected to produce an accurate solution, nor, in many cases, should a solution even be attempted.

We begin with a simple 2×2 example. Consider the system

$$\begin{aligned} 0.832x_1 + 0.448x_2 &= 1.00 \\ 0.784x_1 + 0.421x_2 &= 0 \end{aligned} \tag{3.5.1}$$

and assume that we use a three-digit decimal computer to carry out Gaussian elimination. Note that since a_{11} is the largest element of the matrix, no interchange is required, and the computation of the new elements $a_{22}^{(1)}$ and $b_1^{(1)}$ is

$$\ell_{21} = \frac{0.784}{0.832} = 0.942\,|\,308 \cdots = 0.942$$

$$\begin{aligned} a_{22}^{(1)} &= 0.421 - 0.942 \times 0.448 = 0.421 - 0.422\,|\,016 = -0.001 \\ b_2^{(1)} &= 0 - 1.00 \times 0.942 = -0.942 \end{aligned} \tag{3.5.2}$$

where we have indicated by the vertical bars those digits lost in the computation. Hence, the computed triangular system is

$$\begin{aligned} 0.832x_1 + 0.448x_2 &= 1.00 \\ -\,0.001x_2 &= -0.942 \end{aligned}$$

and the back substitution produces the approximate solution

$$x_1 = -506 \qquad x_2 = 942 \tag{3.5.3}$$

But the exact solution of (3.5.1), correct to three figures, is

$$x_1 = -439 \qquad x_2 = 817 \tag{3.5.4}$$

so the computed solution is incorrect by about 15%. Why has this occurred?

The first easy answer is that we have lost significance in the calculation of $a_{22}^{(1)}$. Indeed, it is clear that the computed value of $a_{22}^{(1)}$ has only one significant figure, so our final computed solution will have no more than one significant figure. But this is only the manifestation of the real problem. We invoke again the principle of backward error analysis. By carrying out a more detailed computation, we can show that the computed solution (3.5.3) is the exact solution of the system

(3.5.5)
$$\begin{aligned} 0.832x_1 + 0.447974\cdots x_2 &= 1.00 \\ 0.783744\cdots x_1 + 0.420992\cdots x_2 &= 0 \end{aligned}$$

The maximum percentage change between the elements of this system and the original system (3.5.1) is only approximately 0.03%. However, these changes cause a change in the solution of 15%; that is, errors in the data are magnified by a factor of about 500.

The root cause of this ill-conditioning is that the coefficient matrix of (3.5.1) is "almost singular." Geometrically, this means that the lines defined by the two equations of (3.5.1) are almost parallel, as indicated in Figure 3.6. Consider now the system of equations

(3.5.6)
$$\begin{aligned} 0.832x_1 + 0.448x_2 &= 1.00 \\ 0.784x_1 + (0.421 + \varepsilon)x_2 &= 0 \end{aligned}$$

The second equation defines a family of lines depending on the parameter ε. As ε increases from zero to approximately 0.0012, the line rotates counterclockwise and its intersection with the line defined by the first equation recedes to infinity until the two lines become exactly parallel and no solution of the linear system exists.

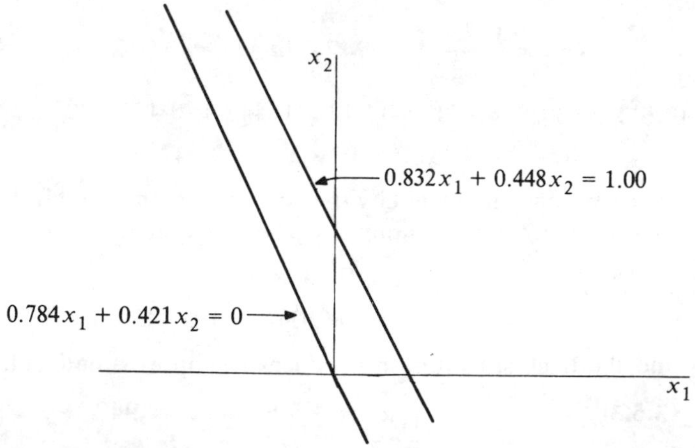

FIGURE 3.6 *Almost-Parallel Lines Defined by* (3.5.1). *The Intersection of the Lines is at* (−439, 817).

It is clear that very small changes in one coefficient of the system (3.5.6) can cause increasingly large changes in the solution as ε approaches the value for which the system is singular. At this point, the determinant of the coefficient matrix is zero, and it is sometimes suggested that the smallness of the determinant is a measure of the ill-conditioning of the system. But this is not true, in general, as the following example shows:

$$\textbf{(3.5.7)} \quad \det\begin{bmatrix} 10^{-10} & 0 \\ 0 & 10^{-10} \end{bmatrix} = 10^{-20} \qquad \det\begin{bmatrix} 10^{10} & 0 \\ 0 & 10^{10} \end{bmatrix} = 10^{20}$$

The values of the two determinants are very different, but the lines defined by the two corresponding sets of equations

$$\textbf{(3.5.8)} \qquad \begin{matrix} 10^{-10}x_1 = 0 & \quad 10^{10}x_1 = 0 \\ 10^{-10}x_2 = 0 & \quad 10^{10}x_2 = 0 \end{matrix}$$

are the same and are simply the coordinate axes. As we shall see more clearly in a moment, if the lines defined by the equations of a system are perpendicular, that system is "perfectly conditioned." Thus, the magnitude of the determinant of the coefficient matrix is not a good measure of the near singularity of the matrix. It can, however, become the basis of such a measure if the matrix is suitably scaled, as we shall now see.

For two equations, it is clear that a good measure of the "almost parallelness" of the corresponding two lines is the angle between them. An essentially equivalent measure is the area of the parallelogram shown in Figure 3.7, in which the sides of the parallelogram are of length 1 and the height is denoted by h. The area of the parallelogram is then simply equal to h since the base is 1, and the angle θ between the lines defined by the two equations is related to h by $h = \sin\theta$. The area, h, varies between zero, when the lines coalesce, and 1, when they are perpendicular, and provides a good measure of the "almost parallelness" of the lines.

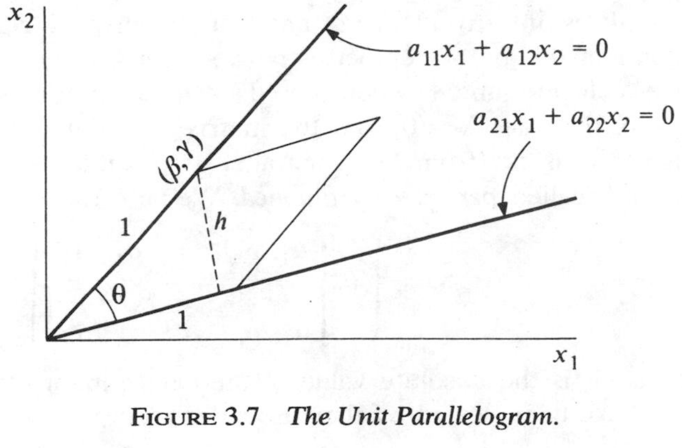

FIGURE 3.7 *The Unit Parallelogram.*

From analytic geometry, the distance from the point (β, γ) to the line $a_{21}x_1 + a_{22}x_2 = 0$ is simply

$$h = \frac{|a_{21}\beta + a_{22}\gamma|}{\alpha_2}, \qquad \alpha_2 = (a_{21}^2 + a_{22}^2)^{1/2}$$

If we assume that $a_{11} \geq 0$, the coordinates (β, γ) are given by

$$\beta = \frac{-a_{12}}{\alpha_1}, \qquad \gamma = \frac{a_{11}}{\alpha_1}, \qquad \alpha_1 = (a_{11}^2 + a_{12}^2)^{1/2}$$

so

(3.5.9) $$h = \frac{|a_{11}a_{22} - a_{21}a_{12}|}{\alpha_1\alpha_2} = \frac{|\det A|}{\alpha_1\alpha_2}$$

Hence, we see that the area, h, is just the determinant divided by the product $\alpha_1\alpha_2$.

This measure easily extends to n equations. Let $A = (a_{ij})$ be the coefficient matrix, and set

(3.5.10) $$V = \frac{|\det A|}{\alpha_1\alpha_2 \cdots \alpha_n}$$

where

$$\alpha_i = (a_{i1}^2 + a_{i2}^2 + \cdots + a_{in}^2)^{1/2}$$

We have called the quantity in (3.5.10) V instead of h because it is the volume of the n-dimensional unit parallelepiped circumscribed by the lines defined by the rows of matrix A; that is,

$$\frac{1}{\alpha_i}(a_{i1}, a_{i2}, \ldots, a_{in}), \qquad i = 1, \ldots, n$$

are the coordinates of n points in n-dimensional space located Euclidean distance 1 from the origin, and these n points define a parallelepiped whose sides are of length 1.

It is intuitively clear, and can be proved rigorously, that the volume of this parallelepiped is between zero, when two or more of the edges coincide, and 1, when the edges are all mutually perpendicular. If $V = 0$, then $\det A = 0$, and the matrix is singular. If $V = 1$, then the edges are as far from being parallel as possible, and in this case, the matrix is called *perfectly conditioned.* We note that

$$V = \left| \det \begin{bmatrix} a_{11}/\alpha_1 & \cdots & a_{1n}/\alpha_1 \\ \vdots & & \vdots \\ a_{n1}/\alpha_n & \cdots & a_{nn}/\alpha_n \end{bmatrix} \right|$$

that is, V is the absolute value of the determinant of the matrix whose rows have been scaled by their Euclidean length.

There are various ramifications of ill-conditioning of a matrix besides the difficulty in computing an accurate solution of the corresponding linear system. Consider again the system (3.5.1) and suppose that (3.5.5) is the "real" system that we wish to solve but that the coefficients of this system must be measured by some physical apparatus that is accurate to only the third decimal place. Thus, (3.5.1) is not the system that we really wish to solve but is the best approximation that we can make to it. Suppose that we can also claim that the coefficients of (3.5.1) are accurate to at least 0.05%, as, indeed, they are, compared with (3.5.5). Then, it is an often-heard argument that we should be able to compute the solution of the system to about the same accuracy. But we have seen that this is not true; the ill-conditioning of the coefficient matrix magnifies small errors in the coefficients by a factor of about 500 in the case of (3.5.1). Hence, no matter how accurately the system (3.5.1) is solved, we will still have the error that has come from the measurement error in the coefficients. If, for example, we need the solution of the "real" system (3.5.5) accurate to less than 1%, we need to measure the coefficients more accurately than three decimal places. Thus, we should not even attempt to solve certain ill-conditioned systems, but rather should reformulate the problem or measure the data more accurately.

In some cases, however, the coefficient matrix may be exact. A famous example of a class of ill-conditioned matrices is the *Hilbert matrices* (or *Hilbert segments*), in which the elements of the matrix are exact rational numbers:

(3.5.11)
$$H_n = \begin{bmatrix} 1 & 1/2 & \cdots & 1/n \\ 1/2 & & & \cdot \\ \cdot & & & \cdot \\ \cdot & & & \cdot \\ \cdot & & & \\ 1/n & & \cdots & 1/(2n-1) \end{bmatrix}$$

These matrices are increasingly ill-conditioned as n increases. To indicate how bad the conditioning is, if for $n = 8$ the coefficients are entered in the computer as binary fractions exact to the extent possible with 27 binary digits (equivalent to about 8 decimal digits), the exact inverse of the matrix in the computer differs from the exact inverse of H_8 in the first figure!

Another manifestation of ill-conditioning is as follows. Suppose that $\hat{\mathbf{x}}$ is a computed solution of the system $A\mathbf{x} = \mathbf{b}$. One way to try to ascertain the accuracy of $\hat{\mathbf{x}}$ is to form the *residual vector*,

(3.5.12)
$$\mathbf{r} = A\hat{\mathbf{x}} - \mathbf{b}$$

If $\hat{\mathbf{x}}$ were the exact solution, then $\mathbf{r}$ would be zero. Thus, we would expect that $\mathbf{r}$ would be "small" if $\hat{\mathbf{x}}$ were a good approximation to the exact solution, and, conversely, that if $\mathbf{r}$ were small, then $\hat{\mathbf{x}}$ would be a good approximation. This is true in some cases, but if A is ill-conditioned, the magnitude of $\mathbf{r}$ can be very misleading. As an example, consider the system

(3.5.13)
$$\begin{aligned} 0.780x_1 + 0.563x_2 &= 0.217 \\ 0.913x_1 + 0.659x_2 &= 0.254 \end{aligned}$$

and the approximate solution

(3.5.14)
$$\hat{\mathbf{x}} = \begin{bmatrix} 0.341 \\ -0.087 \end{bmatrix}$$

Then, the residual vector is

(3.5.15)
$$\mathbf{r} = -\begin{bmatrix} 10^{-6} \\ 0 \end{bmatrix}$$

Now, consider another, very different, approximate solution—

(3.5.16)
$$\hat{\mathbf{x}} = \begin{bmatrix} 0.999 \\ -1.001 \end{bmatrix}$$

and the corresponding residual vector—

(3.5.17)
$$\mathbf{r} = \begin{bmatrix} -0.0013\cdots \\ 0.0015\cdots \end{bmatrix}$$

By comparing the residuals (3.5.15) and (3.5.17), we easily conclude that (3.5.14) is the better approximate solution. However, the exact solution of (3.5.13) is $(1, -1)$, so the residuals give completely misleading information.

A similar phenomenon may occur with inverses. Suppose that

$$A = \begin{bmatrix} 9{,}999 & 9{,}998 \\ 10{,}000 & 9{,}999 \end{bmatrix} \qquad B = \begin{bmatrix} 9{,}999.9999 & -9{,}997.0001 \\ -10{,}001 & 9{,}998 \end{bmatrix}$$

where B is meant to be an approximation to A^{-1}. To test this approximation, we compute the residual matrix

(3.5.18)
$$R_1 = AB - I = \begin{bmatrix} 0.0001 & 0.0001 \\ 0 & 0 \end{bmatrix}$$

where I is the identity. If B were equal to A^{-1}, then this residual should be zero. As it is, the residual is very small, especially compared to the size of the elements of A and B, and would seem to indicate that B is a very good approximation. However, the inverse must also satisfy the relation $A^{-1}A - I = 0$, and if we compute the corresponding residual matrix, we have

$$\textbf{(3.5.19)} \qquad R_2 = BA - I = \begin{bmatrix} 19{,}998 & 19{,}995 \\ -199{,}999 & -19{,}996 \end{bmatrix}$$

Which residual matrix do we believe? Equation (3.5.18) indicates a very good approximation, whereas (3.5.19) indicates a poor approximation. The actual inverse is

$$A^{-1} = \begin{bmatrix} 9{,}999 & -9{,}998 \\ -10{,}000 & 9{,}999 \end{bmatrix}$$

so B is accurate to 1 in the fourth figure. The residual (3.5.19) is completely misleading; again, this is a consequence of the ill-conditioning of the matrix A.

We turn now to another way of measuring the ill-conditioning of a matrix by means of norms (see Appendix 3 for a review of vector and matrix norms). Suppose first that $\mathbf{x}^*$ is the solution of $A\mathbf{x} = \mathbf{b}$ and that $\mathbf{x}^* + \Delta\mathbf{x}$ is the solution of the system with the right-hand side $\mathbf{b} + \Delta\mathbf{b}$; that is,

$$\textbf{(3.5.20)} \qquad A(\mathbf{x}^* + \Delta\mathbf{x}) = \mathbf{b} + \Delta\mathbf{b}$$

Since $A\mathbf{x}^* = \mathbf{b}$, it follows that $A(\Delta\mathbf{x}) = \Delta\mathbf{b}$ and $\Delta\mathbf{x} = A^{-1}(\Delta\mathbf{b})$, assuming, as usual, that A is nonsingular. Thus,

$$\textbf{(3.5.21)} \qquad \|\Delta\mathbf{x}\| \leq \|A^{-1}\|\,\|\Delta\mathbf{b}\|$$

which shows that the change in the solution due to a change in the right-hand side is bounded by $\|A^{-1}\|$. Thus, a small change in $\mathbf{b}$ may cause a large change in $\mathbf{x}^*$ if $\|A^{-1}\|$ is large. The notion of "large" is always relative, however, and it is more useful to deal with the relative change $\|\Delta\mathbf{x}\|/\|\mathbf{x}^*\|$. From $A\mathbf{x}^* = \mathbf{b}$, it follows that

$$\|\mathbf{b}\| \leq \|A\|\,\|\mathbf{x}^*\|$$

and combining this with (3.5.21) yields

$$\|\Delta\mathbf{x}\|\,\|\mathbf{b}\| \leq \|A\|\,\|A^{-1}\|\,\|\Delta\mathbf{b}\|\,\|\mathbf{x}^*\|$$

or, equivalently (if $\mathbf{b} \neq 0$),

$$\textbf{(3.5.22)} \qquad \frac{\|\Delta\mathbf{x}\|}{\|\mathbf{x}^*\|} \leq \|A\|\,\|A^{-1}\|\frac{\|\Delta\mathbf{b}\|}{\|\mathbf{b}\|}$$

This inequality shows that the relative change in $\mathbf{x}^*$ due to a change in $\mathbf{b}$ is bounded by the relative change in $\mathbf{b}$, $\|\Delta\mathbf{b}\|/\|\mathbf{b}\|$, times $\|A\|\,\|A^{-1}\|$. The latter quantity is of great importance and is called the *condition number* of A (with respect to the norm being used); it will be denoted by cond(A). Matrices for which cond(A) is large are ill-conditioned, and those for which it is small are *well-conditioned* (note that cond(A) $\geq$ 1).

Consider next the case in which the elements of A are changed so that the perturbed equations are

$$(3.5.23) \qquad (\mathrm{A} + \delta\mathrm{A})(\mathbf{x}^* + \delta\mathbf{x}) = \mathbf{b}$$

Thus, since $\mathrm{A}\mathbf{x}^* = \mathbf{b}$,

$$\mathrm{A}\delta\mathbf{x} = \mathbf{b} - (\mathrm{A} + \delta\mathrm{A})\mathbf{x}^* - \delta\mathrm{A}\delta\mathbf{x} = -\delta\mathrm{A}(\mathbf{x}^* + \delta\mathbf{x})$$

or

$$-\delta\mathbf{x} = \mathrm{A}^{-1}\delta\mathrm{A}(\mathbf{x}^* + \delta\mathbf{x})$$

Therefore,

$$\|\delta\mathbf{x}\| \le \|\mathrm{A}^{-1}\|\,\|\delta\mathrm{A}\|\,\|\mathbf{x}^* + \delta\mathbf{x}\| = \mathrm{cond}(\mathrm{A})\frac{\|\delta\mathrm{A}\|}{\|\mathrm{A}\|}\|\mathbf{x}^* + \delta\mathbf{x}\|$$

so that

$$(3.5.24) \qquad \frac{\|\delta\mathbf{x}\|}{\|\mathbf{x}^* + \delta\mathbf{x}\|} \le \mathrm{cond}(\mathrm{A})\frac{\|\delta\mathrm{A}\|}{\|\mathrm{A}\|}$$

Once again, the condition number plays a major role in the bound. Note that (3.5.24) expresses the change in $\mathbf{x}^*$ relative to the perturbed solution, $\mathbf{x}^* + \delta\mathbf{x}$, rather than $\mathbf{x}^*$ itself as in (3.5.22), although it is possible to get a bound relative to $\mathbf{x}^*$.

The inequalities (3.5.22) and (3.5.24) need to be interpreted correctly. If A has a small condition number, say close to 1, then small relative changes in the data necessarily mean small changes in the solution. On the other hand, if the condition number is large, then small changes in the data may cause large changes in the solution, but not necessarily, depending on the particular perturbation. The practical effect of a large condition number depends on the accuracy of the data and the word length of the computer being used. If, for example, $\mathrm{cond}(\mathrm{A}) = 10^6$, then possibly the equivalent of 6 decimal digits could be lost, and on a computer with a word length equivalent to 8 decimal digits, that could be disastrous, whereas if the word length were the equivalent of 16 decimal digits, it might not cause much of a problem.

In general, it is very difficult to compute the condition number $\|\mathrm{A}\|\,\|\mathrm{A}^{-1}\|$ without knowing A^{-1}. In some cases of interest, however, it is relatively easy to do, and we give an example of this in the ℓ_2 norm for the $(2, -1)$ tridiagonal matrix A of (3.2.15). As given in Appendix 3, the ℓ_2 norm of a symmetric matrix is its spectral radius. Thus,

$$\|\mathrm{A}\|\,\|\mathrm{A}^{-1}\| = \rho(\mathrm{A})\rho(\mathrm{A}^{-1})$$

As we now show, it is easy to compute all of the eigenvalues of (3.2.15) explicitly, and we are thus able to compute the condition number. The key to the computation is the trigonometric identity

$$(3.5.25) \qquad -\sin\frac{(j-1)(k\pi)}{n+1} - \sin\frac{(j+1)(k\pi)}{n+1} = -2\cos\frac{k\pi}{n+1}\sin\frac{jk\pi}{n+1}$$

which holds for j, $k = 1, \ldots, n$, which is easily verified (exercise 3.5.5). If we add $2\sin[jk\pi/(n+1)]$ to both sides of these equations and then write the equations for $j = 1, \ldots, n$ and fixed k in matrix form, we have

$$\begin{bmatrix} 2 & -1 & & & \\ -1 & \cdot & \cdot & & \\ & \cdot & \cdot & \cdot & \\ & & \cdot & \cdot & -1 \\ & & & -1 & 2 \end{bmatrix} \begin{bmatrix} \sin\frac{k\pi}{n+1} \\ \sin\frac{2k\pi}{n+1} \\ \cdot \\ \cdot \\ \cdot \\ \sin\frac{nk\pi}{n+1} \end{bmatrix} = \left(2 - 2\cos\frac{k\pi}{n+1}\right) \begin{bmatrix} \sin\frac{k\pi}{n+1} \\ \sin\frac{2k\pi}{n+1} \\ \cdot \\ \cdot \\ \cdot \\ \sin\frac{nk\pi}{n+1} \end{bmatrix}$$

which shows that the eigenvalues λ_k, and corresponding eigenvectors, $\mathbf{v_k}$, of A are

$$\textbf{(3.5.26)} \quad \lambda_k = 2 - 2\cos\frac{k\pi}{n+1} \qquad \mathbf{v_k} = \begin{bmatrix} \sin\frac{k\pi}{n+1} \\ \sin\frac{2k\pi}{n+1} \\ \cdot \\ \cdot \\ \cdot \\ \sin\frac{nk\pi}{n+1} \end{bmatrix}, \qquad k = 1, \ldots, n$$

Thus, the largest eigenvalue of A is

$$\rho(A) = \lambda_n = 2 - 2\cos\frac{\pi n}{n+1}$$

and the smallest is

$$\lambda_1 = 2 - 2\cos\frac{\pi}{n+1} > 0$$

(This shows, incidentally, that A is positive-definite.) Since the eigenvalues of A^{-1} are $\lambda_1^{-1}, \ldots, \lambda_n^{-1}$, the spectral radius of A^{-1} is λ_1^{-1}. Thus,

$$\|A\|_2 \|A^{-1}\|_2 = \lambda_n \lambda_1^{-1} = \frac{2 - 2\cos\frac{\pi n}{n+1}}{2 - 2\cos\frac{\pi}{n+1}}$$

For large n, we can approximate the cosine terms by the first-order Taylor expansions

$$\cos\frac{\pi}{n+1} \doteq 1 - \frac{\pi^2}{(n+1)^2}$$

$$\cos\frac{n\pi}{n+1} = -\left(1 - \sin\frac{\pi}{n+1}\right) \doteq -1 + \frac{\pi^2}{(n+1)^2}$$

so

$$\|A\|_2\,\|A^{-1}\|_2 \doteq \frac{2 - \dfrac{\pi^2}{(n+1)^2}}{\dfrac{\pi^2}{(n+1)^2}} = \frac{2(n+1)^2 - \pi^2}{\pi^2} = 0(n^2)$$

This shows that A is moderately ill-conditioned and that the condition number grows approximately as the square of the dimension of the matrix.

To conclude this chapter, we return to the linear two-point boundary-value problems of Section 3.2. As an example, we have chosen the problem

(3.5.27) $$[(1 + x^2)u']' = 2 + 6x^2 + 2x\cos x - (1 + x^2)\sin x$$

(3.5.28) $$u(0) = 1 \qquad u(1) = 2 + \sin 1$$

Note that equation (3.5.27) can be rewritten as

(3.5.29) $$(1 + x^2)u'' + 2xu' = 2 + 6x^2 + 2x\cos x - (1 + x^2)\sin x$$

which is in the general form of (3.2.1). In order to evaluate the accuracy of the differencing methods of Section 3.2, we have chosen a problem whose solution is known—

(3.5.30) $$u(x) = x^2 + \sin x + 1$$

We will use three different schemes for approximating (3.5.27). The first method is given in Section 3.2 by equations (3.2.24) and (3.2.25) and uses a first-order approximation to the first derivative. By comparing (3.5.29) to (3.2.1), we see that $a(x) = 1 + x^2$, $b(x) = 2x$, $c(x) = 0$, and $d(x)$ is the right-hand side of (3.5.29). It follows that $a_i = a(x_i) = a(ih) = 1 + (ih)^2$, $b_i = 2ih$, $c_i = 0$, and $d_i = 2 + 6(ih)^2 + 2ih\cos(ih) - (1 + i^2h^2)\sin(ih)$. Thus, the ith row of the coefficient matrix in (3.2.25) becomes (because $b_i \geq 0$)

(3.5.31) $$-1 - i^2h^2, \qquad 2 + 2i(i+1)h^2, \qquad -1 - i(i+2)h^2$$

and the matrix is

$$(3.5.32)\quad \begin{bmatrix} 2+4h^2 & -1-3h^2 & & & \bigcirc \\ -1-4h^2 & 2+12h^2 & -1-8h^2 & & \\ & \cdot & \cdot & \cdot & \\ & & \cdot & \cdot & \cdot \\ \bigcirc & & \cdot & \cdot & -1-(n-1)^2h^2 \\ & & & -1-n^2h^2 & 2+2n(n+1)h^2 \end{bmatrix}$$

where $(n+1)h = 1$. The right-hand-side vector is given by

$$(3.5.33)\quad -h^2\left[d_1 - \left(1+\frac{1}{h^2}\right), d_2, \ldots, d_n - \left(n^2 + \frac{1}{h^2}\right)(2+\sin 1)\right]^T$$

The second difference approximation is given by (3.2.12), (3.2.13), and (3.2.14). In this case, the ith row of the coefficient matrix reduces to

$$(3.5.34)\quad -1-i(i-1)h^2, \qquad 2+2i^2h^2, \qquad -1-i(i+1)h^2$$

and the matrix and right-hand side are

(3.5.35)

$$\begin{bmatrix} 2+2h^2 & -1-2h^2 & & & \bigcirc \\ -1-2h^2 & 2+8h^2 & -1-6h^2 & & \\ & \cdot & \cdot & \cdot & \\ & & \cdot & \cdot & \cdot \\ \bigcirc & & \cdot & \cdot & -1-n(n-1)h^2 \\ & & & -1-n(n-1)h^2 & 2+2n^2h^2 \end{bmatrix}$$

and

(3.5.36)

$$-h^2\left\{d_1 - \left(1+\frac{1}{h^2}+\frac{1}{h}\right), d_2, \ldots, d_n - \left[n(n-1)+\frac{1}{h^2}\right](2+\sin 1)\right\}^T$$

The third, and final, difference scheme is given by (3.2.29) and (3.2.30), which applied only to equations of the form (3.2.27), as (3.5.27) is. In this case, the ith row of the matrix is

$$(3.5.37)\quad -1-(i-\tfrac{1}{2})^2h^2, \qquad 2+(2i^2+\tfrac{1}{2})h^2, \qquad -1-(i+\tfrac{1}{2})^2h^2$$

and the coefficient matrix becomes

(3.5.38)

$$\begin{bmatrix} 2+\frac{5}{2}h^2 & -1-\frac{9}{4}h^2 & & & \bigcirc \\ -1-\frac{9}{4}h^2 & 2+\frac{17}{2}h^2 & -1-\frac{25}{4}h^2 & & \\ & \cdot & \cdot & \cdot & \\ \bigcirc & & \cdot & \cdot & -1-(n-\frac{1}{2})^2h^2 \\ & & & -1-(n-\frac{1}{2})^2h^2 & 2+(2n^2+\frac{1}{2})h^2 \end{bmatrix}$$

and the right-hand side is

$$\textbf{(3.5.39)} \quad -h^2\left\{d_1 - \left(\frac{1}{4}+\frac{1}{h^2}\right), d_2, \ldots, d_n - \left[(n+\tfrac{1}{2})^2 + \frac{1}{h^2}\right](2+\sin 1)\right\}^T$$

Note that all three tridiagonal matrices (3.5.32), (3.5.35), and (3.5.38) are diagonally dominant, so no pivoting strategy is necessary to assure numerical stability. Furthermore, (3.5.35) and (3.5.38) are symmetric.

All three difference schemes were programmed for various values of h. The computed solutions were so close that their plots were indistinguishable. Figure 3.8 is a plot of the second approximate solution using

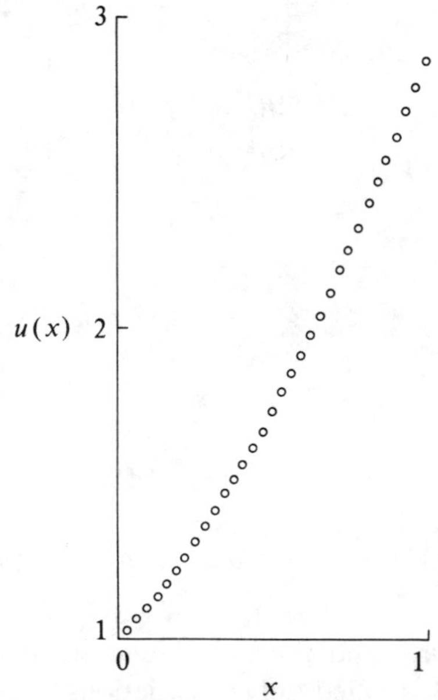

FIGURE 3.8 *The Computed Solution to* (3.5.27)/(3.5.28), *using* $h = 1/32$ *for the Difference Method Corresponding to* (3.5.35)/(3.5.36). *The other methods generated visibly indistinguishable approximate solutions.*

(3.5.35) and (3.5.36) with a step size of $h = 1/32$. This approximate solution agrees very closely with the exact solution, (3.5.30).

Supplementary Discussion and References: 3.5

In a very important paper, Wilkinson [1961] (see also, for example, Forsythe and Moler [1967] and Ortega [1972] for textbook discussions) showed that the effect of rounding errors in Gaussian elimination is such that the computed solution is the exact solution of a perturbed system $(\mathbf{A} + \delta\mathbf{A})\mathbf{x} = \mathbf{b}$. A careful analysis shows that the bound on the matrix is of the form

$$\|\delta\mathbf{A}\|_\infty \leq p(n)g\varepsilon\|\mathbf{A}\|_\infty$$

where $p(n)$ is a cubic polynomial in the size of the matrix, ε is the basic rounding error of the computer (for example, 2^{-27}), and g is the *growth factor* defined by

$$g = \frac{\max\limits_{i,j,k}|a_{ij}^{(k)}|}{a}, \qquad a = \max_{i,j}|a_{ij}|$$

where the $a_{ij}^{(k)}$ are the elements of the successive reduced matrices formed in the elimination process. The growth factor depends crucially on the interchange strategy used. With no interchanges, g may be arbitrarily large. With partial pivoting, g is bounded by 2^{n-1}, which for large n completely dominates $p(n)$. Wilkinson has exhibited matrices for which $g = 2^{n-1}$, but such matrices seem to be very rare in practice; indeed, the actual size of g has been monitored extensively by Wilkinson and others for a large number of practical problems and has seldom exceeded 8 regardless of the size of the matrix. For the complete pivoting strategy, a complicated, but much better bound for g has been given by Wilkinson. Moreover, he has conjectured that in this case, $g \leq n$. This conjecture is still an unsolved problem.

For matrices that are (column) diagonally dominant, the growth factor g is bounded by 2, no matter what interchange strategy, if any, is used. For symmetric positive-definite matrices, g is equal to 1. This explains why for these two important classes of matrices, no interchange strategy is necessary.

One way to attempt to obtain an accurate solution of ill-conditioned systems—and also to detect the ill-conditioning—is by *iterative refinement*, which we now describe. Let $\mathbf{x}_1$ be the computed solution of the system $\mathbf{A}\mathbf{x} = \mathbf{b}$ and $\mathbf{r}_1 = \mathbf{A}\mathbf{x}_1 - \mathbf{b}$. If $\mathbf{x}_1$ is not the exact solution, then $\mathbf{r}_1 \neq 0$. Now, solve the system $\mathbf{A}\mathbf{z}_1 = -\mathbf{r}_1$. If $\mathbf{z}_1$ were the exact solution of this system, then

$$\mathbf{A}(\mathbf{x}_1 + \mathbf{z}_1) = \mathbf{A}\mathbf{x}_1 - \mathbf{r}_1 = \mathbf{b}$$

that is, $\mathbf{x}_1 + \mathbf{z}_1$ is the exact solution of the original system. Of course, we will not be able to compute $\mathbf{z}_1$ exactly, but we hope that $\mathbf{x}_2 = \mathbf{x}_1 + \mathbf{z}_1$ will be a better approximation to the exact solution than $\mathbf{x}_1$. For this to be the case, it is imperative that the residual be computed in higher-precision arithmetic; generally, if single precision is being used for the solution of the linear systems, then the residual should be computed in double precision. The process can be repeated: form $\mathbf{r}_2 = A\mathbf{x}_2 - \mathbf{b}$, solve $A\mathbf{z}_2 = -\mathbf{r}_2$, and set $\mathbf{x}_3 = \mathbf{x}_2 + \mathbf{z}_2$, and so on. Usually, one or two iterations will suffice to obtain an accurate solution, unless the problem is very ill-conditioned.

The state of the art in solving linear equations has now reached a very high level, especially for full and banded systems that can be stored in the computer's fast memory. Probably the best current set of codes is LINPACK, a package of FORTRAN subroutines that was developed with funding from the National Science Foundation and the Department of Energy. LINPACK also contains a method for estimating the condition number of a matrix in a way that avoids the large amount of work necessary to compute $\|A^{-1}\|$. For a discussion of LINPACK, see Dongarra et al. [1979].

EXERCISES 3.5

3.5.1. Compute the determinant and the normalized determinant (3.5.10) for the matrix

$$A = \begin{bmatrix} 1 & 2 & 3 \\ 2 & 3 & 4 \\ 3 & 4 & 4 \end{bmatrix}$$

and for the matrix of (3.5.6).

3.5.2. Using properties of matrix norms, prove that $\text{cond}(A) \geq 1$.

3.5.3. Compute cond(A) for the matrices in exercise 3.5.1 using both the ℓ_1 and ℓ_∞ norms (see Appendix 3 for definitions of these norms).

3.5.4. Solve the system (3.5.1) for different right-hand sides. Compare the differences in these solutions to the bound (3.5.22), using the ℓ_∞ norm.

3.5.5. Verify the identity (3.5.25).

3.5.6. Solve numerically the system with coefficient matrix and right-hand side (3.5.32)/(3.5.33) for $n = 10$ and $n = 20$. Discuss the accuracy of your approximate solutions.

3.5.7. Repeat exercise 3.5.6 for (3.5.35)/(3.5.36) and (3.5.38)/(3.5.39).

4 Life Is Really Nonlinear

4.1 Solution by the Shooting Method

We consider in this chapter the solution of nonlinear problems. Recall that the mathematical model of the problem discussed in Section 3.1 was the nonlinear two-point boundary-value problem

(4.1.1) $$(r^2v')' + r^2g(v) = 0, \qquad 0 \le r \le 1$$

(4.1.2) $$v'(0) = 0 \qquad v(1) = \beta$$

where

(4.1.3) $$g(v) = -\frac{cv}{v + d}$$

There are two basic approaches to such problems. One is to discretize the differential equation as was done in the previous chapter for linear equations; we will study this approach in Section 4.4. In the present section, we will consider a method based on the solution of initial-value problems, and for this purpose, we will first treat as an example the projectile problem of Chapter 2.

Recall that the projectile problem was given by equations (2.1.15), (2.1.17), and (2.1.18) with $\dot{m} = 0$ and $T = 0$:

(4.1.4) $$\dot{x} = v\cos\theta \qquad \dot{y} = v\sin\theta$$
$$\dot{v} = \frac{-1}{2m}c\rho s v^2 - g\sin\theta \qquad \dot{\theta} = -\frac{g}{v}\cos\theta$$

As before, we have the initial conditions

(4.1.5) $$x(0) = y(0) = 0 \qquad v(0) = \bar{v}$$

In Chapter 2, we also prescribed

$$\theta(0) = \bar{\theta} \tag{4.1.6}$$

so (4.1.4)–(4.1.6) was an initial-value problem. Suppose now, however, that in place of (4.1.6) we prescribe

$$x(T) = \bar{x} \qquad y(T) = 0 \tag{4.1.7}$$

That is, we want the projectile to hit the ground at a given range $\bar{x}$. Thus, (4.1.4), (4.1.5), and (4.1.7) now constitute a boundary-value problem. Note that here T is also a free parameter; that is, we do not prescribe the time of flight but only the desired range.

We can base a numerical solution of this problem on the trial-and-error method that an artillery gunner might employ: choose a value of the launch angle, say $\bar{\theta}_1$, and "shoot," which, mathematically, means to solve the initial-value problem (4.1.5)/(4.1.6) together with

$$\theta(0) = \bar{\theta}_1 \tag{4.1.8}$$

We follow the trajectory until y (the altitude) becomes zero and record the corresponding value of x, which we call $\bar{x}_1$. If $\bar{x}_1 < \bar{x}$, we have undershot and we increase $\theta(0)$ to $\bar{\theta}_2$ for the next "shot." If this time we overshoot, then the correct value of $\theta(0)$ is between $\bar{\theta}_1$ and $\bar{\theta}_2$. The situation is depicted in Figure 4.1. If $\bar{x}_1 < \bar{x}_2 < \bar{x}$, we increase $\theta(0)$ again, and so on.

Clearly, this problem has a solution only if $\bar{x}$ is within the range of the projectile; this is determined by v_0 as well as m, c, and s. However, the solution will be unique only if $\bar{x}$ is, in fact, the maximum range; otherwise, we will have the situation depicted in Figure 4.2. Of course, the time T for the two solutions will be different.

We can apply the same procedure to the boundary-value problem (4.1.1)/(4.1.2) even though there is no longer any physical analogy to shooting. In this case, we choose a trial value $\bar{v}_1$ for $v(0)$ and solve the initial-value problem

$$(r^2v')' + r^2g(v) = 0, \qquad v(0) = \bar{v}_1,\ v'(0) = 0 \tag{4.1.9}$$

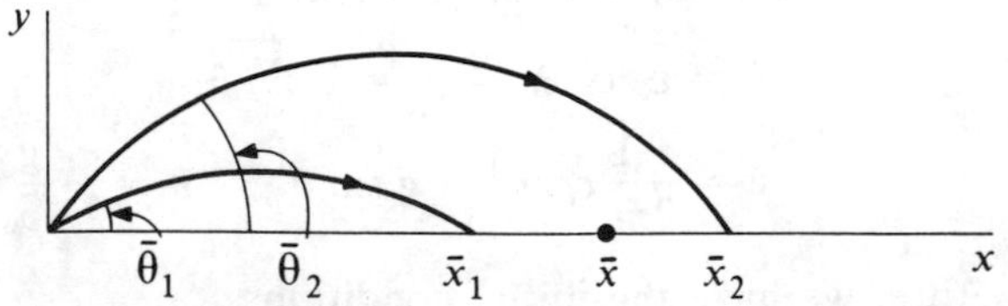

FIGURE 4.1 *The "Shooting" Method.*

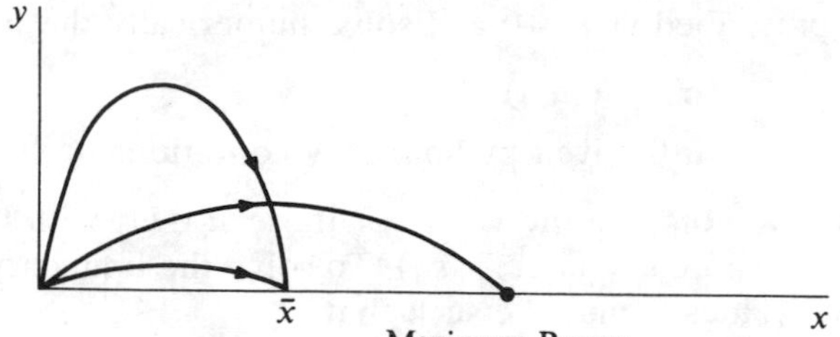

FIGURE 4.2 *Two Possible Solutions.*

up to $r = 1$. For the numerical solution, we would probably first rewrite the second-order differential equation as the first-order system

$$v' = w \qquad (r^2 w)' + r^2 g(v) = 0$$

as discussed in Appendix 2. Here, the initial condition $v'(0) = 0$ becomes $w(0) = 0$. We compare the value of v at 1 to the prescribed condition at 1, namely $v(1) = 1$, adjust $v(0)$ accordingly, and try again. (We note that there is a problem in starting the integration of this system at $r = 0$; this will be discussed later.)

The shooting method as described seems rather ad hoc, but we can systematize it by recognizing that the basic mathematical problem we are solving is finding a root of a nonlinear equation in a single variable. To see why this is, consider the shooting method for (4.1.9) and let s denote the value of the initial condition $v(0)$. Let $v(r; s)$ be the solution of the initial-value problem with $v(0) = s$ and define

$$f(s) = v(1; s) - 1$$

Then, the idea of the shooting method is simply to find a value of s for which $f(s) = 0$. We can, in principle, then apply any number of numerical methods for finding roots of equations; some of these methods will be discussed in the following section.

The shooting method can also be applied to two-point boundary-value problems for general first-order systems. Consider the system

(4.1.10) $$\mathbf{u}' = R(\mathbf{u}, t), \qquad 0 \le t \le 1$$

where $\mathbf{u}(t)$ is the n vector with components $u_i(t)$, $i = 1, \ldots, n$.

Assume that m of the functions $u_1, \ldots, u_n$ are prescribed at $t = 1$ and that $n - m$ are prescribed at $t = 0$ so that we have the correct number, n, of boundary conditions. We will denote the set of functions prescribed at $t = 0$ by U_0 and those prescribed at $t = 1$ by U_1. Note that these sets may overlap; for example, u_1 may be given at both $t = 0$ and $t = 1$, but u_2 not be prescribed at either end point. To apply the shooting method, we select initial values $s_1, \ldots, s_m$ for the m functions not prescribed at $t = 0$ and solve numerically the initial-value problem

$$\mathbf{u}' = R(\mathbf{u}, t)$$
$$\mathbf{u}(0) \text{ given by boundary conditions or } \{s_1, \ldots, s_m\}$$

Next, we compare the values of those $u_i \in \mathrm{U}_1$ with the integrated values $\mathbf{u}(1; \mathbf{s})$, where $\mathbf{s} = (s_1, \ldots, s_m)$. To solve the boundary-value problem, the initial values s_i must be such that

$$u_i(1; \mathbf{s}) = \text{given value}, \qquad u_i \in \mathrm{U}_1$$

This is a system of m nonlinear equations in the m unknowns $s_1, \ldots, s_m$. We will consider methods for the solution of systems of nonlinear equations in Section 4.3.

Although the shooting method is simple in concept, it can suffer from instabilities in the initial-value problems. Instabilities of this type were discussed in Chapter 2, and we give here another simple example similar to the one discussed in Section 2.5. Consider the problem

(4.1.11) $$u'' - 100u = 0$$

with the boundary conditions

(4.1.12) $$u(0) = 1 \qquad u(1) = 0$$

It is easy to verify that the exact solution of this boundary-value problem is

(4.1.13) $$u(t) = \frac{1}{1 - e^{-20}} e^{-10t} - \frac{e^{-20}}{1 - e^{-20}} e^{10t}$$

Now, we attempt to obtain the solution by the shooting method using

(4.1.14) $$u'(0) = s$$

The exact solution of the corresponding initial-value problem is

(4.1.15) $$u(t; s) = \frac{10 - s}{20} e^{-10t} + \frac{10 + s}{20} e^{10t}$$

and we see that the value $u(1; s)$ at the end point $t = 1$ is very sensitive to s. The value of s that will give the exact solution (4.1.13) of the boundary-value problem is

$$s = -10\left(\frac{1 + e^{-20}}{1 - e^{-20}}\right) \doteq -10$$

If we solve the initial-value problem with the value of s correct to two decimal places, say $s = -9.99$, the solution of the initial-value problem is as shown in Figure 4.3. The consequence of this is that obtaining a good approximate solution to the boundary-value problem requires a value of s correct to much higher accuracy than wanted in the boundary-value problem.

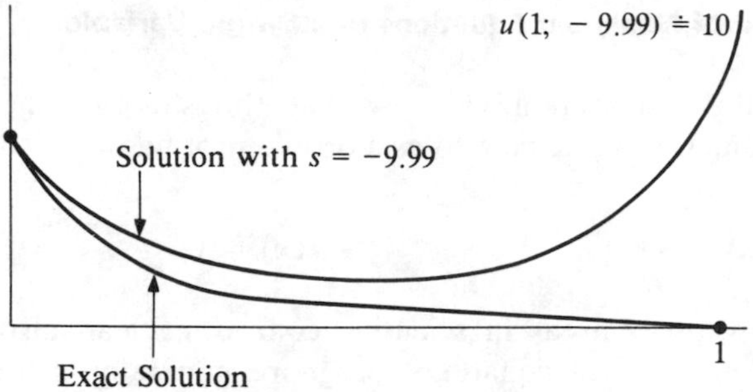

FIGURE 4.3 *Solutions of Exact and Perturbed Problems.*

The difficulty, of course, is that the solution of the initial-value problem grows like e^{10t}, and in order that this fast-growing component be suppressed, it is necessary to obtain a very accurate value of the initial condition.

Supplementary Discussion and References: 4.1

The shooting method for two-point boundary-value problems is described in most books on numerical analysis. A particularly detailed treatment is given in Roberts and Shipman [1972].

Another approach to solving two-point boundary-value problems by means of initial-value problems is the method of invariant imbedding. Here, however, the initial-value problems are for partial differential, rather than ordinary differential, equations. For a thorough discussion of invariant imbedding, see Meyer [1973].

EXERCISES 4.1

4.1.1. Solve the two-point boundary-value problem $y'' + y' + y = -(x^2 + x + 1)$, $y(0) = y(1) = 0$, by the shooting method using one of the methods of Chapter 2 for initial-value problems. Check your numerical results by finding the exact analytical solution to this problem. (*Hint*: For the analytical solution, try the method of undetermined coefficients for a quadratic polynomial.)

4.1.2. Solve the projectile boundary-value problem (4.1.4)/(4.1.5)/(4.1.7) numerically using one of the methods of Chapter 2 for initial-value problems.

4.1.3. Attempt to solve problem (4.1.11)/(4.1.12) using the same method you used for exercise 4.1.2. Compare your best result with the exact solution given by (4.1.15) and discuss the discrepancies. Also discuss any difficulties you encountered in obtaining your numerical solution.

4.2 Solution of Nonlinear Equations in a Single Variable

In the last section, we saw that the shooting method with one free parameter can be viewed as a problem of finding a solution of a nonlinear equation

$$f(x) = 0 \tag{4.2.1}$$

Many other areas in scientific computing lead also to the problem of finding roots of equations, or, more generally, solutions of a system of nonlinear equations, which we will discuss in the next section.

A special—but important—case of (4.2.1) occurs when f is a polynomial

$$f(x) = a_n x^n + \cdots + a_1 x + a_0 \tag{4.2.2}$$

In this case, we know from the fundamental theorem of algebra that f has exactly n real or complex roots if we count multiplicities of the roots.

For a general function f, it is usually difficult to ascertain how many roots equation (4.2.1) has: there may be none, one, finitely many, or infinitely many. A simple condition that ensures that there is at most one root in a given interval (a, b) is that

$$f'(x) > 0 \quad \text{for all } x \in (a, b) \tag{4.2.3}$$

[or $f'(x) < 0$ in the interval], although this does not guarantee that a root exists in the interval. (The proof of these statements is left to exercises 4.2.1 and 4.2.2.) If, however, f is continuous, and

$$f(a) < 0 \qquad f(b) > 0 \tag{4.2.4}$$

then it is intuitively clear (and rigorously proved by a famous theorem of the calculus) that f must have at least one root in the interval (a, b).

Let us now assume that (4.2.4) holds and, for simplicity, that there is just one root in the interval (a, b). [We don't necessarily assume that (4.2.3) holds; the situation might be as shown in Figure 4.4.] One of the

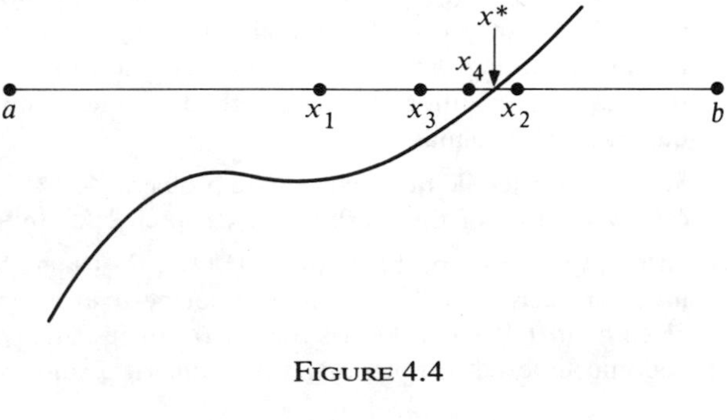

FIGURE 4.4

simplest ways of approximating a root of f in this situation is the *bisection method*, which is simply a systematization of the somewhat ad hoc method suggested in the previous section for adjusting the initial condition.

Let $x_1 = \frac{1}{2}(a + b)$ be the midpoint of the interval (a, b) and evaluate $f(x_1)$. If $f(x_1) > 0$, then the root, which we denote henceforth as x^*, must lie between a and x_1; if $f(x_1) < 0$, which is the situation shown in Figure 4.4, then x^* is between x_1 and b. We now continue this process, always keeping the interval in which x^* is known to lie and evaluating f at its midpoint in order to obtain the next interval. For the function shown in Figure 4.4, the steps would be as follows:

1. $f(x_1) < 0$. Hence, $x^* \in (x_1, b)$. Set $x_2 = \frac{1}{2}(x_1 + b)$
2. $f(x_2) > 0$. Hence, $x^* \in (x_1, x_2)$. Set $x_3 = \frac{1}{2}(x_1 + x_2)$
3. $f(x_3) < 0$. Hence, $x^* \in (x_3, x_2)$. Set $x_4 = \frac{1}{2}(x_2 + x_3)$
4. $f(x_4) < 0$. Hence, $x^* \in (x_4, x_2)$. Set $x_5 = \frac{1}{2}(x_2 + x_4)$

⋮

Clearly, each step of the bisecting procedure reduces the length of the interval known to contain x^* by a factor of 2. Therefore, after m steps, the length of the interval will be $(b - a)2^{-m}$, and this provides a bound on the error in our current approximation to the root. That is, if x_{m+1} is the midpoint of the interval after m steps, then

$$|x_{m+1} - x^*| \leq \frac{|b - a|}{2^{m+1}} \tag{4.2.5}$$

This bound has been obtained under the tacit assumption that the function values $f(x_i)$ are computed exactly. Of course, on a computer this will not be the case because of the rounding error (and possibly discretization error also—recall that the evaluation of the function f for the shooting method requires the numerical integration of the initial-value problem). However, the bisection method does not use the value of $f(x_i)$ but only the *sign* of $f(x_i)$; therefore, the bisection method is impervious to errors in evaluating the function f as long as the sign of $f(x_i)$ is evaluated correctly. One might think that the round-off error could not be so severe as to change even the sign of the function, but this is not the case, as Figure 4.5 demonstrates. If the sign of $f(x_i)$ is incorrect, a wrong decision will be made in choosing the next subinterval, and the error bound (4.2.5) does not necessarily hold.

It is clear that if one makes a maximum error of E in evaluating f at any point in the interval (a, b), then the sign of f will be correctly evaluated as long as

$$|f(x)| > |E|$$

Since the function f will be close to zero near the root x^*, we can also argue the converse: there will be an *interval of uncertainty*, say, $(x^* - \varepsilon, x^* + \varepsilon)$, about the root in which the sign of f may not be correctly evaluated (see Figure 4.6). When our approximations reach this interval,

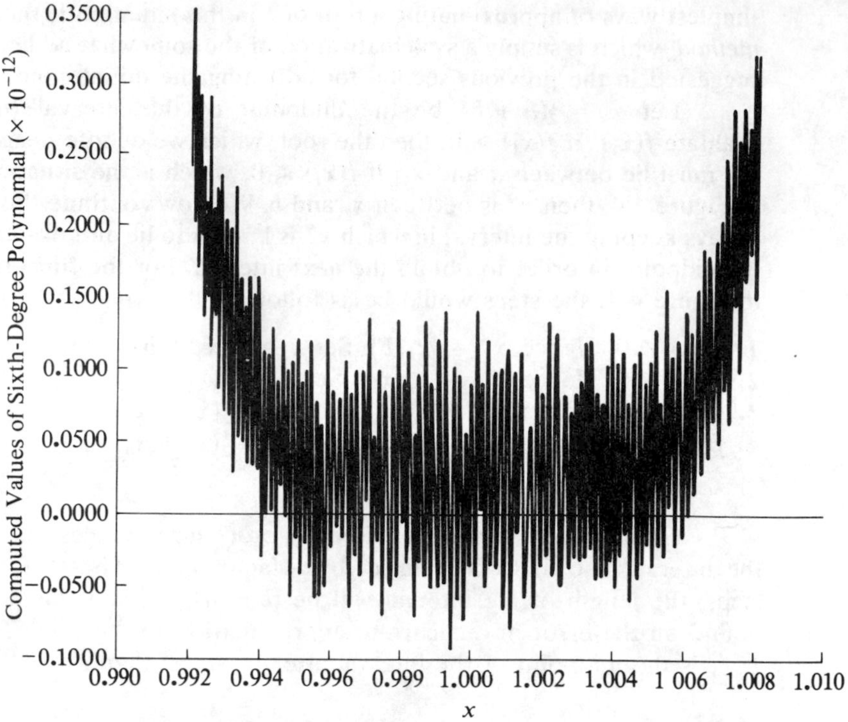

FIGURE 4.5 *Plot of the Values of* $x^6 - 6x^5 + 15x^4 - 20x^3 + 15x^2 - 6x + 1$ *Computed in FORTRAN with 14-Decimal-Digit Accuracy. Theoretically, this polynomial is zero at* $x = 1$ *and positive everywhere else. (Courtesy of Professor John Rice).*

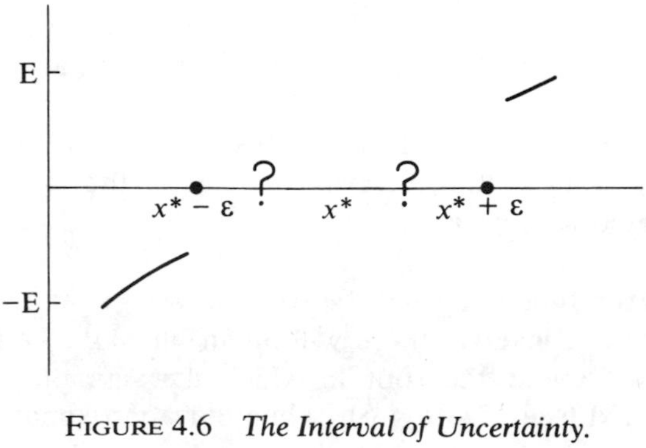

FIGURE 4.6 *The Interval of Uncertainty.*

their further progress toward the root is at best problematical. Unfortunately, it is extremely difficult to determine this interval in advance. It depends on the unknown root x^*, the "flatness" of f in the neighborhood of the root, and the magnitude of the errors made in evaluating f. On the other hand, the interval is usually detectable during the course of the computation by an erratic behavior of the iterates; when this occurs, there is no longer any point in continuing the computation.

The fact that the sign of the function f may not be evaluated correctly near the root affects not only the bisection method but also the other methods we shall discuss, and we will give an example later in the section.

One drawback of the bisection method is that it may be rather slow. To reduce the initial interval by a large factor, say 10^6, which may correspond to about six-decimal-digit accuracy, we would expect to require, from the error bound (4.2.5),

$$m = \frac{6}{\log_{10} 2} \doteq 20$$

evaluations of f. When each evaluation is expensive, as in the case of the shooting method, we would like to keep the number of evaluations as small as possible.

One possibility to speed up the bisection method is to use the values of the function f (instead of only its signs), and the simplest way to utilize this information is to choose the next point x_{i+1} as the zero of the linear function that interpolates at x_{i-1} and x_i. This is shown in Figure 4.7. In the somewhat favorable situation shown in this figure it is clear that x_{i+1} is a considerably better approximation to the root than would be the midpoint of the interval (x_{i-1}, x_i).

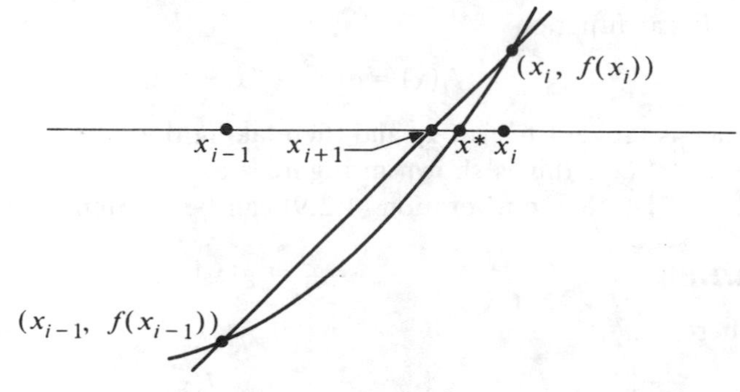

FIGURE 4.7

The linear interpolating function is given by the following (refer to Section 2.3, although it is easily checked directly)

$$\ell(x) = \frac{(x - x_{i-1})}{(x_i - x_{i-1})} f(x_i) - \frac{(x - x_i)}{(x_i - x_{i-1})} f(x_{i-1}) \tag{4.2.6}$$

and the root of this function is then

$$x_{i+1} = \frac{x_{i-1}f(x_i) - x_i f(x_{i-1})}{f(x_i) - f(x_{i-1})} \tag{4.2.7}$$

We may now proceed as in the bisection method, retaining x_{i+1} and either x_i or x_{i-1} so that the function values at the two retained points have different signs. This is the *regula falsi method.* Alternatively, in the *secant method,* we simply carry out (4.2.7) sequentially as indicated, keeping the last two iterates regardless of whether the function values of these two iterates have different signs.

It is convenient to rewrite (4.2.7) as

$$x_{i+1} = x_i - \frac{f(x_i)}{d_i}, \qquad d_i = \frac{f(x_i) - f(x_{i-1})}{x_i - x_{i-1}} \tag{4.2.8}$$

which is easily verified to be mathematically identical to (4.2.7). This form is preferable to (4.2.7) for computation since cancellation effects are less.

We can consider the quantity d_i in (4.2.8) to be a one-sided difference approximation to $f'(x_i)$, and, hence, (4.2.8) may be viewed as a "discrete form" of the iterative method

$$x_{i+1} = x_i - \frac{f(x_i)}{f'(x_i)} \tag{4.2.9}$$

This is known as *Newton's method* and is the most famous iterative method for obtaining roots of equations (as well as for solving systems of nonlinear equations, as we shall see in the next section). Geometrically, Newton's method can be interpreted as approximating the function f by the linear function

$$\ell_i(x) = f(x_i) + (x - x_i)f'(x_i)$$

which is tangent to f at x_i, and then taking the next iterate x_{i+1} to be the zero of $\ell_i(x)$; this is shown in Figure 4.8.

The Newton iteration (4.2.9) can be written in the form

$$x_{i+1} = g(x_i) \tag{4.2.10}$$

where

$$g(x) = x - \frac{f(x)}{f'(x)} \tag{4.2.11}$$

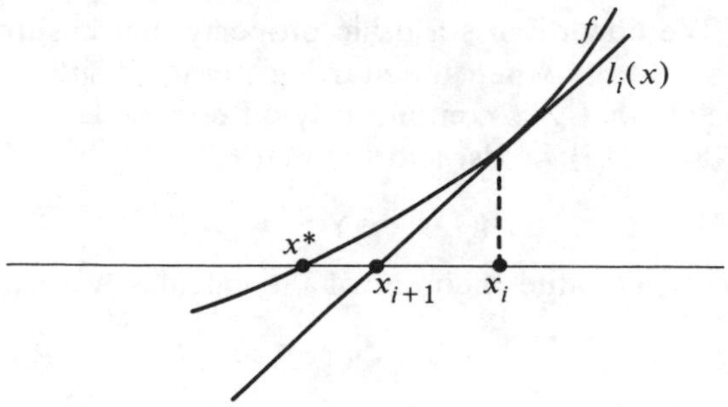

FIGURE 4.8 *Newton's Method.*

Many other iterative methods may also be written in the general form (4.2.10). For example, a very simple method is given by defining g to be

$$g(x) = x - \alpha f(x) \tag{4.2.12}$$

for some scalar α. This is sometimes called the *chord method* and is illustrated in Figure 4.9.

Iterative methods of the form (4.2.10) are called *one-step methods* since x_{i+1} depends only on the previous iterate x_i. On the other hand, the secant method (4.2.8) depends on both x_i and x_{i-1} and is an example of a *multistep method.* (Note the analogy with one-step and multistep methods for initial-value problems.)

In order to be useful, the iteration function g must have the property

$$x^* = g(x^*) \tag{4.2.13}$$

when x^* is a root of f. This is clearly the case for (4.2.11) and (4.2.12). (This is true for (4.2.11) even when $f'(x^*) = 0$, although in this case we must define $g(x^*)$ as the limit as $x \to x^*$; see exercise 4.2.3.). A value of x^* that satisfies (4.2.13) is called a *fixed point* of the function g.

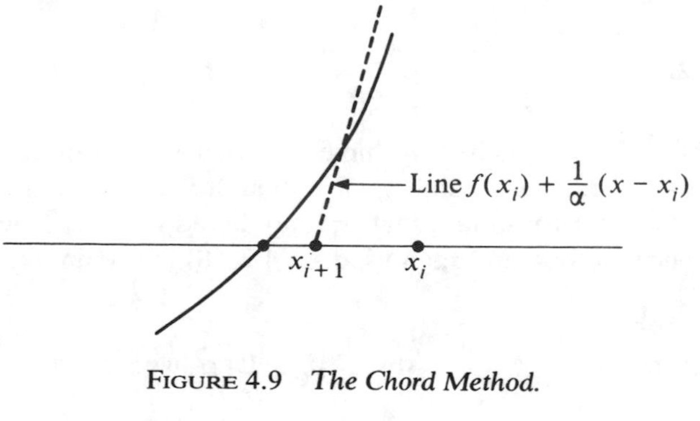

FIGURE 4.9 *The Chord Method.*

We now discuss a basic property that ensures convergence of the iterates, at least when the starting iterate is sufficiently close to x^*. We assume (1) that g is continuously differentiable in a neighborhood of x^*, (2) that (4.2.13) holds, and (3) that

$$|g'(x)| \leq \gamma < 1 \quad \text{if } |x - x^*| \leq \beta \tag{4.2.14}$$

By the mean-value theorem of the calculus, we can then write

$$g(x) - g(x^*) = g'(\xi)(x - x^*) \tag{4.2.15}$$

where ξ is between x and x^*. Therefore, if $|x - x^*| \leq \beta$, then we can apply (4.2.14) to conclude that

$$|g(x) - g(x^*)| \leq \gamma\,|x - x^*|, \quad \text{if } |x - x^*| \leq \beta \tag{4.2.16}$$

Suppose now that $|x_0 - x^*| \leq \beta$. Then, using (4.2.10) and (4.2.13), we see from (4.2.16) that

$$|x_1 - x^*| = |g(x_0) - g(x^*)| \leq \gamma\,|x_0 - x^*|$$

Since $\gamma < 1$, this shows that x_1 is closer to x^* than x_0. Thus, $|x_1 - x^*| \leq \beta$, and we can do the same thing again to obtain

$$|x_2 - x^*| \leq \gamma\,|x_1 - x^*| \leq \gamma^2\,|x_0 - x^*|$$

and, in general,

$$|x_n - x^*| \leq \gamma\,|x_{n-1} - x^*| \leq \cdots \leq \gamma^n\,|x_0 - x^*| \tag{4.2.17}$$

Since $\gamma < 1$, this shows that $x_n \to x^*$ as $n \to \infty$ (assuming no rounding or other errors).

It will be argued that (4.2.14) is an uncheckable condition since it requires knowing something about g′ near x^*, which is unknown. Surprisingly, however, we can obtain valuable information from the preceding analysis even without knowing x^*. As a first illustration of this, we consider an analysis of the second-order Adams–Moulton formula described in Section 2.4 for the solution of the ordinary differential equation $y' = f(y)$. This implicit formula is given in (2.4.9) as

$$y_{k+1} = y_k + \frac{h}{2}[f(y_{k+1}) + f_k] \tag{4.2.18}$$

where, for simplicity, we have dropped the dependence of f on x. This equation defines a value y_{k+1}, although it was used in Section 2.4 only as a "corrector formula"; that is, a predicted value $y_{k+1}^{(0)}$ was computed by an explicit method and then used in (4.2.18) to obtain a new estimate of y_{k+1} by

$$y_{k+1}^{(1)} = y_k + \frac{h}{2}[f(y_{k+1}^{(0)}) + f_k] \tag{4.2.19}$$

Now, we can correct this value again by using it in place of $y_{k+1}^{(0)}$ in (4.2.19). If we do this repeatedly, we obtain the sequence defined by

$$\textbf{(4.2.20)} \qquad y_{k+1}^{(i+1)} = y_k + \frac{h}{2}[f(y_{k+1}^{(i)}) + f_k], \qquad i = 0, 1, \ldots$$

Clearly, (4.2.20) is just the iteration process $y_{k+1}^{(i+1)} = g(y_{k+1}^{(i)})$ where

$$g(y) = y_k + \frac{h}{2}[f(y) + f_k]$$

If y_{k+1} is the exact solution of (4.2.18), we can apply the previous analysis to conclude that the sequence of (4.2.20) will converge to y_{k+1} provided that $y_{k+1}^{(0)}$ (the predicted value) is sufficiently close to y_{k+1} and that

$$|g'(y)| = \left|\frac{h}{2}f'(y)\right| < 1$$

is in a neighborhood of y_{k+1}; this will hold provided that h is sufficiently small.

As another illustration of the use of the convergence analysis, we consider Newton's method. Assume that $f'(x^*) \neq 0$ and that f is twice continuously differentiable in a neighborhood of x^*. Thus, by continuity, $f'(x) \neq 0$ in some neighborhood of x^*, and we can differentiate the Newton iteration function (4.2.11) to obtain

$$g'(x) = 1 - \frac{[f'(x)]^2 - f(x)f''(x)}{[f'(x)]^2} = \frac{f(x)f''(x)}{[f'(x)]^2}$$

so $g'(x^*) = 0$, since $f(x^*) = 0$. Therefore, by continuity, (4.2.14) must hold in a neighborhood of x^*, and we conclude that the Newton iterates converge if x_0 is sufficiently close to x^*.

What the preceding shows is that, under rather mild assumptions, the Newton iterates *must* converge to a root provided that x_0 (or any iterate x_k) is sufficiently close to x^*. Although this type of a convergence theorem, known as a *local convergence theorem*, does not help one decide if the iterates will converge from a given x_0, it gives an important intrinsic property of the iterative method.

When an iterate is not close to a solution, various types of "bad" behavior can occur with Newton's method, as illustrated in Figure 4.10. On the other hand, there are situations where Newton's method will converge for any starting approximation. Perhaps the simplest functions for which this is true are those that are convex; that is, the inequality

$$f(\alpha x + (1 - \alpha)y) \leq \alpha f(x) + (1 - \alpha)f(y)$$

holds for all x, y and all $0 \leq \alpha \leq 1$. If f is twice differentiable, it is convex if and only if $f''(x) \geq 0$ for all x. The behavior of the Newton iterates for a convex function is illustrated in Figure 4.11. Whenever we

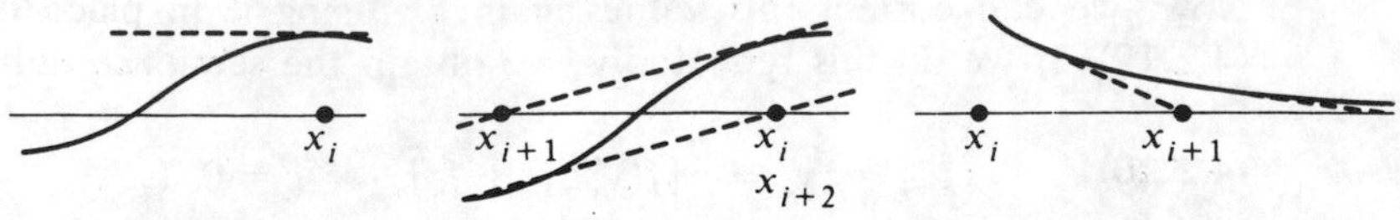

(a) $f'(x_i) = 0$. Next iterate not defined. (b) Oscillation (c) Divergence

FIGURE 4.10 *Possible "Bad" Behavior of Newton's Method.*

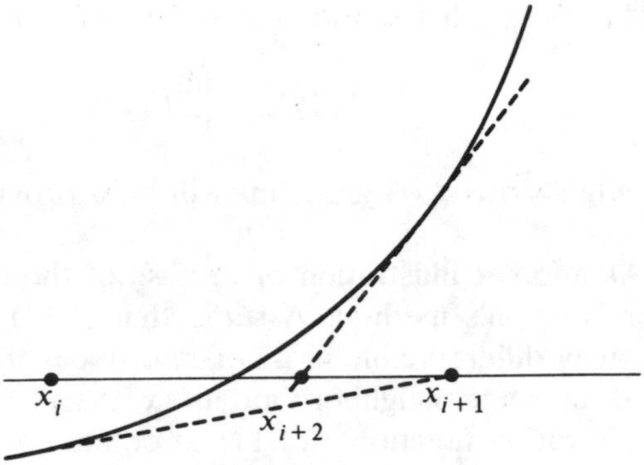

FIGURE 4.11 *Convergence of Newton's Method for a Convex Function.*

can guarantee in advance that an iterative method will converge for *any* starting approximation, we call this *global convergence.* Such results usually require very stringent conditions, such as convexity, on the function f.

From the standpoint of economic computation, the rate at which iterates converge to a root is almost as important as whether they converge at all. Suppose that, analogous to the estimate (4.2.17), the errors behave according to

$$|x^* - x_{i+1}| = \gamma\,|x^* - x_i|$$

where γ is very close to 1, say $\gamma = 0.999$. Then, reducing the error in a given iterate by a factor of 10 would require well over two thousand iterations. Clearly, we wish the γ in the estimate (4.2.17) to be as small as possible, and from the derivation of (4.2.16), we see that it can be no smaller than $|g'(x^*)|$. If $g'(x^*) \neq 0$, then the rate of convergence is said to be *linear* or *geometric.* Recall, however, that for Newton's method, we showed that $g'(x^*) = 0$ [under the assumption that $f'(x^*) \neq 0$]. This does *not* imply, of course, that the iterates converge in one step, but it signals

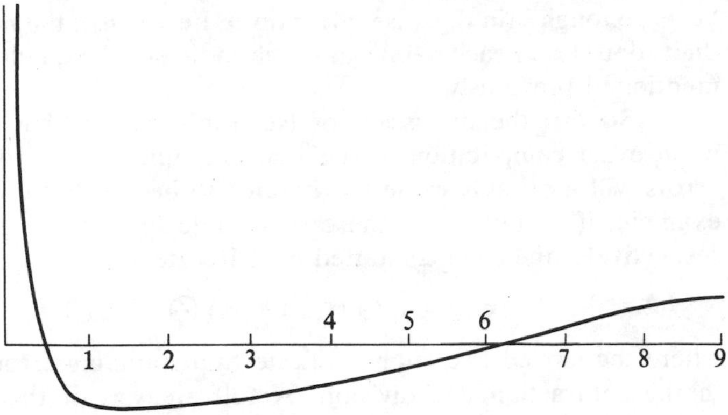

FIGURE 4.12 *The Function* $f(x) = 1/x + \ln 2 - 2$.

that the rate of convergence is of *higher order.* In particular, it can be shown (see Exercise 4.2.4) that the errors in Newton's method satisfy

(4.2.21) $$|x^* - x_{i+1}| \le c\,|x^* - x_i|^2$$

where c is a constant that depends on the ratio of f'' to f' near x^*. Whenever iterates satisfy the relation (4.2.21), we call this *quadratic convergence*; the iterates converge very rapidly once they begin getting close to a root. For example, suppose $c = 1$ and $|x^* - x_i| \doteq 10^{-3}$. Then, $|x^* - x_{i+1}| \doteq 10^{-6}$, so the number of correct decimal places has been doubled in one iteration. It is this property of quadratic convergence that makes Newton's method of central importance.

As a demonstration of Newton's method, consider the problem of finding the zeros of $f(x) = 1/x + \ln x - 2$. This function is defined for all positive values of x and has two zeros: one between $x = 0$ and $x = 1$ and the other between $x = 6$ and $x = 7$, as illustrated in Figure 4.12. Table 4.1 contains a summary of the first six iterations of Newton's method using the starting value of $x = 0.1$. Note that once an approximation is

TABLE 4.1 *Convergence of Newton's Method for* $f(x) = 1/x + \ln x - 2$

Iteration	x	$f(x)$	$x - [f(x)/f'(x)]$	Number of Correct Digits
1	0.1	5.6974149	0.16330461	0
2	0.16330461	2.3113878	0.23697659	0
3	0.23697659	0.7800322	0.29438633	1
4	0.29438633	0.1740346	0.31576121	2
5	0.31576121	0.0141811	0.31782764	4
6	0.31782764	0.0001134	0.31784443	8

"close enough" (in this case, after three iterations), the number of correct digits doubles in each iteration, which indicates the quadratic convergence mentioned previously.

So far, the discussion of Newton's method has been predicated upon exact computation of the iterates, but, clearly, rounding or other errors will inevitably cause the iterates to be computed inaccurately. For example, if ε_i and ε_i' are the errors made in computing $f(x_i)$ and $f'(x_i)$, respectively, then the computed next iterate $\hat{x}_{i+1}$ is

$$\hat{x}_{i+1} = x_i \ominus (f(x_i) + \varepsilon_i) \oplus\!\!\!\!\div\, (f'(x_i) + \varepsilon_i')$$

where the circled operations indicate that rounding errors are also made in the subtraction and division. A full analysis of the effects of these errors is difficult, if even possible, and we content ourselves with the following remarks. If the errors ε_i and ε_i' are small, we can expect the computed iterates to behave roughly as the exact iterates would, at least as long as we are not close to the root. However, when $f(x_i)$ becomes so small that it is comparable in size to ε_i, then the computed iterates no longer behave like the exact ones. In particular, we saw in the case of the bisection method that when the sign of f can no longer be evaluated correctly, the method breaks down in the sense that a wrong decision may be made as to which interval the root is in. An analogous thing happens with Newton's method: if the sign of $f(x_i)$ is evaluated incorrectly, but that of $f'(x_i)$ correctly (a reasonable assumption if $f'(x^*)$ is not particularly small), then the computed value of $f(x_i)/f'(x_i)$ has the wrong sign, and the computed next iterate moves in the wrong direction. As with the bisection method, the notion of an interval of uncertainty about the root x^* applies equally well to Newton's method (as well as to essentially all iterative methods).

In Chapter 3, we discussed the phenomenon of ill-conditioning of a solution of a system of linear equations; an analogous problem can occur with roots of nonlinear equations. The simplest example of this is given by the trivial polynomial equation

$$x^n = 0$$

which has an n-fold root equal to zero, and the polynomial equation

$$x^n = \varepsilon, \qquad \varepsilon > 0$$

whose n roots are $\varepsilon^{1/n}$ times the nth roots of unity and therefore all have absolute value of $\varepsilon^{1/n}$. If, for example, $n = 10$ and $\varepsilon = 10^{-10}$, the roots of the second polynomial have absolute value 10^{-1}; that is, a change of 10^{-10} in one coefficient (the constant term) of the original polynomial has caused changes 10^9 times as much in the roots.

This simple example is a special case of the general observation that if a root x^* of a polynomial f is of multiplicity m, then small changes of order ε in the coefficients of f may cause a change of order $\varepsilon^{1/m}$ in x^*;

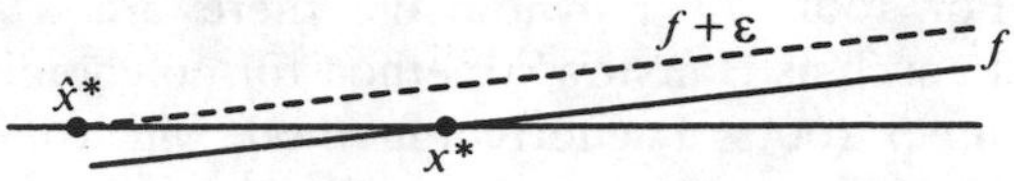

FIGURE 4.13 *A Large Change in x^* Due to a Small Change in f.*

an analogous result holds for functions other than polynomials by expanding in a Taylor series about x^*.

A necessary condition for a multiple root at x^* is that $f'(x^*) = 0$. If $f'(x^*) \neq 0$ but $f'(x)$ is small in the neighborhood of x^*, then small changes in f can still cause large changes in x^*, as Figure 4.13 illustrates.

Perhaps the most famous example of how ill-conditioned nonmultiple roots can be is given by the following. Let f be the polynomial of degree 20 with roots $1, \ldots, 20$, and let $\hat{f}$ be the same polynomial but with the coefficient of x^{19} changed by $2^{-23} \doteq 10^{-7}$. Then, the roots of f to one decimal place are given by

1.0
2.0
3.0
4.0
5.0
6.0
7.0
8.0
8.9
$10.1 \pm 0.6i$
$11.8 \pm 1.7i$
$14.0 \pm 2.5i$
$16.7 \pm 2.8i$
$19.5 \pm 1.9i$
20.8

Since the coefficient of x^{19} in $f(x)$ is 210, we see that a change in this one coefficient of about $10^{-7}\%$ has caused such large changes in the roots that some have even become complex!

Supplementary Discussion and References: 4.2

For a thorough treatment of the theory of iterative methods for roots of equations, see Traub [1964], and for an excellent discussion of rounding error, Wilkinson ([1963], [1965]). In particular, the example of the ill-conditioned polynomial of degree 20 is due to Wilkinson.

For roots of polynomials, there are a number of specialized methods, such as Bairstow's method for polynomials with real coefficients but complex roots; Laguerre's method, which has the property of cubic convergence (that is, an error estimate of the form (4.2.21) holds with $|x^* - x_i|^3$ on the right-hand side); and the Traub–Jenkins algorithm, which exhibits global convergence.

In recent years, there has been a trend toward developing *polyalgorithms*, which are a combination of two or more methods. For example, the bisection method could be used until an approximation is obtained that is sufficiently close to the root that Newton's method will converge, and then Newton's method used to obtain rapid convergence to the root. It is difficult, however, to know when to make the switch, and various heuristic strategies for this and other combinations have been proposed.

Another problem for which there is still no definitive solution is when to stop the iteration. The usual simplest tests are $|f(x_i)| < \varepsilon$ or $|x_{i+1} - x_i| < \varepsilon$, where ε is some given tolerance. The first can be misleading when the function f is very "flat" near the root, as is the case of a multiple root, and the second can fail in a variety of situations depending on the iterative method. For example, for Newton's method, it can fail when the derivative is very large at the current iterate. These two possibilities are depicted in the following figure:

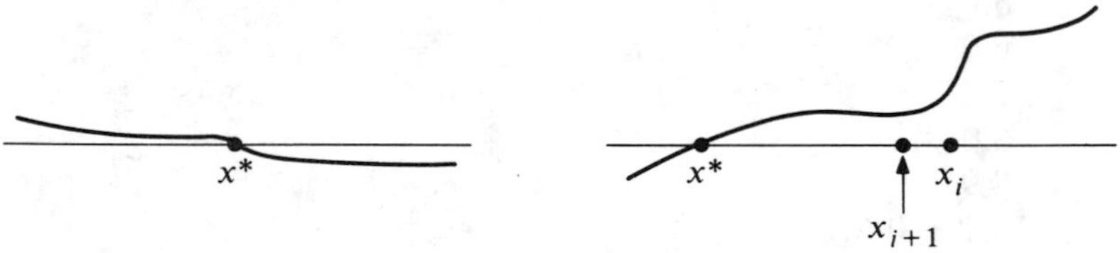

EXERCISES 4.2

4.2.1. If f is a continuously differentiable function, use the mean-value theorem (see Appendix 1) to show that if (4.2.3) holds, then f has, at most, one root in the interval (a, b).

4.2.2. Let $f(x) = e^x$. Show that $f'(x) > 0$ for all x but that f does not have any finite roots.

4.2.3. Let f be twice continuously differentiable and suppose that $f'(x^*) = 0$ at a root x^* of f but $f'(x) \neq 0$ in a neighborhood of x^*. Show that the limit of the iteration function g of (4.2.11) exists and equals x^* as $x \to x^*$.

4.2.4. Let f be twice continuously differentiable and suppose that $f'(x^*) \neq 0$ at a root x^* of f. Show that the error relation (4.2.21) holds for Newton's method in some interval about x^*. (*Hint*: Expand $0 = f(x^*) = f(x) + f'(x)(x^* - x) + \frac{1}{2}f''(\xi)(x^* - x)^2$, solve this for x^*, and then use (4.2.9).

4.2.5. Consider the function $f(x) \equiv x - x^3$ with roots at 0 and ± 1.

a. Show that Newton's method is locally convergent to each of the three roots.

b. Carry out several steps of Newton's method starting with the initial approximation $x_0 = 2$. Discuss the rate of convergence that you observe in your computed iterates.

c. Carry out several steps of both the bisection and secant methods starting with the interval $(\frac{3}{4}, 2)$. Compare the rate of convergence of the iterates from these methods with that of the Newton iterates.

d. Determine the interval for which the Newton iterates will converge (in the absence of rounding errors) to the root 1 for any starting approximation x_0 in the interval. Do the same for the roots 0 and -1.

4.2.6. Consider the equation $x - 2 \sin x = 0$.

a. Show graphically that this equation has precisely three roots: 0, and one in each of the intervals $(\pi/2, 2)$ and $(-2, -\pi/2)$.

b. Show that the iterates $x_{i+1} = 2 \sin x_i$, $i = 0, 1, \ldots$, converge to the root in $(\pi/2, 2)$ for any x_0 in this interval.

c. Apply the Newton iteration to this equation and ascertain for what starting values the iterates will converge to the root in $(\pi/2, 2)$. Compare the rate of convergence of the Newton iterates with those of part b.

4.2.7. Let n be a positive integer and α a positive number. Show that Newton's method for the equation $x^n - \alpha = 0$ is

$$x_{k+1} = \frac{1}{n}\left[(n-1)x_k + \frac{\alpha}{x_k^{n-1}}\right], \qquad k = 0, 1, \ldots$$

and that this Newton sequence converges for any $x_0 > 0$.

4.2.8. Ascertain whether the following statements are true or false and prove your assertions:

a. Let $\{x_k\}$ be a sequence of Newton iterates for a continuously differentiable function f. If for some i, $|f(x_i)| \leq 0.01$ and $|x_{i+1} - x_i| \leq 0.01$, then x_{i+1} is within 0.01 of a root of $f(x) = 0$.

b. The Newton iterates converge to the unique solution of $x^2 - 2x + 1 = 0$ for any $x_0 \neq 1$. (Ignore rounding error.)

4.2.9. Consider the equation $x^2 - 2x + 2 = 0$. What is the behavior of the Newton iterates for various real starting values?

4.2.10. Show that the Newton iterates converge to the unique solution of $e^{2x} + 3x + 2 = 0$ for any starting value x_0.

4.3 Solution of Systems of Nonlinear Equations

We mentioned briefly in Section 4.1 that the shooting method applied to a system of ordinary differential equations can lead to the problem of solving a system of nonlinear algebraic equations in order to supply the missing initial conditions. As we shall see in Section 4.4, the application of the finite difference method to nonlinear boundary-value problems also leads to nonlinear systems of equations. Therefore, we consider in this section the general problem of computing solutions to systems of nonlinear equations and, in particular, how the methods discussed in the previous section for a single equation can be extended to this more general situation.

The problem we consider is obtaining an approximate solution to the system of equations

(4.3.1) $$f_i(x_1, x_2, \ldots, x_n) = 0, \qquad i = 1, \ldots, n$$

where $f_1, f_2, \ldots, f_n$ are given functions of the n variables $x_1, \ldots, x_n$. For ease of writing, we shall usually use vector notation and denote (4.3.1) by

(4.3.2) $$\mathbf{F}(\mathbf{x}) = 0$$

where, as usual, $\mathbf{x}$ is the vector with components $x_1, \ldots, x_n$ and $\mathbf{F}$ is the vector function with components $f_1, \ldots, f_n$. The special case of solving (4.3.1) when $n = 1$ is just the problem of finding roots of a single equation that was considered in the previous section. On the other hand, the special case in which

$$\mathbf{F}(\mathbf{x}) \equiv A\mathbf{x} - \mathbf{b}$$

where A is a given matrix and $\mathbf{b}$ a given vector is that of solving a system of linear equations, which was treated in Chapter 3.

The problem of ascertaining when equation (4.3.2) has solutions, and how many, is, in general, very difficult. In the relatively simple case $n = 2$, it is possible to see geometrically, at least in principle, the various possibilities. For example, if we plot in the x_1, x_2 plane the set of points for which $f_1(x_1, x_2) = 0$, and then the set of points for which $f_2(x_1, x_2) = 0$, the intersection of these sets is precisely the set of solutions of (4.3.2). (Here, and henceforth, we are restricting our attention to only real solutions.) Figure 4.14 illustrates a few possible situations. Later, we shall

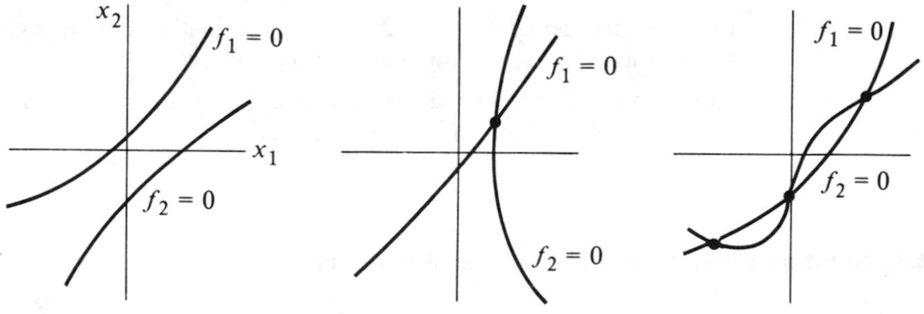

(a) No solutions (b) A unique solution (c) Several solutions

FIGURE 4.14 *Possible Solutions for $n = 2$.*

assume that (4.3.2) has a solution $\mathbf{x}^*$, which is the one of interest to us although the system may have additional solutions.

In many situations—and this will be the case in Section 4.4—the system (4.3.2) has the form

$$\mathbf{F}(\mathbf{x}) \equiv A\mathbf{x} - \mathbf{H}(\mathbf{x}) = 0, \tag{4.3.3}$$

where A is a given nonsingular matrix and $\mathbf{H}$ is a given vector of nonlinear functions. In this case, a somewhat natural (although not necessarily good) iterative procedure is

$$\mathbf{x}^{i+1} = A^{-1}\mathbf{H}(\mathbf{x}^i), \qquad i = 0, 1, \ldots \tag{4.3.4}$$

where the superscript indicates iteration number. Here, as well as later, we mean by (4.3.4) that at each step of the iteration, the linear system of equations

$$A\mathbf{x}^{i+1} = \mathbf{H}(\mathbf{x}^i)$$

is to be solved to obtain the next iterate. The iteration (4.3.4) is usually known as a *Picard iteration.* It may be considered as a special case of the extension of the chord method of the previous section to n equations, which would take the form

$$\mathbf{x}^{i+1} = \mathbf{x}^i - B\mathbf{F}(\mathbf{x}^i), \qquad i = 0, 1, \ldots \tag{4.3.5}$$

for a given nonsingular matrix B. It is easy to see (exercise 4.3.2) that (4.3.5) reduces to (4.3.4) if $\mathbf{F}$ is of the form (4.3.3) and $B = A^{-1}$.

When will iteration (4.3.5) [or (4.3.4)] converge? The situation is precisely analogous to that in the scalar case, but made more complicated by the need to work with vector-valued functions. Let us consider the general one-step iteration

$$\mathbf{x}^{i+1} = \mathbf{G}(\mathbf{x}^i), \qquad i = 0, 1, \ldots \tag{4.3.6}$$

where $\mathbf{G}$ is a given iteration function. For example, for (4.3.5),

$$\mathbf{G}(x) \equiv \mathbf{x} - B\mathbf{F}(\mathbf{x}) \tag{4.3.7}$$

We shall assume that the solution $\mathbf{x}^*$ of $\mathbf{F}(\mathbf{x}) = 0$ satisfies $\mathbf{x}^* = \mathbf{G}(\mathbf{x}^*)$ and, conversely, if $\mathbf{x}^* = \mathbf{G}(\mathbf{x}^*)$, then $\mathbf{F}(\mathbf{x}^*) = 0$; it is clear that this is the case for (4.3.7) if B is nonsingular.

In the previous section, the convergence theory was based on $|g'(x)| < 1$ in a neighborhood of the solution. For systems of equations, the corresponding result is the following. If

$$\|\mathbf{G}'(\mathbf{x})\| \le \gamma < 1, \qquad \text{for } \|\mathbf{x} - \mathbf{x}^*\| \le \beta \tag{4.3.8}$$

then the iterates (4.3.6) converge if $\|\mathbf{x}^0 - \mathbf{x}^*\| \le \beta$ (or if $\|\mathbf{x}^k - \mathbf{x}^*\| \le \beta$ for any k). Here, as in Section 3.5, $\| \ \|$ denotes a vector norm, or the corresponding matrix norm, and $\mathbf{G}'(\mathbf{x})$ is the Jacobian matrix of $\mathbf{G}$ evaluated at $\mathbf{x}$. We shall not prove this convergence statement, but only note that it can be easily proven after a proper extension of the mean-value theorem to n dimensions.

If we apply the criterion (4.3.8) to the iteration (4.3.5), we obtain

$$\|\mathrm{I} - \mathrm{B}\mathbf{F}'(\mathbf{x})\| \leq \gamma < 1 \quad \text{for } \|\mathbf{x} - \mathbf{x}^*\| < \beta \tag{4.3.9}$$

and, in particular, for the iteration (4.3.4),

$$\|\mathrm{A}^{-1}\mathbf{H}'(\mathbf{x})\| \leq \gamma < 1 \quad \text{for } \|\mathbf{x} - \mathbf{x}^*\| \leq \beta \tag{4.3.10}$$

Intuitively, (4.3.10) says that the iteration (4.3.4) will converge provided that $\mathrm{A}^{-1}\mathbf{H}'(\mathbf{x})$ is "small" when $\mathbf{x}$ is close to $\mathbf{x}^*$. Similarly, the iteration (4.3.5) will converge if $\mathrm{B}\mathbf{F}'(\mathbf{x})$ is close to the identity, or, equivalently, if B^{-1} is close to $\mathbf{F}'(\mathbf{x})$. Since x^* is not known, these criteria are not meant to be used to check whether a given iteration will converge, but rather to give some insight as to what factors govern the convergence.

Analogously to the previous section, the size of $\|\mathbf{G}'(\mathbf{x})\|$ will tend to determine the rate of convergence, and we would like this quantity to be as small as possible, at least near the solution $\mathbf{x}^*$. Suppose that for the iteration (4.3.5), we could choose $\mathrm{B} = [\mathbf{F}'(\mathbf{x}^*)]^{-1}$; then, $\mathbf{G}'(\mathbf{x}^*) = 0$, and the rate of convergence will be rapid near the solution. Of course, this choice for B is essentially impossible since $\mathbf{x}^*$ is not known, but we can achieve this effect by the following iteration:

$$\mathbf{x}^{i+1} = \mathbf{x}^i - [\mathbf{F}'(\mathbf{x}^i)]^{-1}\mathbf{F}(\mathbf{x}^i), \qquad i = 0, 1, \ldots \tag{4.3.11}$$

Here, we are assuming, of course, that the Jacobian matrices $\mathbf{F}'(\mathbf{x}^i)$ are nonsingular. We would actually carry out (4.3.11) by the following steps:

1. Solve the linear system

$$\mathbf{F}'(\mathbf{x}^i)\mathbf{y}^i = -\mathbf{F}(\mathbf{x}^i). \tag{4.3.12}$$

2. Set $\mathbf{x}^{i+1} = \mathbf{x}^i + \mathbf{y}^i$.

It is clear that if $n = 1$, the iteration (4.3.12) reduces to Newton's method of the previous section. Of the various possible extensions of the one-dimensional Newton iteration to n dimensions, (4.3.12) is the "correct" one because of the following properties, which we will state without proof:

1. If $\mathbf{F}$ is two times continuously differentiable in a neighborhood of $\mathbf{x}^*$, and if $\mathbf{F}'(\mathbf{x}^*)$ is nonsingular in a neighborhood of $\mathbf{x}^*$, then the iterates (4.3.12) will converge to $\mathbf{x}^*$ provided that $\mathbf{x}^0$ is sufficiently close to $\mathbf{x}^*$ (local convergence theorem), and they will have the property of quadratic convergence

$$\|\mathbf{x}^{i+1} - \mathbf{x}^*\| < c\,\|\mathbf{x}^i - \mathbf{x}^*\|^2 \tag{4.3.13}$$

2. Geometrically, (4.3.12) can be interpreted as follows: The ith function f_i is approximated by a linear function ℓ_i which, considered as a

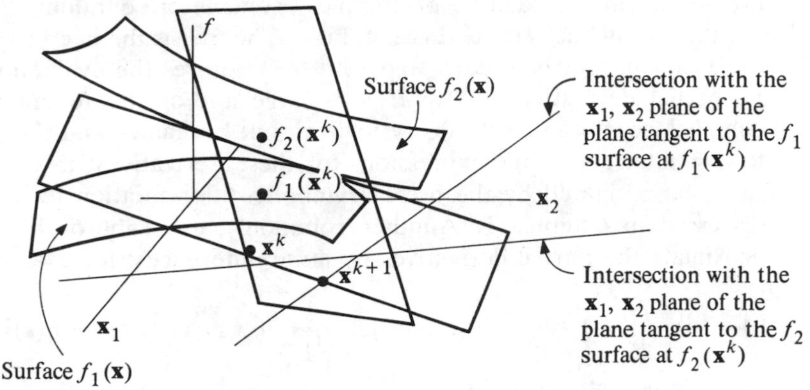

FIGURE 4.15 *Newton's Method for $n = 2$.*

"hyperplane" in $n + 1$-dimensional space, is tangent to f_i at $\mathbf{x}^i$. The intersection of the n sets

$$\{\mathbf{x}: \ell_i(\mathbf{x}) = 0\}$$

is the next iterate $\mathbf{x}^{i+1}$. This is illustrated in Figure 4.15 for $n = 2$.

As an example of Newton's method (4.3.12), for two equations we give in Table 4.2 the first four iterations for the system of nonlinear equations

$$x_1^2 + x_2^2 - 1 = 0 \qquad x_1^2 - x_2 = 0$$

using the starting values $x_1 = 0.5$ and $x_2 = 0.5$. As in the one-dimensional case, we can observe the approximate quadratic behavior of the convergence.

The quadratic convergence property (4.3.13) [which is lost if $\mathbf{F}'(\mathbf{x}^*)$ is singular] is highly desirable and makes Newton's method of central

TABLE 4.2 *Convergence of n-dimensional Newton's Method for $x_1^2 + x_2^2 - 1 = 0$, $x_1^2 - x_2 = 0$*

Iteration	x_1	x_2	Number of Correct Digits
0	0.5	0.5	0, 0
1	0.87499999	0.62499999	1, 2
2	0.79067460	0.61805555	2, 4
3	0.78616432	0.61803399	4, 8
4	0.78615138	0.61803399	8, 8+

importance in the solution of nonlinear systems of equations. But there are three drawbacks to its successful use. The first is the need to compute the Jacobian matrix at each step, and this requires the evaluation of the n^2 partial derivatives $\partial f_i/\partial x_j$. If n is large and/or the functions f_i are complicated, it can be drudgery to work out by hand—and then convert to computer code—the expressions for these derivatives; this can sometimes be mitigated by the use of symbolic differentiation techniques as discussed in Chapter 1. Another commonly used approach is to approximate the partial derivatives by finite differences; for example,

$$\textbf{(4.3.14)} \quad \frac{\partial f_i}{\partial x_j}(\mathbf{x}) \doteq \frac{1}{h}[f_i(x_1, \ldots, x_{j-1}, x_j + h, x_{j+1}, \ldots, x_n) - f_i(\mathbf{x})]$$

This has the advantage of requiring only the expressions for the f_i, which are needed in any case. But the actual numerical evaluation of the Jacobian matrix, either by expressions for the partial derivatives or by approximations such as (4.3.14), can be costly in computer time. This leads to a frequently used modification of Newton's method in which the Jacobian is reevaluated only periodically rather than at each iteration. That is, the iteration would be as follows:

(4.3.15)

1. Evaluate $\mathbf{F}'(\mathbf{x}^0)$.
2. Compute the iterates $\mathbf{x}^{i+1} = \mathbf{x}^i - [\mathbf{F}'(\mathbf{x}^0)]^{-1}\mathbf{F}(\mathbf{x}^i)$, $i = 0, 1, \ldots, k$.
3. Evaluate $\mathbf{F}'(\mathbf{x}^{k+1})$.
4. Compute the iterates $\mathbf{x}^{i+1} = \mathbf{x}^i - [\mathbf{F}'(\mathbf{x}^{k+1})]^{-1}\mathbf{F}(\mathbf{x}^i)$, $i = k + 1, \ldots, 2k$.

.
.
.

The modified Newton iteration (4.3.15) can also be useful in alleviating the second disadvantage of Newton's method: the need to solve a system of linear equations at each step. The advantage of (4.3.15) in this regard is that the actual implementation involves, of course, solving a number of linear systems (as in step 2)

$$\mathbf{F}'(\mathbf{x}^0)\mathbf{y}^i = \mathbf{F}(\mathbf{x}^i), \qquad i = 0, 1, \ldots, k$$

where the coefficient matrix $\mathbf{F}'(\mathbf{x}^0)$ is the same. Hence, as discussed in Section 3.3, the LU factors of $\mathbf{F}'(\mathbf{x}^0)$ from the Gaussian elimination process can be retained and used for all $k + 1$ right-hand sides.

The third—and most troublesome—difficulty with Newton's method is that the iterates may not converge from a given starting approximation $\mathbf{x}^0$; the local convergence theorem only insures convergence once $\mathbf{x}^0$ (or some other iterate) is "sufficiently close" to $\mathbf{x}^*$. One remedy for this difficulty is to obtain the best possible first approximation using any physical or other knowledge about the problem. However, this is not always sufficient. A more or less systematic approach that often—but certainly not always—works is the *continuation method*, which we now describe.

In many scientific problems, the equations are to be solved for various values of one or more parameters. Suppose there is a single parameter α and we write the system of equations as

$$\textbf{(4.3.16)} \qquad \mathbf{F}(\mathbf{x}; \alpha) = 0$$

Assume that we wish solutions $\mathbf{x}_i^*$ for values $\alpha_0 < \alpha_1 < \cdots < \alpha_N$, where α_0 corresponds to a trivial, or at least an easy, problem; for example, the equations for α_0 may be linear. If $\mathbf{x}_0^*$ can be computed and if $|\alpha_1 - \alpha_0|$ is small, then we hope that $\mathbf{x}_0^*$ is sufficiently close to $\mathbf{x}_1^*$ that $\mathbf{x}_0^*$ is a suitable starting approximation for the equation $\mathbf{F}(\mathbf{x}; \alpha_1) = 0$. Continuing in this way, we use each previous solution as a starting approximation for the next problem.

If the equations to be solved do not contain such a parameter, we can always introduce one artificially. For example, let $\mathbf{F}(\mathbf{x}) = 0$ be the equations to be solved and let $\mathbf{x}^0$ be our best approximation to the solution (but not good enough that the Newton iteration will converge). Define a new set of equations depending on a parameter α by

$$\textbf{(4.3.17)} \qquad \hat{\mathbf{F}}(\mathbf{x}; \alpha) = \mathbf{F}(\mathbf{x}) + (\alpha - 1)\mathbf{F}(\mathbf{x}^0) = 0, \qquad 0 \le \alpha \le 1$$

Then, $\hat{\mathbf{F}}(\mathbf{x}; 0) = \mathbf{F}(\mathbf{x}) - \mathbf{F}(\mathbf{x}^0) = 0$, for which $\mathbf{x}^0$ is a solution, and $\hat{\mathbf{F}}(\mathbf{x}; 1) = \mathbf{F}(\mathbf{x}) = 0$, which are the equations to be solved. Hence, we proceed as in the previous paragraph for a sequence $0 = \alpha_0 < \alpha_1 < \cdots < \alpha_N = 1$.

Supplementary Discussion and References: 4.3

For a more detailed discussion of a variety of methods for solving systems of nonlinear equations numerically, see Ortega and Rheinboldt [1970] and Ostrowski [1973]. In particular, these references contain various discrete forms of Newton's method where the Jacobian matrix is approximated in some fashion. Certain of these approximations lead to natural generalizations of the secant method to systems of equations, and others give what are now known as quasi-Newton methods and seem to be among the most promising of current methods for this problem. For a review of the status of these quasi-Newton methods, see Dennis and Moré [1977].

Many systems of equations arise in the attempt to minimize (or maximize) a function g of n variables. From the calculus, we know that if g is continuously differentiable, then a necessary condition for a local minimum is that

$$\left(\frac{\partial g}{\partial x_1}, \ldots, \frac{\partial g}{\partial x_n}\right) = 0$$

That is, the gradient vector of g vanishes. Thus, by solving this system of equations, one obtains a possible local minimizer of g, and, in many situations, it will be known that this vector must indeed minimize g. Alternatively, if we are given an arbitrary system of equations $f_i = 0$, $i = 1, \ldots, n$, we can convert the solution of this system to a minimization problem by defining a function

$$g(\mathbf{x}) = \sum_{i=1}^{n} [f_i(\mathbf{x})]^2$$

Clearly, g takes on a minimum value of zero only when all f_i vanish. This conversion is usually not recommended for obtaining a numerical solution of the system since the ill-conditioning of the problem will be increased.

The continuation method is closely related to what is known as *Davidenko's method.* For illustration, consider (4.3.17) and assume that for each $\alpha \in [0, 1]$, the equation defines a solution $\mathbf{x}(\alpha)$ that is continuously differentiable in α. Then, if we differentiate

$$\mathbf{F}(\mathbf{x}(\alpha)) + (\alpha - 1)\mathbf{F}(\mathbf{x}^0) = 0$$

with respect to α, we obtain by the chain rule

$$\mathbf{F}'(\mathbf{x})(\alpha))\mathbf{x}'(\alpha) + \mathbf{F}(\mathbf{x}^0) = 0$$

or, assuming that the Jacobian matrix $\mathbf{F}'(\mathbf{x}(\alpha))$ is nonsingular,

$$\mathbf{x}'(\alpha) = -[\mathbf{F}'(\mathbf{x}(\alpha))]^{-1}\mathbf{F}(\mathbf{x}^0)$$

with the initial condition $\mathbf{x}(0) = \mathbf{x}^0$. The solution $x(\alpha)$ of this initial-value problem at $\alpha = 1$ will, we hope, be the desired solution of the original system of equations $\mathbf{F}(\mathbf{x}) = 0$. In practice, we will have to solve the differential equations numerically, and for this, we can, in principle, use any of the methods of Chapter 2. Although Davidenko's method and the continuation method are attractive possibilities, their reliability in practice has been less than desired. In particular, it is possible that the Jacobian matrix will become singular for some $\mathbf{x}(\alpha)$ with $\alpha < 1$, or even that the solution curve itself will blow up prematurely.

In the last few years, there have been important developments in overcoming some of these difficulties; for a recent review, see Allgower and Georg [1980].

EXERCISES 4.3

4.3.1. Show graphically that the system of equations $x_1^2 + x_2^2 = 1$, $x_1^2 - x_2 = 0$ has precisely two solutions.

4.3.2. Show that (4.3.5) reduces to (4.3.4) when $\mathbf{F}$ is of the form (4.3.3) and $B = A^{-1}$.

4.3.3. Compute the Jacobian matrix $\mathbf{G}'(\mathbf{x})$ for

$$\mathbf{G}(\mathbf{x}) = \begin{bmatrix} x_1^2 + x_1x_2x_3 + x_3^3 \\ x_1^3x_2 + x_2x_3^2 \\ x_1/x_3^2 \end{bmatrix}$$

4.3.4. If $\mathbf{G}(\mathbf{x}) = \mathbf{x} - \mathbf{BF}(\mathbf{x})$, shown that $\mathbf{G}'(\mathbf{x}) = \mathbf{I} - \mathbf{BF}'(\mathbf{x})$ and conclude that (4.3.9) and (4.3.10) follow from (4.3.8).

4.3.5. For the functions of exercise 4.3.1, compute the tangent planes at $x_1 = 2$, $x_2 = 2$.

4.3.6. Write down the Newton iteration for the equations of exercise 4.3.1. For what points $\mathbf{x}$ is the Jacobian matrix nonsingular?

4.3.7. Write a program for Newton's method to handle n equations in n unknowns. Use Gaussian elimination with partial pivoting to solve the linear equations.

4.4 Finite Difference Methods for Nonlinear Boundary-Value Problems

We turn now to an extension to nonlinear two-point boundary-value problems of the finite difference method discussed in Chapter 3. We shall consider first the rather simple equation

(4.4.1) $$v'' = g(x, v), \qquad 0 \le x \le 1$$

with the boundary conditions

(4.4.2) $$v(0) = \alpha \qquad v(1) = \beta$$

Here, g is a given function of two variables, and α and β are given constants.

We proceed exactly as in Section 3.2. The interval $[a, b]$ is partitioned by grid points

$$0 = x_0 < x_1 < \cdots < x_n < x_{n+1} = 1$$

with spacing h. Next, at each interior grid point $x_1, \ldots, x_n$, we approximate the second derivative by central differences and use these approximations in (4.4.1). This leads to the system of equations [corresponding to (3.2.12)]

(4.4.3) $$v_{i+1} - 2v_i + v_{i-1} = h^2 g(x_i, v_i), \qquad i = 1, \ldots, n$$

where $v_0 = \alpha$ and $v_{n+1} = \beta$ are known by the boundary conditions (4.4.2). This is a system of n equations in the n unknowns $v_1, \ldots, v_n$ and is nonlinear if the function g is nonlinear in v. A solution $v_1^*, \ldots, v_n^*$ of (4.4.3), if it exists, is an approximation to the corresponding solution v of (4.4.1)/(4.4.2) at the grid points $x_1, \ldots, x_n$.

We can write (4.4.3) in matrix-vector form as follows. Let A be the tridiagonal matrix (4.4.10) with 2 on the main diagonal and -1 on the neighboring off-diagonals, and let $\mathbf{H}$ be the vector function of $\mathbf{v} = (v_1, \ldots, v_n)$ defined by

(4.4.4)
$$\mathbf{H}(\mathbf{v}) = h^2 \begin{bmatrix} g(x_1, v_1) \\ \cdot \\ \cdot \\ \cdot \\ g(x_n, v_n) \end{bmatrix} + \begin{bmatrix} \alpha \\ 0 \\ \cdot \\ \cdot \\ \cdot \\ 0 \\ \beta \end{bmatrix}$$

Then, the system (4.4.3) is

(4.4.5)
$$\mathbf{F}(\mathbf{v}) \equiv \mathrm{A}\mathbf{v} + \mathbf{H}(\mathbf{v}) = 0$$

As an example, consider the problem

(4.4.6)
$$v''(x) = 3v(x) + x^2 + 10[v(x)]^3, \qquad 0 \le x \le 1, v(0) = v(1) = 0$$

Here,

(4.4.7)
$$g(x, v) = 3v + x^2 + 10v^3$$

and with

(4.4.8)
$$x_i = ih, \qquad i = 0, 1, \ldots, n + 1, h = \frac{1}{n+1}$$

the difference equations (4.4.3) are

(4.4.9)
$$v_{i+1} - 2v_i + v_{i-1} = h^2(3v_i + i^2h^2 + 10v_i^3), \quad i = 1, \ldots, n$$

where, from the boundary conditions, $v_0 = v_{n+1} = 0$. For this problem, the matrix A and vector function $\mathbf{H}$ of (4.4.5) are given by

(4.4.10)
$$\mathrm{A} = \begin{bmatrix} 2 & -1 & & \\ -1 & \cdot & \cdot & \\ & \cdot & \cdot & \cdot \\ & & \cdot & \cdot & -1 \\ & & & -1 & 2 \end{bmatrix} \qquad \mathbf{H}(\mathbf{v}) = h^2 \begin{bmatrix} 3v_1 + h^2 + 10v_1^3 \\ 3v_2 + 4h^2 + 10v_2^3 \\ \cdot \\ \cdot \\ \cdot \\ 3v_n + n^2h^2 + 10v_n^3 \end{bmatrix}$$

We now consider some numerical methods for the system (4.4.5). The Picard iteration discussed in Section 4.3 is

(4.4.11)
$$\mathrm{A}\mathbf{v}^{k+1} = -\mathbf{H}(\mathbf{v}^k)$$

The time to carry out one of these iterative steps depends almost entirely on the complexity of $\mathbf{H}$ since, as we saw in Section 3.4, the solution of tridiagonal linear systems is very rapid. Moreover, in this case, the LU decomposition of A can be done once and for all and need not be done at each step. Whether the iteration (4.4.11) even converges, however, will depend upon the properties of H.

Let us next consider Newton's method for (4.4.5). As we saw in Section 4.3, the Jacobian matrix in this case will be

(4.4.12)
$$\mathbf{F}'(\mathbf{v}) = A + \mathbf{H}'(\mathbf{v})$$

Thus, the kth step of the Newton iteration is as follows:

(4.4.13)
1. Solve $[A + \mathbf{H}'(\mathbf{v}^k)]\mathbf{y}^k = -[A\mathbf{v}^k + \mathbf{H}(\mathbf{v}^k)]$.
2. Set $\mathbf{v}^{k+1} = \mathbf{v}^k + \mathbf{y}^k$.

Since the ith component H_i of $\mathbf{H}$,

$$H_i(\mathbf{v}) = h^2 g(x_i, v_i)$$

depends on only v_i, we have that

(4.4.14)
$$\frac{\partial H_i}{\partial v_j} \equiv 0, \qquad j \neq i$$

That is, the Jacobian matrix $\mathbf{H}'(\mathbf{v})$ is diagonal, so the linear systems of (4.4.13) to be solved for Newton's method are all tridiagonal and hence require a relatively negligible amount of work, even if row interchanges are used. Specifically, the Jacobian matrix $A + \mathbf{H}'(\mathbf{v})$ is

(4.4.15)

$$\begin{bmatrix} 2 + h^2\frac{\partial}{\partial v}g(x_1, v_1) & -1 & & & \\ -1 & 2 + h^2\frac{\partial}{\partial v}g(x_2, v_2) & -1 & & \\ & \ddots & \ddots & \ddots & \\ & & \ddots & \ddots & -1 \\ & & & -1 & 2 + h^2\frac{\partial}{\partial v}g(x_n, v_n) \end{bmatrix}$$

We note that to carry out Newton's method, we need to evaluate the partial derivatives of g used in (4.4.15). If g is a complicated function of v, it may be beneficial to use the symbolic computation techniques discussed in Chapter 1 to produce explicit expressions for these partial derivatives. These expressions would then be written as part of the program to evaluate the Jacobian matrix (4.4.15).

Let us return to the boundary-value problem (4.4.6) and corresponding difference equations (4.4.9). Here, g is given by (4.4.7), so

$$\frac{\partial g}{\partial v}(x, v) = 3 + 30v^2$$

and the ith diagonal element of the Jacobian matrix (4.4.15) is just $2 + h^2(3 + 30v_i^2)$. Since the matrix A of (4.4.10) is diagonally dominant, it is clear that the addition of the positive terms $h^2(3 + 30v_i^2)$ to the diagonal only enhances the diagonal dominance. More generally, whenever

$$\frac{\partial g}{\partial v}(x, v) \geq 0, \qquad 0 \leq x \leq 1$$

and A is given by (4.4.10), then

(4.4.16) $\quad \mathrm{A} + \mathbf{H}'(\mathbf{v})$ is diagonally dominant

(4.4.17) $\quad \mathrm{A} + \mathbf{H}'(\mathbf{v})$ is positive-definite

As we saw in Section 3.3, either of these properties is sufficient to ensure that the solution of the tridiagonal systems (4.4.13) of Newton's method can be carried out by Gaussian elimination without any need for interchanging rows to preserve numerical stability. It is also true (but beyond the scope of this book to prove) that either of the conditions (4.4.16) or (4.4.17) ensures that the system (4.4.5) has a unique solution.

For the difference equation (4.4.9), we tabulate in Table 4.3 the results of Newton's method at the grid points $0.1, 0.2, \ldots, 0.9$ for $h = 0.1$, 0.01, and 0.001 ($n = 9$, 99, and 999). In all cases, the initial approximation for Newton's method was taken to be $\mathbf{v}^0 = 0$, and the iteration terminated when all components of the Newton correction vector $\mathbf{y}^k$ of (4.4.13) were less than 10^{-6} in magnitude.

TABLE 4.3 *Newton's Method for the Difference Equations* (4.4.9)

x	$h = 0.1$	$h = 0.01$	$h = 0.001$
0.1	−0.0058	−0.0058	−0.0058
0.2	−0.0116	−0.0118	−0.0118
0.3	−0.0174	−0.0176	−0.0176
0.4	−0.0223	−0.0230	−0.0230
0.5	−0.0274	−0.0276	−0.0276
0.6	−0.0302	−0.0304	−0.0304
0.7	−0.0303	−0.0305	−0.0305
0.8	−0.0265	−0.0266	−0.0266
0.9	−0.0170	−0.0171	−0.0171

Suppose, now, that the equation (4.4.1) has the more general form

(4.4.18) $$(a(x)v')' = g(x, v), \qquad 0 \le x \le 1$$

together with the boundary conditions (4.4.2). For the left-hand side of this equation, we use the difference approximation (3.2.29), and the difference equations then take the form

(4.4.19)

$$a_{i-1/2}v_{i-1} - (a_{i+1/2} + a_{i-1/2})v_i + a_{i+1/2}v_{i+1} = h^2 g(x_i, v_i), \qquad i = 1, \ldots, n$$

where $a_{i\pm 1/2} = a(x_i \pm \frac{1}{2}h)$ and, again, $v_0 = \alpha$, $v_{n+1} = \beta$. If we now denote by A the tridiagonal matrix corresponding to (4.4.19) [the matrix A is written out explicitly in (3.2.30)], then, again, the system of equations is given by (4.4.5), the Picard iteration by (4.4.6), and the Newton iteration by (4.4.13). The Jacobian matrix is again symmetric and tridiagonal. Moreover, if the conditions

(4.4.20) $$\frac{\partial g}{\partial v}(x, v) \ge 0 \qquad a(x) \ge 0 \qquad 0 < x < 1$$

hold, then both of the properties (4.4.16) and (4.4.17) are true.

The formulation (4.4.19) holds, in principle, for the equation

(4.4.21) $$(x^2 v')' = \frac{cvx^2}{v + d}, \qquad 0 \le x \le 1$$

which arose from the diffusion-reaction problem discussed in Section 3.1. In this case, the boundary conditions are

(4.4.22) $$v'(0) = 0 \qquad v(1) = 1$$

in place of (4.4.2). (We note that we have changed notation slightly from Section 3.1: we use x as the independent variable in place of r.)

With the grid points x_i again given by (4.4.8), we have

(4.4.23) $$a_{i\pm 1/2} = (i \pm \tfrac{1}{2})^2 h^2$$

and thus the difference equations (4.4.19) become

(4.4.24) $$(i - \tfrac{1}{2})^2 v_{i-1} - (2i^2 + \tfrac{1}{2})v_i + (i + \tfrac{1}{2})^2 v_{i+1} = \frac{cv_i(ih)^2}{v_i + d}$$

for $i = 1, \ldots, n$. Again, $v_{n+1} = 1$ by the boundary condition $v(1) = 1$. Now, however, the other boundary condition, $v'(0) = 0$, does not yield a value for v_0. Rather, we approximate $v'(0)$ by the one-sided difference

$$v'(0) \doteq \frac{1}{h}(v_1 - v_0)$$

Since $v'(0) = 0$, this gives the additional equation $v_0 = v_1$, which we use in the first equation ($i = 1$) of (4.4.24) to obtain

$$-\tfrac{9}{4}(v_1 - v_2) = \frac{cv_1h^2}{v_1 + d} \tag{4.4.25}$$

This equation and (4.4.24) for $i = 2, \ldots, n$ now constitute the system of equations to be solved for $v_1, \ldots, v_n$.

Since $g(x, v) = cvx^2/(v + d)$,

$$\frac{\partial g}{\partial v} = \frac{cdx^2}{(v + d)^2} \tag{4.4.26}$$

and the Jacobian matrix of the system is

$$\frac{1}{4}\begin{bmatrix} 9 + \dfrac{4cdh^2}{(v_1 + d)^2} & -9 & & & \\ -9 & 34 + \dfrac{4cd(2h)^2}{(v_2 + d)^2} & -25 & & \\ & -25 & \ddots & \ddots & \\ & & \ddots & \ddots & -(2n - 1)^2 \\ & & & -(2n - 1)^2 & (8n^2 + 2) + \dfrac{4cd(nh)^2}{(v_n + d)^2} \end{bmatrix}$$

We see that the Jacobian matrix is symmetric. Moreover, since c and d are assumed to be positive constants, (4.4.26) shows that $\partial g/\partial v \geq 0$, so, as before, the Jacobian matrix is also positive-definite. Hence, we can again carry out Newton's method by solving the tridiagonal systems without interchanging.

Supplementary Discussion and References: 4.4

The proof that the system (4.4.5) has a unique solution under the conditions given in (4.4.16) or (4.4.17) can be found, for example, in Ortega and Rheinboldt [1970, Section 4.4].

The diffusion-reaction equation (4.4.26) has been treated numerically in Keller [1968], and we have followed his development. As discussed in the Supplementary Discussion of Section 3.1, this equation is singular because the coefficient of v' becomes infinite at the origin.

EXERCISES 4.4

4.4.1. Write out the difference equations (4.4.3) and the corresponding Jacobian matrix for:

a. $g(x, v) = v + v^2$

b. $g(x, v) = xv^3$

4.4.2. Write out the Newton iteration (4.4.13) explicitly for the difference equations (4.4.3) with g given by exercise 4.4.1.

4.4.3. Repeat exercise 4.4.1 for the difference equations (4.4.19) with:

a. $a(x) = e^x$

b. $a(x) = 1 + x^2$

4.4.4. Under the assumptions (4.4.20), verify that (4.4.16) and (4.4.17) are both true.

4.4.5. Consider the two-point boundary-value problem $v'' = e^v + 2 - e^{x^2}$, $0 \leq x \leq 1$, $v(0) = 0$, $v(1) = 1$.

a. Write the standard finite difference equations for this problem in matrix-vector form for $h = 0.01$.

b. Discuss in detail how you would solve the system of equations in part a on a computer. The discussion should include a clear description of the method, what if any problems you expect the method to have, how much computer time you would expect the method to use, and so on.

c. Describe in detail the shooting method for the boundary-value problem and discuss any problems you expect to have in carrying it out on a computer.

5 Is There More to Computing Than Finite Differences?

5.1 Introduction to Projection Methods

In the last three chapters, we have studied in some detail the application of finite difference methods to the approximate solution of differential equations. In this chapter, we will consider another approach which has several variants known by such names as the finite element method, Galerkin's method, the Rayleigh–Ritz method, and so on. The underlying theme of all of these methods is that one attempts to approximate the solution of the differential equation by a finite linear combination of known functions. These known functions, usually called the *basis functions* (or *trial functions*), have the common property that they are relatively simple: polynomials, trigonometric functions, and, most importantly, the spline functions, which will be studied in the following section. Conceptually, we regard the solution as lying in some appropriate (infinite-dimensional) function space, and we attempt to obtain an approximate solution that lies in the finite-dimensional subspace that is determined by the basis functions. The "projection" of the solution onto the finite-dimensional subspace is the approximate solution.

We will illustrate these general ideas with the linear two-point boundary-value problem

(5.1.1) $$(p(x)v')' + q(x)v = f(x), \qquad 0 \le x \le 1$$

with

(5.1.2) $$v(0) = 0 \qquad v(1) = 0$$

where, for simplicity, we have taken the interval to be $[0, 1]$ and the boundary conditions to be zero.

Suppose that we look for an approximate solution of (5.1.1)/(5.1.2) of the form

$$u(x) = \sum_{j=1}^{n} c_j \phi_j(x) \tag{5.1.3}$$

where the basis functions ϕ_j satisfy the boundary conditions; that is,

$$\phi_j(0) = \phi_j(1) = 0, \qquad j = 1, \ldots, n \tag{5.1.4}$$

If (5.1.4) holds, then the approximate solution u given by (5.1.3) satisfies the boundary conditions. A classical example of a set of basis functions that satisfy (5.1.4) is

$$\phi_j(x) = \sin j\pi x, \qquad j = 1, \ldots, n \tag{5.1.5}$$

Another example is the set of polynomials

$$\phi_j(x) = x^j(1 - x), \qquad j = 1, \ldots, n \tag{5.1.6}$$

In the latter case, the approximate solution (5.1.3) is of the form

$$u(x) = x(1 - x)(c_1 + c_2 x + \cdots + c_n x^{n-1})$$

which is a polynomial of degree $n + 1$ with the property that it vanishes at zero and 1. Our main example of a set of basis functions, however, is the spline functions, which, as mentioned previously, will be studied in the following section.

Given a set of basis functions, we need to specify in what sense (5.1.3) is to be an approximate solution; that is, what is the criterion for determining the coefficients c_k in the linear combination. There are several possible approaches, and we will discuss here only two, both of which are generally applicable and widely used.

The first criterion is that of *collocation*. Let $x_1, \ldots, x_n$ be n (not necessarily equally spaced) grid points in the interval $[0, 1]$. We then require that the approximate solution satisfy the differential equation at these n points. Thus, for the equation (5.1.1) and the approximation (5.1.3), we require that

$$\frac{d}{dx}\left[p(x)\frac{d}{dx}\left(\sum_{j=1}^{n} c_j\phi_j(x)\right)\right]\Bigg|_{x_i} + q(x_i)\sum_{j=1}^{n} c_j\phi_j(x_i) = f(x_i), \qquad i = 1, \ldots, n \tag{5.1.7}$$

and we assume, of course, that the basis functions are twice differentiable. If we carry out the differentiation in (5.1.7) and collect coefficients of the c_j, we have

$$\sum_{j=1}^{n} c_j[p(x_i)\phi_j''(x_i) + p'(x_i)\phi_j'(x_i) + q(x_i)\phi_j(x_i)] = f(x_i), \qquad i = 1, \ldots, n \tag{5.1.8}$$

This is a system of n linear equations in the n unknowns $c_1, \ldots, c_n$. The computational problem is first to evaluate the coefficients

$$a_{ij} \equiv p(x_i)\phi_j''(x_i) + p'(x_i)\phi_j'(x_i) + q(x_i)\phi_j(x_i) \tag{5.1.9}$$

and then solve the system of linear equations

$$\mathbf{A}\mathbf{c} = \mathbf{f} \tag{5.1.10}$$

where A is the $n \times n$ matrix (a_{ij}), $\mathbf{c} = (c_1, \ldots, c_n)$, and $\mathbf{f} = (f(x_1), \ldots, f(x_n))$.

We give a simple example of this. Consider the problem

$$[(1 + x^2)v'(x)]' + x^2v(x) = x^3, \qquad 0 \le x \le 1 \tag{5.1.11}$$

with, again, the boundary conditions (5.1.2). Here, $p(x) = 1 + x^2$ and $q(x) = x^2$. Let us first use the basis functions (5.1.5). Then,

$$\phi_j'(x) = j\pi \cos j\pi x \qquad \phi_j''(x) = -(j\pi)^2 \sin j\pi x$$

so that the coefficients (5.1.9) are

$$\begin{aligned} a_{ij} &= -(1 + x_i^2)(j\pi)^2 \sin j\pi x_i + 2j\pi x_i \cos j\pi x_i + x_i^2 \sin j\pi x_i \\ &= [-(1 + x_i^2)(j\pi)^2 + x_i^2] \sin j\pi x_i + 2j\pi x_i \cos j\pi x_i \end{aligned}$$

The coefficients of the right-hand side of the system (5.1.10) are simply $f(x_i) = x_i^3$. If we use the basis functions (5.1.6), then

$$\phi_j'(x) = x^{j-1}[j - (j + 1)x] \qquad \phi_j''(x) = jx^{j-2}[j - 1 - (j + 1)x]$$

so that the coefficients (5.1.9) are now

$$a_{ij} = (1 + x_i^2)jx_i^{j-2}[j - 1 - (j + 1)x_i] + 2x_i^j[j - (j + 1)x_i] + x_i^{j+2}(1 - x_i)$$

Again, the components of the right-hand side are x_i^3. In both cases, the system (5.1.10) is easily constructed once the grid points $x_1, \ldots, x_n$ are specified.

We will return to a discussion of the collocation method after we consider another approach to determining the coefficients $c_1, \ldots, c_n$. This is known as *Galerkin's method* and is based on the concept of orthogonality of functions.

Recall that two vectors $\mathbf{f}$ and $\mathbf{g}$ are *orthogonal* if the inner product

$$(\mathbf{f}, \mathbf{g}) \equiv \mathbf{f}^T\mathbf{g} = \sum_{j=1}^{n} f_j g_j = 0 \tag{5.1.12}$$

Now, suppose that the components of the vectors $\mathbf{f}$ and $\mathbf{g}$ are the values of two functions f and g at n equally spaced grid points in the interval [0, 1]; that is,

$$\mathbf{f} = (f(h), f(2h), \ldots, f(nh))$$

where $h = (n + 1)^{-1}$ is the grid-point spacing, and similarly for **g**. Then, the orthogonality relation (5.1.12) is

$$\sum_{j=1}^{n} f(jh)g(jh) = 0$$

and this relation is unchanged if we multiply by h:

$$h \sum_{j=1}^{n} f(jh)g(jh) = 0 \tag{5.1.13}$$

Now, let $n \to \infty$ (or, equivalently, let $h \to 0$). Then, assuming that the functions f and g are integrable, the sum in (5.1.13) will tend to the integral

$$\int_0^1 f(x)g(x)\,dx = 0 \tag{5.1.14}$$

With this motivation, we *define* two functions f and g to be *orthogonal* on the interval $[0, 1]$ if the relation (5.1.14) holds.

The rationale for the Galerkin approach is as follows. Let the *residual function* for $u(x)$ be defined by

$$r(x) = (p(x)u'(x))' + q(x)u(x) - f(x), \qquad 0 \le x \le 1 \tag{5.1.15}$$

If $u(x)$ were the exact solution to (5.1.1), then the residual function would be identically zero. Obviously, the residual would be orthogonal to every function, and, in particular, it would be orthogonal to the set of basis functions. However, we cannot expect $u(x)$ to be the exact solution because we restrict $u(x)$ to be a linear combination of the basis functions. What the Galerkin method does is to choose that $u(x)$ which has a residual that is orthogonal to all of the basis functions $\phi_1, \ldots, \phi_n$; that is,

$$\int_0^1 [(p(x)u'(x))' + q(x)u(x) - f(x)]\phi_i(x)\,dx = 0, \qquad i = 1, \ldots, n \tag{5.1.16}$$

or, if we put in (5.1.3) and interchange the summation and integration,

$$\sum_{j=1}^{n} c_j \int_0^1 [(p(x)\phi_j'(x))' + q(x)\phi_j(x)]\phi_i(x)\,dx = \int_0^1 f(x)\phi_i(x)\,dx, \qquad i = 1, \ldots, n$$

Again, this is a system of linear equations of the form (5.1.10) with

$$f_i = \int_0^1 f(x)\phi_i(x)\,dx, \qquad i = 1, \ldots, n \tag{5.1.17}$$

and

$$a_{ij} = \int_0^1 [(p(x)\phi_j'(x)]' + q(x)\phi_j(x)]\phi_i(x)\,dx$$

If we integrate the first term in this integral by parts,

$$\int_0^1 (p(x)\phi_j'(x))'\phi_i(x)\,dx = p(x)\phi_j'(x)\phi_i(x)|_0^1 - \int_0^1 p(x)\phi_j'(x)\phi_i'(x)\,dx$$

and note that the first term vanishes because ϕ_i is zero at the end points, we can rewrite a_{ij} as

$$\textbf{(5.1.18)} \qquad a_{ij} = -\int_0^1 p(x)\phi_i'(x)\phi_j'(x)\,dx + \int_0^1 q(x)\phi_i(x)\phi_j(x)\,dx$$

Thus, the system of equations to solve for the coefficients $c_1, \ldots, c_n$ in Galerkin's method is $A\mathbf{c} = \mathbf{f}$, with the elements of A given by (5.1.18) and those of $\mathbf{f}$ by (5.1.17).

As an example of the system of equations obtained from Galerkin's method, consider again the differential equation (5.1.11) with the boundary conditions (5.1.2). For the basis functions (5.1.6), the coefficients a_{ij} of (5.1.18) are

$$\begin{aligned} a_{ij} &= -\int_0^1 x^{i+j-2}(1 + x^2)[i - (i+1)x][j - (j+1)x]\,dx \\ &\quad + \int_0^1 x^{i+j+2}(1 - x)^2\,dx \\ &= \frac{ij}{i+j-1} - \frac{(2ij + i + j)}{i+j} + \frac{(i+1)(j+1) + ij}{i+j+1} - \frac{(2ij + i + j)}{i+j+2} \\ &\quad + \frac{(i+1)(j+1) + 1}{i+j+3} - \frac{2}{i+j+4} + \frac{1}{i+j+5} \end{aligned}$$

and the coefficients of the right-hand side are

$$f_i = \int_0^1 x^{i+2}(1 - x)\,dx = \frac{1}{i+3} - \frac{1}{i+4}$$

Although somewhat messy, these coefficients are easily evaluated to form the system of equations $A\mathbf{c} = \mathbf{f}$. The determination of the system for the basis functions (5.1.5) is left to exercise 5.1.5.

Let us now make several comments regarding the finite difference, collocation, and Galerkin methods as applied to (5.1.1). In each case, the central computational problem is to solve a system of linear equations. In the case of the finite difference and collocation methods, these linear systems are determined by n grid points in the interval, although the nature of the solution of the respective linear systems is quite different, that of the finite difference method being an approximation to the solution of the differential equation at the grid points, and that of the collocation method being the coefficients of the representation (5.1.3) of the approximate solution. Thus, with the collocation (or Galerkin) method, the value of the approximate solution at any point $\bar{x}$ in the interval is obtained by the additional evaluation

$$u(\bar{x}) = \sum_{j=1}^{n} c_j \phi_j(\bar{x})$$

Whereas the finite difference method requires no additional work to obtain the approximate solution at the grid points, it is defined *only* at the grid points, and obtaining an approximation at other points in the interval necessitates an interpolation process. The collocation and Galerkin methods, on the other hand, give an approximate solution on the whole interval.

As we saw in Chapter 3, the linear system of equations of the finite difference method is easily obtained and has the important property (for the second-order difference approximations used there) that the coefficient matrix is tridiagonal; thus, the solution of the linear system requires relatively little computation, the number of arithmetic operations required being proportional to n (Section 3.3). For the collocation method, the elements of the coefficient matrix are also evaluated relatively easily by (5.1.9) provided that the basis functions ϕ_j are suitably simple. However, the coefficient matrix will now, in general, be full, which means not only that all n^2 elements be evaluated but also that the solution time will be proportional to n^3. One of the very important properties of the spline basis functions—to be discussed in the next section—is that ϕ_i will be identically zero except in a subinterval about x_i. In the cases considered in Section 5.4, this subinterval will extend only from x_{i-2} to x_{i+2}, and the coefficient matrix will be tridiagonal.

These same comments apply to Galerkin's method: the coefficient matrix will, in general, be full, but the use of an appropriate spline function basis will allow us to recover a tridiagonal matrix. However, there is now another complication. The evaluation of the matrix coefficients (5.1.18) and elements of the right-hand side (5.1.17) requires integration over the whole interval. Only if the functions p, q, and f are very simple will one be able to evaluate these integrals explicitly in closed form. Often, they must be approximated, and this leads us to the topic of numerical integration, which we consider in Section 5.3. Computer-based symbolic computation systems may also be used under certain circumstances. Finally, one advantage of the Galerkin method is that it always yields a symmetric matrix, as can be seen by examining (5.1.18). Collocation does not necessarily yield a symmetric matrix. No method has a clear advantage over the others. For each method, there are problems for which that method is best. Given a particular problem, analyses of the three methods applied to that problem may be necessary in order to evaluate their relative effectivenesses.

We end this section by indicating briefly how the collocation and Galerkin methods can be applied to nonlinear problems. For this purpose, we will consider only the simple equation

$$v'' = g(v), \qquad v(0) = v(1) = 0 \tag{5.1.19}$$

where g is a given nonlinear function of a single variable. For the collocation method applied to (5.1.19), we put in the approximate solution (5.1.3) and evaluate at the grid points $x_1, \ldots, x_n$ as before. This then leads to the system of equations

$$\sum_{j=1}^{n} c_j\phi_j''(x_i) = g\left(\sum_{j=1}^{n} c_j\phi_j(x_i)\right), \qquad i = 1, \ldots, n \tag{5.1.20}$$

for the coefficients $c_1, \ldots, c_n$. Since g is a nonlinear function, this is then a nonlinear system of equations for the c_j's.

Similarly, for the Galerkin method, the residual function (5.1.15) now becomes

$$r(x) = \sum_{j=1}^{n} c_j\phi_j''(x) - g\left(\sum_{j=1}^{n} c_j\phi_j(x)\right)$$

so the system of equations corresponding to (5.1.15) is

$$\int_0^1 \left[\sum_{j=1}^{n} c_j\phi_j''(x) - g\left(\sum_{j=1}^{n} c_j\phi_j(x)\right)\right]\phi_i(x)\,dx = 0, \qquad i = 1, \ldots, n \tag{5.1.21}$$

As before, we can integrate the first term by parts to put (5.1.21) in the form

$$-\sum_{j=1}^{n} c_j \int_0^1 \phi_i'(x)\phi_j'(x)\,dx = \int_0^1 g\left(\sum_{j=1}^{n} c_j\phi_j(x)\right)\phi_i(x)\,dx \tag{5.1.22}$$

which is again a nonlinear system for $c_1, \ldots, c_n$.

Supplementary Discussion and References: 5.1

A related approach to projection methods is by means of a *variational principle.* Consider the problem

$$\text{Minimize}_{v \in V} \int_0^1 \{p(x)[v'(x)]^2 - q(x)[v(x)]^2 - 2f(x)v(x)\}\,dx \tag{5.1.23}$$

where V is a set of suitably differentiable functions that vanish at the end points $x = 0$ and $x = 1$. By results in the calculus of variations, the solution of (5.1.23) is also the solution of the differential equation (5.1.1), which is known as the *Euler equation* for (5.1.23). Thus, we can solve (5.1.1) by solving (5.1.23), and we can attempt to approximate a solution to (5.1.23) in a manner analogous to the Galerkin method. This is known as the *Rayleigh–Ritz method.*

Let $\phi_1, \ldots, \phi_n$ be a set of basis functions such that $\phi_i(0) = \phi_i(1) = 0$, $i = 1, \ldots, n$. Then,

$$\text{(5.1.24)} \quad \underset{c_1,\ldots,c_n}{\text{Minimize}} \int_0^1 \left\{ p(x)\left[\sum_{i=1}^n c_i\phi_i'(x)\right]^2 - q(x)\left[\sum_{i=1}^n c_i\phi_i(x)\right]^2 - 2f(x)\sum_{i=1}^n c_i\phi_i(x)\right\} dx$$

is a finite-dimensional minimization problem for the coefficients $c_1, \ldots, c_n$. If $c_1^*, \ldots, c_n^*$ is the solution of this minimization problem, then

$$U(x) = \sum_{i=1}^n c_i^*\phi_i(x)$$

is taken as an approximate solution for (5.1.23). If we use the same basis functions for the Galerkin method applied to (5.1.1), we will obtain the same approximate solution. A good reference for the Rayleigh–Ritz and Galerkin methods is Strang and Fix [1973].

An important question is when does the system of linear equations obtained by the discretization methods of this section have a unique solution. This is generally easier to ascertain in the case of the Rayleigh–Ritz method since the question reduces to when the functional (5.1.24) has a minimum. In Section 5.4, we will give some simple examples of when the system of equations for the collocation and Galerkin methods have unique solutions when the basis functions are the spline functions discussed in the next section. For an introduction to these existence and uniqueness theorems as well as the important question of discretization error for the Galerkin and collocation methods, see, for example, Prenter [1975], Lucas and Reddien [1972], Russell [1977], and Russell and Shampine [1972].

EXERCISES 5.1

5.1.1. **a.** For the two-point boundary-value problem $y''(x) = y(x) + x^2$, $0 \le x \le 1$, $y(0) = y(1) = 0$, write out explicitly the system of equations (5.1.8) for $n = 3$ where $\phi_j(x) = \sin j\pi x$, and $x_i = i/3$, $i, j = 1, 2, 3$.

b. Repeat part a with $\phi_j(x) = x^j(1 - x)$, $j = 1, 2, 3$.

c. Write out the systems for general n in matrix form using both (5.1.5) and (5.1.6) as the basis functions.

d. Repeat parts a–c for the problem $(1 + x^2)y'' + 2xy' + x^2y = e^x$, $y(0) = y(1) = 0$.

5.1.2. Show that the functions $\sin k\pi x$ are mutually orthogonal on the interval $[0, 1]$, that is, $\int_0^1 \sin k\pi x \sin j\pi x \, dx = 0$, $j, k = 0, 1, \ldots, j \neq k$.

5.1.3. Repeat exercise 5.1.1 for the Galerkin equations $\mathbf{Ac} = \mathbf{f}$ where $\mathbf{f}$ is given by (5.1.17), and $\mathbf{A}$ by (5.1.18).

5.1.4. Let $g(v) = e^v$.

a. For $n = 3$ and $\phi_j(x) = \sin j\pi x$, $j = 1, 2, 3$, write out explicitly the equations (5.1.20) and (5.1.22) for the two-point boundary-value problem (5.1.19).

b. Repeat part a for the basis functions $\phi_j(x) = x^j(1 - x)$, $j = 1, 2, 3$.

5.1.5. For the basis functions (5.1.5), show that the coefficients a_{ij} of (5.1.18) are

$$a_{ij} = \frac{ij\pi^2 - 1}{(i - j)^2\pi^2}[1 - \cos(i - j)\pi] + \frac{ij\pi^2 + 1}{(i + j)^2\pi^2}[1 - \cos(i + j)\pi]$$

if $i \neq j$ and $a_{ii} = -1/12 - i^2\pi^3/2 - i^2\pi^2/6 - 1/4\pi^2 i^2$.

5.2 Spline and Least-Squares Approximation

In Section 2.3, we considered the problem of approximating a function by polynomials or piecewise polynomials. In the present section, we will extend these ideas in two directions. The first is to approximate by interpolation using piecewise polynomials that have additional properties. The second is to approximate by polynomials or piecewise polynomials using a criterion other than interpolation.

Let $a \le x_1 < x_2 < \cdots < x_n \le b$ be nodes subdividing the interval $[a, b]$, and let $y_1, \ldots, y_n$ be corresponding function values. In Section 2.3, we used piecewise polynomials that matched at certain of the grid points. For example, the function of (2.3.8) was a piecewise quadratic that agreed with given data at seven nodes; it was composed of three quadratics and was continuous but failed to be differentiable at the nodes where the different quadratics met.

Now, suppose that we wish to approximate by piecewise quadratics, but we require that the approximating function be differentiable everywhere. Then, we need a different approach from that of Section 2.3. To illustrate this approach, let $n = 4$, $I_i = [x_i, x_{i+1}]$, $i = 1, 2, 3$, and

(5.2.1) $$q_i(x) = a_{i2}x^2 + a_{i1}x + a_{i0}, \qquad i = 1, 2, 3$$

Then, we will define a piecewise quadratic function q such that $q(x) = q_i(x)$ if $x \in I_i$, $i = 1, 2, 3$, as illustrated in Figure 5.1. In order that q be continuous and take on the prescribed values $\{y_i\}$ at the nodes requires that

(5.2.2) $$\begin{matrix} q_1(x_1) = y_1 & q_1(x_2) = y_2 & q_2(x_2) = y_2 \\ q_2(x_3) = y_3 & q_3(x_3) = y_3 & q_3(x_4) = y_4 \end{matrix}$$

If we also wish that q be differentiable at the nodes, then q_1' must equal q_2' at x_2, and q_2' must equal q_3' at x_3; that is,

(5.2.3) $$q_1'(x_2) = q_2'(x_2) \qquad q_2'(x_3) = q_3'(x_3)$$

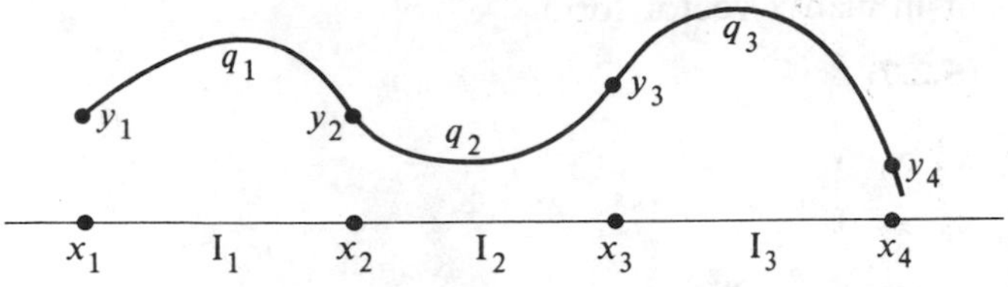

FIGURE 5.1 *A Piecewise Quadratic Function.*

The function q is determined by the nine coefficients that define q_1, q_2, and q_3. The relations (5.2.2) and (5.2.3) give only eight conditions that these nine coefficients must satisfy, and hence another relation must be specified to determine q uniquely. Usually, a value of q' at some node is specified, for example,

(5.2.4) $$q_1'(x_1) = d_1$$

where d_1 is some given value. The nine relations (5.2.2), (5.2.3), and (5.2.4) are simply a system of nine linear equations for the coefficients of the q_i, and can be solved by Gaussian elimination.

This approach is easily extended to an arbitrary number, n, of nodes. In this case, there will be $n - 1$ intervals I; and $n - 1$ quadratics q_i defined on these intervals. The conditions (5.2.2) and (5.2.3) become

(5.2.5) $$q_i(x_i) = y_i \qquad q_i(x_{i+1}) = y_{i+1}, \qquad i = 1, \ldots, n-1$$

and

(5.2.6) $$q_i'(x_{i+1}) = q_{i+1}'(x_{i+1}), \qquad i = 1, \ldots, n-2$$

These relations give $3n - 4$ linear equations for the $3n - 3$ unknown coefficients of the polynomials $q_1, \ldots, q_{n-1}$. Again, one additional condition is needed, and we can use, for example, (5.2.4). Thus, to determine the piecewise quadratic, we need to solve $3n - 3$ linear equations.

If we write out the equations (5.2.5), (5.2.6), and (5.2.4) in detail for the quadratic (5.2.1), we have

$$a_{i2}x_i^2 + a_{i1}x_i + a_{i0} = y_i, \qquad i = 1, \ldots, n-1$$

$$a_{i2}x_{i+1}^2 + a_{i1}x_{i+1} + a_{i0} = y_{i+1}, \qquad i = 1, \ldots, n-1$$

$$2a_{i2}x_{i+1} + a_{i1} = 2a_{i+1,2}x_{i+1} + a_{i+1,1}, \qquad i = 1, \ldots, n-2$$

$$2a_{12}x_1 + a_{11} = d_1$$

or in matrix-vector form,

(5.2.7)

$$
\begin{bmatrix}
x_1^2 & x_1 & 1 & & & & & & & \\
x_2^2 & x_2 & 1 & & & & & & & \\
 & & & x_2^2 & x_2 & 1 & & & & \\
 & & & x_3^2 & x_3 & 1 & & & & \\
 & & & & & & \ddots & & & \\
 & & & & & & x_{n-1}^2 & x_{n-1} & 1 & \\
 & & & & & & x_n^2 & x_n & 1 & \\
2x_2 & 1 & 0 & -2x_2 & -1 & & & & & \\
 & & & 2x_3 & 1 & 0 & -2x_3 & -1 & & \\
 & & & & & \ddots & & & & \\
 & & & & & 2x_{n-1} & 1 & 0 & -2x_{n-1} & -1 \quad 0 \\
2x_1 & 1 & & & & & & & &
\end{bmatrix}
\begin{bmatrix}
a_{12} \\ a_{11} \\ a_{10} \\ a_{22} \\ a_{21} \\ a_{20} \\ \cdot \\ \cdot \\ \cdot \\ a_{n-1,2} \\ a_{n-1,1} \\ a_{n-1,0}
\end{bmatrix}
=
\begin{bmatrix}
y_1 \\ y_2 \\ y_2 \\ y_3 \\ \vdots \\ y_{n-1} \\ y_n \\ 0 \\ 0 \\ \vdots \\ 0 \\ d_1
\end{bmatrix}
$$

This shows rather clearly the structure of this system of equations.

For the purpose of approximating solutions to differential equations—as well as for many other situations—it is useful that the approximating functions be at least two times continuously differentiable. This is not possible with piecewise quadratics unless the data are such that a single quadratic will suffice. We are thus led to consider a piecewise cubic polynomial $C(x)$, with the following properties:

(5.2.8) C is twice continuously differentiable

(5.2.9) In each interval $I_i = [x_i, x_{i+1}]$, $i = 1, \ldots, n-1$, C is a cubic polynomial

Such a function is called a *cubic spline*, the name being derived from a flexible piece of wood used by draftsmen for drawing curves.

The function C will be represented by

(5.2.10) $$C(x) = C_i(x) = a_{i3}x^3 + a_{i2}x^2 + a_{i1}x + a_{i0}, \qquad x \in I_i$$

The condition (5.2.8) of course implies that both C and C' are also continuous on the whole interval I. Hence, we must have

(5.2.11) $$C_{i-1}(x_i) = C_i(x_i) \qquad C'_{i-1}(x_i) = C'_i(x_i) \qquad C''_{i-1}(x_i) = C''_i(x_i), \qquad i = 2, \ldots, n-1$$

which are $3n - 6$ conditions. Since there are $4n - 4$ unknown coefficients a_{ij} to be obtained for the function C of (5.2.10), we need $n + 2$ additional conditions. Especially for the purpose of interpolation or approximation, we will require that C take on prescribed values:

(5.2.12)
$$C(x_i) = y_i, \qquad i = 1, \ldots, n$$

which gives another n conditions. We still need two more conditions, and there are various possibilities for this. The *natural cubic spline* satisfies the additional conditions

(5.2.13)
$$C''(x_1) = C''(x_n) = 0$$

It can be shown that if $\hat{C}$ is any other cubic spline that satisfies (5.2.8)/(5.2.9)/(5.2.12), and is twice continuously differentiable, then

(5.2.14)
$$\int_a^b [C''(x)]^2\,dx \le \int_a^b [\hat{C}''(x)]^2\,dx$$

We could determine C by solving the system of linear equations given by (5.2.11)–(5.2.13) for the unknown coefficients a_{ij}. However, there is another approach that will lead to a simple tridiagonal system of equations in which the unknowns are the values of the second derivatives of C at the nodes. Then, by integration, we can determine C itself. Obtaining this tridiagonal system requires a good deal of manipulation, which we now begin.

We first note that each C_i'' is linear since C_i is a cubic. Therefore, the formula for linear interpolation yields

(5.2.15)
$$C_i''(x) = C_i''(x_i) + \frac{(x - x_i)}{h_i}[C_i''(x_{i+1}) - C_i''(x_i)]$$

where we have set $h_i = x_{i+1} - x_i$, $i = 1, \ldots, n-1$. We now integrate this twice to obtain an expression for $C(x)$:

(5.2.16)
$$C_i'(x) = C_i'(x_i) + \int_{x_i}^{x} C_i''(t)\,dt = C_i'(x_i) + C_i''(x_i)(x - x_i) + \frac{[C_i''(x_{i+1}) - C_i''(x_i)]}{2h_i}(x - x_i)^2$$

(5.2.17)
$$C_i(x) = C_i(x_i) + \int_{x_i}^{x} C_i'(t)\,dt = C_i(x_i) + C_i'(x_i)(x - x_i) + C_i''(x_i)\frac{(x - x_i)^2}{2} + \frac{[C_i''(x_{i+1}) - C_i''(x_i)]}{6h_i}(x - x_i)^3$$

For convenience, we will henceforth use the notations

(5.2.18)
$$y_i = C_i(x_i) = C_{i-1}(x_i) \qquad y_i' = C_i'(x_i) = C_{i-1}'(x_i)$$
$$y_i'' = C_i''(x_i) = C_{i-1}''(x_i)$$

where we have invoked the conditions (5.2.11) and (5.2.12). Now, replace i by $i - 1$ in (5.2.16) and then set $x = x_i$ to obtain

(5.2.19)
$$y_i' = y_{i-1}' + (y_i'' + y_{i-1}'')\frac{h_{i-1}}{2}$$

Next, set $x = x_{i+1}$ in (5.2.17) and solve for y_i':

(5.2.20)
$$y_i' = \frac{y_{i+1} - y_i}{h_i} - y_{i+1}''\frac{h_i}{6} - y_i''\frac{h_i}{3}$$

Equating the right-hand sides of (5.2.19) and (5.2.20) gives

(5.2.21)
$$y_{i-1}' + (y_i'' + y_{i-1}'')\frac{h_{i-1}}{2} = \frac{y_{i+1} - y_i}{h_i} - y_{i+1}''\frac{h_i}{6} - y_i''\frac{h_i}{3}$$

We next wish to eliminate y_{i-1}' from (5.2.21). To do this, replace i by $i - 1$ in (5.2.20) and substitute the resulting expression for y_{i-1}' into (5.2.21):

$$\frac{y_i - y_{i-1}}{h_{i-1}} - y_i''\frac{h_{i-1}}{6} - y_{i-1}''\frac{h_{i-1}}{3} + (y_i'' + y_{i-1}'')\frac{h_{i-1}}{2}$$
$$= \frac{y_{i+1} - y_i}{h_i} - y_{i+1}''\frac{h_i}{6} - y_i''\frac{h_i}{3}$$

which, after rearranging, becomes

(5.2.22)
$$y_{i-1}''h_{i-1} + 2y_i''(h_i + h_{i-1}) + y_{i+1}''h_i = 6\left[\frac{y_{i+1} - y_i}{h_i} - \frac{y_i - y_{i-1}}{h_{i-1}}\right], \quad i = 2, \ldots, n-1$$

This is a system of $n - 2$ linear equations in the $n - 2$ unknowns $y_2'', \ldots, y_{n-1}''$; recall that $y_1'' = y_n'' = 0$ by the condition (5.2.13). If we set

(5.2.23)
$$\gamma_i = 6\left[\frac{y_{i+1} - y_i}{h_i} - \frac{y_i - y_{i-1}}{h_{i-1}}\right], \qquad i = 2, \ldots, n-1$$

the system (5.2.22) is of the form $\mathbf{Hy} = \boldsymbol{\gamma}$ where $\mathbf{y} = (y_2'', \ldots, y_{n-1}'')$, $\boldsymbol{\gamma} = (\gamma_2, \ldots, \gamma_{n-1})$ and

(5.2.24)
$$\mathrm{H} = \begin{bmatrix} 2(h_1 + h_2) & h_2 & & & \bigcirc \\ h_2 & 2(h_2 + h_3) & h_3 & & \\ & h_3 & \ddots & \ddots & \\ & & \ddots & \ddots & h_{n-2} \\ \bigcirc & & & h_{n-2} & 2(h_{n-2} + h_{n-1}) \end{bmatrix}$$

The matrix H is tridiagonal and clearly diagonally dominant. (It is also symmetric and positive-definite.) Hence, the system $\mathbf{Hy} = \boldsymbol{\gamma}$ can be easily and efficiently solved by Gaussian elimination with no interchanges.

After the y_i'' are computed, we still need to obtain the polynomials $C_1, \ldots, C_{n-1}$. The first derivatives y_i' at the node points can be obtained from (5.2.20) since the y_i are also known; that is,

$$\textbf{(5.2.25)} \quad y_i' = C_i'(x_i) = C_{i-1}'(x_i)$$
$$= \frac{y_{i+1} - y_i}{h_i} - y_{i+1}''\frac{h_i}{6} - y_i''\frac{h_i}{3}, \qquad i = 1, \ldots, n-1$$

Then, the C_i themselves can be computed from (5.2.17), which we write in terms of y_i, y_i', and y_i'':

$$\textbf{(5.2.26)} \quad C_i(x) = y_i + y_i'(x - x_i) + y_i''\frac{(x - x_i)^2}{2} + (y_{i+1}'' - y_i'')\frac{(x - x_i)^3}{6h_i}, \qquad i = 1, \ldots, n-1$$

Note that if we wish to evaluate C for some particular value $\hat{x}$, we first need to ascertain the interval I_i in which the point $\hat{x}$ lies and thus select the correct C_i for the evaluation.

We now give a simple example of the computation of a cubic spline. Suppose that we have the following nodes and function values:

$$x_1 = 0 \qquad x_2 = \tfrac{1}{4} \qquad x_3 = \tfrac{1}{2} \qquad x_4 = \tfrac{3}{4} \qquad x_5 = 1$$
$$y_1 = 1 \qquad y_2 = 2 \qquad y_3 = 1 \qquad y_4 = 0 \qquad y_5 = 1$$

Here, $n = 5$ and the h_i are all equal to $\frac{1}{4}$. The matrix H of (5.2.24) and the vector $\boldsymbol{\gamma}$ whose components are given by (5.2.23) are

$$\mathbf{H} = \frac{1}{4}\begin{bmatrix} 4 & 1 & 0 \\ 1 & 4 & 1 \\ 0 & 1 & 4 \end{bmatrix} \qquad \boldsymbol{\gamma} = \begin{bmatrix} -48 \\ 0 \\ 48 \end{bmatrix}$$

Hence, the quantities y_2'', y_3'', and y_4'' are obtained as the solution of the linear system

$$\begin{aligned} 4y_2'' + y_3'' \quad\quad &= -192 \\ y_2'' + 4y_3'' + y_4'' &= 0 \\ y_3'' + 4y_4'' &= 192 \end{aligned}$$

which is easily solved by elimination. Since $y_1'' = y_5'' = 0$ by the condition (5.2.13), we have

$$y_1'' = 0 \qquad y_2'' = -48 \qquad y_3'' = 0 \qquad y_4'' = 48 \qquad y_5'' = 0$$

Using these values of the y_i'', we next compute the y_i' from (5.2.25):

$$y_1' = 6 \qquad y_2' = 0 \qquad y_3' = -6 \qquad y_4' = 0$$

and with these, we obtain the cubic polynomials C_1, C_2, C_3, and C_4 from (5.2.26). This then gives the cubic spline:

$$\begin{aligned} C(x) &= C_1(x) = 1 + 6x - 32x^3, & 0 \le x \le \tfrac{1}{4} \\ &= C_2(x) = 2 - 24(x - \tfrac{1}{4})^2 + 32(x - \tfrac{1}{4})^3, & \tfrac{1}{4} \le x \le \tfrac{1}{2} \\ &= C_3(x) = 1 - 6(x - \tfrac{1}{2}) + 32(x - \tfrac{1}{2})^3, & \tfrac{1}{2} \le x \le \tfrac{3}{4} \\ &= C_4(x) = 24(x - \tfrac{3}{4})^2 - 32(x - \tfrac{3}{4})^3, & \tfrac{3}{4} \le x \le 1 \end{aligned}$$

If we wish to evaluate C at some point, say $x = 0.35$, we first note that $0.35 \in [\tfrac{1}{4}, \tfrac{1}{2}]$ and thus use C_2 for the evaluation:

$$C(0.35) = C_2(0.35) = 2 - 24(0.1)^2 + 32(0.1)^3 = 1.792$$

In Section 5.4, we will return to the collocation and Galerkin methods using cubic splines as the basis functions. In the remainder of the present section, we wish to consider another type of approximation by polynomials or other functions in which the criterion is no longer a matching of function values. This will be the method of least-squares approximation.

Recall from Section 2.3 that if $x_0, x_1, \ldots, x_n$ are $n + 1$ distinct points and f is a given function, then there is a unique polynomial p of degree n such that

$$p(x_i) = f(x_i), \qquad i = 0, \ldots, n$$

Now, suppose that f itself is a polynomial of degree n, and that we wish to determine its coefficients. Then, by the preceding interpolation result, it suffices to know f at $n + 1$ distinct points provided that the determination of the values $f(x_i)$ can be made exactly. In many situations, however, the values of f can be found only by measurements and may be in error. In this case, it is common to take many more than $n + 1$ measurements in the hope that these measurement errors will "average out." How these errors "average out" is determined by the method used to combine the measurements to obtain the coefficients of f. For statistical reasons, the method of choice is often that of least squares, and this method also enjoys an elegant mathematical simplicity.

We now assume that we have m points $x_1, \ldots, x_m$ where $m \ge n + 1$ and at least $n + 1$ of the points are distinct. Let $f_1, \ldots, f_m$ be approximate values of a function f at the points $x_1, \ldots, x_m$. Then, we wish to find a polynomial $p(x) = a_0 + a_1 x + \cdots + a_n x^n$ such that

(5.2.27)
$$\sum_{i=1}^{m} [f_i - p(x_i)]^2$$

is a minimum over all polynomials of degree n. That is, we wish to find $a_0, a_1, \ldots, a_n$ so that the sum of the squares of the "errors" $f_i - p(x_i)$ is minimized.

The simplest case of such a problem is when $n = 0$, when p is simply a constant. Suppose, for example, that we have m measurements $w_1, \ldots, w_m$ of the weight of some object, where the measurements are obtained from m different scales. Here, the points $x_1, \ldots, x_m$ are all identical and, indeed, do not enter explicitly. If we invoke the least-squares principle, then we wish to minimize

$$g(w) = \sum_{i=1}^{m} (w_i - w)^2$$

From the calculus, we know that g takes on a (relative) minimum at a point $\hat{w}$ such that $g'(\hat{w}) = 0$ and $g''(w) \geq 0$. Since

$$g'(w) = -2 \sum_{i=1}^{m} (w_i - w) \qquad g''(w) = 2m$$

it follows that

$$\hat{w} = \frac{1}{m} \sum_{i=1}^{m} w_i$$

and because this is the only solution of $g'(w) = 0$, it must be the unique point that minimizes g. Thus, the least-squares approximation to w is simply the average of the measurements $w_1, \ldots, w_m$.

The next-simplest situation is if we use a linear polynomial $p(x) = a_0 + a_1 x$. Problems of this type arise very frequently under the assumption that our data are obeying some linear relationship. In this case, the function (5.2.27) is

(5.2.28)
$$g(a_0, a_1) = \sum_{i=1}^{m} (f_i - a_0 - a_1 x_i)^2$$

which we wish to minimize over the coefficients a_0 and a_1. Again from the calculus, we know that a necessary condition for g to be minimized is that the relations

$$\frac{\partial g}{\partial a_0} = -2 \sum_{i=1}^{m} (f_i - a_0 - a_1 x_i) = 0$$

$$\frac{\partial g}{\partial a_1} = -2 \sum_{i=1}^{m} x_i (f_i - a_0 - a_1 x_i) = 0$$

hold. Collecting coefficients of a_0 and a_1 gives the system of two linear equations

$$m a_0 + \left(\sum_{i=1}^{m} x_i\right) a_1 = \sum_{i=1}^{m} f_i \qquad \left(\sum_{i=1}^{m} x_i\right) a_0 + \left(\sum_{i=1}^{m} x_i^2\right) a_1 = \sum_{i=1}^{m} x_i f_i$$

for the unknowns a_0 and a_1, which can be solved explicitly by

$$a_0 = \frac{\sum x_i^2 \sum f_i - \sum x_i f_i \sum x_i}{m \sum x_i^2 - (\sum x_i)^2} \qquad a_1 = \frac{m \sum x_i f_i - \sum f_i \sum x_i}{m \sum x_i^2 - (\sum x_i)^2}$$

where the summations are all from 1 to m.

For polynomials of degree n, we wish to minimize the function of (5.2.27); that is, we wish to minimize

(5.2.29) $$g(a_0, a_1, \ldots, a_n) = \sum_{i=1}^{m} (a_0 + a_1 x_i + \cdots + a_n x_i^n - f_i)^2$$

Proceeding as in the $n = 2$ case, we know from the calculus that a necessary condition for g to be minimized is that the first partial derivatives all vanish:

$$\frac{\partial g}{\partial a_j}(a_0, a_1, \ldots, a_n) = 0, \quad j = 0, 1, \ldots, n$$

Writing these partial derivatives out explicitly gives the conditions

(5.2.30) $$\sum_{i=1}^{m} x_i^j (a_0 + a_1 x_i + \cdots + a_n x_i^n - f_i) = 0, \qquad j = 0, 1, \ldots, n$$

which is a system of $n + 1$ linear equations in the $n + 1$ unknowns $a_0, a_1, \ldots, a_n$; these equations are usually known as the *normal equations*. Collecting the coefficients of the a_i and rewriting (5.2.30) in matrix-vector form gives the system

(5.2.31) $$\begin{bmatrix} m & \sum x_i & \sum x_i^2 & \cdots & \sum x_i^n \\ \sum x_i & & & & \cdot \\ \sum x_i^2 & & & & \cdot \\ \cdot & & & & \cdot \\ \cdot & & & & \\ \cdot & & & & \\ \sum x_i^n & & \cdots & & \sum x_i^{2n} \end{bmatrix} \begin{bmatrix} a_0 \\ a_1 \\ \cdot \\ \cdot \\ \cdot \\ \\ a_n \end{bmatrix} = \begin{bmatrix} \sum f_i \\ \sum x_i f_i \\ \cdot \\ \cdot \\ \cdot \\ \\ \sum x_i^n f_i \end{bmatrix}$$

where all summations are from 1 to m.

We note that the system (5.2.31) can be rewritten in the form

(5.2.32) $$E^T E\mathbf{a} = E^T \mathbf{f}$$

where

(5.2.33) $$E = \begin{bmatrix} 1 & x_1 & \cdots & x_1^n \\ 1 & x_2 & \cdots & x_2^n \\ \cdot & & & \cdot \\ \cdot & & & \cdot \\ \cdot & & & \cdot \\ 1 & x_m & \cdots & x_m^n \end{bmatrix} \qquad \mathbf{a} = \begin{bmatrix} a_0 \\ a_1 \\ \cdot \\ \cdot \\ \cdot \\ a_n \end{bmatrix} \qquad \mathbf{f} = \begin{bmatrix} f_1 \\ f_2 \\ \cdot \\ \cdot \\ \cdot \\ f_m \end{bmatrix}$$

The matrix E is $m \times (n + 1)$ and is of Vandermonde type. Under the assumption that at least $n + 1$ of the points x_i are distinct, it can be shown that E has rank $n + 1$ and, therefore, the matrix $E^T E$ is positive-definite. This implies, in particular, that the solution of the system

(5.2.31) gives the unique minimizing point of the function g of (5.2.29); that is, the least-squares problem has a unique solution.

The preceding procedure extends immediately to more general least-squares problems in which the approximating function is not necessarily a polynomial. Let $\phi_0, \phi_1, \ldots, \phi_n$ be given functions of a single variable; let $w_1, \ldots, w_m$ be given positive numbers called *weights*; and let $x_1, \ldots, x_n$ and $f_1, \ldots, f_m$ be as before. Then, the general linear least-squares approximation problem is to find numbers $a_0, a_1, \ldots, a_n$ such that

(5.2.34) $$g(a_0, a_1, \ldots, a_n) \equiv \sum_{i=1}^{m} w_i[a_0\phi_0(x_i) + a_1\phi_1(x_i) + \cdots + a_n\phi_n(x_i) - f_i]^2$$

is minimized. If $w_1 = w_2 = \cdots = w_m = 1$ and $\phi_j(x) = x^j$, then g is simply the function of (5.2.29). Other common choices for the "basis functions" ϕ_i are

$$\phi_j(x) = \sin j\pi x, \qquad j = 0, 1, \ldots, n$$

and

$$\phi_j(x) = e^{\alpha_j x}, \qquad j = 0, 1, \ldots, n$$

where the α_j are given numbers.

The weights w_i are usually used to assign greater or lesser emphasis to the terms of (5.2.34). For example, if the f_i are measurements and we have great confidence in, say, $f_1, \ldots, f_{10}$, but rather little confidence in the rest, we might set $w_1 = w_2 = \cdots = w_{10} = 5$ and $w_{11} = \cdots = w_m = 1$.

We can proceed exactly as before in obtaining the normal equations for (5.2.34). The first partial derivatives of g are

$$\frac{\partial g}{\partial a_j} = 2\sum_{i=1}^{m} w_i\phi_j(x_i)[a_0\phi_0(x_i) + a_1\phi_1(x_1) + \ldots + a_n\phi_n(x_i) - f_i]$$

Setting these equal to zero, collecting coefficients of the a_i, and writing the resulting linear system in matrix-vector form gives the system

(5.2.35)

$$\begin{bmatrix} \sum w_i\phi_0(x_i)\phi_0(x_i) & \sum w_i\phi_1(x_i)\phi_0(x_i) & \cdots & \sum w_i\phi_n(x)\phi_0(x_i) \\ \sum w_i\phi_0(x_i)\phi_1(x_i) & \cdots & & \\ \cdot & & & \cdot \\ \cdot & & & \cdot \\ \cdot & & & \cdot \\ \sum w_i\phi_0(x_i)\phi_n(x_i) & \cdots & & \sum w_i\phi_n(x_i)\phi_n(x_i) \end{bmatrix} \begin{bmatrix} a_0 \\ a_1 \\ \cdot \\ \cdot \\ \cdot \\ a_n \end{bmatrix} = \begin{bmatrix} \sum w_i\phi_0(x_i)f_i \\ \sum w_i\phi_1(x_i)f_i \\ \cdot \\ \cdot \\ \cdot \\ \sum w_i\phi_n(x_i)f_i \end{bmatrix}$$

where the summations are all from 1 to m. As before, we can rewrite this system in the form (5.2.32), where now

(5.2.36)

$$E = \begin{bmatrix} \sqrt{w_1}\phi_0(x_1) & \sqrt{w_1}\phi_1(x_1) & \cdots & \sqrt{w_1}\phi_n(x_1) \\ \sqrt{w_2}\phi_0(x_2) & \sqrt{w_2}\phi_1(x_2) & \cdots & \sqrt{w_2}\phi_n(x_2) \\ \vdots & & & \vdots \\ \sqrt{w_m}\phi_0(x_m) & & \cdots & \sqrt{w_m}\phi_n(x_m) \end{bmatrix} \qquad \mathbf{f} = \begin{bmatrix} \sqrt{w_1}f_1 \\ \sqrt{w_2}f_2 \\ \vdots \\ \sqrt{w_m}f_m \end{bmatrix}$$

In order that there be a unique solution to the system (5.2.35), it is necessary and sufficient that the matrix E of (5.2.36) have rank $n + 1$. This, in turn, imposes conditions on both the points $x_1, \ldots, x_m$ and the functions $\phi_0, \phi_1, \ldots, \phi_n$.

The normal equations are very useful for theoretical purposes, or for computation purposes when n is small. But they have a tendency to become very ill-conditioned for n at all large, even $n \geq 5$. We now describe an alternative approach to computing the least-squares polynomial by means of orthogonal polynomials.

Let $q_0, q_1, \ldots, q_n$ be polynomials of degree $0, 1, \ldots, n$, respectively. Then, we will say that the q_i are mutually *orthogonal* with respect to the points $x_1, \ldots, x_m$ if

(5.2.37) $$\sum_{i=1}^{m} q_k(x_i)q_j(x_i) = 0, \qquad k, j = 0, 1, \ldots, n, \; k \neq j$$

We shall return shortly to the question of how one obtains such a set of orthogonal polynomials. For the moment, assume that we have them and take $\phi_i = q_i$, $i = 0, 1, \ldots, n$, in the normal equations (5.2.35), in which the weights w_i are all equal to 1. Then, because of (5.2.37), all elements of the coefficient matrix of (5.2.35) off the main diagonal are zero, and the system of equations reduces to

$$\sum_{i=1}^{m} [q_k(x_i)]^2 a_k = \sum_{i=1}^{m} q_k(x_i) f_i, \qquad k = 0, 1, \ldots, n$$

so

(5.2.38) $$a_k = \frac{\sum_{i=1}^{m} q_k(x_i) f_i}{\sum [q_k(x_i)]^2}, \qquad k = 0, 1, \ldots, n$$

Thus, the least-squares polynomial is

(5.2.39) $$q(x) = \sum_{k=0}^{n} a_k q_k(x)$$

An obvious question is whether the polynomial q of (5.2.39) is the same as the polynomal obtained from the normal equations (5.2.31). The answer is yes, under our standard assumption that at least $n + 1$ of the points x_i are distinct. This follows from the fact that—as observed earlier—the least-squares problem has a unique solution; that is, there is a unique polynomial of degree n or less that minimizes (5.2.27). Therefore, to show that the polynomial q of (5.2.39) is this same minimizing polynomial, it suffices to show that any polynomial of degree n can be written as a linear combination of the q_i; that is, given a polynomial

(5.2.40) $$\hat{p}(x) = b_0 + b_1 x + \cdots + b_n x^n$$

we can find coefficients $c_0, c_1, \ldots, c_n$ so that

(5.2.41) $$\hat{p}(x) = c_0 q_0(x) + c_1 q_1(x) + \cdots + c_n q_n(x)$$

This can be done as follows. Let

$$q_i(x) = d_{i,0} + d_{i,1} x + \cdots + d_{i,i} x^i, \qquad i = 0, 1, \ldots, n$$

where $d_{i,i} \neq 0$. Equating the right-hand sides of (5.2.40) and (5.2.41) gives

$$\begin{aligned} & b_0 + b_1 x + \cdots + b_n x^n \\ & \qquad = c_0 d_{0,0} + c_1(d_{1,0} + d_{1,1}x) + \cdots + c_n(d_{n,0} + \cdots + d_{n,n}x^n) \end{aligned}$$

and equating coefficients of powers of x then gives

(5.2.42) $$\begin{aligned} b_n &= c_n d_{n,n} \\ b_{n-1} &= c_n d_{n-1} + c_{n-1} d_{n-1,n-1} \\ &\;\;\vdots \\ b_0 &= c_n d_{0,0} + c_{n-1} d_{n-1,0} + \cdots + c_0 d_{0,0} \end{aligned}$$

which are necessary and sufficient conditions that the polynomials of (5.2.40) and (5.2.41) be identical. Given $b_0, b_1, \ldots, b_n$, (5.2.42) is a triangular linear system of equations for the c_i and is solvable since $d_{i,i} \neq 0$, $i = 0, 1, \ldots, n$. Hence, the polynomial of (5.2.39) is just another representation of the unique least-squares polynomial obtained by solving the normal equations (5.2.31).

The use of orthogonal polynomials reduces the normal equations to a trivial diagonal system of equations. However, the burden is now shifted to the computation of the q_i. There are several possible ways to construct orthogonal polynomials, but we will describe only one, which is particularly suitable for computation.

Let

(5.2.43) $$q_0(x) \equiv 1 \qquad q_1(x) \equiv x - \alpha_1$$

where α_1 is to be determined so that q_0 and q_1 are orthogonal with respect to the x_i. Thus, we must have

$$0 = \sum_{i=1}^{m} q_0(x_i)q_1(x_i) = \sum_{i=1}^{m} (x_i - \alpha_1) = \sum_{i=1}^{m} x_i - m\alpha_1$$

so that

$$\alpha_1 = \frac{1}{m}\sum_{i=1}^{m} x_i \tag{5.2.44}$$

Now, let

$$q_2(x) = xq_1(x) - \alpha_2 q_1(x) - \beta_1$$

where α_2 and β_1 are to be determined so that q_2 is orthogonal to both q_0 and q_1; that is,

$$\sum_{i=1}^{m} [x_i q_1(x_i) - \alpha_2 q_1(x_i) - \beta_1] = 0$$

$$\sum_{i=1}^{m} [x_i q_1(x_i) - \alpha_2 q_1(x_i) - \beta_1] q_1(x_i) = 0$$

Recalling that $\sum q_1(x_i) = 0$, these relations reduce to

$$\sum_{i=1}^{m} x_i q_1(x_i) - m\beta_1 = 0 \qquad \sum_{i=1}^{m} x_i[q_1(x_i)]^2 - \alpha_2 \sum_{i=1}^{m} [q_1(x_i)]^2$$

so that

$$\beta_1 = \frac{1}{m}\sum_{i=1}^{m} x_i q_1(x_i) \qquad \alpha_2 = \frac{\sum_{i=1}^{m} x_i[q_1(x_i)]^2}{\sum_{i=1}^{m} [q_1(x_i)]^2}$$

The computation for the remaining q_i proceeds in an analogous fashion. Assume that we have determined $q_0, q_1, \ldots, q_j$ and set

$$q_{j+1}(x) = xq_j(x) - \alpha_{j+1}q_j(x) - \beta_j q_{j-1}(x) \tag{5.2.45}$$

where α_{j+1} and β_j are to be determined from the orthogonality requirements. In particular, we must have

$$\sum_{i=1}^{m} q_{j+1}(x_i)q_j(x_i) = 0 \qquad \sum_{i=1}^{m} q_{j+1}(x_i)q_{j-1}(x_i) = 0 \tag{5.2.46}$$

Note that if these two relations are satisfied, then q_{j+1} must also be orthogonal to all the previous q_k, $k < j - 1$, since by (5.2.45),

$$\sum_{i=1}^{m} q_{j+1}(x_i)q_k(x_i) = \sum_{i=1}^{m} x_i q_j(x_i)q_k(x_i) - \alpha_{j+1}\sum_{i=1}^{m} q_j(x_i)q_k(x_i) - \beta_j \sum_{j=1}^{m} q_{j-1}(x_i)q_k(x_i) \tag{5.2.47}$$

The last two terms in (5.2.47) are zero by assumption, whereas $xq_k(x)$ is a polynomial of degree $k + 1$ and can be expressed as a linear combination of $q_0, q_1, \ldots, q_{k+1}$. Hence, the first term on the right-hand side of (5.2.47) is zero also.

Returning to the conditions (5.2.46) and putting in q_{j+1} from (5.2.45) leads to the expressions

(5.2.48)
$$\alpha_{j+1} = \frac{\sum_{i=1}^{m} x_i [q_j(x_i)]^2}{\sum_{i=1}^{m} [q_j(x_i)]^2}$$

(5.2.49)
$$\beta_j = \frac{\sum_{i=1}^{m} x_i q_j(x_i) q_{j-1}(x_i)}{\sum_{i=1}^{m} [q_{j-1}(x_i)]^2}$$

for α_{j+1} and β_j. Note that the denominator in (5.2.48) can vanish only if $q_j(x_i) = 0$, $i = 1, \ldots, m$. But since at least $n + 1$ of the x_i are assumed to be distinct, and $j \le n$, this would imply that q_j is identically zero, which contradicts the definition of q_j. Hence, the denominator cannot vanish.

We can summarize the orthogonal polynomial algorithm as follows:

1. Set $q_0(x) \equiv 1$, $q_1(x) = x - \frac{1}{m} \sum_{i=1}^{m} x_i$.
2. For $j = 1, \ldots, n - 1$, set $q_{j+1}(x) = xq_j(x) - \alpha_{j+1}q_j(x) - \beta_j q_{j-1}(x)$, where α_{j+1} is given by (5.2.48), and β_j by (5.2.49).
3. Compute the coefficients $a_0, a_1, \ldots, a_n$ of the least-squares polynomial $a_0q_0(x) + a_1q_1(x) + \cdots + a_nq_n(x)$ by (5.2.38).

As mentioned previously, this approach is to be preferred numerically because it avoids the necessity of solving the (possibly) ill-conditioned system (5.2.31). Another advantage is that we are able to build up the least-squares polynomial degree by degree. For example, if we do not really know what degree polynomial we wish to use, we might start with a first-degree polynomial, then a second-degree, and so on, until we obtain a fit that we believe is suitable. With the orthogonal polynomial algorithm, the coefficients a_i are independent of n, and as soon as we compute q_j, we can compute a_j, and hence the least-squares polynomial of degree j.

We now give a simple example, using again the data

$$\begin{array}{ccccc} x_1 = 0 & x_2 = \frac{1}{4} & x_3 = \frac{1}{2} & x_4 = \frac{3}{4} & x_5 = 1 \\ y_1 = 1 & y_2 = 2 & y_3 = 1 & y_4 = 0 & y_5 = 1 \end{array}$$

which we used in the example of a cubic spline. Since there are five points x_i, these data will uniquely determine a fourth-degree interpolating polynomial. Let us compute the linear and quadratic least-squares polynomials by both the normal equations and the orthogonal polynomial approaches.

To compute the linear least-squares polynomial by the normal-equations approach, we will need the following quantities:

$$\textbf{(5.2.50)} \quad \sum_{i=1}^{5} x_i = \tfrac{5}{2} \qquad \sum_{i=1}^{5} x_i^2 = \tfrac{15}{8} \qquad \sum_{i=1}^{5} f_i = 5 \qquad \sum_{i=1}^{5} x_i f_i = 2$$

Then, the coefficients a_0 and a_1—as given previously—are

$$a_0 = \frac{(\frac{15}{8})(5) - (2)(\frac{5}{2})}{(5)(\frac{15}{8}) - (\frac{25}{4})} = \frac{7}{5} \qquad a_1 = \frac{(5)(2) - (5)(\frac{5}{2})}{(5)(\frac{15}{8}) - (\frac{25}{4})} = \frac{-4}{5}$$

Thus, the linear least-squares polynomial for these data is

$$\textbf{(5.2.51)} \qquad p_1(x) = \tfrac{7}{5} - \tfrac{4}{5}x$$

If we compute the same polynomial by orthogonal polynomials, the polynomial is given in the form

$$\textbf{(5.2.52)} \qquad a_0 q_0(x) + a_1 q_1(x) = a_0 + a_1(x - \alpha_1)$$

where a_0 and a_1 are given by (5.2.38), and α_1 by (5.2.44):

$$a_0 = \frac{\sum_{i=1}^{5} f_i}{5} = 1 \qquad \alpha_1 = \frac{\sum x_i}{5} = \frac{1}{2}$$

$$a_1 = \frac{\sum (x_i - \frac{1}{2}) f_i}{\sum (x_i - \frac{1}{2})^2} = \frac{\sum x_i f_i - \frac{1}{2}\sum f_i}{\sum x_i^2 - \sum x_i + \frac{5}{4}} = \frac{2 - \frac{5}{2}}{\frac{15}{8} - \frac{5}{2} + \frac{5}{4}} = \frac{-4}{5}$$

Thus, the polynomial (5.2.52) is $1 - \frac{4}{5}(x - \frac{1}{2})$, which is, as expected, identical to (5.2.51).

To compute the least-squares quadratic polynomial by the normal equations, we need to solve the system (5.2.31) for $n = 2$:

$$\begin{bmatrix} m & \sum x_i & \sum x_i^2 \\ \sum x_i & \sum x_i^2 & \sum x_i^3 \\ \sum x_i^2 & \sum x_i^3 & \sum x_i^4 \end{bmatrix} \begin{bmatrix} a_0 \\ a_1 \\ a_2 \end{bmatrix} = \begin{bmatrix} \sum f_i \\ \sum x_i f_i \\ \sum x_i^2 f_i \end{bmatrix}$$

which, for our data is:

$$\begin{bmatrix} 640 & 320 & 240 \\ 320 & 240 & 200 \\ 240 & 200 & 177 \end{bmatrix} \begin{bmatrix} a_0 \\ a_1 \\ a_2 \end{bmatrix} = \begin{bmatrix} 640 \\ 256 \\ 176 \end{bmatrix}$$

The solution of this system is

(5.2.53) $$a_0 = \tfrac{7}{5} \qquad a_1 = \tfrac{-4}{5} \qquad a_2 = 0$$

Thus, the best least-squares quadratic polynomial approximation turns out to be the linear least-squares polynomial; that is, no improvement to the linear approximation can be made by adding a quadratic term. That (5.2.53) is correct is verified by computing the least-squares quadratic by orthogonal polynomials. The orthogonal-polynomial representation will be

$$a_0q_0(x) + a_1q_1(x) + a_2q_2(x) = \tfrac{7}{5} - \tfrac{4}{5}x + a_2[x(x - \tfrac{1}{2}) - \alpha_2(x - \tfrac{1}{2}) - \beta_1]$$

where α_2 and β_1 are computed from (5.2.48) and (5.2.49) as

$$\alpha_2 = \frac{\sum x_i(x_i - \frac{1}{2})^2}{\sum (x_i - \frac{1}{2})^2} = \tfrac{1}{2} \qquad \beta_1 = \tfrac{1}{5}\sum x_i(x_i - \tfrac{1}{2}) = \tfrac{1}{8}$$

Thus, $q_2(x) = x^2 - x - \frac{1}{8}$, and from (5.2.38), we find that $a_2 = 0$.

Supplementary Discussion and References: 5.2

For further reading on spline functions, see Prenter [1975] and deBoor [1978]. In particular, splines using polynomials of degree higher than cubic are sometimes very useful and are developed in these references.

An alternative approach to solving the least-squares polynomial problem is to deal directly with the system of linear equations E**a** = **f**, where E and **f** are given in (5.2.33). This is an $m \times (n + 1)$ system, where m is usually greater than $n + 1$; hence, the matrix E is not square. Techniques for dealing with this type of system are given, for example, in Stewart [1973] and Dongarra et al. [1979].

EXERCISES 5.2

5.2.1. Assume that f is a given function for which the following values are known: $f(1) = 2$, $f(2) = 3$, $f(3) = 5$, $f(4) = 3$.

a. Find the interpolating polynomial of degree 3 for these data and write it in the form $a_0 + a_1x + a_2x^2 + a_3x^3$.

b. Find the quadratic spline function for these data that satisfies the condition $q'(1) = 0$. (*Hint*: Start from the left.)

c. Find the cubic spline function for these data that satisfies $C''(1) = 6$, $C''(4) = -9$. (*Hint*: Try the polynomial of part a.)

5.2.2. Reorder the unknowns in the system of equations (5.2.7) so as to obtain a coefficient matrix with as small a bandwidth as you can.

5.2.3. Use (5.2.11)–(5.2.13) to write out the system of equations for the unknown coefficients a_{ij} of the cubic spline (5.2.9).

5.2.4. For the function of exercise 5.2.1, find the cubic spline C that satisfies $C'(1) = 1$, $C'(4) = -1$, rather than the condition (5.2.13). (*Hint*: Think.)

5.2.5. Write a computer program to obtain the natural cubic spline for a given set of nodes $x_1 < \cdots < x_n$ and corresponding function values $y_1, \ldots, y_n$ by first solving the tridiagonal system with the coefficient matrix (5.2.24) and then using (5.2.25) and (5.2.26). Also write a program for evaluating this cubic spline at a given value x. Test your program on the example given in the text.

5.2.6. For the data of exercise 5.2.1, find the constant, linear, and quadratic least-squares polynomials by both the normal-equation and orthogonal-polynomial approaches.

5.2.7. Write a computer program to obtain the least-squares polynomial of degree n using $m \geq n + 1$ data points by the orthogonal-polynomial approach. Test your program on the polynomials of exercise 5.2.6.

5.3 Numerical Integration

The Galerkin method described in Section 5.1 requires the evaluation of definite integrals of the form

$$I(f) = \int_a^b f(x)\,dx$$

and the need to evaluate such integrals also arises in a number of other problems. The integrand, $f(x)$, may be given in one of three ways:

1. An explicit formula for $f(x)$ is given; for example, $f(x) = \sin xe^{-x^2}$.
2. The function $f(x)$ is not given explicitly but can be computed for any value of x in the interval $[a, b]$, usually by means of a given computer program.
3. A table of values $\{x_i, f(x_i)\}$ is given for a fixed, finite set of points x_i in the interval.

Functions in the first category are sometimes amenable to methods of symbolic computation, either by hand or by computer systems. The integrals of functions that fall into the second and third categories—as well as the first category if symbolic methods are not used—are usually

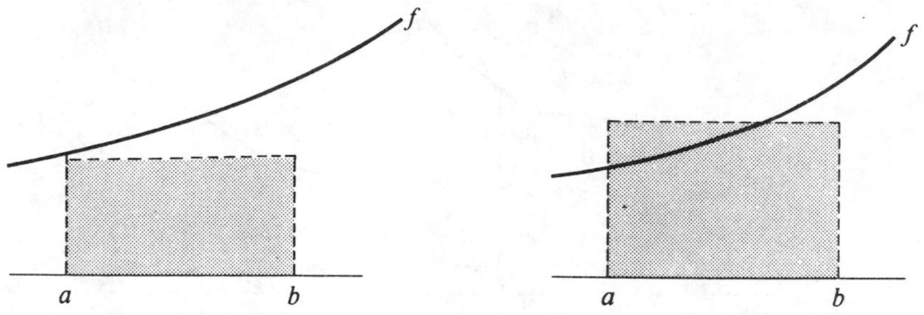

(a) Rectangle rule (b) Midpoint rule

FIGURE 5.2

approximated by numerical methods; such methods are called *quadrature rules* and are derived by approximating the function $f(x)$ by some other function, $\tilde{f}(x)$, whose integral is relatively easy to evaluate. Any class of simple functions may be used to approximate $f(x)$, such as polynomials, piecewise polynomials, and trigonometric, exponential, or logarithmic functions. The choice of the class of functions used may depend on some particular properties of the integrand but the most common choice, which we will use here, is polynomials.

The simplest polynomial is a constant. In the *rectangle rule*, f is approximated by its value at the end point a (or, alternatively, at b); that is,

(5.3.1) $$I(f) \doteq R(f) = (b - a)f(a)$$

We could also approximate f by another constant obtained by evaluating f at a point interior to the interval; the most common choice is $(a + b)/2$, the center of the interval, which gives the *midpoint rule*

(5.3.2) $$I(f) \doteq M(f) = (b - a)f\left(\frac{a + b}{2}\right)$$

The rectangle and midpoint rules are illustrated in Figure 5.2.

The next simplest polynomial is a linear function. If it is chosen so that it agrees with f at the end points a and b, then a trapezoid is formed, as illustrated in Figure 5.3. The area of this trapezoid—the integral of the linear function—is the approximation to the integral of f and is given by

(5.3.3) $$I(f) \doteq T(f) = \frac{(b - a)}{2}[f(a) + f(b)]$$

This is known as the *trapezoid rule*.

To obtain one further formula, we next approximate f by an interpolating quadratic polynomial that agrees with f at the end points a

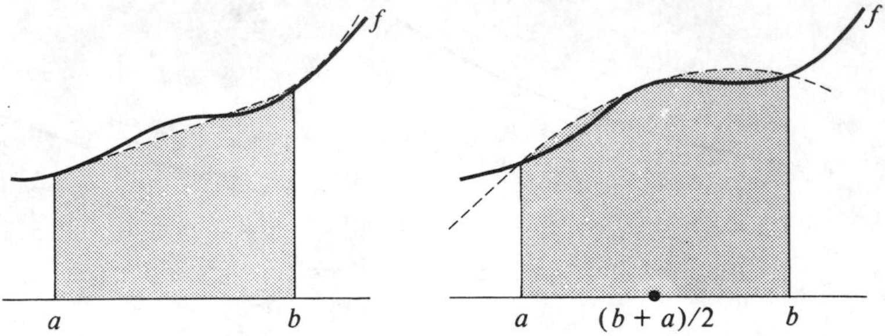

(a) Trapezoid rule (b) Simpson's rule

FIGURE 5.3

and b and the midpoint $(a + b)/2$. The integral of this quadratic is given by (see exercise 5.3.1)

$$I(f) \doteq S(f) = \frac{(b-a)}{6}\left[f(a) + 4f\left(\frac{a+b}{2}\right) + f(b)\right] \tag{5.3.4}$$

which is *Simpson's rule* and is illustrated in Figure 5.3. We note that Simpson's rule may also be viewed as a linear combination of one-third of the trapezoid rule and two-thirds of the midpoint rule since

$$\frac{1}{6}\left[f(a) + 4f\left(\frac{a+b}{2}\right) + f(b)\right] = \frac{1}{3}\left[\frac{f(a) + f(b)}{2}\right] + \frac{2}{3}f\left(\frac{a+b}{2}\right)$$

We can continue the preceding method of generating quadrature formulas by using polynomials of still higher degree. The interval $[a, b]$ is divided by m equally spaced points, an interpolating polynomial of degree $m + 1$ is constructed to agree with f at these m points plus the two end points, and this polynomial is then integrated from a to b to give an approximation to the integral. Such quadrature formulas are called the *Newton–Cotes formulas* (See the Supplementary Discussion.)

We consider next the error made in using the quadrature rules that have been described. In all cases, f is approximated by an interpolating polynomial p over the interval $[a, b]$ and $\int_a^b p(x)\,dx$ is the approximation to the integral. Hence, the error in this approximation is simply

$$E = \int_a^b [f(x) - p(x)]\,dx \tag{5.3.5}$$

By the basic interpolation error theorem 2.3.2, this can be written as

$$E = \frac{1}{(n+1)!}\int_a^b (x - x_0)\cdots(x - x_n)f^{(n+1)}(z(x))\,dx \tag{5.3.6}$$

where $x_0, x_1, \ldots, x_n$ are the interpolation points, and $z(x)$ is a point in the interval $[a, b]$ that depends on x. We now apply (5.3.6) to the specific cases of interest.

For the rectangle rule (5.3.1), $n = 0$ and $x_0 = a$; hence, (5.3.6) becomes

(5.3.7) $$|E_R| = \left|\int_a^b (x-a)f'(z(x))\,dx\right| \le M_1 \int_a^b (x-a)\,dx = \frac{M_1}{2}(b-a)^2$$

where $M_1 = \max\limits_{a \le x \le b} |f'(x)|$. This error bound would be the same if the other end point, b, were used instead of a in the rectangle rule. Note that this error will not be small unless M_1 is small, which means that f is close to constant, or the length of the interval is small; we shall return to this point later when we discuss the practical use of these quadrature formulas.

For the trapezoid rule (5.3.3), $n = 1$, $x_0 = a$, and $x_1 = b$. Hence, again applying (5.3.6), we have

(5.3.8) $$|E_T| = \frac{1}{2}\left|\int_a^b (x-a)(x-b)f''(z(x))\,dx\right| \le \frac{M_2}{12}(b-a)^3$$

where $M_2 = \max\limits_{a \le x \le b} |f''(x)|$.

Consider now the midpoint rule (5.3.2), in which $n = 0$ and $x_0 = (a+b)/2$. If we apply (5.3.6) and proceed as in (5.3.7), we obtain

(5.3.9) $$|E_M| = \left|\int_a^b \left[x - \frac{(a+b)}{2}\right] f'(z(x))\,dx\right| \le M_1 \int_a^b \left|x - \frac{(a+b)}{2}\right| dx$$
$$\le M_1(b-a)(b+a)$$

This, however, is not a satisfactory bound since it contains only the first power of $b - a$. To obtain the bound that we desire, we shall instead expand the integral of (5.3.5) in a Taylor series about $m = (a+b)/2$. Since the interpolating polynomial is simply the constant $p(x) = f(m)$, this gives

$$f(x) - p(x) = f'(m)(x-m) + \tfrac{1}{2}f''(z(x))(x-m)^2$$

where z is a point in the interval and depends on x. Thus, the error in the midpoint rule is

(5.3.10) $$|E_M| = \left|\int_a^b [f(x) - p(x)]\,dx\right|$$
$$= \left|\int_a^b [f'(m)(x-m)\,dx + \tfrac{1}{2}f''(z(x))(x-m)^2]\,dx\right|$$
$$\le \left|f'(m)\int_a^b (x-m)\,dx\right| + \frac{1}{2}\left|\int_a^b f''(z(x))(x-m)^2\,dx\right|$$
$$\le \frac{M_2}{24}(b-a)^3$$

since

$$\int_a^b (x - m)\,dx = 0 \qquad \int_a^b (x - m)^2\,dx = \frac{(b-a)^3}{12}$$

In a similar way, we can derive the following bound for the error in Simpson's rule (5.3.4), which we state without proof (M_4 is the bound for the fourth derivative):

(5.3.11)
$$|E_S| \le \frac{M_4}{2880}(b-a)^5$$

The error bounds that we have derived all involve powers of the length $b - a$ of the interval, and unless this length is small, the bounds will not, in general, be small. However, in practice, we will only apply these quadrature formulas to sufficiently small intervals which we obtain by subdividing the given interval $[a, b]$. Thus, we partition the interval $[a, b]$ into n subintervals $[x_{i-1}, x_i]$, $i = 1, \ldots, n$, where $x_0 = a$ and $x_n = b$. Then

$$I(f) = \int_a^b f(x)\,dx = \sum_{i=1}^{n} \int_{x_{i-1}}^{x_i} f(x)\,dx$$

If we apply the rectangle rule to each subinterval $[x_{i-1}, x_i]$, we obtain the *composite rectangle rule*

(5.3.12)
$$I(f) \doteq I_{CR}(f) = \sum_{i=1}^{n} h_i f(x_{i-1})$$

where $h_i = x_i - x_{i-1}$. Similarly, the *composite midpoint, trapezoid,* and *Simpson's rules* are obtained in the same way by applying the basic rule to each subinterval; they are given by

(5.3.13) $$I_{CM}(f) = \sum_{i=1}^{n} h_i f\left(\frac{x_i + x_{i-1}}{2}\right)$$ (Composite midpoint rule)

(5.3.14) $$I_{CT}(f) = \sum_{i=1}^{n} \frac{h_i}{2}[f(x_{i-1}) + f(x_i)]$$ (Composite trapezoid rule)

(5.3.15) $$I_{CS}(f) = \frac{1}{6}\sum_{i=1}^{n} h_i \left[f(x_{i-1}) + 4f\left(\frac{x_{i-1} + x_i}{2}\right) + f(x_i)\right]$$

(Composite Simpson's rule)

We note that the composite rules may all be viewed as approximating the integrand f on the interval $[a, b]$ by a piecewise polynomial function (see Section 2.3) and then integrating the piecewise polynomial to obtain an approximation to the integral. For the midpoint and rectangle rules, the approximating function is piecewise constant; for the trapezoid rule, it is piecewise linear, and for Simpson's rule, it is piecewise quadratic.

We can now apply the previous error bounds on each subinterval. For example, for the rectangle rule, we use (5.3.7) to obtain the following bound on the error in the composite rule:

(5.3.16)
$$E_{CR} \le \frac{M_1}{2} \sum_{i=1}^{n} h_i^2$$

Note that we have used the maximum M_1 of $|f'(x)|$ on the whole interval $[a, b]$; perhaps a better bound in (5.3.16) could be obtained if we used the maximum of $|f'(x)|$ separately on each subinterval.

In the special case that the subintervals are all of the same length, $h_i = h = (b - a)/n$, (5.3.16) becomes

(5.3.17) $$E_{CR} \le \frac{M_1}{2}(b - a)h$$ (Composite rectangle rule error)

which shows that the composite rectangle rule is a first-order method; that is, the error reduces only linearly in h. In a similar fashion, we can obtain bounds for the errors in the other composite rules by using (5.3.8), (5.3.10), and (5.3.11). The following bounds are given in the case that the intervals are all of the same length h:

(5.3.18) $$E_{CM} \le \frac{M_2}{24}(b - a)h^2$$ (Composite midpoint rule error)

(5.3.19) $$E_{CT} \le \frac{M_2}{12}(b - a)h^2$$ (Composite trapezoid rule error)

(5.3.20) $$E_{CS} \le \frac{M_4}{2880}(b - a)h^4$$ (Composite Simpson's rule error)

Thus, the composite midpoint and trapezoid rules are both second order, whereas the composite Simpson rule is fourth order. Because of its relatively high accuracy and simplicity, the composite Simpson's rule is an often-used method.

A difficulty with quadrature rules, as well as with other numerical approximations that we have encountered several times earlier, is that some choice of the step size, h_j, must be made. If the numerical integration schemes were to be used as described previously, the user would be required to specify h_j a priori. In practice, high-quality quadrature software will employ some automatic adaptive scheme that will vary the step size depending on estimates of the error obtained during the computation. The user will be required to specify an acceptable tolerance for the error, and the program will automatically specify the step size as it is computing.

Supplementary Discussion and References: 5.3

The solution at $x = b$ of the initial-value problem

$$y'(x) = f(x), \qquad y(a) = 0, \qquad a \le x \le b \tag{5.3.21}$$

is simply $y(b) = \int_a^b f(x)\,dx$. Hence, integration may be viewed as the trivial subcase of solving an initial-value problem in which the right-hand side is independent of y. Any of the methods discussed in Chapter 2 may be applied to (5.3.21), in principle. In fact, most of those methods reduce to some quadrature rule that we have discussed. For example, Euler's method is simply the composite rectangle rule, the second-order Runge–Kutta method is the composite trapezoid rule, and the fourth-order Runge–Kutta method is the composite Simpson's rule.

The Newton–Cotes formulas, mentioned in the text as being derived by integrating an interpolating polynomial of degree n, can be written in the form

$$I(f) \doteq \sum_{i=0}^{n} \alpha_i f(x_i) \tag{5.3.22}$$

where the x_i are equally spaced points in the interval $[a, b]$, with $x_0 = a$, $x_n = b$; Simpson's rule is the case $n = 2$. For $n < 7$, the coefficients α_i are all positive, but beginning with $n = 8$, certain coefficients will be negative; this has a deleterious effect on rounding error since cancellations will occur. The Newton–Cotes formulas also have the unsatisfactory theoretical property that as $n \to \infty$, convergence to the integral will not necessarily occur, even for infinitely differentiable functions.

The representation (5.3.22) provides another approach to the derivation of quadrature formulas—the *method of undetermined coefficients*. Assume first that the x_i are given. If we seek to determine the α_i so that the formula is exact for polynomials of as high a degree as possible, then in particular it must be exact for $1, x, x^2, \ldots, x^m$ where m is to be as large as possible. This means that we must have

$$\sum_{i=0}^{n} \alpha_i x_i^j = \frac{b^{j+1} - a^{j+1}}{j+1}, \qquad j = 0, 1, \ldots, m \tag{5.3.23}$$

(The right-hand sides of these relations are simply the exact integrals of the powers of x.) The relations (5.3.23) constitute a system of linear equations for the unknown coefficients. If $m = n$, then the coefficient matrix is simply the Vandermonde matrix discussed in Section 2.3. It is nonsingular (if the x_i are all distinct), and hence the C_i are uniquely determined for $m = n$. If the x_i are equally spaced, then this approach again gives the Newton–Cotes formulas.

Now, assume that we do not specify the points x_i in advance but consider them to be unknown in the relations (5.3.23). Then, if $m = 2n + 1$, (5.3.23) is a system of $2n + 2$ equations in the $2n + 2$ unknowns

$\alpha_0, \alpha_1, \ldots, \alpha_n$ and $x_0, x_1, \ldots, x_n$. Even though these equations are nonlinear, they have a solution; the resulting α_i and x_i give the *Gaussian quadrature formulas.* For example, in the case $n = 1$ on the interval $[a, b] = [-1, 1]$, the formula is

$$\int_{-1}^{1} f(x)\,dx \doteq f\left(-\frac{1}{\sqrt{3}}\right) + f\left(\frac{1}{\sqrt{3}}\right)$$

In general, the abscissas x_i of these quadrature formulas are roots of certain orthogonal polynomials. Gaussian quadrature rules are popular because of their high-order accuracy.

We remarked in the text that Simpson's rule can be viewed as a linear combination of the trapezoid and midpoint rules. By taking suitable linear combinations of the trapezoid rule for different spacings h, we can also derive higher-order quadrature formulas; this is known as *Romberg integration.* The basis for the derivation of Romberg integration is that the trapezoid approximation can be shown to satisfy

$$\textbf{(5.3.24)} \quad T(h) = I(f) + C_2h^2 + C_4h^4 + \cdots + C_{2m}h^{2m} + 0(h^{2m+2})$$

where the C_i depend only on f and the interval, and are independent of h. The relation (5.3.24) holds provided that f has $2m + 2$ derivatives. Now, define a new approximation to the integral by

$$\textbf{(5.3.25)} \qquad T_1(h) = \tfrac{1}{3}\left[4T\left(\frac{h}{2}\right) - T(h)\right]$$

The coefficients of this linear combination are chosen so that when the error in (5.3.25) is computed using (5.3.24), the coefficient of the h^2 term is zero. Thus,

$$T_1(h) = I(f) + C_4^{(1)}h^4 + \cdots + 0(h^{2m+2})$$

so T_1 is a fourth-order approximation to the integral. One can continue the process by combining $T_1(h)$ and $T_1(h/2)$ in a similar fashion to eliminate the h^4 term in the error for T_1. More generally, we can construct the triangular array

$$\begin{array}{lll} T(h) & & \\ T(h/2) & T_1(h) & \\ T(h/4) & T_1(h/2) & T_2(h) \\ \vdots & \vdots & \ddots \end{array}$$

where

$$T_k\left(\frac{h}{2^{j-1}}\right) = \frac{4^j T_{k-1}\left(\frac{h}{2^j}\right) - T_{k-1}\left(\frac{h}{2^{j-1}}\right)}{4^j - 1}$$

The elements in the ith column of this array converge to the integral at a rate depending on h^{2i}. But, provided that f is infinitely differentiable, the elements on the diagonal of the array converge at a rate that is superlinear, that is, faster than any power of h.

We have not touched at all upon several other important topics in numerical integration: techniques for handling integrands with a singularity, integrals over an infinite interval, multiple integrals, and adaptive procedures that attempt to fit the grid spacing automatically to the integrand. For a discussion of these matters as well as further reading on the topics covered in this section, see Davis and Rabinowitz [1975] and Stroud [1971].

EXERCISES 5.3

5.3.1. Write down explicitly the interpolating quadratic polynomial that agrees with f at the three points a, b, and $(a + b)/2$. Integrate this quadratic from a to b to obtain Simpson's rule (5.3.4).

5.3.2. Show that the trapezoid rule integrates any linear function exactly and that Simpson's rule integrates any cubic polynomal exactly. (*Hint*: Expand the cubic about the midpoint.)

5.3.3. Apply the rectangle, midpoint, trapezoid, and Simpson's rules to the function $f(x) = x^4$ on the interval $[0, 1]$. Compare the actual error in the approximations to the bounds given by (5.3.7), (5.3.8), (5.3.10), and (5.3.11).

5.3.4. Based on the bound (5.3.19), how small would h need to be in order to guarantee an error no larger than 10^{-6} in the composite trapezoid rule approximation for $f(x) = x^4$ on $[0, 1]$. How small for the composite Simpson's rule?

5.3.5. Write a computer program to carry out the composite trapezoid and Simpson's rules for an "arbitrary" function on the interval $[a, b]$ and with an arbitrary subdivision of $[a, b]$. Test your program on $f(x) = x^4$ on $[0, 1]$ and find the actual h needed, in the case of an equal subdivision, to achieve an error of less than 10^{-6} with the composite trapezoid rule.

5.4 The Discrete Problem Using Splines

We now return to the original problem of this chapter: for the two-point boundary-value problem

$$(p(x)v'(x))' + q(x)v(x) = f(x), \qquad 0 \le x \le 1 \tag{5.4.1}$$

and

$$v(0) = v(1) = 0 \tag{5.4.2}$$

we wish to find an approximate solution of the form

$$u(x) = \sum_{j=1}^{n} c_j\phi_j(x) \tag{5.4.3}$$

where $\phi_1, \ldots, \phi_n$ are given functions.

Recall from Section 5.1 that the collocation method for (5.4.1) requires solving the linear system of equations

$$\mathbf{Ac} = \mathbf{f} \tag{5.4.4}$$

where the elements of the matrix A are

$$a_{ij} = p(x_i)\phi_j''(x_i) + p'(x_i)\phi_j'(x_i) + q(x_i)\phi_j(x_i), \qquad i, j = 1, \ldots, n \tag{5.4.5}$$

$\mathbf{c}$ is the vector of unknown coefficients $c_1, \ldots, c_n$, $\mathbf{f}$ is the vector of values $f(x_1), \ldots, f(x_n)$, and $x_1, \ldots, x_n$ are given points in the interval $[0, 1]$. In Section 5.1, we considered the choice of the basis functions ϕ_j as either polynomials or trigonometric functions and saw that, in general, the coefficient matrix A was dense—that is, it had few zero elements—in contrast to the tridiagonal coefficient matrix that was obtained in Chapter 3 using the finite difference method. In the present section, we shall use the spline functions described in Section 5.2, and we will see that, in the simplest case, this again leads to a tridiagonal coefficient matrix.

Since the coefficients a_{ij} use $\phi_j''(x_i)$, it is necessary that the basis functions have a second derivative at the nodes $x_1, \ldots, x_n$. Thus, linear and quadratic splines will not suffice; cubic splines, however, are twice differentiable, and we will consider them first as our basis functions. We will need to choose the basis functions so that they are linearly independent in a sense to be made clear shortly. We would also like to choose them so that the coefficient matrix A has as small a bandwidth as possible. To illustrate this last point, let us attempt to make the coefficient matrix tridiagonal. Assuming that the functions p and q have no special properties, we see from (5.4.5) that this will be achieved if we can choose the ϕ_j so that

$$\phi_j''(x_i) = \phi_j'(x_i) = \phi_j(x_i) = 0, \qquad |i - j| > 1 \tag{5.4.6}$$

This, in turn, will be achieved if we could choose ϕ_i such that it vanishes identically outside the interval $[x_{i-2}, x_{i+2}]$, and if

$$\begin{aligned} \phi_i''(x_{i-2}) &= \phi_i'(x_{i-2}) = \phi_i(x_{i-2}) = 0 \\ \phi_i''(x_{i+2}) &= \phi_i'(x_{i+2}) = \phi_i(x_{i+2}) = 0 \end{aligned} \tag{5.4.7}$$

Now, recall that a cubic spline was defined by the conditions (5.2.8) and (5.2.9). These conditions, together with a specification of the function values at the node points $x_1, \ldots, x_n$, give $4n - 6$ relations to determine the $4n - 4$ unknown coefficients that define uniquely the cubic spline. In Section 5.2, we used the additional two conditions (5.2.13), which determine a natural cubic spline; however, this natural cubic spline cannot satisfy the condition (5.4.6) unless it is identically zero. However, if we do not impose the additional conditions (5.2.13), we can obtain a cubic spline that does, indeed, satisfy the conditions (5.4.6). We can write down this spline explicitly as

(5.4.8)
$$
\begin{aligned}
B_i(x) &= \frac{1}{4h^3}(x - x_{i-2})^3, && x_{i-2} \le x \le x_{i-1} \\
&= \frac{1}{4} + \frac{3}{4h}(x - x_{i-1}) + \frac{3}{4h^2}(x - x_{i-1})^2 - \frac{3}{4h^3}(x - x_{i-1})^3, && \\
& && x_{i-1} \le x \le x_i \\
&= \frac{1}{4} + \frac{3}{4h}(x_{i+1} - x) + \frac{3}{4h^2}(x_{i+1} - x)^2 - \frac{3}{4h^3}(x_{i+1} - x)^3, && \\
& && x_i \le x \le x_{i+1} \\
&= \frac{1}{4h^3}(x_{i+2} - x)^3, && x_{i+1} \le x \le x_{i+2} \\
&= 0, && \text{otherwise}
\end{aligned}
$$

where we have now assumed that the node points $x_1, \ldots, x_n$ are equally spaced with spacing h. It is straightforward (exercise 5.4.1) to verify that this function is a cubic spline with the function values

$$B_i(x_i) = 1 \qquad B_i(x_{i\pm1}) = \tfrac{1}{4}$$

and zero at the other nodes. Moreover, it satisfies the conditions (5.4.6) and (5.4.7) (exercise 5.4.1). Such a spline function, which is illustrated in Figure 5.4, is called a *cubic basis spline*, or *cubic B-spline* for short, since any cubic spline on the interval $[a, b]$ may be written as a linear combination of B-splines. More precisely, we state the following theorem without proof:

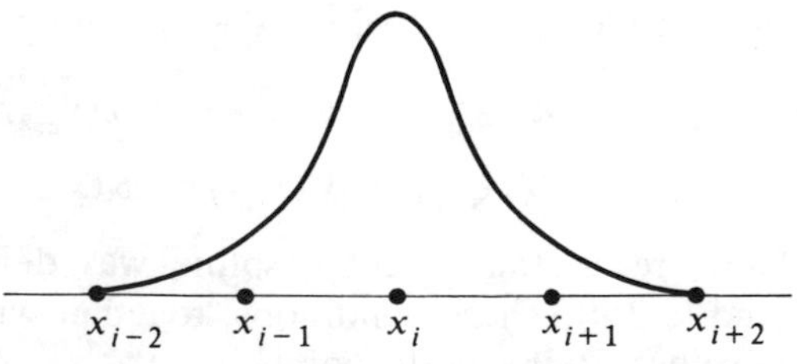

FIGURE 5.4 *A Cubic B Spline.*

THEOREM 5.4.1 *Let $C(x)$ be a cubic spline for the equally spaced node points $x_1 < \cdots < x_n$. Then, there are constants $\alpha_0, \alpha_1, \ldots, \alpha_{n+1}$ such that*

$$C(x) = \sum_{i=0}^{n+1} \alpha_i B_i(x) \tag{5.4.9}$$

Note that the functions B_0, B_1, B_n, and B_{n+1} used in (5.4.9) require the introduction of the auxiliary grid points x_{-2}, x_{-1}, x_0 and $x_{n+1}, x_{n+2}, x_{n+3}$.

We now return to the boundary-value problem (5.4.1). Again, we assume that the node points are equally spaced and that $x_0 = 0$, $x_{n+1} = 1$. We wish to take the basis functions $\phi_1, \ldots, \phi_n$ to be the B-splines $B_1, \ldots, B_n$. However, although $B_2, \ldots, B_{n-1}$ satisfy the zero boundary conditions, B_1 and B_n do not. Therefore, we take the basis functions ϕ_i to be

$$\begin{aligned} &\phi_i(x) = B_i(x), \qquad i = 2, \ldots, n-1 \\ &\phi_1(x) = 4B_1(x) - B_0(x),\ \phi_n(x) = 4B_n(x) - B_{n+1}(x) \end{aligned} \tag{5.4.10}$$

It is easy to verify from the definition (5.4.8) that $\phi_1(0) = \phi_n(1) = 0$. Moreover, it is clear that any linear combination (5.4.3) is a cubic spline for the nodes $x_0, x_1, \ldots, x_{n+1}$ and satisfies $u(0) = u(1) = 0$.

We next need to evaluate the coefficients (5.4.5), and for this, we will need B_i, B_i', and B_i'' evaluated at the nodal points. This is easily done (exercise 5.4.2), and we summarize the results in Table 5.1. Note that by the definition of the B_i, all values at node points not indicated in Table 5.1 are zero. This implies, in particular, that the coefficients a_{ij} of (5.4.5) are all zero unless $|i - j| \le 1$ or, possibly, if $i = 1$ or n. For the evaluation of the nonzero coefficients a_{ij}, we make the designations $p_i = p(x_i)$, $p_i' = p'(x_i)$, and $q_i = q(x_i)$. Then, by (5.4.5) and using Table 5.1, we have

$$\begin{aligned} a_{ii} &= p_i B_i''(x_i) + p_i' B_i'(x_i) + q_i B_i(x_i) \\ &= \frac{-3p_i}{h^2} + q_i, \qquad i = 2, \ldots, n-1 \\ a_{i,i+1} &= p_i B_{i+1}''(x_i) + p_i' B_{i+1}'(x_i) + q_i B_{i+1}(x_i) \\ &= \frac{3p_i}{2h^2} + \frac{3p_i'}{4h} + \frac{q_i}{4}, \qquad i = 1, \ldots, n-2 \\ a_{i,i-1} &= p_i B_{i-1}''(x_i) + p_i' B_{i-1}'(x_i) + q_i B_{i-1}(x_i) \\ &= \frac{3p_i}{2h^2} - \frac{3p_i'}{4h} + \frac{q_i}{4}, \qquad i = 3, \ldots, n \end{aligned} \tag{5.4.11}$$

For the remaining coefficients, we use the functions ϕ_1 and ϕ_n of (5.4.10)

TABLE 5.1

	x_{i-1}	x_i	x_{i+1}
B_i	$1/4$	1	$1/4$
B_i'	$3/(4h)$	0	$-3/(4h)$
B_i''	$3/(2h^2)$	$-3/h^2$	$3/(2h^2)$

and obtain

(5.4.12)

$$\begin{aligned}
a_{11} &= -\frac{27}{2h^2}p_1 + \frac{3}{4h}p_1' + \frac{15}{4}q_1, \\
a_{21} &= \frac{6}{h^2}p_2 - \frac{3}{h}p_2' + q_2 \\
a_{nn} &= -\frac{27}{2h^2}p_n - \frac{3}{4h}p_n' + \frac{15}{4}q_n \\
a_{n-1,n} &= \frac{6}{h^2}p_{n-1} + \frac{3}{h}p_{n-1}' + q_{n-1}
\end{aligned}$$

The components of the right-hand side $\mathbf{f}$ of the system (5.4.4) are simply $f(x_1), \ldots, f(x_n)$. Then, the solution of the system (5.4.4) with the coefficients of the tridiagonal matrix A defined by (5.4.11) and (5.4.12) yields the coefficients $c_1, \ldots, c_n$ of the linear combination (5.4.3).

We note that in the special case $p(x) \equiv 1$ and $q(x) \equiv 0$ [that is, equation (5.4.1) is simply $v''(x) = f(x)$], the coefficient matrix A reduces to

$$A = -\frac{3}{2h^2}\begin{bmatrix} 9 & -1 & & & & \\ -4 & 2 & -1 & & & \\ & -1 & 2 & \ddots & & \\ & & \ddots & \ddots & \ddots & \\ & & & \ddots & \ddots & -1 \\ & & & & -1 & 2 & -4 \\ & & & & & -1 & 9 \end{bmatrix}$$

which, aside from the factor $-3/(2h^2)$ and the elements of the first and last rows and columns, is simply the coefficient matrix obtained by the finite difference method of Section 3.2.

It can be shown that, provided the solution v of (5.4.1) is sufficiently differentiable, the preceding method has a discretization error of order h^2, the same as the finite difference method of Section 3.2 using centered differences. Higher-order accuracy can be obtained by using splines of higher degree. For example, with quintic splines, that is, functions that are four times continuously differentiable and that reduce to fifth-degree polynomials on each subinterval $[x_i, x_{i+1}]$, fourth-order accuracy can be obtained.

We now turn to the Galerkin method. Again, we will assume that we wish to approximate a solution of problem (5.4.1)/(5.4.2) by a linear combination of the form (5.4.3), where now the coefficients $c_1, \ldots, c_n$ are determined by the Galerkin criterion discussed in Section 5.1. This leads us to the solution of the linear system (5.4.4) where, from (5.1.17) and (5.1.18),

$$\textbf{(5.4.13)} \quad a_{ij} = -\int_0^1 p(x)\phi_i'(x)\phi_j'(x)\,dx + \int_0^1 q(x)\phi_i(x)\phi_j(x)\,dx, \qquad i, j = 1, \ldots, n$$

and

$$\textbf{(5.4.14)} \qquad f_i = \int_0^1 f(x)\phi_i(x)\,dx, \qquad i = 1, \ldots, n$$

For the basis functions, we will again use piecewise polynomials. As the simplest possibility, let us first consider piecewise linear functions. In particular, assuming as before that the grid points $0 = x_0, x_1, \ldots, x_n, x_{n+1} = 1$, are equally spaced with spacing h, we will take the basis functions ϕ_i, $i = 1, \ldots, n$, to be

$$\textbf{(5.4.15)} \qquad \begin{aligned} \phi_i(x) &= \frac{1}{h}(x - x_{i-1}), && x_{i-1} \le x \le x_i \\ &= -\frac{1}{h}(x - x_{i+1}), && x_i \le x \le x_{i+1} \\ &= 0, && \text{otherwise} \end{aligned}$$

These particular piecewise linear functions are called *hat functions*, or *linear B-splines*, and are illustrated in Figure 5.5. It is intuitively clear, and easily shown (exercise 5.4.4), that any piecewise linear function defined

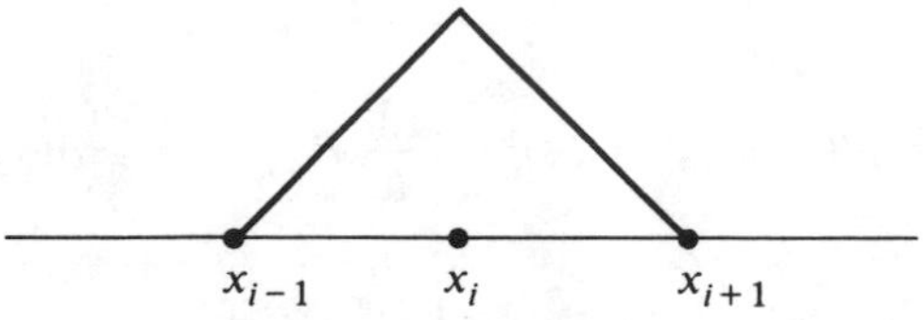

FIGURE 5.5 *A Hat Function.*

on the nodes $x_0, x_1, \ldots, x_{n+1}$ and that vanishes at x_0 and x_{n+1} can be expressed as a linear combination of these $\phi_1, \ldots, \phi_n$.

We now wish to use the basis functions (5.4.15) in Galerkin's method. At first glance, it would seem that there is a difficulty in using the ϕ_i in the computation of the a_{ij} since this requires ϕ_i', which doesn't exist at the points x_{i-1}, x_i, and x_{i+1}. Note, however, that ϕ_i' is simply the piecewise constant function

(5.4.16)
$$\begin{aligned} \phi_i'(x) &= \frac{1}{h}, \qquad x_{i-1} \le x \le x_i \\ &= -\frac{1}{h}, \qquad x_i \le x \le x_{i+1} \\ &= 0, \qquad \text{otherwise} \end{aligned}$$

There are discontinuities in this function at the points x_{i-1}, x_i, and x_{i+1}, but these do not affect the integration, and the integrations in (5.4.13) can be carried out on each subinterval to give

(5.4.17)
$$a_{ij} = \sum_{k=0}^{n} \int_{x_k}^{x_{k+1}} [-p(x)\phi_i'(x)\phi_j'(x) + q(x)\phi_i(x)\phi_j(x)]\, dx$$

By the definition of the ϕ_i, the products $\phi_i\phi_j$ and $\phi_i'\phi_j'$ vanish identically unless $i - 1 \le j \le i + 1$. Thus,

(5.4.18)
$$a_{ij} = 0, \qquad \text{if } |i - j| > 1$$

To evaluate the other a_{ij}, we first introduce the designations

(5.4.19)
$$\begin{aligned} P_i &= \int_{x_{i-1}}^{x_i} p(x)\, dx \qquad Q_i = \int_{x_{i-1}}^{x_i} q(x)(x - x_{i-1})^2\, dx \\ R_i &= \int_{x_i}^{x_{i+1}} q(x)(x - x_{i+1})^2\, dx \\ S_i &= \int_{x_{i-1}}^{x_i} q(x)(x - x_{i-1})(x - x_i)\, dx \end{aligned}$$

and note that

$$\int_{x_i}^{x_{i+1}} p(x)\phi_i'(x)\phi_i'(x)\, dx = \frac{1}{h^2} P_{i+1} \qquad \int_{x_{i-1}}^{x_i} p(x)\phi_i'(x)\phi_i'(x)\, dx = \frac{1}{h^2} P_i$$

$$\int_{x_i}^{x_{i+1}} p(x)\phi_i'(x)\phi_{i+1}'(x)\, dx = -\frac{1}{h^2} P_{i+1} \qquad \int_{x_i}^{x_{i+1}} q(x)\phi_i(x)\phi_i(x)\, dx = \frac{1}{h^2} R_i$$

$$\int_{x_{i-1}}^{x_i} q(x)\phi_i(x)\phi_i(x)\, dx = \frac{1}{h^2} Q_i \qquad \int_{x_{i-1}}^{x_i} q(x)\phi_{i-1}(x)\phi_i(x)\, dx = -\frac{1}{h^2} S_i$$

Therefore, from (5.4.17),

$$a_{ii} = \frac{-1}{h^2}(P_i + P_{i+1} - Q_i - R_i), \qquad i = 1, \ldots, n$$

(5.4.20)
$$a_{i,i+1} = \frac{1}{h^2}(P_{i+1} - S_{i+1}), \qquad i = 1, \ldots, n-1$$

$$a_{i,i-1} = \frac{1}{h^2}(P_i - S_i), \qquad i = 2, \ldots, n$$

and the right-hand-side components of system (5.4.4) are given by

(5.4.21)
$$f_i = \frac{1}{h}\int_{x_{i-1}}^{x_i} f(x)(x - x_{i-1})\,dx + \frac{1}{h}\int_{x_i}^{x_{i+1}} f(x)(x_{i+1} - x)\,dx, \qquad i = 1, \ldots, n$$

Thus, the linear system (5.4.4) to be solved for the coefficients c_1, c_n of (5.4.3) consists of the tridiagonal matrix A whose components are given by (5.4.20) and the right-hand-side **f** with components given by (5.4.21).

We note that in the special case $p(x) \equiv 1$ and $q(x) \equiv 0$, all Q_i, R_i, and S_i are zero, while $P_i = h$; hence,

$$a_{ii} = \frac{-2}{h} \qquad a_{i,i+1} = \frac{1}{h} \qquad a_{i-1,i} = \frac{1}{h}$$

Therefore, the coefficient matrix A is simply

$$A = \frac{-1}{h}\begin{bmatrix} 2 & -1 & & & \\ -1 & 2 & -1 & & \\ & \cdot & \cdot & \cdot & \\ & & \cdot & \cdot & \cdot \\ & & & \cdot & \cdot & -1 \\ & & & & -1 & 2 \end{bmatrix}$$

which, except for the factor h^{-1}, is exactly the same matrix as arises in the finite difference approximation to $v'' = f$, as we saw in Chapter 3.

Provided that the solution of (5.4.1) is sufficiently differentiable, it can be shown that the Galerkin procedure using the piecewise linear functions (5.4.16) is second-order accurate; that is, the discretization error is $0(h^2)$. By using cubic splines, it is possible to increase the order of accuracy by two, that is, to make the discretization error $0(h^4)$.

We will end this section with an example of collocation applied to the boundary-value problem

(5.4.22)
$$v''(x) - 3v(x) = x^2 + 10[v(x)]^3, \qquad 0 \le x \le 1,\ v(0) = v(1) = 0$$

which was treated in Section 4.4.

We first consider this equation without the nonlinear term $10v^3$; that is, we consider the linear equation

(5.4.23) $$v''(x) - 3v(x) = x^2, \qquad 0 \le x \le 1,\ v(0) = v(1) = 0$$

which is of the form (5.4.1) with $p(x) \equiv 1$, $q(x) \equiv -3$, and $f(x) = x^2$. We choose the basis functions $\phi_1, \ldots, \phi_n$ of (5.4.3) to be the cubic splines defined by (5.4.10) in terms of the B-splines (5.4.8), and with the points $x_i = ih$, $i = 1, \ldots, n$, $h = 1/(n+1)$. Then, the coefficients a_{ij} of the matrix A of (5.4.4) are given by (5.4.11) and (5.4.12), so

(5.4.24)

$$A = -\frac{1}{4h^2}\begin{bmatrix} 54+45h^2 & -6+3h^2 & & & & \\ -24+12h^2 & 12+12h^2 & -6+3h^2 & & & \\ & -6+3h^2 & \ddots & \ddots & & \\ & & \ddots & \ddots & -6+3h^2 & \\ & & & \ddots & 12+12h^2 & -24+12h^2 \\ & & & & -6+3h^2 & 54+45h^2 \end{bmatrix}$$

Hence, for the linear problem (5.4.23), we would solve the system of linear equations $\mathbf{Ac} = \mathbf{f}$ with A given by (5.4.24) and

(5.4.25) $$\mathbf{f} = (f(x_1), \ldots, f(x_n)) = h^2(1, 2^2, 3^2, \ldots, n^2)$$

For the nonlinear problem (5.4.22), we need to add to the system $\mathbf{Ac} = \mathbf{f}$ the vector of nonlinear terms

(5.4.26) $$10\left\{\left[\sum_{j=1}^{n} c_j\phi_j(x_1)\right]^3, \left[\sum_{j=1}^{n} c_j\phi_j(x_2)\right]^3, \ldots, \left[\sum_{j=1}^{n} c_j\phi_j(x_n)\right]^3\right\}$$

The values of the $\phi_j(x_i)$ are given by (5.4.10) and Table 5.1 as

$$\begin{aligned} \phi_1(x_1) &= 4B_1(x_1) - B_0(x_1) = \tfrac{15}{4} \\ \phi_i(x_i) &= 1, \qquad i = 2, \ldots, n-1 \\ \phi_n(x_n) &= 4B_n(x_n) - B_{n+1}(x_n) = \tfrac{15}{4} \\ \phi_1(x_2) &= 4B_1(x_2) - B_0(x_2) = 1 \\ \phi_{i-1}(x_i) &= \tfrac{1}{4}, \qquad i = 3, \ldots, n \\ \phi_{i+1}(x_i) &= \tfrac{1}{4}, \qquad i = 1, \ldots, n-2 \\ \phi_n(x_{n-1}) &= 4B_n(x_{n-1}) - B_{n+1}(x_{n-1}) = 1 \end{aligned}$$

and $\phi_j(x_i) = 0$ otherwise. Putting these values of the $\phi_j(x_i)$ into (5.4.26) gives the system of equations

(5.4.27) $$-\mathbf{Ac} + \mathbf{f} + \mathbf{H}(\mathbf{c}) \equiv \mathbf{F}(\mathbf{c}) = 0$$

where

$$\mathbf{H}(\mathbf{c}) = \frac{10}{64}\begin{bmatrix} (15c_1 + c_2)^3 \\ (4c_1 + 4c_2 + c_3)^3 \\ (c_2 + 4c_3 + c_4)^3 \\ \cdot \\ \cdot \\ \cdot \\ (c_{n-3} + 4c_{n-2} + c_{n-1})^3 \\ (c_{n-2} + 4c_{n-1} + 4c_n)^3 \\ (c_{n-1} + 15c_n)^3 \end{bmatrix}$$

and A and $\mathbf{f}$ are given by (5.4.24) and (5.4.25).

We now wish to apply Newton's method to the system (5.4.27). The Jacobian matrix is $\mathbf{F}'(\mathbf{c}) = -A + \mathbf{H}'(\mathbf{c})$ where the first two rows and last two rows of $\mathbf{H}'(\mathbf{c})$ as given by 15/32 times

$$\begin{matrix} 15(15c_1 + c_2)^2 & (15c_1 + c_2)^2 & 0 & 0\ldots0 \\ 4(4c_1 + 4c_2 + c_3)^2 & 4(4c_1 + 4c_2 + c_3)^2 & (4c_1 + 4c_2 + c_3)^2 & 0\ldots0 \\ 0\ldots0 \quad (c_{n-2} + 4c_{n-1} + 4c_n)^2 & 4(c_{n-2} + 4c_{n-1} + 4c_n)^2 & & 4(c_{n-2} + 4c_{n-1} + 4c_n)^2 \\ 0\ldots \quad\quad 0 & (c_{n-1} + 15c_n)^2 & & 15(c_{n-1} + 15c_n)^2 \end{matrix}$$

and otherwise the ith row is 15/32 times

$$0\ldots0 \quad (c_{i-1} + 4c_i + c_{i+1})^2 \quad 4(c_{i-1} + 4c_i + c_{i+1})^2 \quad (c_{i-1} + 4c_i + c_{i+1})^2 \quad 0\ldots0$$

Note that both $\mathbf{H}'(\mathbf{c})$ and $-A$ are tridiagonal and column diagonally dominant. Hence, the solution of the linear systems

$$\mathbf{F}'(\mathbf{c}^k)\mathbf{c}^{k+1} = \mathbf{F}'(\mathbf{c}^k)\mathbf{c}^k - \mathbf{F}(\mathbf{c}^k)$$

in Newton's method can be carried out by Gaussian elimination without interchanges.

In Table 5.2, we give the results of the computation for $h = 0.01$ ($n = 99$). We see that this computed solution agrees with that computed by the finite difference method in Chapter 4 (Table 4.3) to within a few units in the last place shown.

We now compare the three methods that we have discussed for two-point boundary-value problems: finite difference, collocation, and Galerkin. The finite difference method is conceptually simple and easy to implement and yields second-order accuracy with the centered differences that we discussed in Chapter 3. The collocation method using cubic splines is slightly more difficult to implement but still relatively easy. For the Galerkin method, however, we must evaluate the integrals of (5.4.19)

TABLE 5.2 *Solution of Equation (5.4.22) by the Collocation Method with Cubic Splines and h = 0.01*

x	$u(x)$
0.1	−0.0059
0.2	−0.0116
0.3	−0.0176
0.4	−0.0229
0.5	−0.0278
0.6	−0.0306
0.7	−0.0307
0.8	−0.0268
0.9	−0.0172

and (5.4.21), and generally this will require the use of numerical integration or symbolic computation systems. In all three cases, the system of linear equations to be solved has a tridiagonal coefficient matrix. All three methods have higher-order versions, which are, naturally, more complicated. It is probably fair to say that for ordinary differential equations, the simplicity of the finite difference method allows it to be preferred in most cases. The real power of the Galerkin method becomes more apparent for partial differential equations.

Supplementary Discussion and References: 5.4

The books by deBoor [1978] and Prenter [1975] are good sources for further reading on the material of this section and for a proof of theorem 5.4.1. See also Strang and Fix [1973] for further discussion of the Galerkin method.

There is a phenomenon known as "superconvergence" that occurs in the collocation and Galerkin methods. By using judiciously selected node points $x_1, \ldots, x_n$, the order of accuracy of the methods can be significantly increased. For a discussion of this, see Dupont [1976].

EXERCISES 5.4

5.4.1. Show that the function defined by (5.4.8) is a cubic spline on the interval $[0, 1]$ and satisfies the conditions (5.4.6) and (5.4.7).

5.4.2. Show that the values of B_i, B_i', and B_i'' at x_{i-1}, x_i, x_{i+1} are as given in Table 5.1.

5.4.3. Consider the two-point boundary-value problem $(1 + x^2)v'' + 2xv' + v = x^2$, $v(0) = 0$, $v(1) = 0$.

a. Let $h = \frac{1}{4}$ and write out the coefficients a_{ij} of (5.4.11) and (5.4.12) for the collocation method and then the complete system of linear equations (5.4.4). Ascertain whether the coefficient matrix is symmetric and/or diagonally dominant. Solve the system and express the approximate solution in the form (5.4.3) where the basis functions are given by (5.4.10).

b. Repeat part a for the Galerkin method using basis functions (5.4.15).

5.4.4. Let $f(x)$ be a piecewise linear function with nodes $x_i = ih$, $i = 0, 1, \ldots, n + 1$, $h = (n + 1)^{-1}$, and that vanishes at x_0 and x_{n+1}. Show that there are constants $\alpha_1, \ldots, \alpha_n$ such that $f(x) = \sum_{i=1}^{n} \alpha_i \phi_i(x)$, where the ϕ_i are defined by (5.4.15).

5.4.5. Carry out the calculations indicated in the text to solve the boundary-value problem (5.4.22) by the collocation method, and verify the results of Table 5.2. Do the calculation also for $h = 0.1$ and $h = 0.02$ and comment on how much discretization error you believe your computed solution has. Repeat the problem using Galerkin's method with piecewise linear basis functions.

6 n Important Numbers: Eigenvalue Computations

6.1 Examples of Eigenvalue Problems and Mathematical Background

In this chapter, we shall consider the numerical solution of eigenvalue problems. Such problems occur frequently in engineering, physics, chemistry, economics, and demography, as well as in other areas. In this section, we shall discuss a few example problems, classify different types of eigenvalue problems, and give some mathematical background that supplements that given in Appendix 3.

By the standard *matrix eigenvalue problem*, we mean to find real or complex numbers $\lambda_1, \lambda_2, \ldots, \lambda_n$ and corresponding nonzero vectors $\mathbf{x}_1, \ldots, \mathbf{x}_n$ that satisfy the equation

(6.1.1) $$A\mathbf{x} = \lambda \mathbf{x}$$

where A is a given real or complex $n \times n$ matrix. As mentioned in Appendix 3, the solutions $\lambda_1, \ldots, \lambda_n$ of (6.1.1) are the roots of the characteristic polynomial $\det(A - \lambda I) = 0$, which is a polynomial of degree n and, therefore, has exactly n roots, provided that the multiplicity of each root is counted. Once an eigenvalue λ_i is known, the corresponding eigenvector $\mathbf{x}_i$ can be determined, in principle, as a solution of the homogeneous system of equations

(6.1.2) $$(A - \lambda_i I)\mathbf{x} = 0$$

Note that even if the matrix A is real, its eigenvalues—and consequently also its eigenvectors—may be complex.

The preceding mathematical procedure—form the characteristic polynomial, compute its roots, and solve the homogeneous equations

(6.1.2)—is not a viable computational procedure in practice except for the most trivial problems. The main purpose of this chapter is to give alternative computational methods.

As a first example of how eigenvalue problems arise, consider the system of n ordinary differential equations

$$\frac{d\mathbf{y}}{dt} = \mathrm{A}\mathbf{y} \tag{6.1.3}$$

for a given constant $n \times n$ matrix A. Let us try a solution of (6.1.3) of the form

$$\mathbf{y}(t) = e^{\lambda t}\mathbf{x} \tag{6.1.4}$$

for some constant unknown vector $\mathbf{x}$ and unknown parameter λ. If (6.1.4) is to satisfy equation (6.1.3), then we must have

$$\frac{d\mathbf{y}}{dt} = \lambda e^{\lambda t}\mathbf{x} = \mathrm{A}(e^{\lambda t}\mathbf{x})$$

or, since $e^{\lambda t}$ is always nonzero, $\mathrm{A}\mathbf{x} = \lambda\mathbf{x}$; that is, (6.1.4) is a solution of (6.1.3) if and only if λ and $\mathbf{x}$ are an eigenvalue and a corresponding eigenvector of A, respectively.

An important type of matrix is one that has n linearly independent eigenvectors (see theorem A.3.1 in Appendix 3 for the definition of linear independence). If this is the case, and $\lambda_1, \ldots, \lambda_n$ and $\mathbf{x}_1, \ldots, \mathbf{x}_n$ are the eigenvalues and corresponding eigenvectors, then

$$\mathbf{y}_1(t) = e^{\lambda_1 t}\mathbf{x}_1 \qquad \mathbf{y}_2(t) = e^{\lambda_2 t}\mathbf{x}_2 \qquad \cdots \qquad \mathbf{y}_n(t) = e^{\lambda_n t}\mathbf{x}_n \tag{6.1.5}$$

is a complete set of linearly independent solutions of the differential equation (6.1.3), and any solution of (6.1.3) may be written in the form

$$\mathbf{y}(t) = \sum_{i=1}^{n} c_i\mathbf{y}_i(t) = \sum_{i=1}^{n} c_i e^{\lambda_i t}\mathbf{x}_i \tag{6.1.6}$$

for suitable constants $c_1, \ldots, c_n$. Thus, the general solution of (6.1.3) may be obtained by solving the eigenvalue problem for the matrix A. In case A does not have n linearly independent eigenvectors, a similar, but more complicated representation of the solution may be given.

We now discuss in more detail the property of a matrix having n linearly independent eigenvectors. As mentioned in Appendix 3, a similarity transformation of the matrix A is of the form PAP^{-1} where P is any nonsingular matrix. A similarity transformation of A arises from a change of variables; that is, consider the system of equations $\mathrm{A}\mathbf{x} = \mathbf{b}$ and make the change of variables $\mathbf{y} = \mathrm{P}\mathbf{x}$, $\mathbf{c} = \mathrm{P}\mathbf{b}$, where P is a nonsingular matrix. In the new variables, the system of equations is $\mathrm{AP}^{-1}\mathbf{y} = \mathrm{P}^{-1}\mathbf{c}$, or upon multiplying through by P, $\mathrm{PAP}^{-1}\mathbf{y} = \mathbf{c}$. Thus, the coefficient matrix of the system in the new variables is the similarity transform PAP^{-1}

An important property of similarity transformations is that they preserve the eigenvalues of A; that is, the matrices A and PAP^{-1} have the same eigenvalues. This is easily seen by considering the characteristic polynomial and the fact that the determinant of a product of matrices is the product of the determinants. Thus,

$$\det(A - \lambda I) = \det(PP^{-1})\det(A - \lambda I) = \det(P)\det(A - \lambda I)\det(P^{-1})$$
$$= \det(PAP^{-1} - \lambda I)$$

which shows that the characteristic polynomials, and hence the eigenvalues, of A and PAP^{-1} are identical. However, the eigenvectors change under a similarity transformation. Indeed,

$$PAP^{-1}\mathbf{y} = \lambda\mathbf{y} \quad \text{or} \quad AP^{-1}\mathbf{y} = P^{-1}\mathbf{y}$$

shows that the eigenvector $\mathbf{y}$ of PAP^{-1} is related to the eigenvector $\mathbf{x}$ of A by $P^{-1}\mathbf{y} = \mathbf{x}$ or $\mathbf{y} = P\mathbf{x}$.

An important question is how "simple" the matrix A may be made under a similarity transformation. A basic result in this regard that brings us back to linear independence of the eigenvectors is the following:

THEOREM 6.1.1 *A matrix A is similar to a diagonal matrix if and only if A has n linearly independent eigenvectors.*

The proof of this theorem is both simple and illustrative. Let $\mathbf{x}_1, \ldots, \mathbf{x}_n$ be n linearly independent eigenvectors of A with corresponding eigenvalues $\lambda_1, \ldots, \lambda_n$ and let P be the matrix with columns $\mathbf{x}_1, \ldots, \mathbf{x}_n$; then, P is nonsingular since its columns are linearly independent. By the basic definition $A\mathbf{x}_i = \lambda_i\mathbf{x}_i$ applied to each column of P, we have

$$\textbf{(6.1.7)} \qquad AP = A(\mathbf{x}_1, \mathbf{x}_2, \ldots, \mathbf{x}_n) = (\lambda_1\mathbf{x}_1, \ldots, \lambda_n\mathbf{x}_n) = PD$$

where D is the diagonal matrix

$$D = \begin{bmatrix} \lambda_1 & & & & \\ & \lambda_2 & & & \\ & & \cdot & & \\ & & & \cdot & \\ & & & & \cdot \\ & & & & & \lambda_n \end{bmatrix}$$

Thus, (6.1.7) is equivalent to $A = PDP^{-1}$, which shows that A is similar to a diagonal matrix whose diagonal entries are the eigenvalues of A. Conversely, if A is similar to a diagonal matrix, then (6.1.7) shows that the columns of the similarity matrix P must be eigenvectors of A, and they are linearly independent by the nonsingularity of P.

Two important special cases of the preceding result are the following:

THEOREM 6.1.2 *If* A *has distinct eigenvalues, then* A *is similar to a diagonal matrix.*

THEOREM 6.1.3 *If* A *is a real symmetric matrix* (that is, $A = A^T$), *then* A *is similar to a diagonal matrix, and the similarity matrix may be taken to be orthogonal* (that is, $PP^T = I$).

We will not prove these results. We do point out that symmetric matrices are extremely important in applications and that they have many nice properties as regards their eigenvalues. In particular, the eigenvalues of a symmetric matrix are always real, and are positive if A is positive-definite (that is, if $\mathbf{x}^T A\mathbf{x} > 0$ for all nonzero vectors $\mathbf{x}$).

Theorem 6.1.2 shows that if a matrix A does not have n linearly independent eigenvectors, then necessarily it has multiple eigenvalues. (But note that a matrix may have n linearly independent eigenvectors even though it has multiple eigenvalues; the identity matrix is such an example.)

The matrix

(6.1.8)
$$A = \begin{bmatrix} 1 & 1 \\ 0 & 1 \end{bmatrix}$$

is a simple example of a matrix that does not have two linearly independent eigenvectors (see exercise 6.1.4) and is not similar to a diagonal matrix. In general, the closest to diagonal that a matrix may be made by a similarity transformation is a matrix of the form

$$J = \begin{bmatrix} \lambda_1 & \delta_1 & 0 & \cdots & 0 \\ 0 & \lambda_2 & \delta_2 & & \vdots \\ \vdots & & \ddots & \ddots & 0 \\ \vdots & & & \ddots & \delta_{n-1} \\ 0 & \cdots & & 0 & \lambda_n \end{bmatrix}$$

where the λ_i are the eigenvalues of A and the δ_i are either 0 or 1. If q is the number of δ_i that are nonzero, then A has $n - q$ linearly independent eigenvectors, and whenever a δ_i is nonzero, then the eigenvalues λ_i and λ_{i+1} are identical. Thus, the matrix J can be partitioned as

(6.1.9)
$$J = \begin{bmatrix} J_1 & & \\ & \ddots & \\ & & J_p \end{bmatrix}$$

where p is the number of linearly independent eigenvectors, and each J_i is a matrix of the form

$$J_i = \begin{bmatrix} \lambda_i & 1 & & \\ & \ddots & \ddots & \\ & & \ddots & 1 \\ & & & \lambda_i \end{bmatrix}$$

with identical eigenvalues and all 1's on the first superdiagonal. The matrix J of (6.1.9) is called the *Jordan canonical form* of A. Note that in case A has n linearly independent eigenvectors then $p = n$, each J_i reduces to a 1×1 matrix, and J is diagonal.

For many computational purposes, it is very desirable to work with orthogonal or unitary matrices (a unitary matrix U is a complex matrix that satisfies $U^H U = I$, where U^H is the conjugate transpose of U; a real unitary matrix is an orthogonal matrix). We next state without proof two basic results on transformations with unitary matrices.

Schur's Theorem *For an arbitrary* $n \times n$ *matrix* A, *there is a unitary matrix* U *such that* UAU^H *is triangular.*

Singular Value Decomposition *For an arbitrary* $n \times n$ *matrix* A, *there are unitary matrices* U *and* V *such that* UAV *is diagonal.*

In the case of Schur's theorem, UAU^H is a similarity transformation, and hence the diagonal elements of the triangular matrix are the eigenvalues of A. In the singular value decomposition, however, UAV is *not* a similarity transformation except in the special case that $U = V^H$, and the diagonal elements of the diagonal matrix are not necessarily the eigenvalues of A. It turns out that they are the (positive) square roots of the eigenvalues of A^TA. (Note that A^TA is always symmetric and positive-semidefinite; that is, $\mathbf{x}^T A^T A \mathbf{x} \geq 0$ for all vectors $\mathbf{x}$, and hence all the eigenvalues of A^TA are real and nonnegative.) These numbers are called the *singular values* of A and play an important role in many statistical and computational problems, although we shall not consider them further.

We now return to further examples of eigenvalue problems. Such problems also arise for differential equations, but in a different way than in the earlier example. As we will see in Section 7.1, the problem of a vibrating string leads in certain simple cases to the ordinary differential equation

(6.1.10) $$y''(x) = \lambda y(x), \qquad y(0) = 0, \qquad y(1) = 0$$

Here, we wish to find values—again called eigenvalues—of the scalar parameter λ so that (6.1.10) has corresponding nonzero solutions—called eigenfunctions—that satisfy the given zero boundary conditions. This particularly simple problem can be solved explicitly. There are infinitely many eigenvalues and corresponding eigenfunctions that are given by

(6.1.11) $$\lambda_k = -k^2\pi^2 \qquad y_k(x) = \sin k\pi x, \qquad k = 1, 2, \ldots$$

as is easily checked by substitution into (6.1.10).

Next, suppose that (6.1.10) is modified by adding a nonconstant coefficient of y, that is,

(6.1.12) $$y''(x) = \lambda C(x)y(x), \qquad y(0) = 0, \qquad y(1) = 0$$

where C is a given positive function. Now, it is no longer possible, in general, to obtain the eigenvalues and eigenfunctions of (6.1.12) explicitly, but we can approximate them numerically by the following procedure. Just as in the treatment of boundary-value problems in Chapter 3, we can discretize the interval [0, 1] with grid points $x_i = ih$, $i = 0, 1, \ldots, n+1$, $h = 1/(n+1)$, and replace the second derivative in (6.1.12) by the corresponding difference quotient. This gives the discrete equations

(6.1.13) $$\frac{1}{h^2}(y_{i+1} - 2y_i + y_{i-1}) = \lambda C_i y_i, \qquad i = 1, \ldots, n$$

where $C_i = C(x_i)$, $y_0 = y_{n+1} = 0$, and y_i is an approximation to $y(x_i)$.

The equations (6.1.13) constitute a matrix eigenvalue problem. If we define the matrices

(6.1.14) $$A = \begin{bmatrix} 2 & -1 & & & 0 \\ -1 & 2 & -1 & & \\ & \cdot & \cdot & \cdot & \\ & & \cdot & \cdot & -1 \\ 0 & & & -1 & 2 \end{bmatrix} \qquad B = h^2 \begin{bmatrix} C_1 & & & & 0 \\ & C_2 & & & \\ & & \cdot & & \\ & & & \cdot & \\ 0 & & & & C_n \end{bmatrix}$$

then (6.1.13) may be written in matrix-vector form as

(6.1.15) $$A\mathbf{y} = \lambda B\mathbf{y}$$

This is an example of a *generalized eigenvalue* problem in which the matrix B on the right-hand side of the equation is not the identity matrix. Of course, if the matrix B is not singular, (6.1.15) may be converted to a standard eigenvalue problem by multiplying the equation through by B^{-1}. In most cases, however, it is not desirable to make this type of conversion.

Equation (6.1.15) is also an example of a *sparse* eigenvalue problem since the matrices A and B are sparse—that is, they have few nonzero elements.

Next, let us return to the system (6.1.3) of ordinary differential equations. An important property of this system is whether all solutions are *asymptotically stable*, that is, all solutions tend to zero as t tends to infinity. Assuming again that the matrix A has n linearly independent eigenvectors, then any solution can be represented in the form (6.1.6). Therefore, every solution will go to zero as t goes to infinity if and only if each of the solutions (6.1.5) does, and since the vectors $\mathbf{x}_i$ are constant, this will be the case if and only if $e^{\lambda_i t}$ approaches zero as t approaches infinity for each i. If λ_i is real, this will be the case if and only if $\lambda_i < 0$, and if λ_i is complex, we need the real part of λ_i, denoted by $\mathrm{Re}(\lambda_i)$, to be negative. Thus, all solutions of (6.1.3) are stable if and only if

(6.1.16) $$\mathrm{Re}(\lambda_i) < 0, \qquad i = 1, \ldots, n$$

In many cases, we might wish only to know whether all solutions are stable and not wish to compute any particular solutions. In that case, we only need to compute the eigenvalues with sufficient accuracy to ascertain whether (6.1.16) holds. We will return to this point shortly.

Similar problems of determining the asymptotic stability of solutions of *difference* equations—as opposed to differential equations—arise in a number of disciplines. We will outline one such problem from the field of demography which is concerned with population projection. Given the human population distribution today, what can be predicted about the population distribution in the future? Admittedly, the particular model we shall develop makes several assumptions and simplifications. However, it is indicative of mathematical models in the field of population dynamics.

In this demographic model, time is broken up into discrete units such as five-year periods, males are ignored, and females are divided into age classes that are separated by a common time unit. We shall let $p_i^{(0)}$ represent the number of females in age group i, $i = 1, \ldots, n$, at some starting time $t = 0$ and let $p_i^{(k)}$ be the number of females in age group i, k units of time later. Then, the vector

$$\mathbf{p}^{(k)} = (p_1^{(k)}, \ldots, p_n^{(k)})$$

will represent the age distribution of all females (group n, the oldest group, will contain all females above a certain age).

Next, let b_i represent the average rate of female births for age group i, and likewise d_i for the death rate. These parameters can be approximated using census data. Assuming that these rates remain constant, what happens to the population as time passes?

The number of newborn females at time $k + 1$ will be the sum of births produced by each of the age groups at time k. That is,

$$p_1^{(k+1)} = \sum_{j=1}^{n} b_j p_j^{(k)}$$

Likewise, the number of females in group i will be

$$p_i^{(k+1)} = (1 - d_{i-1}) p_{i-1}^{(k)}, \qquad i = 2, \ldots, n - 1$$

the number of surviving females from class $i - 1$ at time k. A modification is required for the case $i = n$. For this case, there are survivors from class $n - 1$ and class n. It follows that

$$p_n^{(k+1)} = (1 - d_{n-1})p_{n-1}^{(k)} + (1 - d_n)p_n^{(k)}$$

Matrix notation is very convenient for representing these relations. If we let A be the matrix

$$\text{(6.1.17)}\quad A = \begin{bmatrix} b_1 & b_2 & \cdots & b_{n-1} & b_n \\ (1-d_1) & 0 & \cdots & 0 & 0 \\ 0 & (1-d_2) & \cdots & 0 & 0 \\ & \cdot & & \vdots & \vdots \\ & & \cdot & & \\ & & & 0 & 0 \\ & & 0 & (1-d_{n-1}) & (1-d_n) \end{bmatrix}$$

then all n equations can be written as

$$\text{(6.1.18)}\qquad \mathbf{p}^{(k+1)} = A\mathbf{p}^{(k)}$$

Now, suppose that a demographer is interested in the behavior of $\mathbf{p}^{(k)}$ as k increases. Let us assume, again, that A has n linearly independent eigenvectors $\mathbf{x}_1, \ldots, \mathbf{x}_n$ and corresponding eigenvalues $\lambda_1, \ldots, \lambda_n$. Since the $\mathbf{x}_i$ are linearly independent, we can express an arbitrary vector as a linear combination of these eigenvectors; in particular, we can write

$$\text{(6.1.19)}\qquad \mathbf{p}^{(0)} = c_1\mathbf{x}_1 + \cdots + c_n\mathbf{x}_n$$

for certain constants $c_1, \ldots, c_n$. Then, since $A\mathbf{x}_i = \lambda_i\mathbf{x}_i$, we have

$$\text{(6.1.20)}\qquad \begin{aligned} \mathbf{p}^{(1)} &= A\mathbf{p}^{(0)} = c_1\lambda_1\mathbf{x}_1 + \cdots + c_n\lambda_n\mathbf{x}_n \\ \mathbf{p}^{(2)} &= A\mathbf{p}^{(1)} = c_1\lambda_1^2\mathbf{x}_1 + \cdots + c_n\lambda_n^2\mathbf{x}_n \\ &\;\;\vdots \\ \mathbf{p}^{(k)} &= A\mathbf{p}^{(k-1)} = c_1\lambda_1^k\mathbf{x}_1 + \cdots + c_n\lambda_n^k\mathbf{x}_n \end{aligned}$$

From the representation (6.1.20), we can immediately obtain certain qualitative information about the population. Let $\rho = \rho(A) = \max_{i=1,2,\ldots,n} |\lambda_i|$ denote the spectral radius of A. Then, it is clear that if $\rho < 1$, the population will decrease to zero as k approaches infinity, whereas if $\rho > 1$, the population will increase without bound. Again, if this is the only information that is desired, it is only necessary to compute the eigenvalues accurately enough to determine if $\rho < 1$ or $\rho > 1$.

We can summarize the preceding matrix-theoretic results in the following important theorem, which will be useful in Chapter 8 in the study of iterative methods. We have indicated its proof only in the case that the matrix A has n linearly independent eigenvectors, but it holds in the generality stated.

THEOREM 6.1.4 *If the spectral radius of A satisfies $\rho(A) < 1$, then any sequence of vectors $\{\mathbf{x}^{(k)}\}$ for which*

$$\mathbf{x}^{(k+1)} = A\mathbf{x}^{(k)}, \qquad k = 0, 1, \ldots \tag{6.1.21}$$

converges to zero; that is $\mathbf{x}^{(k)} \to \mathbf{0}$ as $k \to \infty$. Conversely, if $\rho(A) > 1$, there is at least one sequence of vectors $\{\mathbf{x}^{(k)}\}$ satisfying (6.1.21) for which $\|\mathbf{x}^{(k)}\| \to \infty$ as $k \to \infty$.

Crude approximations to the eigenvalues of a matrix may sometimes be obtained very easily by what are known as *localization theorems.* We next discuss the most famous such result, Gerschgorin's theorem. Let $A = (a_{ij})$ be a real or complex $n \times n$ matrix and let

$$r_i = \sum_{\substack{j=1 \\ j \neq i}}^{n} |a_{ij}|, \qquad i = 1, \ldots, n$$

That is, r_i is the sum of the absolute values of the off-diagonal elements in the ith row of A. Next, define the disks in the complex plane centered at a_{ii} and with radius r_i:

$$\Lambda_i = \{z : |z - a_{ii}| \leq r_i\}, \qquad i = 1, \ldots, n$$

Then, we have the following:

THEOREM 6.1.5 (Gerschgorin's Theorem) *All the eigenvalues of A lie in the union of the disks $\Lambda_1, \ldots, \Lambda_n$.*

As a simple example of the use of Gerschgorin's theorem, consider the matrix

$$A = \frac{1}{16}\begin{bmatrix} -8 & -2 & 4 \\ -1 & -4 & 2 \\ 2 & 2 & -10 \end{bmatrix}$$

for which the Gerschgorin disks are illustrated in Figure 6.1. Note that we can immediately conclude that all eigenvalues of A have negative real part; hence, if A were the coefficient matrix of the system of differential equations (6.1.3), all solutions of that system would be asymptotically stable. Similarly, we can immediately conclude that the eigenvalues of A are all less than 1 in absolute value, so the vectors $p^{(k)}$ defined by

$$\mathbf{p}^{(k)} = A\mathbf{p}^{(k-1)}, \qquad k = 1, 2, \ldots$$

tend to zero as k approaches infinity for any $\mathbf{p}^{(0)}$.

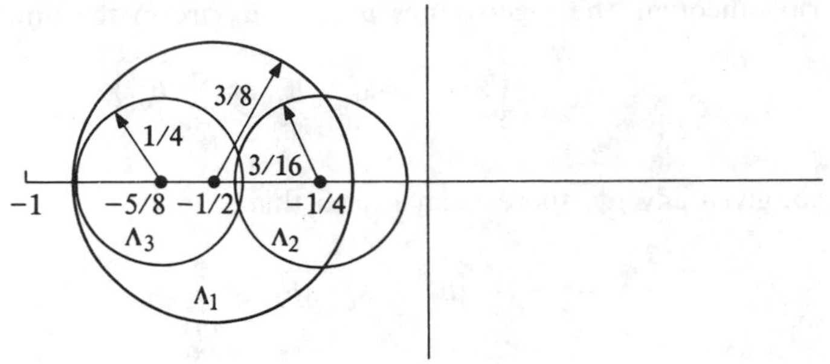

FIGURE 6.1 *Gerschgorin's Disks in the Complex Plane.*

The proof of Gerschgorin's theorem is very easy. Let λ be any eigenvalue of A, and $\mathbf{x}$ a corresponding eigenvector. Then, by definition,

$$(\lambda - a_{ii})x_i = \sum_{\substack{j=1 \\ j \neq i}}^{n} a_{ij}x_j, \qquad i = 1, \ldots, n$$

If we let x_k be the component of largest absolute value in the vector $\mathbf{x}$, then

$$|\lambda - a_{kk}| \leq \sum_{\substack{j=1 \\ j \neq k}}^{n} |a_{kj}| \frac{|x_j|}{|x_k|} \leq \sum_{\substack{j=1 \\ j \neq k}}^{n} |a_{kj}|$$

so λ is in the disk centered at a_{kk}.

Another important use of Gerschgorin's theorem is in ascertaining the change in the eigenvalues of a matrix due to changes in the coefficients. Let A be a given $n \times n$ matrix with eigenvalues $\lambda_1, \ldots, \lambda_n$, and suppose that E is a matrix whose elements are in some sense small compared to those of A; for example, E may be the rounding errors committed in entering the matrix A into a computer. Suppose that $\mu_1, \ldots, \mu_n$ are the eigenvalues of A + E. Then, what can one say about the changes $|\lambda_i - \mu_i|$? We next give a relatively simple result in the case that A has n linearly independent eigenvectors. Recall, from Appendix 3, that the infinitity norm of a matrix is simply the maximum value of the sums of the absolute values of the elements in each row.

THEOREM 6.1.6 *Assume that* $A = PDP^{-1}$, *where* D *is the diagonal matrix of eigenvalues of* A, *and let* $d = \|P^{-1}EP\|_\infty$. *Then, every eigenvalue of* A + E *is within* d *of an eigenvalue of* A.

The proof of this theorem is a simple consequence of Gerschgorin's theorem. Set $C = P^{-1}(A + E)P$. Then, C has the same eigenvalues $\mu_1, \ldots, \mu_n$ as A + E. Let $B = P^{-1}EP$. Then, $C = D + B$, and the diagonal elements of C are $\lambda_i + b_{ii}$, $i = 1, \ldots, n$. Hence, by Gerschgorin's theorem, the eigenvalues $\mu_1, \ldots, \mu_n$ are in the union of the disks

$$\left\{ z : |z - \lambda_i - b_{ii}| \le \sum_{\substack{j=1 \\ j \ne i}}^{n} |b_{ij}| \right\}$$

so, given any μ_k, there is an i such that

$$|\mu_k - \lambda_i - b_{ii}| \le \sum_{\substack{j=1 \\ j \ne i}}^{n} |b_{ij}|$$

or

$$|\mu_k - \lambda_i| \le \sum_{j=1}^{n} |b_{ij}| \le d$$

which was to be shown.

Note that the quantity d need not be small even though $\|E\|_\infty$ is small; this will depend on P. In general, the more ill-conditioned the matrix P (in the sense of Chapter 3), the more ill-conditioned will be the eigenvalues of A; that is, the more the eigenvalues may change because of small changes in the coefficients of A. We give a simple example of this. Let

$$A = \begin{bmatrix} 1 & 1 \\ 0 & 1 + 10^{-10} \end{bmatrix} \qquad A + E = \begin{bmatrix} 1 & 1 \\ 10^{-10} & 1 + 10^{-10} \end{bmatrix}$$

Then, the eigenvalues of A are 1 and $1 + 10^{-10}$, and those of A + E are approximately 1 ± 10^{-5}. Thus, a change of 10^{-10} in one element of A has caused a change 10^5 times as much in the eigenvalues. The reason for this is that the matrix P of eigenvectors of A is very ill-conditioned. It is easy to verify that

$$P = \begin{bmatrix} 1 & 1 \\ 0 & 10^{-10} \end{bmatrix} \qquad P^{-1} = \begin{bmatrix} 1 & -10^{10} \\ 0 & 10^{10} \end{bmatrix}$$

Therefore, the matrix $P^{-1}EP$ of theorem 6.1.6 is

$$P^{-1}EP = \begin{bmatrix} 1 & -10^{10} \\ 0 & 10^{10} \end{bmatrix} \begin{bmatrix} 0 & 0 \\ 10^{-10} & 0 \end{bmatrix} \begin{bmatrix} 1 & 1 \\ 0 & 10^{-10} \end{bmatrix} = \begin{bmatrix} -1 & -1 \\ 1 & 1 \end{bmatrix}$$

and thus $d = \|P^{-1}EP\|_\infty = 2$. Note that the actual change in the eigenvalues is far smaller than this bound.

It is an interesting and important fact that the eigenvalues of a symmetric matrix are always well-conditioned, which is the interpretation of the following theorem, stated without proof.

THEOREM 6.1.7 *Let* A *and* B *be real symmetric* $n \times n$ *matrices with eigenvalues* $\lambda_1, \ldots, \lambda_n$ *and* $\mu_1, \ldots, \mu_n$, *respectively. Then, given any* μ_j, *there is a* λ_i *such that*

$$|\lambda_i - \mu_j| \le \|A - B\|_2$$

Note that in this theorem, it is the 2-norm (see Appendix 3) that is used, and hence the result does not follow directly from theorem 6.1.6.

In this section, we have given various examples of eigenvalue problems and some of the basic mathematical theory. In the remainder of this chapter, we will discuss the foundation of various methods for computing eigenvalues and eigenvectors.

Supplementary Discussion and References: 6.1

Further discussion of the use of eigenvalues for solving linear ordinary differential equations can be found in most elementary differential equation textbooks. The mathematical study of population dynamics has an extensive literature, most of which is not related to eigenvalues. For a review of this field, see the books by Hoppensteadt [1975] and Keyfitz [1968].

A detailed discussion of the theory of eigenvalue problems, in a form most suitable for numerical analysis, may be found in Wilkinson [1965]. See also Householder [1964], Stewart [1973], and Parlett [1980].

The basic theorem 6.1.4 is really a result on when powers of a matrix tend to zero. Equation (6.1.21) can be written as $\mathbf{x}^{(k)} = A^k\mathbf{x}^{(0)}$. From this, it is clear that $\mathbf{x}^{(k)} \to \mathbf{0}$ as $k \to \infty$ for all $\mathbf{x}^{(0)}$ if and only if $A^k \to 0$ as $k \to \infty$. The convergence of the powers of A can be analyzed, in principle, through the Jordan canonical form. Thus, if $A = PJP^{-1}$, then $A^k = PJ^kP^{-1}$ and $A^k \to 0$ as $k \to \infty$ if and only if $J^k \to 0$ as $k \to \infty$. If J is diagonal, the analysis is trivial. Otherwise, one needs to analyze the behavior of powers of a Jordan block. It is easy to show that

$$\begin{bmatrix} \lambda & 1 & & \\ & \lambda & \ddots & \\ & & \ddots & 1 \\ & & & \lambda \end{bmatrix}^k = \begin{bmatrix} \lambda^k & k\lambda^{k-1} & \binom{k}{2}\lambda^{k-2} & \cdots & \binom{k}{n-1}\lambda^{k-n+1} \\ & \lambda^k & k\lambda^{k-1} & \cdots & \vdots \\ & & \ddots & \ddots & \vdots \\ & & & \ddots & k\lambda^{k-1} \\ & & & & \lambda^k \end{bmatrix}$$

which shows that the powers tend to zero if and only if $|\lambda| < 1$.

EXERCISES 6.1

6.1.1. Compute the characteristic equation for the matrix

$$A = \begin{bmatrix} 2 & -1 \\ -1 & 2 \end{bmatrix}$$

that is, compute

$$\det\begin{bmatrix} 2-\lambda & -1 \\ -1 & 2-\lambda \end{bmatrix}$$

Next, compute the eigenvalues of A by obtaining the roots of this polynomial, and then compute the eigenvectors by solving the homogeneous equations (6.1.2).

6.1.2. Give the solution of the initial-value problem

$$\mathbf{y}'(t) = \mathrm{A}\mathbf{y}(t), \qquad \mathbf{y}(0) = \begin{bmatrix} 1 \\ 1 \end{bmatrix}$$

in terms of the eigenvalues and eigenvectors that were computed in exercise 6.1.1.

6.1.3. If A is the matrix

$$\mathrm{A} = \frac{1}{4}\begin{bmatrix} 1 & 1 \\ -1 & 2 \end{bmatrix}$$

determine whether the solutions of $\mathbf{y}' = \mathrm{A}\mathbf{y}$ are asymptotically stable.

6.1.4. Compute an eigenvector of the matrix of (6.1.8) and show that there are no other linearly independent eigenvectors.

6.1.5. Consider the population problem that has time-dependent birthrates and death rates; that is, replace A in (6.1.17) with

$$\mathrm{A}(t) = \begin{bmatrix} b_1(t) & b_2(t) & \cdots & & b_n(t) \\ 1-d_1(t) & 0 & \cdot & & 0 \\ \cdot & \cdot & & \cdot & \\ \cdot & & \cdot & & \\ \cdot & & & \cdot & \cdot \\ 0 & & & 1-d_{n-1}(t) & 1-d_n(t) \end{bmatrix}$$

Derive the corresponding expression that would replace (6.1.18) in this case.

6.1.6. Let

$$\mathrm{A} = \begin{bmatrix} 2 & 0.1 & 0.1 \\ 0.1 & 1 & 0.1 \\ 0.1 & 0.1 & 1.01 \end{bmatrix}$$

Find the Gerschgorin disks for A and sketch them.

6.1.7. Using Gerschgorin's theorem, prove that a symmetric, strictly diagonally dominant matrix with positive diagonal elements is positive-definite.

6.1.8. By direct substitution and use of trigonometric identities, show that the $n \times n$ real symmetric matrix

$$\mathrm{A} = \begin{bmatrix} a & b & & & & \\ b & a & b & & & \\ & b & a & b & & \\ & & \cdot & \cdot & \cdot & \\ & & & \cdot & \cdot & \cdot \\ & & & b & a & b \\ & & & & b & a \end{bmatrix}$$

has eigenvalues $\lambda_k = a + 2b\cos[k\pi/(n+1)]$, $k = 1, \ldots, n$, and corresponding eigenvectors $\mathbf{x}_k = \{\sin[k\pi/(n+1)], \sin[2k\pi/(n+1)], \ldots, \sin[nk\pi/(n+1)]\}$, $k = 1, \ldots, n$.

6.2 The Symmetric Eigenvalue Problem

The best available methods for the computation of eigenvalues of nonsparse matrices begin by reducing the given matrix to a simpler form. We consider in this section the basic method for real symmetric matrices, in which the first step is to reduce the matrix by orthogonal similarity transformations to a tridiagonal matrix that has the same eigenvalues. The second step is then to compute the eigenvalues of the tridiagonal matrix. Finally, the eigenvectors are computed, if desired.

Let A be a real $n \times n$ symmetric matrix. We will define $n - 2$ orthogonal matrices $P_1, \ldots, P_{n-2}$ and the matrices $A_1 = A, A_2, \ldots, A_{n-1}$ by

(6.2.1)
$$A_{i+1} = P_i A_i P_i^T, \qquad i = 1, \ldots, n-2$$

such that A_{n-1} is a tridiagonal matrix. Since each P_i is orthogonal, all of the matrices $A_1, \ldots, A_{n-1}$ are similar and, hence, have the same eigenvalues. Moreover, each A_i retains the symmetry of A_1.

We now concentrate on the construction of the matrix P_1. Our goal is to choose P_1 so that the matrix A_2 has zeros in its first row and column outside of the tridiagonal positions; that is, we wish A_2 to have the form

(6.2.2)
$$A_2 = \begin{bmatrix} * & * & 0 & \cdots & 0 \\ * & * & * & \cdots & * \\ 0 & * & & & \cdot \\ \cdot & \cdot & & & \cdot \\ \cdot & \cdot & & & \\ \cdot & \cdot & & & \cdot \\ 0 & * & & \cdots & * \end{bmatrix}$$

where an $*$ indicates an element that is not necessarily zero. We can achieve this by choosing P_1 to be a matrix of the form

(6.2.3)
$$P_1 = I - 2\mathbf{w}\mathbf{w}^T = \begin{bmatrix} 1 - 2w_1^2 & -2w_1w_2 \cdots & & -2w_1w_n \\ -2w_2w_1 & & & \\ \cdot & & & \cdot \\ \cdot & & & \cdot \\ \cdot & & & \cdot \\ -2w_nw_1 & \cdot & \cdot & \cdot \quad 1 - 2w_n^2 \end{bmatrix}$$

where the vector $\mathbf{w}$ satisfies $\mathbf{w}^T\mathbf{w} = \|\mathbf{w}\|_2^2 = 1$. Such a matrix is always orthogonal, as is seen by the computation

$$P_1^T P_1 = (I - 2\mathbf{w}\mathbf{w}^T)(I - 2\mathbf{w}\mathbf{w}^T) = I - 4\mathbf{w}\mathbf{w}^T + 4\mathbf{w}^T\mathbf{w}\mathbf{w}\mathbf{w}^T = I$$

Similarly, the similarity transformation $P_1AP_1^T$ is given by

$$\begin{aligned} A_2 = P_1AP_1^T &= (I - 2\mathbf{w}\mathbf{w}^T)A(I - 2\mathbf{w}\mathbf{w}^T) \\ &= A - 2\mathbf{w}\mathbf{w}^TA - 2A\mathbf{w}\mathbf{w}^T + 4\mathbf{w}^TA\mathbf{w}\mathbf{w}\mathbf{w}^T \end{aligned}$$

Now, suppose that the first component of $\mathbf{w}$ is zero. Then, the matrix $\mathbf{w}\mathbf{w}^T$ has zeros in its first row and column, and the matrix $A\mathbf{w}\mathbf{w}^T$ has zeros in its first column. Therefore, if we denote the first column of A by $\mathbf{a}$, the first column of A_2 is simply $\mathbf{a}$ minus the first column of $2\mathbf{w}\mathbf{w}^TA$, which is given by

$$\mathbf{a} - 2\mathbf{w}\mathbf{w}^T\mathbf{a} = \begin{bmatrix} a_{11} \\ a_{21} - 2w_2\mathbf{w}^T\mathbf{a} \\ \cdot \\ \cdot \\ \cdot \\ a_{n1} - 2w_n\mathbf{w}^T\mathbf{a} \end{bmatrix}$$

We wish to choose $\mathbf{w}$ so that the third through nth components of $\mathbf{a}$ are zero, and we can achieve this by defining

(6.2.4)
$$\mathbf{w}^T = \mu(0, a_{21} - s, a_{31}, \ldots, a_{n1}),$$
$$s = \pm\left(\sum_{j=2}^{n} a_{j1}^2\right)^{1/2}, \qquad \mu = \frac{1}{\sqrt{2s(s - a_{21})}}$$

where the sign of s is chosen to be the same as that of $-a_{21}$.

Let us verify that this choice of $\mathbf{w}$ achieves our goals. First, we need that $\mathbf{w}^T\mathbf{w} = 1$; this is shown by

$$\mathbf{w}^T\mathbf{w} = \mu^2\left[(a_{21} - s)^2 + \sum_{j=3}^{n} a_{j1}^2\right] = \mu^2(a_{21}^2 - 2a_{21}s + s^2 + s^2 - a_{21}^2) = 1$$

Next,

$$\mathbf{w}^T\mathbf{a} = \mu\left[(a_{21} - s)a_{21} + \sum_{j=3}^{n} a_{j1}^2\right] = \mu(s^2 - a_{21}s) = \frac{1}{2\mu}$$

so

$$a_{21} - 2w_2\mathbf{w}^T\mathbf{a} = a_{21} - \frac{2(a_{21} - s)\mu}{2\mu} = s$$

and

$$a_{i1} - 2w_i\mathbf{w}^T\mathbf{a} = a_{i1} - \frac{2a_{i1}\mu}{2\mu} = 0, \qquad i = 3, 4, \ldots, n$$

Therefore, the first column of A_2 has the desired form, and since A_2 is symmetric, the first row of A_2 has also. That is, A_2 has the structure (6.2.2) with the (1, 1) element equal to a_{11} and the (2, 1) and (1, 2) elements equal to s.

To complete the reduction to tridiagonal form, we simply observe that the next step is completely analogous to the one just completed. Define

$$P_2 = I - 2\mathbf{w}_2\mathbf{w}_2^T$$

where $\mathbf{w}_2$ is a vector with its first two components equal to zero. Then, it is easy to see that the transformation $P_2A_2P_2^T$ does not disturb the first row and column of A_2 and affects only the submatrix defined by the last $n - 1$ rows and columns of A_2. Hence, the elements of $\mathbf{w}_2$ may be defined in a way analogous to the definition of $\mathbf{w}$, and the resulting matrix A_3 has the form

$$A_3 = \begin{bmatrix} * & * & 0 & \cdot & \cdot & \cdot & 0 \\ * & * & * & 0 & \cdot & \cdot & 0 \\ 0 & * & * & * & * & \cdots & * \\ \cdot & 0 & * & & & & \cdot \\ \cdot & \cdot & \cdot & & & & \cdot \\ \cdot & \cdot & \cdot & & & & \cdot \\ 0 & 0 & * & \cdot & \cdot & \cdot & * \end{bmatrix}$$

After $n - 4$ further transformations of this type using vectors $\mathbf{w}_i$, $i = 3, \ldots, n - 2$, with zeros in the first i positions, the reduction to tridiagonal form will be complete:

$$A_{n-1} = \begin{bmatrix} a_1 & b_1 & & & \\ b_1 & a_2 & b_2 & & \\ & \ddots & \ddots & \ddots & \\ & & \ddots & \ddots & b_{n-1} \\ & & & b_{n-1} & a_n \end{bmatrix} \tag{6.2.5}$$

The matrices $I - 2\mathbf{w}\mathbf{w}^T$ are known as *Householder matrices*, or *Householder transformations*, and the procedure just described is called the *Householder reduction to tridiagonal form*.

The next task is to calculate the eigenvalues of this tridiagonal matrix. There are a number of ways to accomplish this, and in the next section, we will give a method based on the QR transformation. In this section, we will outline the classic method of Sturm sequences.

We now shall assume that the off-diagonal elements $b_1, \ldots, b_{n-1}$ are all nonzero; this is no loss of generality since if some

$b_i = 0$, the characteristic polynomial trivially factors into two polynomials which can be handled separately.

We define the polynomials

(6.2.6)
$$p_0(\lambda) \equiv 1 \qquad p_1(\lambda) = a_1 - \lambda$$
$$p_i(\lambda) = (a_i - \lambda)p_{i-1}(\lambda) - b_{i-1}^2 p_{i-2}(\lambda), \qquad i = 2, \ldots, n$$

where the a_i are the diagonal elements and the b_i are the off-diagonal elements of A_{n-1}. Clearly, p_i is a polynomial of degree i. Moreover, p_n is the characteristic polynomial of A_{n-1}; for example, for $n = 3$, using expansion by minors, we have

$$\det\begin{bmatrix} a_1 - \lambda & b_1 & 0 \\ b_1 & a_2 - \lambda & b_2 \\ 0 & b_2 & a_3 - \lambda \end{bmatrix} = (a_3 - \lambda)\det\begin{bmatrix} a_1 - \lambda & b_1 \\ b_1 & a_2 - \lambda \end{bmatrix}$$
$$-b_2\det\begin{bmatrix} a_1 - \lambda & 0 \\ b_1 & b_2 \end{bmatrix} = (a_3 - \lambda)p_2(\lambda) - b_2^2 p_1(\lambda)$$

More generally, p_i is the characteristic polynomial of the $i \times i$ submatrix obtained from the first i rows and columns of A_{n-1}. Since each of these submatrices is also symmetric, all of the roots of all the p_i are real.

We next show that the polynomials p_i have the following property:

(6.2.7) $\qquad$ If $p_i(\lambda_0) = 0$, then $p_{i+1}(\lambda_0)p_{i-1}(\lambda_0) < 0$

which states that if λ_0 is a root of some p_i, then it is not also a root of p_{i-1} or p_{i+1}, and, moreover, p_{i-1} and p_{i+1} have different signs at λ_0. For example, if $p_1(\lambda_0) = 0$, then

$$p_2(\lambda_0)p_0(\lambda_0) = -b_1^2 p_0^2(\lambda_0) = -b_1^2 < 0$$

In a similar way, the general statement (6.2.7) is proved by induction. If $p_{k+1}(\lambda_0) = 0$, then by the induction hypothesis, it follows that $p_k(\lambda_0) \neq 0$, and since

$$p_{k+2}(\lambda_0) = -b_{k+1}^2 p_k(\lambda_0)$$

we must have

$$p_k(\lambda_0)p_{k+2}(\lambda_0) = -b_{k+1}^2 p_k^2(\lambda_0) < 0$$

The property (6.2.7) is known as the *Sturm sequence property*, and the polynomials (6.2.6) are called a *Sturm sequence.*

From (6.2.7), there follows an important separation property of the roots of the polynomials p_i, which we illustrate for the case $n = 3$. Let $\lambda_1 \le \lambda_2 \le \lambda_3$, $\mu_1 \le \mu_2$, and v_1 be the roots of p_3, p_2, and p_1, respectively. We note first that

(6.2.8) $\qquad p_i(\lambda) > 0$ as $\lambda \to -\infty, \qquad i = 1, \ldots, n$

which follows immediately from the definition (6.2.6). Thus, $p_2(\lambda) > 0$ for $|\lambda| \to +\infty$ since p_2 is a quadratic. Moreover, by (6.2.7), $p_2(v_1) < 0$, so

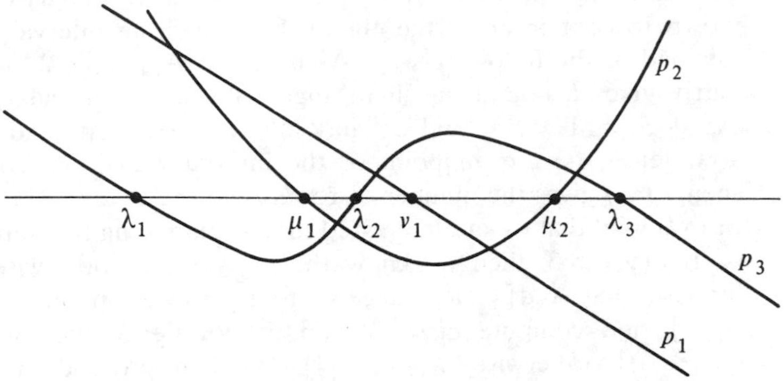

FIGURE 6.2 *The Root Separation Property.*

that $\mu_1 < v_1 < \mu_2$. Similarly, p_3 is a cubic with $p_3(\lambda) > 0$ as $\lambda \to -\infty$, and since $p_1(\mu_1) > 0$ while $p_1(\mu_2) < 0$, then again by (6.2.7), we have $p_3(\mu_1) < 0$ and $p_3(\mu_2) > 0$. Therefore, p_3 must have a root in each of the intervals $(-\infty, \mu_1)$, (μ_1, μ_2), and $(\mu_2, +\infty)$, and we must have the separation property

$$\textbf{(6.2.9)} \qquad \mu_1 < v_1 < \mu_2, \qquad \lambda_1 < \mu_1 < \lambda_2 < \mu_2 < \lambda_3$$

The polynomials p_1, p_2, and p_3 are depicted in Figure 6.2. Note that the root-separation property implies that the roots of p_n (that is, the eigenvalues of A_{n-1}) are distinct. This is a consequence of the assumption that the off-diagonal elements b_i are nonzero.

We can now use the root-separation property as a basis for a numerical method for approximating the eigenvalues. For any λ, we define $c(\lambda)$ to be the number of agreements in sign between consecutive terms in the sequence

$$1, p_1(\lambda), p_2(\lambda), \ldots, p_n(\lambda)$$

where if some $p_i(\lambda) = 0$, we take its sign to be that of $p_{i-1}(\lambda)$. As an example, suppose that $n = 3$, $p_1(\lambda) = 2 - \lambda$, $p_2(\lambda) = (2 - \lambda)^2 - 1$, $p_3(\lambda) = (2 - \lambda)p_2(\lambda) - p_1(\lambda)$. By evaluating the Sturm sequence at $\lambda = 0$, we obtain the values $\{+1, +2, +2, +3\}$, for which there are three agreements in sign between consecutive terms. Thus, $c(0) = 3$. Similarly, $c(2) = 2$, and $c(5) = 0$.

It turns out that the following remarkable fact holds for $c(\lambda)$; this follows directly from the root-separation property:

THEOREM 6.2.1. *$c(\lambda)$ is the number of roots of p_n greater than or equal to λ.*

This result can be used as the basis of a numerical method for approximating the roots $\lambda_1 < \cdots < \lambda_n$ of p_n. Let $[\ell, u]$ be an interval known to contain all of the eigenvalues. Such an interval can be easily obtained in the following way. As noted in Appendix 2, any norm of a matrix gives a bound on all its eigenvalues. In particular, then, $|\lambda_i| \leq \|A_{n-1}\|_\infty$, $i = 1, \ldots, n$, and we may take $\ell = -\|A_{n-1}\|_\infty$ and $u = \|A_{n-1}\|_\infty$. Now, let γ_1 be the midpoint of the interval $[\ell, u]$ and compute $c(\gamma_1)$. Then, $c(\gamma_1)$ gives the number of roots λ_i in the interval $[\gamma_1, u]$. Suppose, for example, that we are interested in approximating the third largest root λ_3. If $c(\gamma_1) \geq 3$, then we know that $\lambda_3 \in [\gamma_1, u]$; otherwise, $\lambda_3 \in [\ell, \gamma_1]$. Suppose that $\lambda_3 \in [\gamma_1, u]$, take γ_2 to be the midpoint of the interval $[\gamma_1, u]$, and compute $c(\gamma_2)$. Again, if $c(\gamma_2) \geq 3$, then we know that $\lambda_3 \in [\gamma_2, u]$; otherwise, $\lambda_3 \in [\gamma_1, \gamma_2]$. We can proceed in this fashion, retaining the interval in which λ_3 is known to lie and using the midpoint of this interval for the next evaluation of the function $c(\lambda)$. After k bisections, we will have an interval of length $2^{-k}(u - \ell)$ known to contain the root, and we can make this interval as small as we please by further bisections.

Note that the method just described is very similar to the bisection method discussed in Section 4.2. However, $c(\lambda)$ gives information about all of the roots, and this can be utilized to cut down considerably the overall calculation time. For example, if in the context of the previous paragraph, $c(\gamma_1) = 7$, we know that all of $\lambda_1, \ldots, \lambda_7$ are in the interval $[\gamma_1, u]$. As subsequent values of $c(\gamma_i)$ are computed, they can be utilized to begin isolating several roots rather than only one particular one.

We next turn to the problem of computing the eigenvectors of A. Suppose that we have obtained an approximation $\hat{\lambda}_k$ to the eigenvalue λ_k and we wish to approximate a corresponding eigenvector $\mathbf{x}$. The first step is to obtain an approximate eigenvector of the tridiagonal matrix A_{n-1}. Suppose that $\hat{\lambda}_k$ were the exact eigenvalue λ_k. Then, the eigenvector would be a nonzero solution of the homogeneous system of equations

(6.2.10)
$$(A_{n-1} - \hat{\lambda}_k I)\mathbf{x} = 0$$

If $\hat{\lambda}_k$ is not exact, the equations (6.2.10) in general will not have a non-trivial solution. Instead, we will solve the system

(6.2.11)
$$(A_{n-1} - \hat{\lambda}_k I)\mathbf{x} = \mathbf{d}$$

for an appropriately chosen right-hand-side $\mathbf{d}$.

To see under what conditions this will suitably approximate an eigenvector, recall that our assumption that all $b_i \neq 0$ in (6.2.4) implies that the eigenvalues of A_{n-1} are distinct, and therefore by theorems 6.1.1 and 6.1.2, A_{n-1} has n linearly independent eigenvectors.† Let these

† The symmetry of A_{n-1} also guarantees this. However, the following arguments hold for nonsymmetric matrices as well.

eigenvectors be $\mathbf{v}_1, \ldots, \mathbf{v}_n$ corresponding to the eigenvalues $\lambda_1, \ldots, \lambda_n$. Then, we can expand $\mathbf{d}$ in terms of the eigenvectors as

$$\mathbf{d} = \gamma_1 \mathbf{v}_1 + \cdots + \gamma_n \mathbf{v}_n$$

Now, the eigenvalues of the matrix $A_{n-1} - \hat{\lambda}_k I$ are $\lambda_i - \hat{\lambda}_k$, $i = 1, \ldots, n$, and the corresponding eigenvectors are simply the $\mathbf{v}_i$ of A_{n-1}; moreover, $(A_{n-1} - \hat{\lambda}_k I)^{-1}$ has eigenvalues $(\lambda_i - \hat{\lambda}_k)^{-1}$ and corresponding eigenvectors $\mathbf{v}_i$. (See exercise 6.2.1 for these facts in a more general context.) Therefore, we can write

$$\mathbf{x} = (A_{n-1} - \hat{\lambda}_k I)^{-1}\, \mathbf{d} = \sum_{i=1}^{n} \gamma_i (A_{n-1} - \hat{\lambda}_k)^{-1} \mathbf{v}_i$$

(6.2.12)

$$= \sum_{i=1}^{n} \frac{\gamma_i}{\lambda_i - \hat{\lambda}_k} \mathbf{v}_i = \frac{\gamma_k}{\lambda_k - \hat{\lambda}_k} \mathbf{v}_k + \sum_{\substack{i=1 \\ i \neq k}}^{n} \frac{\gamma_i}{\lambda_i - \hat{\lambda}_k} \mathbf{v}_i$$

Now, suppose that $\hat{\lambda}_k$ is close to λ_k, say $|\hat{\lambda}_k - \lambda_k| = 0(10^{-6})$, and that λ_k is not particularly close to any other eigenvalue λ_i. Then, provided that γ_k is not too small, the dominant term in (6.2.12) will be $\gamma_k(\lambda_k - \hat{\lambda}_k)^{-1}\mathbf{v}_k$. It is only the direction of $\mathbf{v}_k$ that we need to compute, since we can scale this to any desired length, and the effect of solving the system (6.2.11) will be to approximate the desired eigenvector.

Two factors will affect how accurate this approximation will be. First, if λ_k is very close to another eigenvalue, say λ_{k+1}, then $\lambda_{k+1} - \hat{\lambda}_k$ will also be small, and the first term of (6.2.12) will no longer be dominant; that is, we will tend to approximate some linear combination of $\mathbf{v}_k$ and $\mathbf{v}_{k+1}$. Closeness of the eigenvalues is an intrinsic problem of the particular matrix and hampers any numerical method in the calculation of the eigenvectors. The second factor is the possibility that γ_k is very small, and if this is the case, then, again, the first term of (6.2.12) may not be sufficiently dominant to give a good approximation to the desired eigenvector. In principle, we can insure that this will not happen by choosing the vector $\mathbf{d}$ so that γ_k is not small. However, we can do that with certainty only if the eigenvectors are known, and, of course, that is not the case. It has been found that choosing $\mathbf{d}$ to be the vector with components all equal to 1 usually works very satisfactorily. A similar strategy that sometimes works even better is to do Gaussian elimination on the coefficient matrix $A_{n-1} - \hat{\lambda}_k I$ to produce the upper-triangular matrix U and then solve the system $U\mathbf{y} = \mathbf{z}$ where $\mathbf{z}$ is a vector all of whose components are equal to 1. In this case, the vector $\mathbf{d}$ is not specified explicitly, but, implicitly, it is the vector that would give rise to a vector of all 1s under the Gaussian elimination calculation. Obviously, there is a great deal of flexibility in choosing the vector $\mathbf{d}$. Indeed, any "randomly" chosen vector would be very unlikely to yield a particularly small γ_k.

It is usually a good strategy to do one more solution of the tridiagonal system using as a right-hand side the approximate eigenvector just computed. Even if the original choice of **d** is such that γ_k is very small, the approximate eigenvector will have a $\hat{\gamma}_k$ that is larger, and another solution of the system may then give a suitable approximation. This iterative procedure could be repeated as many times as desired, but one extra solution is generally sufficient.

Once an approximate eigenvector of A_{n-1} is known, it must be transformed to an approximate eigenvector of A itself. Now, by (6.2.1), $A_{n-1} = PAP^T$, where $P = P_{n-2} \cdots P_2P_1$. If $\mathbf{x}$ is an eigenvector of A_{n-1}, then $\mathbf{y} = P^T\mathbf{x}$ is an eigenvector of A, as is seen by

$$A\mathbf{y} = AP^T\mathbf{x} = P^TPAP^T\mathbf{x} = P^TA_{n-1}\mathbf{x} = \lambda P^T\mathbf{x} = \lambda\mathbf{y}$$

Therefore, we use the same transformation if $\mathbf{x}$ is an approximate eigenvector of A_{n-1}:

$$\textbf{(6.2.13)}\quad \mathbf{y} = P^T\mathbf{x} = (P_{n-2} \cdots P_2P_1)^T\mathbf{x} = P_1^TP_2^T \cdots P_{n-2}^T\mathbf{x}$$
$$= P_1P_2 \cdots P_{n-2}\mathbf{x} = (I - 2\mathbf{w}_1\mathbf{w}_1^T) \cdots (I - 2\mathbf{w}_{n-2}\mathbf{w}_{n-2}^T)\mathbf{x}$$

This is very easy to carry out, assuming, of course, that we have retained the vectors $\mathbf{w}_1, \ldots, \mathbf{w}_{n-2}$ from the reduction to tridiagonal form. Thus,

$$(I - 2\mathbf{w}_{n-2}\mathbf{w}_{n-2}^T)\mathbf{x} = \mathbf{x} - 2(\mathbf{w}_{n-2}^T\mathbf{x})\mathbf{w}_{n-2}$$

and then the next transformation with $(I - 2\mathbf{w}_{n-3}\mathbf{w}_{n-3}^T)$ is applied to this vector, and so on.

We now carry out an example that is easily verified on a hand calculator. Let

$$\textbf{(6.2.14)}\qquad A = \begin{bmatrix} 120 & 80 & 40 & -16 \\ 80 & 120 & 16 & -40 \\ 40 & 16 & 120 & -80 \\ -16 & -40 & -80 & 120 \end{bmatrix}$$

This is a very special matrix for which the eigenvalues and eigenvectors are known explicitly, and thus we will be able to know exactly the accuracy of our calculation. The eigenvalues are 16, 64, 144, and 256, and the corresponding eigenvectors are

$$\mathbf{v}_1 = \begin{bmatrix} 1 \\ -1 \\ -1 \\ -1 \end{bmatrix}, \quad \mathbf{v}_2 = \begin{bmatrix} -1 \\ 1 \\ -1 \\ -1 \end{bmatrix}, \quad \mathbf{v}_3 = \begin{bmatrix} -1 \\ -1 \\ 1 \\ -1 \end{bmatrix}, \quad \mathbf{v}_4 = \begin{bmatrix} -1 \\ -1 \\ -1 \\ 1 \end{bmatrix}$$

We now begin the Householder reduction to the tridiagonal form. First, we compute the vector $\mathbf{w}_1$ from (6.2.4):

$$s = -90.86 \qquad \mathbf{w}_1^T = (0, 0.9696, 0.2270, -0.0908)$$

Then, carrying out the first transformation of (6.2.1), we obtain

$$A_2 = \begin{bmatrix} 120 & -90.86 & 0 & 0 \\ -90.86 & 157.2 & -16.17 & 65.63 \\ 0 & -16.17 & 102.9 & -51.44 \\ 0 & 65.63 & -51.44 & 99.89 \end{bmatrix}$$

Next,

$$s = 67.59 \qquad \mathbf{w}_2^T = (0, 0, -0.7872, 0.6168)$$

$$A_3 = \begin{bmatrix} 120 & -90.86 & 0 & 0 \\ -90.86 & 157.2 & 67.59 & 0 \\ 0 & 67.59 & 124.0 & -46.26 \\ 0 & 0 & -46.26 & 78.84 \end{bmatrix}$$

which is the desired tridiagonal matrix.

We next compute the eigenvalues of A_3 by the Sturm sequence method. Since $\|A_3\|_\infty = 315.7$, we may take the interval $[\ell, u]$ to be $[-315.7, 315.7]$, and this contains all the eigenvalues of A_3. Now, set $\lambda = 0$, the midpoint of the interval $[\ell, u]$. In general, it is possible to have severe overflow or underflow problems in computing the polynomial values $p_1(\lambda), \ldots, p_n(\lambda)$. This problem is mitigated to a large extent by computing the ratios

$$r_i(\lambda) = \frac{p_i(\lambda)}{p_{i-1}(\lambda)}, \qquad i = 1, \ldots, n$$

or

$$r_i(\lambda) = a_i - \lambda - b_{i-1}^2 \frac{p_{i-2}(\lambda)}{p_{i-1}(\lambda)}, \qquad i = 2, \ldots, n,$$

$$r_1(\lambda) = p_1(\lambda) = a_1 - \lambda$$

Since $p_0(\lambda) \equiv 1$, $c(\lambda)$, the number of sign agreements in the sequence $p_0(\lambda), p_1(\lambda), \ldots, p_n(\lambda)$, is just the number of nonnegative terms in the sequence $r_1(\lambda), \ldots, r_n(\lambda)$.

For A_3 and $\lambda = 0$, we then have

$$r_1(0) = 120 \qquad r_2(0) = 157.2 - \frac{(-90.86)^2}{120} = 88.42$$

$$r_3(0) = 124.0 - \frac{(67.59)^2}{88.42} = 72.34$$

$$r_4(0) = 78.84 - \frac{(-46.26)^2}{72.34} = 49.25$$

Since all $r_i(0)$ are nonnegative, $c(0) = 4$, and all eigenvalues of A_3 are in the interval $[0, 315.7]$. We next take $\lambda = 157.8$, the midpoint of this new interval, and compute the sequence $r_i(157.8)$, $i = 1, 2, 3, 4$. This yields $c(157.8) = 1$, so that one eigenvalue of A_3 is in the interval

[157.8, 315.7], and the remainder are in the interval [0, 157.8]. If we now concentrate on the largest eigenvalue λ_1, we have the sequence of steps

$$\begin{aligned}
\lambda &= 236.7, \ c(\lambda) = 1, \ \lambda_1 \in [236.7, 315.7] \\
\lambda &= 276.2, \ c(\lambda) = 0, \ \lambda_1 \in [236.7, 276.2] \\
\lambda &= 256.5, \ c(\lambda) = 0, \ \lambda_1 \in [236.7, 256.5] \\
\lambda &= 246.6, \ c(\lambda) = 1, \ \lambda_1 \in [246.5, 256.5] \\
&\vdots \qquad\qquad\qquad\qquad \vdots
\end{aligned}$$

We can continue this calculation as long as we wish to obtain a smaller and smaller interval that contains λ_1. It will take about twenty more steps to produce eight-place accuracy in the approximation to λ_1. To compute the remaining eigenvalues, we return to the interval [0, 157.8] which we saw before contained the lowest three eigenvalues. We then proceed in the analogous fashion to isolate the lowest three eigenvalues.

Finally, we consider the calculation of the eigenvector corresponding to the largest eigenvalue. Suppose that we have obtained the approximation $\hat{\lambda}_1 = 255.99998$ to the largest eigenvalue; this is correct to 2 in the last place since the exact eigenvalue is 256. If we apply Gaussian elimination to the system $(A_3 - \hat{\lambda}_1 I)\mathbf{x} = \mathbf{d}$, we obtain the upper triangular matrix

$$U = \begin{bmatrix} -136.0 & -90.86 & 0 & 0 \\ & 67.59 & -132.0 & -46.27 \\ & & -46.26 & -177.2 \\ & & & 0.9298 \cdot 10^{-5} \end{bmatrix}.$$

We use the strategy, discussed previously, of choosing $\mathbf{d}$ implicitly so that the right-hand side of the reduced triangular system is a vector $\mathbf{z}$ all of whose elements are equal to 1. Thus, we solve the system $U\mathbf{x} = \mathbf{z}$ and call the solution $\hat{\mathbf{x}}$. It is

$$\hat{\mathbf{x}}^T = 10^5(4.884, -7.310, -4.119, 1.075)$$

We then solve again the system $(A_3 - \hat{\lambda}_1 I)\mathbf{x} = \hat{\mathbf{x}}$, in which the right-hand side is the approximate eigenvector just obtained. This gives

$$\mathbf{x}^T = 10^{10}(5.250, -7.862, -4.430, 1.157)$$

and after the transformations (6.2.13), the corresponding eigenvector of A is

$$\mathbf{y}^T = 10^{10}(5.250, 5.250, 5.250, -5.250)$$

which, if we scale by 5.250×10^{10}, agrees with the exact eigenvector to four places. The other eigenvectors, corresponding to λ_2, λ_3, and λ_4, can be calculated in an analogous fashion.

We now make some general comments on errors in the methods of this section. The transformations that carry out the reduction to tridiagonal form are numerically very stable, and rounding error is not a serious problem. In the computation of the eigenvalues of the tridiagonal matrix, rounding error can affect the results only when the sign of some $p_i(\lambda)$ [or $r_i(\lambda)$] is incorrectly evaluated, so that $c(\lambda)$ is in error. This is essentially the same problem as with the bisection method, as discussed in Section 4.2. In general, this error will affect the eigenvalues only if very high accuracy is desired. The calculation of the eigenvectors is the most prone to error, and is particularly difficult when there are very close eigenvalues. In this case, we cannot hope to obtain the individual eigenvectors correctly but, rather, we try to determine the correct subspace associated with the cluster of eigenvalues.

Except for this possible difficulty in obtaining some of the eigenvectors, the methods are very satisfactory and experience little difficulty with respect to errors. Moreover, since the coefficient matrix is symmetric, its eigenvalues are well-conditioned. In the next section, we shall consider the problem of computing eigenvalues of nonsymmetric matrices, in which possible ill-conditioning of the eigenvalues is a severe problem.

Supplementary Discussion and References 6.2

The idea of computing the eigenvalues of a symmetric matrix by first reducing the matrix to tridiagonal form was put forth in the early 1950s by J. W. Givens, who used elementary rotation matrices that zeroed one off-tridiagonal element at a time. Subsequently, A. S. Householder noted that the reduction could be done in about half the number of arithmetic operations using orthogonal matrices of the form (6.2.3). Givens also developed the idea of using Sturm sequences—a classical concept—for computing the eigenvalues of the tridiagonal matrix. J. Wilkinson contributed immensely to the understanding of the behavior of these methods on a computer, and a detailed discussion including rounding-error analysis may be found in his classic book (Wilkinson [1965]). For a more theoretical treatment, see Householder [1964], and for a recent review, see Parlett [1980].

Excellent codes for Householder's method and the bisection method as well as the QR algorithm of the next section are available from the EISPACK package. (See Smith, et al. [1977] and Garbow, et al. [1979].)

It was mentioned previously that if the matrix B is nonsingular, then the generalized eigenvalue problem $A\mathbf{x} = \lambda B\mathbf{x}$ can be reduced to the standard problem $B^{-1}A\mathbf{x} = \lambda\mathbf{x}$. However, even if A and B are symmetric, the product $B^{-1}A$ need not be symmetric. If B is also positive-definite, an alternative reduction can be based on the Cholesky decomposition $B = LL^T$. Then, with the change of variable $\mathbf{y} = L^T\mathbf{x}$, the generalized problem is reduced to $L^{-1}AL^{-T}\mathbf{y} = \lambda\mathbf{y}$, and the coefficient matrix is again symmetric. This reduction is often a good way to proceed, especially if the decomposition of B is easily carried out. Alternatively, we will mention in the Supplementary discussion of the next section the QZ method, which can be applied directly to the generalized problem.

EXERCISES 6.2

6.2.1. Let B be a nonsingular matrix with eigenvalues $\lambda_1, \ldots, \lambda_n$ and corresponding eigenvectors $\mathbf{v}_1, \ldots, \mathbf{v}_n$.

a. Show that the eigenvalues of B^{-1} are $\lambda_1^{-1}, \ldots, \lambda_n^{-1}$ and the eigenvectors are $\mathbf{v}_1, \ldots, \mathbf{v}_n$.

b. Show that for any scalar μ, the eigenvalues of $B - \mu I$ are $\lambda_1 - \mu, \ldots, \lambda_n - \mu$ and the eigenvectors are $\mathbf{v}_1, \ldots, \mathbf{v}_n$.

6.2.2. Carry out the Householder reduction to tridiagonal form for the matrix

$$A = \begin{bmatrix} 2 & 1 & 1 \\ 1 & 2 & 1 \\ 1 & 1 & 2 \end{bmatrix}$$

6.2.3. Write a computer program for carrying out the Householder reduction to tridiagonal form for a general $n \times n$ real, symmetric matrix.

6.2.4. Let $P = I - \mu\mathbf{w}\mathbf{w}^T$ where $\mathbf{w}$ is a vector satisfying $\mathbf{w}^T\mathbf{w} = 1$. Show that P is orthogonal if and only if $\mu = 2$.

6.2.5. Compute the polynomials p_i of (6.2.6) for the matrix

$$B = \begin{bmatrix} 2 & -1 & \\ -1 & 2 & -1 \\ & -1 & 2 \end{bmatrix}$$

and verify that the properties (6.2.7)–(6.2.9) hold.

6.2.6. Using a hand calculator, carry out the Sturm sequence process for the matrix of exercise 6.2.5 until the three eigenvalues are isolated in intervals of width less than 0.01.

6.2.7. Using the approximate eigenvalues obtained in exercise 6.2.6, compute the corresponding approximate eigenvectors of the matrix of exercise 6.2.5.

6.3 The QR Method

We now turn to the problem of computing the eigenvalues of nonsymmetric matrices. This is inherently a much more difficult problem than when the matrix is symmetric, and the best methods are more complicated than the methods presented in the previous section. More importantly, the eigenvalues may be very ill-conditioned; we give a simple example of this. Let A and B be the $n \times n$ matrices

$$(6.3.1)\quad A = \begin{bmatrix} 0 & 1 & & & \\ & 0 & \cdot & & \\ & & \cdot & \cdot & \\ & & & \cdot & 1 \\ & & & & 0 \end{bmatrix} \qquad B = \begin{bmatrix} 0 & 1 & & & \\ & 0 & \cdot & & \\ & & \cdot & \cdot & \\ & & & \cdot & 1 \\ \varepsilon & & & & 0 \end{bmatrix}$$

Clearly, the matrix A has an n-fold eigenvalue equal to zero whereas the eigenvalues of B satisfy the characteristic equation $\lambda^n - \varepsilon = 0$, so

$$(6.3.2)\qquad |\lambda_i| = |\varepsilon|^{1/n}, \qquad i = 1, \ldots, n$$

Now, suppose, for example, that $n = 100$ and $\varepsilon = 10^{-100}$. Then, $|\lambda_i| = 10^{-1}$. That is, a change in one element of the matrix has produced changes in its eigenvalues that are 10^{99} times as large. Note that this is the same example, restated in terms of an eigenvalue problem, that was given in Section 4.2 to show the possible ill-conditioning of the roots of a polynomial.

Because of this possible ill-conditioning of the eigenvalues, it is impossible to expect any method to be able to compute accurate eigenvalues for all nonsymmetric matrices. For a given matrix, the best that we can hope is that the method will give the exact eigenvalues of a matrix of the form A + E, where E is a matrix with suitably "small" elements. If the computed eigenvalues then differ appreciably from the exact eigenvalues, it is because these eigenvalues are ill-conditioned.

We now begin the discussion of two closely related methods—the LR and QR methods. Given the matrix A, we use the Gaussian elimination process to factor the matrix A as

$$(6.3.3)\qquad A = LR$$

where L is a lower triangular matrix with 1's on its main diagonal and R is upper-triangular. Note that we have assumed that the decomposition of A into upper- and lower-triangular factors can be performed; as we saw in Chapter 3, this is not always the case. Now, define a new matrix by reversing the order of the factors L and R, that is,

$$(6.3.4)\qquad A_1 = RL$$

Since L is lower-triangular with 1's on the main diagonal, it is nonsingular, and we can write

$$(6.3.5)\qquad A = LR = L(RL)L^{-1} = LA_1L^{-1}$$

which shows that A and A_1 are similar and, hence, have the same eigenvalues. (See exercise 6.3.1 for a more general result of this type.)

Now, assume that we can decompose A_1 into lower- and upper-triangular factors L_1 and R_1; then, reverse the order of the factors to form a new matrix, A_2:

(6.3.6) $$A_1 = L_1R_1 \qquad A_2 = R_1L_1$$

Once again, A_2 is similar to A_1. We continue the procedure, alternately decomposing into the L and R factors and then reversing the order of the factors. Thus, we generate the sequence of matrices

(6.3.7) $$A_k = L_kR_k \qquad A_{k+1} = R_kL_k, \qquad k = 1, 2, \ldots$$

All of the matrices A_k are similar and, hence, have the same eigenvalues as the original matrix A. We then have the following theorem, the proof of which is beyond our scope:

THEOREM 6.3.1. *Assume the following:*

1. *The* LR *process* (6.3.7) *can be carried out.*
2. *The eigenvalues* $\lambda_1, \ldots, \lambda_n$ *of* A *have distinct absolute values; that is,* $|\lambda_1| > \cdots > |\lambda_n|$.
3. *If* $A = PDP^{-1}$, *where* D *is the diagonal matrix of eigenvalues of* A, *then* P *and* P^{-1} *both have* LU *decompositions.*

Then the matrices A_k of (6.3.7) converge to the triangular matrix

(6.3.8) $$\begin{bmatrix} \lambda_1 & * & \cdot & \cdot & * \\ & \lambda_2 & & & \cdot \\ & & \cdot & & \cdot \\ & & & \cdot & \cdot \\ & & & & * \\ & & & & \lambda_n \end{bmatrix}$$

where $*$ indicates an element that is, in general, nonzero.

Note that condition 2 precludes not only multiple eigenvalues but also complex eigenvalues if A is real, while the other assumptions are restrictive as well as difficult to verify. Although some of these restrictions may be circumvented, we will concentrate instead on a related method.

The basic idea of the QR method is the same as the LR method except that now the decompositions are to be into the product of an orthogonal matrix times an upper-triangular matrix. That is, starting with $A_0 = A$, we form sequence A_k by alternatively decomposing and then multiplying the factors in reverse order:

(6.3.9) $$A_k = Q_kR_k \qquad A_{k+1} = R_kQ_k, \qquad k = 0, 1, \ldots$$

where each of the Q_k is an orthogonal matrix. (We assume that A is real; if A were complex, the Q_k would be unitary matrices.)

We next show that the QR decompositions can be done very easily using the Householder transformations of the previous section. If we choose the vector $\mathbf{w}_1$ to be

$$\textbf{(6.3.10)}\qquad \mathbf{w}_1^T = \mu(a_{11} - s, a_{21}, \ldots, a_{n1}) \qquad s = \left(\sum_{j=1}^{n} a_{j1}^2\right)^{1/2},$$

$$\mu = \frac{1}{\sqrt{2s(s - a_{11})}}$$

then it is easy to verify (exercise 6.3.3) that

$$\textbf{(6.3.11)}\qquad A^{(2)} = (I - 2\mathbf{w}_1\mathbf{w}_1^T)A = \begin{bmatrix} s & * & \cdots & * \\ 0 & * & \cdots & * \\ \vdots & \vdots & & \vdots \\ 0 & * & & * \end{bmatrix}$$

where, as usual, the $*$ indicates an element that is, in general, nonzero. Next, choose the vector $\mathbf{w}_2$ as

$$\mathbf{w}_2^T = \hat{\mu}(0, \hat{a}_{22} - \hat{s}, \hat{a}_{32}, \ldots, \hat{a}_{n2}), \qquad \hat{s} = \pm\left(\sum_{j=2}^{n} \hat{a}_{j2}^2\right)^{1/2},$$

$$\hat{\mu} = \frac{1}{\sqrt{2\hat{s}(\hat{s} - \hat{a}_{22})}}$$

where the $\hat{}$ denotes the elements of $A^{(2)}$. Then, the matrix $(I - 2\mathbf{w}_2\mathbf{w}_2^T)A^{(2)}$ has zeros in its first two columns below the main diagonal. Continuing in this way with vectors $\mathbf{w}_i$ that have zeros in their first $i - 1$ positions, we obtain

$$\textbf{(6.3.12)}\qquad (I - 2\mathbf{w}_{n-1}\mathbf{w}_{n-1}^T) \cdots (I - 2\mathbf{w}_2\mathbf{w}_2^T)(I - 2\mathbf{w}_1\mathbf{w}_1^T)A = R$$

where R is upper-triangular. If we define

$$\textbf{(6.3.13)}\qquad Q = (I - 2\mathbf{w}_1\mathbf{w}_1^T)(I - 2\mathbf{w}_2\mathbf{w}_2^T) \cdots (I - 2\mathbf{w}_{n-1}\mathbf{w}_{n-1}^T)$$

then (6.3.12) may be written as $Q^TA = R$. Since each matrix $I - 2\mathbf{w}_i\mathbf{w}_i^T$ is orthogonal, the product Q is also orthogonal (see exercise 6.3.4). Therefore, $Q^{-1} = Q^T$, and (6.3.12) is equivalent to

$$\textbf{(6.3.14)}\qquad A = QR$$

which is the QR decomposition of the matrix A. We note that this decomposition can always be carried out without any conditions on the matrix A. Moreover, it is numerically stable, and no serious problem with rounding error can develop.

We now state a theorem for the QR method, analogous to theorem 6.3.1, and again without proof.

THEOREM 6.3.2. *Assume that conditions* 2 *and* 3 *of theorem* 6.3.1 *hold. Then, the matrices* A_k *produced by the* QR *method* (6.3.9) *converge to an* *upper-triangular matrix of the form* (6.3.8). *Moreover, the subdiagonal elements* $a_{ij}^{(k)}$ *of the matrices* A_k *converge to zero with a linear rate of convergence determined by the ratios of the eigenvalues of* A; *that is*

$$a_{ij}^{(k)} = 0\left(\frac{|\lambda_i|^k}{|\lambda_j|^k}\right), \qquad k \to \infty,\ i > j \tag{6.3.15}$$

This theorem provides the theoretical basis for the QR method. However, there are a number of restrictions in both the theorem and in the formulation of the method that limit its usefulness. We will next address these difficulties and ways to circumvent them, at least partially.

First, consider condition 2 of theorem 6.3.1 that the eigenvalues of A have distinct absolute values. This not only precludes multiple eigenvalues but also complex conjugate pairs of eigenvalues if the matrix is real. However, the situation is not really that bad. If the matrix A is real, then all the factors Q_k and R_k are also real, and there is, of course, no possibility that the A_k could converge to a triangular matrix with complex eigenvalues. However, what does occur—which is the best that we could hope—is that the A_k will "converge" to an almost-triangular form illustrated by the matrix

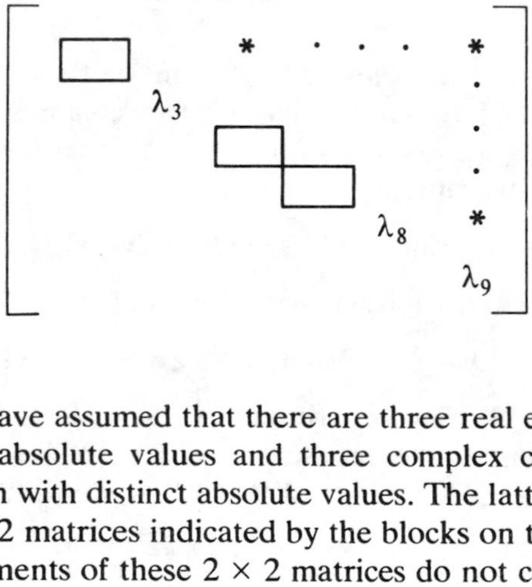

In this case, we have assumed that there are three real eigenvalues λ_3, λ_8, λ_9 with distinct absolute values and three complex conjugate pairs of eigenvalues, again with distinct absolute values. The latter are determined by the three 2×2 matrices indicated by the blocks on the main diagonal. Actually, the elements of these 2×2 matrices do not converge, but their eigenvalues do converge to eigenvalues of A. Hence, the computation of complex eigenvalues of real matrices does not present any problem.

The QR algorithm as described so far is too inefficient to be effective in practice, and two important modifications must be made. The first problem is that the decomposition (6.3.14) requires $0(n^3)$ operations, which makes each step of the process very slow. We can circumvent this difficulty by making a preliminary reduction of the matrix A to a form for which the decomposition can be more rapidly computed. Indeed, we would like first to reduce A to tridiagonal form, as in the previous section, and then perform the QR method on this tridiagonal matrix. Unfortunately, the reduction to tridiagonal form, while possible, may be numerically unstable for nonsymmetric matrices. The best that we can achieve with guaranteed numerical stability is reduction to what is called a *Hessenberg matrix*, which has the form

$$\text{(6.3.16)} \qquad A = \begin{bmatrix} a_{11} & a_{12} & \cdots & & a_{1n} \\ a_{21} & & \cdot & & \cdot \\ 0 & \cdot & & & \cdot \\ \cdot & \cdot & \cdot & & \cdot \\ \cdot & & \cdot & \cdot & \cdot \\ 0 & \cdots & 0 & a_{n,n-1} & a_{nn} \end{bmatrix}$$

That is, it has one nonzero diagonal below the main diagonal while the elements above the main diagonal are, in general, nonzero. The reduction of the original matrix A to Hessenberg form can be effected by the Householder transformations of the previous section. Indeed, if we define the vectors $\mathbf{w}_i$, $i = 1, \ldots, n-2$, precisely as in that section and carry out the similarity transformations (6.2.1) with the orthogonal matrices $P_i = I - 2\mathbf{w}_i\mathbf{w}_i^T$, the result will be a matrix of the form (6.3.16); the verification of this is left to exercise 6.3.6.

Now, assume that the matrix A is in the Hessenberg form (6.3.16) and consider the QR method applied to it. First of all, the decomposition (6.3.14) into the Q and R factors becomes particularly simple. It can be carried out by Householder transformations as before, but it is somewhat better to use what are known as *Givens transformations*, or *plane rotations*. These are orthogonal matrices of the form

$$\text{(6.3.17)} \qquad P_i = \begin{bmatrix} 1 & & & & & & \\ & \ddots & & & & & \\ & & 1 & & & & \\ & & & \sin\theta & \cos\theta & & \\ & & & -\cos\theta & \sin\theta & & \\ & & & & & 1 & \\ & & & & & & \ddots \\ & & & & & & & 1 \end{bmatrix}$$

where the first sin term is in the i, i position.

Now, the multiplication of the Hessenberg matrix (6.3.16) by the rotation matrix P_1 with the sine and cosine terms in the first 2×2

submatrix gives

$$\begin{bmatrix} \sin\theta & \cos\theta & & & \\ -\cos\theta & \sin\theta & & & \\ & & 1 & & \\ & & & \ddots & \\ & & & & 1 \end{bmatrix} \begin{bmatrix} a_{11} & & \cdots & & a_{1n} \\ a_{21} & & & & \cdot \\ & \ddots & & & \vdots \\ & & \ddots & & \cdot \\ & & & a_{n,n-1} & a_{nn} \end{bmatrix}$$

$$= \begin{bmatrix} a_{11}\sin\theta + a_{21}\cos\theta & & \cdots & & a_{1n}\sin\theta + a_{2n}\cos\theta \\ -a_{11}\cos\theta + a_{21}\sin\theta & & \cdots & & -a_{1n}\cos\theta + a_{2n}\sin\theta \\ & a_{32} & & \cdots & a_{3n} \\ & & \ddots & & \vdots \\ & & & a_{n,n-1} & a_{nn} \end{bmatrix}$$

The (2, 1) element of the product will then be zero provided that θ is chosen to satisfy

$$-a_{11}\cos\theta + a_{21}\sin\theta = 0 \quad \text{or} \quad \theta = \tan^{-1}\left(\frac{a_{11}}{a_{21}}\right)$$

Therefore, by a sequence of multiplications with the plane rotation matrices P_i, $i = 1, \ldots, n-1$, with the angles properly chosen, the subdiagonal elements of the Hessenberg matrix are successively set to zero. Thus, the decomposition is $A = QR$, where $Q^T = P_{n-1} \cdots P_1$, and hence $Q = P_1^T \cdots P_{n-1}^T$. The decomposition can be carried out in $0(n^2)$ operations, which is suitably efficient.

The initial reduction of A to Hessenberg form would not, of course, be effective if the QR method itself did not preserve the Hessenberg form from step to step. But it does. Note first that since each P_i has off-diagonal elements only in the $(i + 1, i)$ and $(i, i + 1)$ positions, the product Q is itself a Hessenberg matrix, as is easily verified (exercise 6.3.7). Then, since R is upper-triangular, the product RQ is a Hessenberg matrix (exercise 6.3.8). Thus, all of the matrices A_k generated by the QR method retain the Hessenberg form.

Even with the initial reduction of the matrix to Hessenberg form and the resulting economy in carrying out the generation of the matrices A_k, the QR method is still inefficient due to the possibly slow rate of convergence to zero of the subdiagonal elements. This rate of convergence is indicated by (6.3.15), which shows that if two eigenvalues, say λ_i and λ_{i+1}, are very close in absolute value, then the off-diagonal element in position $(i + 1, i)$ will converge to zero very slowly.

We will attempt to mitigate this convergence problem in the following way. Suppose that $\hat{\lambda}_n$ is a good approximation to λ_n and consider the matrix $\hat{A} = A - \hat{\lambda}_n I$ that has eigenvalues $\lambda_1 - \hat{\lambda}_n, \ldots, \lambda_n - \hat{\lambda}_n$. If we apply the QR method to $\hat{A}$, then the off-diagonal elements in the last row of the matrices A_k will converge to zero as powers of the quotients $(\lambda_n - \hat{\lambda}_n)/(\lambda_i - \hat{\lambda}_n)$ as opposed to the quotients λ_n/λ_i, $i = 1, \ldots, n-1$. The element with the slowest rate of convergence will be in the $(n, n-1)$ position, and here the convergence will be determined by the ratio $(\lambda_n - \hat{\lambda}_n)/(\lambda_{n-1} - \hat{\lambda}_n)$ for $\hat{A}$ as opposed to λ_n/λ_{n-1} for the original matrix. For example, suppose that $\lambda_n = 0.99$, $\lambda_{n-1} = 1.1$, and $\hat{\lambda}_n = 1.0$. Then, $\lambda_n/\lambda_{n-1} = 0.9$ while $|\lambda_n - \hat{\lambda}_n|/|\lambda_{n-1} - \lambda_n| = 0.1$, so the convergence of the $(n, n-1)$ element is approximately 20 times faster for the shifted matrix $\hat{A}$.

Of course, we will usually not know a good approximation $\hat{\lambda}_n$ to use as the shift parameter. However, as the QR process proceeds, the (n, n) elements $a_{nn}^{(k)}$ of the matrices A_k will be converging to the eigenvalue λ_n, and we can use them as the shift parameters; that is, at the kth stage, do the next QR step on the matrix $\hat{A}_k = A_k - a_{n,n}^{(k)}I$. There is then no reason not to continue using the (n, n) element of the current matrix to make a shift at each stage. Each shift changes the eigenvalues of the original matrix by the amount of the shift, so we need to keep track of the accumulation of shifts that are made; indeed, it is this accumulation that converges to the eigenvalue λ_n. The convergence is signaled by the elements in the last row becoming sufficiently small. When this occurs, the last row and column of the matrix may be dropped, and to determine the eigenvalue λ_{n-1}, we proceed with the resulting $(n-1) \times (n-1)$ submatrix. Note that the eigenvalues of this submatrix, and hence of the original matrix, have been changed by the total accumulation of shifts (which is the approximation to λ_n), and this must be added back to the other computed eigenvalues at the end of the computation. Alternatively, the shifts may be added back in at each stage, as illustrated by (6.3.18) in a different context, so that all of the matrices A_k retain the same eigenvalues.

The preceding discussion has been predicated on the assumption that the matrix A, as well as the smallest eigenvalue λ_n, is real. Now, suppose that A is real but λ_n is complex. Then, shifting by $a_{nn}^{(k)}$, which remains real, is not a particularly good strategy since the imaginary part of the eigenvalue cannot be approximated. Instead, as was discussed earlier, the eigenvalues of the lower right 2×2 submatrices of the matrices A_k produced by the unshifted QR algorithm will converge to the eigenvalue pair λ_n, $\lambda_{n-1} = \bar{\lambda}_n$. Hence, it would seem natural to use the eigenvalues of these 2×2 submatrices as shift parameters. Consider the first step applied to the matrix A_1 and let k_1, $k_2 = \bar{k}_1$ be the eigenvalues of the lower right 2×2 submatrix. If we add back the shifts, we obtain

(6.3.18)
$$\begin{aligned} A_1 - k_1 I &= Q_1 R_1 \qquad & A_2 &= R_1 Q_1 + k_1 I \\ A_2 - k_2 I &= Q_2 R_2 \qquad & A_3 &= R_2 Q_2 + k_2 I \end{aligned}$$

Since k_1 and k_2 are complex, the matrices A_1, A_2, Q_1, Q_2, R_1, and R_2 will, in general, be complex, and consequently the QR steps need to be carried out in complex arithmetic. However, an interesting fact is that A_3 is real (exercise 6.3.10). Indeed, it is possible to carry out the transformation from A_1 to A_3 entirely in real arithmetic, although we will not go into the details of this here. This procedure is called the *double-shift QR method.*

Even if the eigenvalues are real, it is a good strategy to shift twice using the eigenvalues of the lower right 2×2 submatrix. With this choice of shifts, as with the one of shifting by the (n, n) element, the rate of convergence is usually at least quadratic.

Once the eigenvalues are obtained, we still need to compute the eigenvectors, and this can be done in a manner analogous to that of the previous section but using, in the present case, the Hessenberg matrix. That is, assume that $\hat{A}$ is the Hessenberg matrix obtained from the original matrix A and that $\hat{\lambda}$ is an approximate eigenvalue. Then, we solve the system of linear equations

(6.3.19) $$(\hat{A} - \hat{\lambda}I)\mathbf{x} = \mathbf{d}$$

where, again, $\mathbf{d}$ is some suitably chosen right-hand side. The conditions under which the solution of (6.3.19) will be a suitable approximation to an eigenvector can be analyzed as in the previous section by expanding $\mathbf{d}$ in terms of the eigenvectors of $\hat{A}$. Once $\mathbf{x}$ has been computed, it still needs to be converted to an eigenvector of A itself. If $\hat{A} = PAP^T$, then, as in the previous section, $\mathbf{y} = P^T\mathbf{x}$ will be an approximate eigenvector of A.

We now summarize briefly the main points of our discussion of the QR method. In order for the method to be efficient, we must first reduce the original matrix to Hessenberg form, and then incorporate shifts into the basic QR algorithm to be applied to this Hessenberg matrix. As the iteration proceeds, the eigenvalues are obtained one by one (or two at a time in the case of a complex conjugate pair), the matrix is reduced in size, and the iteration proceeds toward the remaining eigenvalues. Properly implemented, the QR algorithm is the best general-purpose method for nonsymmetric matrices whose size is such that they can be contained in the main memory of the computer. We have not been able to give all of the details necessary for such an implementation but have tried only to present the basic flavor of the method. The Supplementary Discussion gives various references for further reading.

The QR algorithm is also an attractive alternative to the Sturm sequence method for symmetric tridiagonal matrices, especially where all eigenvalues of the matrix are desired. For tridiagonal matrices, the method simplifies considerably; and for symmetric matrices, the eigenvalues are all real, so the shift strategy does not need to involve complex numbers. Moreover, the rate of convergence is generally faster in the symmetric case.

Supplementary Discussion and References: 6.3

The LR algorithm was introduced by H. Rutishauser in 1958, and the QR algorithm was published independently by Francis [1961, 1962] and Kublanovskaya [1961]. Subsequently, J. Wilkinson continued the development and analysis of these algorithms, and a wealth of material, including proofs of theorems 6.3.1 and 6.3.2, may be found in his book (1965). See also Stewart [1973] for further discussion of the QR method; in particular, this book discusses an implicitly shifted version of the method as well as relationships between the QR method and the power, inverse power, and Rayleigh quotient methods to be presented in the next section. Probably the best programs now available are contained in EISPACK (see Smith et al. [1977] and Garbow et al. [1979]).

For symmetric positive-definite matrices, a variant of the LR method is the LL^T method, in which the decompositions are those of Cholesky. Thus, the basic method is to decompose $A = A_1$ into $L_1L_1^T$, compute $A_2 = L_1^TL_1$, decompose A_2 into $L_2L_2^T$, and so on.

There is an interesting connection between the LL^T algorithm and the QR algorithm. If A_i and $\hat{A}_i$, $i = 1, 2, \ldots$, are the matrices generated by the LL^T and QR methods, respectively, then $\hat{A}_{k+1} = A_{2k+1}$.

An extension of the QR method for the generalized eigenvalue problem $A\mathbf{x} = \lambda B\mathbf{x}$ has been developed by Moler and Stewart [1973]; see also Ward [1975]. It is known as the QZ algorithm. A similar extension of the LR method—the LZ method—has been given by Kaufman [1974].

EXERCISES 6.3

6.3.1. Let B and C be $n \times n$ matrices. Show that BC and CB are similar.

6.3.2. Show that the matrix

$$A = \begin{bmatrix} 0 & 1 \\ 1 & 1 \end{bmatrix}$$

has no LR decomposition, and hence the LR method cannot be carried out. Show that although the matrix

$$A = \begin{bmatrix} 1 & 1 \\ -1 & 1 \end{bmatrix}$$

has an LR decomposition, the matrix A_1 of (6.3.4) does not, and hence the LR method cannot be carried out.

6.3.3. Verify that if $\mathbf{w}_1$ is given by (6.3.10), then the form of the matrix in (6.3.11) is correct.

6.3.4. Show that if A and B are $n \times n$ real orthogonal matrices, then AB is also orthogonal. Then, show that the product Q of (6.3.13) is orthogonal if each $\mathbf{w}_i$ satisfies $\mathbf{w}_i^T\mathbf{w}_i = 1$.

6.3.5. Carry out the QR decomposition for the matrix

$$A = \begin{bmatrix} 2 & -1 & 1 \\ 2 & 3 & 1 \\ 1 & -1 & 2 \end{bmatrix}$$

6.3.6. Verify, in detail, that the orthogonal similarly transformations $P_i = I - 2\mathbf{w}_i\mathbf{w}_i^T$, where the $\mathbf{w}_i$ are defined as in Section 6.2, reduce a nonsymmetric matrix A to the Hessenberg form (6.3.16).

6.3.7. Show that if P_i is a diagonal matrix except for nonzero elements in the $(i + 1, i)$ and $(i, i + 1)$ positions, then the product $P_1 \cdots P_{n-1}$ is a Hessenberg matrix.

6.3.8. Show that if Q is a Hessenberg matrix and R is upper-triangular, then the product RQ is a Hessenberg matrix.

6.3.9. Let A be a banded matrix. Show that both the LR and the QR method preserve the bandwidth of A.

6.3.10. Let A_1 be real and k_1, $k_2 = \bar{k}_1$ be complex scalars. Show that the matrix A_3 defined by (6.3.18) is real.

6.4 Methods for Large Sparse Matrices

The Householder and QR methods of the previous sections are of primary value when the matrix A can be held in main memory, the matrix is not particularly sparse except that it may be banded, and all or a large number of the eigenvalues are desired. Conversely, they are not very useful for very large sparse matrices for which only a few eigenvalues are desired. Problems such as this arise in partial differential equations, as well as in other areas. A typical problem of this type might involve a 5,000 × 5,000 matrix with only ten or fewer nonzero elements in each row, and for which only a few eigenvalues, perhaps four or five, are desired. For such a problem, the previous methods are completely unsuitable.

A classical method that has certain usefulness—but also serious defects—for large sparse problems is the *power method.* Let A have eigenvalues $\lambda_1, \ldots, \lambda_n$, which we assume for the moment are real and satisfy

$$|\lambda_1| > |\lambda_2| \geq \cdots \geq |\lambda_n| \tag{6.4.1}$$

For a given vector $\mathbf{x}_0$, consider the sequence of vectors generated by

$$\mathbf{x}_{k+1} = A\mathbf{x}_k, \qquad k = 0, 1, \ldots \tag{6.4.2}$$

The analysis of the behavior of the sequence $\{\mathbf{x}_k\}$ can be done in precisely the same way as for the demography problem in Section 6.1. For simplicity, assume that A has n linearly independent eigenvectors

$\mathbf{v}_1, \ldots, \mathbf{v}_n$, corresponding to the eigenvalues $\lambda_1, \ldots, \lambda_n$, and expand $\mathbf{x}_0$ in terms of these eigenvectors:

$$\mathbf{x}_0 = c_1\mathbf{v}_1 + \cdots + c_n\mathbf{v}_n$$

Then, as in (6.1.20),

$$\textbf{(6.4.3)} \qquad \begin{aligned} \mathbf{x}_k &= c_1\lambda_1^k\mathbf{v}_1 + c_2\lambda_2^k\mathbf{v}_2 + \cdots + c_n\lambda_n^k\mathbf{v}_n \\ &= \lambda_1^k\left[c_1\mathbf{v}_1 + c_2\left(\frac{\lambda_2}{\lambda_1}\right)^k\mathbf{v}_2 + \cdots + c_n\left(\frac{\lambda_n}{\lambda_1}\right)^k\mathbf{v}_n\right] \end{aligned}$$

and, because of (6.4.1), the terms $(\lambda_i/\lambda_1)^k$, $i = 2, \ldots, n$, all tend to zero as k goes to infinity. Therefore,

$$\textbf{(6.4.4)} \qquad \lambda_1^{-k}\mathbf{x}_k \to c_1\mathbf{v}_1 \quad \text{as } k \to \infty$$

which shows that the vectors $\mathbf{x}_k$ tend to the direction of the eigenvector $\mathbf{v}_1$. The magnitudes of vectors $\mathbf{x}_k$, however, will tend to zero if $|\lambda_1| < 1$, or become unbounded if $|\lambda_1| > 1$. Therefore, scaling of the vectors $\mathbf{x}_k$ is required, and the scaling process will also give approximations to the eigenvalue λ_1.

There are numerous ways to choose the scaling factors. One convenient modification of (6.4.2) is

$$\textbf{(6.4.5)} \qquad \begin{aligned} \hat{\mathbf{x}}_k &= A\mathbf{x}_{k-1}, & k &= 1, 2, \ldots \\ \mathbf{x}_k &= \frac{\hat{\mathbf{x}}_k}{\sigma_k}, & k &= 1, 2, \ldots \end{aligned}$$

where σ_k is an element of $\hat{\mathbf{x}}_k$ of maximum modulus. Then, one can show that

$$\textbf{(6.4.6)} \qquad \sigma_k \to \lambda_1 \quad \text{and} \quad \mathbf{x}_k \to c\mathbf{v}_1 \qquad \text{as } k \to \infty$$

where the last relation says that $\mathbf{x}_k$ tends to some multiple of the eigenvector $\mathbf{v}_1$.

The main advantage of the power method is that the vectors $\mathbf{x}_k$ can be generated by only matrix-vector multiplications (plus the work needed to compute the scaling factors); operations on the matrix A itself are unnecessary. The main disadvantage is the possibly slow rate of convergence, which, as shown by (6.4.3), is determined primarily by the ratio λ_2/λ_1. If this ratio is close to 1, as is typical for many problems, the convergence will be slow. One way to attempt to mitigate this problem is by the use of origin shifts as was done with the QR algorithm. If the power method is applied to the matrix $A - \sigma I$, whose eigenvalues are $\lambda_1 - \sigma, \ldots, \lambda_n - \sigma$, then the rate of convergence will be determined by the ratio $|\lambda_2 - \sigma|/|\lambda_1 - \sigma|$ provided that $\lambda_1 - \sigma$ remains the dominant eigenvalue. Under the assumption that the λ_i are real, it can be shown that the optimum value of σ to minimize this ratio is $\sigma = (\lambda_2 + \lambda_n)/2$. But even with this optimum choice—which would be hard to obtain in practice—the convergence may still be painfully slow. For example, suppose that a $1,000 \times 1,000$ matrix has the eigenvalues 1,000, 999, . . . , 1. Then, the optimum value of the ratio after this shift by σ is 0.998, which is barely better than the unshifted ratio of 0.999.

The power method also has other disadvantages. If there is more than one dominant eigenvalue, for example, $|\lambda_1| = |\lambda_2| > |\lambda_3| \geq |\lambda_n|$, which would be the case for a real matrix with a dominant complex conjugate pair of roots, the sequence (6.4.5) does not converge. There are ways to circumvent this difficulty, but in the case of complex roots, acceleration of the convergence by origin shifts is even less satisfactory. Another problem is in computing the subdominant eigenvalues. Once we have approximated λ_1, we need to remove it in some fashion from the matrix or subsequent iterations will again converge to λ_1 rather than λ_2. There are various ways to accomplish this, but we will not discuss them here.

Many of the disadvantages of the power method are overcome to some extent by the *inverse power method* (also called *inverse iteration*), but at the expense of new difficulties. This method was the basis for our computation of an eigenvector of a tridiagonal or Hessenberg matrix in the previous two sections under the assumption that an approximate eigenvalue was already known.

Consider the sequence $\{\mathbf{x}_k\}$ defined by

$$(A - \sigma I)\mathbf{x}_k = \mathbf{x}_{k-1}, \qquad k = 1, 2, \ldots \tag{6.4.7}$$

That is, $\mathbf{x}_k$ is defined as the solution of the linear system (6.4.7). This is simply the power method for the matrix $(A - \sigma I)^{-1}$. If A again has eigenvalues $\lambda_1, \ldots, \lambda_n$ and corresponding eigenvectors $\mathbf{v}_1, \ldots, \mathbf{v}_n$, then $(A - \sigma I)^{-1}$ has eigenvalues $(\lambda_i - \sigma)^{-1}$ and eigenvectors $\mathbf{v}_i$, and the sequence $\{\mathbf{x}_k\}$ of (6.4.7) obeys the relationship (6.4.3) with the λ_i replaced by $(\lambda_i - \sigma)^{-1}$:

$$\begin{aligned} \mathbf{x}_k &= \frac{c_1}{(\lambda_1 - \sigma)^k}\mathbf{v}_1 + \cdots + \frac{c_n}{(\lambda_n - \sigma)^k}\mathbf{v}_n \\ &= \frac{1}{(\lambda_1 - \sigma)^k}\left[c_1\mathbf{v}_1 + c_2\left(\frac{\lambda_1 - \sigma}{\lambda_2 - \sigma}\right)^k\mathbf{v}_2 + \cdots + c_n\left(\frac{\lambda_1 - \sigma}{\lambda_n - \sigma}\right)^k\mathbf{v}_n\right] \end{aligned} \tag{6.4.8}$$

Now, if (6.4.1) holds and if σ is a sufficiently good approximation to λ_1 that $|\lambda_1 - \sigma| < |\lambda_2 - \sigma|$, the vectors $\mathbf{x}_k$ will again converge in direction to the eigenvector $\mathbf{v}_1$. Moreover, the rate of convergence is determined by the ratio $(\lambda_1 - \sigma)/(\lambda_2 - \sigma)$, and in contrast to the power method itself, the better σ approximates the eigenvalue λ_1, the smaller will be this ratio.

Each step of inverse iteration can greatly improve the approximation to the eigenvector if σ is a good approximation to λ_1. However, there remains the problem of approximating the eigenvalue itself, and we now describe a sometimes-useful way to do this. We will restrict our discussion now to symmetric matrices, but the majority of large sparse matrices that arise in applications—especially those from differential equations—are symmetric.

For a given vector $\mathbf{v}$, the *Rayleigh quotient* is the quantity

$$\sigma = \frac{\mathbf{v}^T A \mathbf{v}}{\mathbf{v}^T \mathbf{v}} \tag{6.4.9}$$

If $\mathbf{v}$ is a good approximation to the eigenvector $\mathbf{v}_1$ of A, then σ will be a good approximation to the corresponding eigenvalue λ_1. To see why this is so, again expand $\mathbf{v}$ in terms of the eigenvectors as

$$\mathbf{v} = \gamma_1 \mathbf{v}_1 + \cdots + \gamma_n \mathbf{v}_n$$

and assume that the $\mathbf{v}_i$ are normalized so that $\mathbf{v}_i^T \mathbf{v}_i = 1$, $i = 1, \ldots, n$. Then, since $A\mathbf{v}_i = \lambda_i \mathbf{v}_i$, (6.4.9) becomes

$$\begin{aligned} \sigma &= \frac{(\gamma_1 \mathbf{v}_1 + \cdots + \gamma_n \mathbf{v}_n)^T (\gamma_1 \lambda_1 \mathbf{v}_1 + \cdots + \gamma_n \lambda_n \mathbf{v}_n)}{\gamma_1^2 + \cdots + \gamma_n^2} \\ &= \frac{\lambda_1 \gamma_1^2 + \cdots + \lambda_n \gamma_n^2}{\gamma_1^2 + \cdots + \gamma_n^2} \\ &= \lambda_1 \left[\frac{1 + \frac{\lambda_2}{\lambda_1}\left(\frac{\gamma_2}{\gamma_1}\right)^2 + \cdots + \frac{\lambda_n}{\lambda_1}\left(\frac{\gamma_n}{\gamma_1}\right)^2}{1 + \left(\frac{\gamma_2}{\gamma_1}\right)^2 + \cdots + \left(\frac{\gamma_n}{\gamma_1}\right)^2} \right] \end{aligned} \tag{6.4.10}$$

Now, the assumption that $\mathbf{v}$ is a good approximation to the direction of $\mathbf{v}_1$ means that γ_1 is large relative to the other γ_i. Therefore, the quantity in brackets in (6.4.10) is close to 1, so σ is an approximation to λ_1, and, clearly, the smaller the ratios γ_i/γ_1, the better the approximation will be.

We can now consider a combined inverse power/Rayleigh quotient iteration. Given $\mathbf{x}_0$, compute

$$\sigma_k = \frac{\mathbf{x}_k^T A \mathbf{x}_k}{\mathbf{x}_k^T \mathbf{x}_k}, \qquad k = 0, 1, \ldots \tag{6.4.11a}$$

$$(A - \sigma_k I)\mathbf{x}_{k+1} = \mathbf{x}_k, \qquad k = 0, 1, \ldots \tag{6.4.11b}$$

That is, at each stage, compute a new Rayleigh quotient approximation σ_k to the eigenvalue, and then a new approximation to the eigenvector by an inverse iteration step. This procedure can be very rapidly convergent where it is successful; indeed, it can be shown that there is a cubic rate of convergence of the sequence $\{\sigma_k\}$ to a simple eigenvalue. However, there are several drawbacks. The first is that of obtaining a satisfactory starting vector $\mathbf{x}_0$, since if $\mathbf{x}_0$ is not a reasonable approximation to the direction $\mathbf{v}_1$, the sequences (6.4.11) will not necessarily converge to the eigenvalue and eigenvector pair $\lambda_1, \mathbf{v}_1$. One way to obtain a suitable $\mathbf{x}_0$ is to use the power method itself for several steps and then switch to (6.4.11).

Another drawback to the process (6.4.11) is the necessity to solve the linear systems (6.4.11b) at each stage. For large sparse coefficient matrices, this in itself is a major problem, which will be discussed in Chapter 8.

We have summarized in this section two classical methods for approximating eigenvalues and vectors of large sparse matrices. Although both are useful in certain circumstances, neither is a viable method in general. There are newer, more complicated methods available, but they are beyond the scope of this book. However, there is as yet no really satisfactory method for computing the eigenvalues and vectors of general large sparse matrices.

Supplementary Discussion and References: 6.4

As with the other sections of this chapter, the books by Stewart [1973] and Wilkinson [1965] provide excellent information on more advanced points. See also Bathe and Wilson [1976], Jennings [1977], and Parlett [1980]. The analysis of the algorithms of this section was restricted to matrices with n linearly independent eigenvectors, but it can be extended to general matrices; see Wilkinson [1965] for a complete analysis of the power and inverse power methods, and Kahan and Parlett [1968] for the Rayleigh quotient method.

Two potentially promising methods are the Lanczos algorithm and the "subspace" method. For a review of these methods, see Parlett [1980].

EXERCISES 6.4

6.4.1. The matrix

$$A = \begin{bmatrix} 2 & 1 \\ 1 & 2 \end{bmatrix}$$

has eigenvalues 1 and 3 with corresponding eigenvectors $(1, -1)$ and $(1, 1)$. Apply several steps of the power method (6.4.5) to this matrix, starting with the vector $\mathbf{x}_0^T = (1, 0)$. Carry the iteration sufficiently far that the rate of convergence is becoming apparent.

6.4.2. Write a computer program to carry out the power method (6.4.5). Test the code on the matrix of the previous exercise and on the matrix (6.2.14).

6.4.3. Apply the power method to the shifted matrix $A - \frac{1}{2}I$ where A is given in exercise 6.4.1. Discuss the improvement in the rate of convergence.

6.4.4. If $\{\mathbf{x}_k\}$ is the sequence generated by (6.4.2), and (6.4.1) holds, show that $\|\mathbf{x}_{k+1}\|/\|\mathbf{x}_k\| \to |\lambda_1|$ as $k \to \infty$ in any norm.

6.4.5. Apply the inverse power iteration (6.4.7) with shift parameters $\sigma = 2$, 2.5, and 2.9 to the matrix of exercise 6.4.1. Discuss the rate of convergence to the eigenvector corresponding to the eigenvalue 3. Analyze the rate of convergence for each of the shift parameters by using (6.4.8).

6.4.6. Carry out several steps of the iteration (6.4.11) for the matrix A of exercise 6.4.1 and $\mathbf{x}_0^T = (1, 0)$. Discuss your results vis-à-vis those of exercise 6.4.1.

7 Space and Time

7.1 Partial Differential Equations

In the previous chapters, we have considered ordinary differential equations, that is, differential equations in a single independent variable. This independent variable was either time—as in the case of the trajectory or predator–prey problems of Chapter 2—or a space variable as in the problem of Chapter 3. We now begin the study of the numerical solution of differential equations in two or more independent variables—partial differential equations. In the present chapter, the two independent variables will be time and a single space variable, and in the next chapter, we shall treat problems in more than one space variable.

As two examples, we shall concentrate on

(7.1.1) $$u_t = cu_{xx}$$

and

(7.1.2) $$u_{tt} = cu_{xx}$$

which are known, respectively, as the *heat* (or *diffusion*) *equation* and the *wave equation.* The heat equation (7.1.1) is the prototype example of a *parabolic equation,* and (7.1.2) is the standard example of a *hyperbolic equation.* The third standard type of partial differential equation is called *elliptic,* and the simplest example of this type is the *potential* or *Laplace's equation*

(7.1.3) $$u_{xx} + u_{yy} = 0$$

which will be treated in Chapter 8.

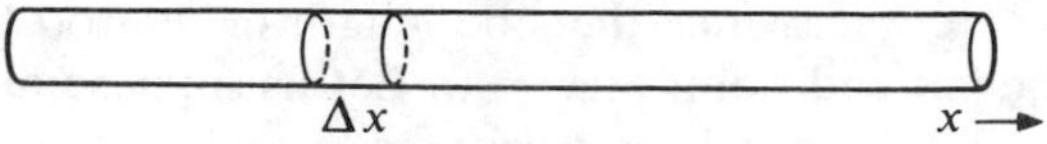

FIGURE 7.1

We will first sketch how (7.1.1) arises as a mathematical model of heat conduction. Let us consider a narrow rod aligned with the x-axis as indicated in Figure 7.1. We assume that the rod is perfectly insulated except, perhaps, at the two ends and that the flow of heat is only in the x-direction. Let $u = u(t, x)$ be the temperature (in degrees Kelvin) at time t and at a point x in the rod, and let a be the cross-sectional area of the rod. By elementary physics, the time rate of change of heat across a surface perpendicular to the direction of the rod is given by $-kau_x$, where $k > 0$ is the thermal conductivity; that is, if the temperature gradient, u_x, across the surface is negative, so that the temperature is higher to the left than to the right, then heat is flowing across the surface to the right, in accord with one's intuition. Therefore, if we consider a small element of the rod of length Δx, the rate at which heat is flowing into the element at the point x is $-(kau_x)|_x$, and the rate at which it is flowing out at $x + \Delta x$ is $(-kau_x)|_{x+\Delta x}$; thus, the net rate of change in the element is given by

(7.1.4)
$$(-kau_x)|_x - (-kau_x)|_{x+\Delta x}$$

On the other hand, again by elementary physics, the heat in such an element is proportional to the mass of the element times the temperature; more precisely, it is equal to $sa\Delta x\rho u$, where s is the specific heat of the material and ρ is the mass density (mass per unit volume). Therefore, the derivative with respect to time of the heat in the element is equal to the quantity of (7.1.4); that is,

$$sa\Delta x\rho u_t = (kau_x)|_{x+\Delta x} - (kau_x)_x$$

or, letting $\Delta x \to 0$ and simplifying,

(7.1.5)
$$u_t = \frac{1}{s\rho}(ku_x)_x$$

If k is independent of x, then this reduces to equation (7.1.1) with $c = k/(s\rho)$. Thus, in this case, (7.1.1) shows that the time rate of change of the temperature in such a thin rod is proportional to the second spatial derivative of the temperature within the rod.

As we saw with ordinary differential equations, a solution of a differential equation is not determined without giving appropriate initial and/or boundary conditions, and we expect the same to be true for partial differential equations. Let us see how we can impose suitable conditions for the heat equation in the case of the problem of the rod. Suppose that at some time that we call $t = 0$, the rod has a temperature distribution

$g(x)$ where we assume that the length of the rod has been taken to be 1 with the left end point at $x = 0$. Let us suppose also that the ends of the rod are held at fixed temperatures α and β; that is,

(7.1.6) $$u(t, 0) = \alpha, \qquad u(t, 1) = \beta$$

which provide boundary conditions in the space variable x. The initial temperature distribution provides an initial condition

(7.1.7) $$u(0, x) = g(x), \qquad 0 \le x \le 1$$

Thus, the physical problem is: Given a rod whose ends are held at fixed temperatures α and β, and whose initial temperature distribution is given by $g(x)$, then what is the temperature at any point x in the rod at any time $t > 0$? And the mathematical model for this problem is given by the partial differential equation

(7.1.8) $$u_t = cu_{xx}, \qquad c = \frac{k}{s\rho}, \qquad 0 \le x \le 1$$

together with the boundary conditions (7.1.6) and the initial condition (7.1.7).

There are several variations on this problem that can be modeled by changing the boundary conditions or the equation itself. For example, suppose that we assume that the right end of the rod is, like the sides, perfectly insulated; by definition, then, we expect no heat loss or change in temperature across this end, so the boundary conditions (7.1.6) are changed to

(7.1.9) $$u(t, 0) = \alpha \qquad u_x(t, 1) = 0$$

Another variation is to suppose that the rod is not homogeneous—as has been tacitly assumed—but is made of an alloy whose components vary slowly as a function of x. Then, the density as well as the thermal conductivity and specific heat will, in general, also vary with x, so the proper equation is now (7.1.5) where $\rho = \rho(x)$, $s = s(x)$, and $k = k(x)$. Thus, the differential equation is now one with variable rather than constant coefficients. Going one step further, the thermal conductivity will, in general, depend not only on the material but also on the temperature itself. For many problems, this dependence is so slight that it can be ignored, but for others, it cannot. Thus, we may have $k = k(u)$ so that the equation (7.1.5) is now nonlinear.

The heat equation is also a mathematical model of various other physical phenomena such as diffusion of a gas.

Let us turn now to the wave equation (7.1.2): $u_{tt} = cu_{xx}$. This equation, or more general forms of it, models various types of wave propagation phenomena, as, for example, in acoustics. One of the classical situations that it models is that of a vibrating string—for example, a violin string—and we shall discuss this problem rather briefly.

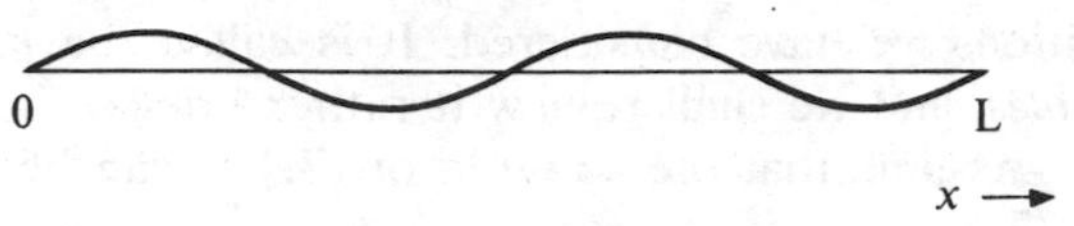

FIGURE 7.2 *A Vibrating String.*

Consider a taut string along the x-axis that is fastened at $x = 0$ and $x = L$, as in Figure 7.2. If the string is plucked, it will vibrate, as indicated.

We will assume that the string is "ideal"—that is, it is perfectly flexible and the tension T is constant as a function of both x and t and is large compared to the weight of the string. We denote the deflection of the string at a point x and time t by $u(t, x)$ and we assume that the deflections u we are studying are small compared to the length L of the string. We assume, moreover, that the slope of the deflected string at any point is small compared to unity and that the horizontal displacement of the string is negligible compared to the vertical displacement (this is sometimes called *transverse motion*). We are also tacitly assuming that the motion of the string is only in a plane.

By application of Newton's second law of motion—force equals mass times acceleration—it can be shown by fairly elementary arguments that the deflection of the string satisfies the equation

(7.1.10) $$u_{tt} = cu_{xx}, \qquad c = \frac{gT}{w}$$

where g is the gravitational constant and w is the weight of the string per unit length. In addition to the differential equation, we again, of course, need suitable initial and boundary conditions in order to specify completely the problem. Since the ends of the string are fixed at $x = 0$ and $x = L$, we have the boundary conditions

(7.1.11) $$u(t, 0) = 0 \qquad u(t, L) = 0$$

For the initial conditions, we must specify the initial deflection as well as the initial velocity of the string; thus,

(7.1.12) $$u(0, x) = f(x) \qquad u_t(0, x) = 0$$

With the differential equation (7.1.10), the boundary conditions (7.1.11), and the initial conditions (7.1.12), the problem is now fully specified.

The purpose of this book is, of course, to study techniques for the numerical solution of problems. It is worth recalling here, however, that there is a classical analytical technique for representing the solution of both (7.1.1) and (7.1.2)—by means of Fourier series. This technique is only valid under very restrictive conditions, but it does apply to the heat and wave equations together with the types of initial and boundary conditions we have considered. It is called the *method of separation of variables*, and we shall review it rather briefly.

Assume that the solution of (7.1.1) can be written as

(7.1.13) $$u(t, x) = v(t)w(x)$$

that is, as a product of a function that depends only on t together with a function that depends only on x; hence, the term *separation of variables.* If we substitute (7.1.13) into (7.1.1), we obtain

(7.1.14) $$v'(t)w(x) = cv(t)w''(x)$$

or, assuming that neither v nor w is zero,

(7.1.15) $$\frac{v'(t)}{v(t)} = c\frac{w''(x)}{w(x)}$$

Since the left side of (7.1.15) is a function only of t and the right side is a function only of x, it follows that both sides must be equal to some constant, say μ; that is,

(7.1.16) $$v'(t) = \mu v(t) \qquad cw''(x) = \mu w(x)$$

Now, the general solution of the first equation is

(7.1.17) $$v(t) = c_1 e^{\mu t}, \qquad c_1 = \text{constant}$$

The second equation of (7.1.16) is simply the eigenvalue problem discussed in Section 6.1. As we saw there, the eigenfunctions are

(7.1.18) $$w(x) = \sin k\pi x, \qquad 0 \le x \le 1,\ k = 1, 2, \ldots$$

and the eigenvalues are $-k^2\pi^2$. Because of the constant c, the corresponding values of μ are

(7.1.19) $$\mu = -ck^2\pi^2, \qquad k = 1, 2, \ldots$$

That is, any function w of the form (7.1.18) is a solution of $cw'' = \mu w$ provided μ is given by (7.1.19). Note that such a solution would vanish at certain points in the interval [0, 1], and (7.1.15) would not be valid there. However, the use of (7.1.15) is meant only to be suggestive; the final criterion is whether v and w satisfy (7.1.14), and this will be the case provided that (7.1.16) holds. Thus, any function of the form

(7.1.20) $$u(t, x) = e^{-ck^2\pi^2 t}\sin k\pi x,$$

where k is any positive integer, satisfies the heat equation (7.1.1), as may be verified directly.

Even though (7.1.20) satisfies the differential equation, it need not satisfy initial or boundary conditions that may also be given. Let us consider the special case of the boundary conditions (7.1.6) for which

(7.1.21) $$u(t, 0) = 0 \qquad u(t, 1) = 0$$

and let us suppose that the initial condition can be written as a finite trigonometric polynomial

$$u(0, x) = \sum_{k=1}^{n} a_k \sin k\pi x \tag{7.1.22}$$

It is then easy to verify that

$$u(t, x) = \sum_{k=1}^{n} a_k e^{-ck^2\pi^2 t} \sin k\pi x \tag{7.1.23}$$

is a solution of (7.1.1) [any linear combination of solutions of (7.1.1) is again a solution] and, moreover, satisfies the boundary and initial conditions (7.1.21) and (7.1.22).

The solution (7.1.23) is predicated on the finite expansion (7.1.22), but by the theory of Fourier series, a very large class of functions, and hence initial conditions, can be represented by the infinite series

$$g(x) = \sum_{k=1}^{\infty} a_k \sin k\pi x \tag{7.1.24}$$

where

$$a_k = 2\int_0^1 g(z)\sin(k\pi z)\,dz$$

In this case, the solution can be represented, analogously to (7.1.23), by

$$u(t, x) = \sum_{k=1}^{\infty} a_k e^{-ck^2\pi^2 t} \sin k\pi x \tag{7.1.25}$$

although it is no longer as simple as in the case of (7.1.23) to verify rigorously that this is a solution.

The method of separation of variables can also be applied to the wave equation, and we will just indicate the result corresponding to (7.1.25) for equation (7.1.10) together with the boundary and initial conditions (7.1.11) and (7.1.12). Again, if we assume that the first initial condition of (7.1.12) can be represented by

$$f(x) = \sum_{k=1}^{\infty} a_k \sin\left(\frac{k\pi x}{L}\right) \tag{7.1.26}$$

then the solution is

$$u(t, x) = \sum_{k=1}^{\infty} a_k \sin\left(\frac{k\pi}{L} x\right)\cos\left(\frac{k\pi}{L}\sqrt{c}t\right) \tag{7.1.27}$$

In the case that (7.1.26) is a finite sum, analogous to (7.1.22), it is easy to verify this result directly, without any technical difficulties.

We have not meant to imply that these series expansions are to be the basis for numerical methods, although in certain special cases they can be. Rather, such representations are sometimes useful in ascertaining qualitative information about the solution of the differential equation. For example, (7.1.23) clearly shows, since $c > 0$, that $u(t, x) \to 0$ as $t \to \infty$, and this same conclusion can be reached from the infinite series (7.1.25). We shall use this information in the following section on finite difference methods. On the other hand, we see that the solution (7.1.27) has no exponential decay with time, and, in fact, $u(t, x)$ does *not* tend to zero as t tends to infinity. This shows that the wave equation is an incomplete mathematical model of a real vibrating string since we have neglected friction forces, which will cause the string's motion to subside eventually.

Supplementary Discussion and References: 7.1

The method of separation of variables together with the use of Fourier series is a classical technique for solving certain simple equations and is discussed in most beginning textbooks on partial differential equations. Similarly, most such books will contain additional examples and derivations of equations. See, for example, Berg and McGregor [1966], Dennemeyer [1968], and Powers [1972], and, for more advanced treatments, Carrier and Pearson [1976], Courant and Hillbert [1953, 1962], and Garabedian [1964].

Many, if not most, partial differential equation models of physical phenomena involve systems of equations rather than a single equation. The classification system of elliptic, hyperbolic, and parabolic can be extended to systems of equations, although relatively few systems that model realistic physical situations fit this nice classification.

EXERCISES 7.1

7.1.1. Show that the function of (7.1.20) satisfies (7.1.1) for any integer k. Then, verify that (7.1.23) is a solution of (7.1.1) that satisfies the initial and boundary conditions (7.1.21) and (7.1.22).

7.1.2. a. Show that

(7.1.28)
$$u(x, t) = \sum_{k=1}^{n} a_k \sin\left(\frac{k\pi}{L} x\right)\cos\left(\frac{k\pi}{L}\sqrt{c}\, t\right)$$

satisfies the wave equation (7.1.2) as well as the boundary and initial conditions $u(t, 0) = 0$, $u(t, L) = 0$, $u_t(0, x) = 0$, and $u(0, x) = \sum_{k=1}^{n} a_k \sin(k\pi x/L)$.

b. Write a program to display the special solution $u(x, t) = \sin(\pi x)\cos(\pi t)$ on a graphics terminal in such a way that the motion of the string is clear. Do the same for more complicated solutions consisting of two and three terms of (7.1.28).

7.2 Explicit Methods and the Stability Problem

We begin in this section the study of finite difference methods for partial differential equations and, in particular, for the equations discussed in the previous section. We will treat first the heat equation

$$u_t = cu_{xx}, \qquad 0 \le x \le 1, t \ge 0 \tag{7.2.1}$$

with the initial and boundary conditions

$$u(0, x) = g(x), \qquad 0 \le x \le 1 \tag{7.2.2}$$

$$u(t, 0) = \alpha \qquad u(t, 1) = \beta, \qquad t \ge 0 \tag{7.2.3}$$

We set up a grid in the x, t plane with grid spacings Δx and Δt as illustrated in Figure 7.3. The basis of the simplest finite difference method for (7.2.1) is to replace the second derivative on the right-hand side of (7.2.1) by a central difference quotient in x, and replace u_t by a forward difference in time. Then, one advances the approximate solution forward in time, one time level after another. More precisely, if we let u_j^m denote the approximate solution at $x_j = j\Delta x$ and $t_m = m\Delta t$, then the finite difference analog of (7.2.1) is

$$\frac{u_j^{m+1} - u_j^m}{\Delta t} = \frac{c}{(\Delta x)^2}(u_{j+1}^m - 2u_j^m + u_{j-1}^m) \tag{7.2.4}$$

or

$$u_j^{m+1} = u_j^m + \mu(u_{j+1}^m - 2u_j^m + u_{j-1}^m), \qquad j = 1, \ldots, n \tag{7.2.5}$$

where

$$\mu = \frac{c\Delta t}{(\Delta x)^2} \tag{7.2.6}$$

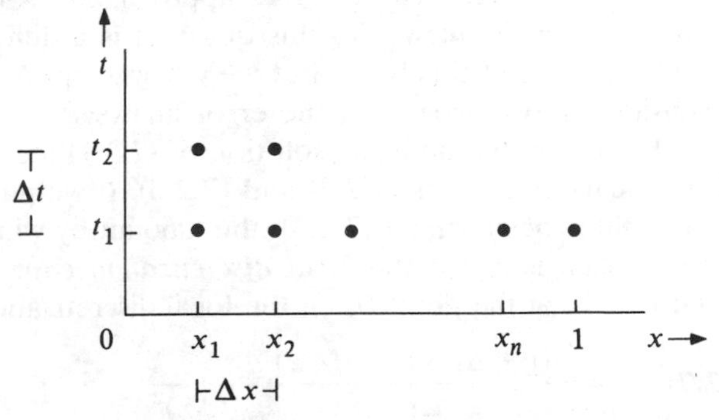

FIGURE 7.3 *Grid Spacings.*

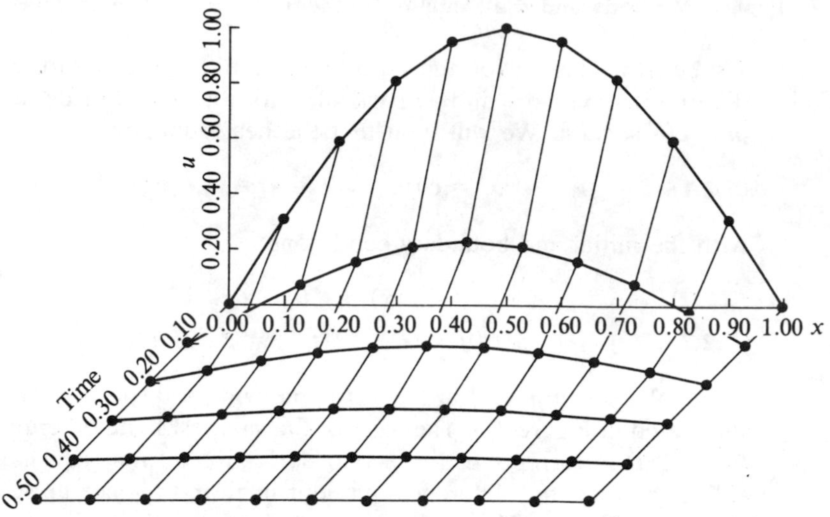

FIGURE 7.4 *A Finite Difference Solution for* $u_t = u_{xx}$.

The boundary conditions (7.2.3) give the values

$$u_0^m = \alpha \qquad u_{n+1}^m = \beta,\ m = 0, 1, \ldots$$

and the initial condition (7.2.2) furnishes

$$u_j^0 = g(x_j), \qquad j = 1, \ldots, n$$

Therefore, (7.2.5) provides a prescription for marching the approximate solution forward one time step after another: the values u_j^1, $j = 1, \ldots, n$, are first all obtained, and knowing these, we can obtain u_j^2, $j = 1, \ldots, n$, and so on. An approximate solution obtained in this way is depicted in Figure 7.4 for the case $c = 1$, $g(x) = \sin \pi x$, and $\alpha = \beta = 0$, with $\Delta x = 0.1$ and $\Delta t = 0.005$.

How accurate will be the approximate solution obtained by (7.2.5)? A rigorous answer to this question is a difficult problem that is beyond the scope of this book, but we will attempt to obtain some insight by considering two aspects of the error analysis.

Let $u(t, x)$ be the exact solution of (7.2.1) together with the initial and boundary conditions (7.2.2) and (7.2.3). If we put this exact solution into the difference formula (7.2.4), the amount by which the formula fails to be satisfied is called the *local discretization error* (or *local truncation error*); that is, at the point (t, x), the local discretization error, e, is

(7.2.7) $$e = \frac{u(t + \Delta t, x) - u(t, x)}{\Delta t} - \frac{c}{(\Delta x)^2} \times [u(t, x + \Delta x) - 2u(t, x) + u(t, x - \Delta x)]$$

This is entirely analogous to the previous definitions of local discretization error for ordinary differential equations and enjoys similar properties. For example, suppose that we know the exact solution $u(t, x)$ for some t and all $0 \leq x \leq 1$ and we use (7.2.4) to estimate the solution at $t + \Delta t$. Call this estimate $\hat{u}(t + \Delta t, x)$. Then, by definition,

$$0 = \frac{\hat{u}(t + \Delta t, x) - u(t, x)}{\Delta t} - \frac{c}{(\Delta x)^2}[u(t, x + \Delta x) - 2u(t, x) + u(t, x - \Delta x)]$$

so, if we subtract this from (7.2.7), we obtain

$$\hat{u}(t + \Delta t, x) - u(t + \Delta t, x) = \Delta t e \tag{7.2.8}$$

That is, the error caused by one time step using the difference scheme (7.2.4) is Δt times the local discretization error.

It is easy to estimate the quantity e of (7.2.7) in terms of Δt and Δx. Indeed, if we consider u as only a function of t for fixed x, we can apply the Taylor expansion

$$u(t + \Delta t, x) = u(t, x) + u_t(t, x)\Delta t + 0[(\Delta t)^2]$$

to conclude that

$$\frac{u(t + \Delta t, x) - u(t, x)}{\Delta t} = u_t(t, x) + 0(\Delta t)$$

Similarly, in a manner completely analogous to what was done to obtain (3.2.8), we have

$$\frac{u(t, x + \Delta x) - 2u(t, x) + u(t, x - \Delta x)}{(\Delta x)^2} = u_{xx}(t, x) + 0[(\Delta x)^2]$$

If we put these expressions into (7.2.7) and use $u_t = cu_{xx}$ (since u is the exact solution of the differential equation), we obtain

$$e = 0(\Delta t) + 0[(\Delta x)^2] \tag{7.2.9}$$

The fact that Δt appears to the first power and Δx to the second power in this expression for the local discretization error is usually described by the statement that the finite difference method (7.2.4) is *first-order accurate in time* and *second-order accurate in space*.

It is tempting to conclude from (7.2.8) and (7.2.9) that the discretization error in u_j^m, as obtained from (7.2.5), converges to zero as Δt and Δx tend to zero. Unfortunately, this conclusion is not warranted since (7.2.8) gives the error in the approximate solution only for a single time step. To show that the discretization error tends to zero on a whole time interval $[0, T]$ is difficult and, in general, requires additional conditions on how Δt and Δx tend to zero. A relationship of the type (7.2.9), or more generally a statement that the local discretization error tends to zero with Δt and Δx, is essentially a necessary condition for the global discretization error itself to tend to zero and is called *consistency* of the difference scheme. The reason that consistency of the difference method does not necessarily imply convergence of the discretization error is bound up with the phenomenon known as *stability* of the difference scheme, and we now discuss certain aspects of this for the difference scheme (7.2.5).

In a way exactly analogous to the method of separation of variables and the use of Fourier series that was applied to the differential equation $u_t = cu_{xx}$ in the previous section, we can obtain the exact solution of (7.2.5) together with the boundary and initial conditions

(7.2.10)
$$u_0^m = u_{n+1}^m = 0, \qquad m = 1, 2, \ldots$$
$$u_j^0 = \text{given}, \; j = 1, \ldots, n$$

Assume that the solution u_j^m can be written as

(7.2.11)
$$u_j^m = v_m w_j, \qquad j = 1, \ldots, n, \qquad m = 0, 1, \ldots$$

This is the paradigm of separation of variables for difference equations. Putting (7.2.11) into (7.2.5) and collecting terms yields

$$\frac{v_{m+1} - v_m}{\mu v_m} = \frac{w_{j+1} - 2w_j + w_{j-1}}{w_j}, \qquad j = 1, \ldots, n, \qquad m = 0, 1, \ldots$$

Since the left side is independent of j and the right side is independent of m, both sides must be equal to some constant, say $-\lambda$; that is,

(7.2.12)
$$v_{m+1} - v_m = -\lambda\mu v_m, \qquad m = 0, 1, \ldots$$

(7.2.13)
$$w_{j+1} - 2w_j + w_{j-1} = -\lambda w_j, \qquad j = 1, \ldots, n$$

where the values $w_0 = w_{n+1} = 0$ follow from the boundary conditions (7.2.10). Equation (7.2.13) represents the eigenvalue problem for the tridiagonal matrix

(7.2.14)
$$A = \begin{bmatrix} 2 & -1 & & & \\ -1 & 2 & \cdot & & \\ & \cdot & \cdot & \cdot & \\ & & \cdot & \cdot & -1 \\ & & & -1 & 2 \end{bmatrix}$$

(which is why we chose the sign of the constant λ to be negative). We obtained the eigenvalues of this matrix in Section 3.5 [see (3.5.26)] as

(7.2.15)
$$\lambda_k = 2 - 2\cos\frac{k\pi}{n+1}, \qquad k = 1, \ldots, n$$

with corresponding eigenvectors

$$\mathbf{w}_k = [\sin(k\pi\Delta x), \sin(2k\pi\Delta x), \ldots, \sin(nk\pi\Delta x)], \qquad k = 1, \ldots, n$$

since $\Delta x = 1/(n+1)$. Thus, for each $\lambda = \lambda_k$,

(7.2.16)
$$w_j = \sin(jk\pi\Delta x), \qquad j = 0, 1, \ldots, n+1$$

is a solution of (7.2.13). Clearly,

$$v_m = (1 - \lambda\mu)^m v_0, \qquad m = 0, 1, \ldots$$

is a solution of (7.2.12) for any λ, so

$$v_m w_j = (1 - \lambda_k\mu)^m \sin(jk\pi\Delta x), \qquad m = 0, 1, \ldots, j = 0, 1, \ldots, n + 1$$

is a solution of (7.2.5) for each k. As with the differential equation, any linear combination of these solutions is also a solution; that is,

(7.2.17)
$$u_j^m = \sum_{k=1}^{n} a_k(1 - \lambda_k\mu)^m \sin(jk\pi\Delta x),$$
$$m = 0, 1, \ldots, j = 0, 1, \ldots, n + 1$$

is a solution of (7.2.5) for any constants a_k. If the a_k are chosen so that

(7.2.18)
$$a_k = \sum_{\ell=1}^{n} g(x_\ell)\sin k\pi\ell\Delta x$$

then u_j^m also satisfies the initial condition

(7.2.19)
$$u_j^0 = g(x_j), \qquad j = 1, \ldots, n$$

Now, we wish to use the representation (7.2.17) in the following way. From our discussion in the previous section, the equation $u_t = cu_{xx}$ together with the boundary conditions $u(t, 0) = u(t, 1) = 0$ is a model of the temperature distribution in a thin insulated rod whose ends are held at zero temperature. Since there is no source of heat, we expect that the temperature of the rod will decrease to zero; that is, $u(t, x) \to 0$ as $t \to \infty$. As mentioned in the previous section, this conclusion can also be obtained mathematically from the series representations (7.1.23) or (7.1.25) of the solution since the exponential terms all tend to zero. Therefore, it is reasonable to demand that the finite difference approximations u_j^m also tend to zero as m tends to infinity, and for any initial conditions, by (7.2.17), this will be the case if and only if

(7.2.20)
$$|1 - \mu\lambda_k| < 1, \qquad k = 1, \ldots, n$$

Since μ and all the λ_k are positive, (7.2.15) will hold if and only if

$$-(1 - \mu\lambda_k) < 1, \qquad k = 1, \ldots, n$$

or

(7.2.21)
$$\mu < \min_k \frac{2}{\lambda_k} = \frac{1}{1 - \cos\dfrac{\pi n}{n+1}} = \frac{1}{1 + \cos\dfrac{\pi}{n+1}}$$

since the largest λ_k is λ_n. Thus, with $\mu = c\Delta t/(\Delta x)^2$ from (7.2.6), (7.2.21)

TABLE 7.1 *Unstable Behavior*

t/x	0.1	0.2	0.3	0.4	0.5	0.6	0.7	0.8	0.9
0	0.31	0.59	0.81	0.95	1.0	0.95	0.81	0.59	0.31
0.04	0.19	0.36	0.49	0.57	0.61	0.58	0.49	0.36	0.19
0.08	0.11	0.22	0.29	0.35	0.37	0.35	0.29	0.22	0.11
0.12	0.07	0.13	0.18	0.21	0.23	0.21	0.18	0.13	0.07
0.16	0.04	0.08	0.11	0.13	0.14	0.13	0.11	0.08	0.04
0.20	0.026	0.05	0.07	0.08	0.08	0.08	0.07	0.05	0.03
0.24	0.016	0.03	0.04	0.05	0.05	0.05	0.04	0.03	0.01
0.28	0.009	0.02	0.02	0.03	0.03	0.02	0.03	0.004	0.02
0.32	0.006	0.01	0.01	0.02	−0.01	0.09	−0.13	0.20	−0.13
0.36	0.004	0.005	0.04	−0.14	0.53	−1.22	2.09	−2.43	1.70
0.40	−0.007	0.12	−0.77	3.20	−9.13	19.0	−29.3	32.2	−21.6
0.44	0.537	−3.97	18.7	−62.0	152.9	−286.9	409.	−428.	279.

becomes

(7.2.22)
$$\Delta t < \frac{(\Delta x)^2}{c\left(1 + \cos\dfrac{\pi}{n+1}\right)}$$

This gives a restriction on the relative sizes of Δt and Δx, which if not satisfied, will, in general, mean that the approximate solution u_j^m of the difference scheme will ultimately diverge as m tends to infinity and, obviously, will become an increasingly poor approximation to the solution of the differential equation, which tends to zero. In Table 7.1, we give an example of this instability for the same problem as in Figure 7.4, but now with $\Delta x = 0.1$ and $\Delta t = 0.04$ so that (7.2.22) is not satisfied. Note that the instability has begun to develop noticeably by the time $t = 0.32$ and then rapidly worsens.

We can replace (7.2.22) by the slightly stronger condition

(7.2.23)
$$\Delta t \le \frac{(\Delta x)^2}{2c}$$

which always implies (7.2.22). This relation is called the *stability condition* for the difference method (7.2.5). Our derivation of it has been in the context of the behavior of u_j^m as $m \to \infty$ for fixed Δt and Δx. But it is also relevant to the problem of the convergence of the discretization error to zero as Δt and Δx tend to zero. In fact, although it is beyond our scope to prove, the approximate solutions will converge to the exact solution as Δt and Δx tend to zero if (7.2.23) holds as Δt and Δx are tending to zero. This is a special case of a more general principle known as the *Lax Equivalence Theorem*, which states that for quite general differential equations and consistent difference schemes, the global discretization error will tend to zero if and only if the method is stable.

TABLE 7.2 *Maximum Time Steps for Given Δx and $c = 1$*

Δx	Δt
0.1	$0.5 \cdot 10^{-2}$
0.01	$0.5 \cdot 10^{-4}$
0.001	$0.5 \cdot 10^{-6}$

The condition (7.2.23) imposes an increasingly stringent limitation on the time step Δt as the space increment Δx becomes small, as Table 7.2 shows for the case $c = 1$. Thus, we may require a time step far smaller than otherwise necessary to resolve the time-dependent nature of the solution of the differential equation itself. Although the analysis that we have done has been restricted to the simplest differential equation and simplest difference scheme, the requirement of small time steps for explicit finite difference methods for parabolic and similar equations is a general problem and is a primary motivation for the so-called implicit methods to be discussed in the next section.

We turn now to hyperbolic equations, and in particular to the wave equation

(7.2.24) $$u_{tt} = cu_{xx}, \qquad 0 \le x \le 1, \qquad t \ge 0$$

together with the initial and boundary conditions

(7.2.25) $$u(0, x) = f(x) \qquad u_t(0, x) = g(x) \qquad u(t, 0) = \alpha \qquad u(t, 1) = \beta$$

As we discussed in the previous section, the problem (7.2.24)/(7.2.25) is a mathematical model for a vibrating string.

Probably the simplest finite difference scheme for (7.2.24) is

(7.2.26) $$\frac{u_j^{m+1} - 2u_j^m + u_j^{m-1}}{(\Delta t)^2} = \frac{c}{(\Delta x)^2}(u_{j+1}^m - 2u_j^m + u_{j-1}^m)$$

To obtain (7.2.26), we have used the usual centered difference formula for u_{xx}, just as in (7.2.4), as well as for u_{tt}. Note that (7.2.26) now involves three time levels and requires that both u_j^m and u_j^{m-1} be known in order to advance to the $(m + 1)$st time level. This requires additional storage for u_j^{m-1}, as opposed to the method (7.2.5) for $u_t = cu_{xx}$, but is a natural consequence of the fact that the differential equation contains a second derivative in time. We also require both u_j^0 and u_j^1 in order to start, but these can be obtained from the initial conditions (7.2.5):

(7.2.27) $$u_j^0 = f(x_j) \qquad u_j^1 = f(x_j) + \Delta t g(x_j), \qquad j = 1, \ldots, n$$

where the second condition is obtained by approximating $u_t(0, x) = g(x)$ by $[u(\Delta t, x) - u(0, x)]/\Delta t = g(x)$. From the boundary conditions, we have

(7.2.28) $$u_0^m = \alpha \qquad u_{n+1}^m = \beta, \qquad m = 0, 1, \ldots$$

Thus, the values at the $(m + 1)$st time level are obtained by

(7.2.29) $$u_j^{m+1} = 2u_j^m - u_j^{m-1} + \mu(u_{j+1}^m - 2u_j^m + u_{j-1}^m)$$

where

$$\mu = \frac{c(\Delta t)^2}{(\Delta x)^2}$$

It is easy to show that the local discretization error for (7.2.26) is $0[(\Delta t)^2, (\Delta x)^2]$, that is, the method is second-order accurate in both space and time (exercise 7.2.4). For the stability analysis, we can again proceed by the method of separation of variables and assume that the boundary conditions α and β are zero. Let $u_j^m = v_m w_j$. Putting this into (7.2.26) leads to the two conditions

(7.2.30) $$v_{m+1} - 2v_m + v_{m-1} = -\lambda\mu v_m, \qquad m = 1, \ldots$$

(7.2.31) $$w_{j+1} - 2w_j + w_{j-1} = -\lambda w_j, \qquad j = 1, \ldots, n$$

The second set of equations is the same as (7.2.13), and thus its solutions are given by (7.2.15)/(7.2.16). Equations (7.2.30), although ostensibly of the same form as (7.2.31), are for an initial-value problem in which v_0 and v_1 are known. From Section 2.5, [see (2.5.11)–(2.5.14)], the solution of (7.2.30) is given by

$$v_m = \gamma_1\eta_+^m + \gamma_2\eta_-^m, \qquad m = 0, 1, \ldots$$

where $\eta_\pm$ are the roots of the characteristic equation $\eta^2 + (\lambda\mu - 2)\eta + 1 = 0$ and are given by

$$\eta_\pm = \tfrac{1}{2}(2 - \lambda\mu \pm \sqrt{\lambda^2\mu^2 - 4\lambda\mu})$$

and the γ_i can be obtained from the initial conditions v_0 and v_1. Thus, the solution of (7.2.26) can be written as

(7.2.32) $$u_j^m = \sum_{k=1}^{n} a_k(\gamma_{k,1}\eta_{k,+}^m + \gamma_{k,2}\eta_{k,-}^m)\sin(jk\pi\Delta x)$$

where the subscript k indicates that the corresponding γ and η have been computed for $\lambda = \lambda_k$. In order that u_j^m remain bounded for arbitrary a_k and initial conditions, it is necessary and sufficient that $|\eta_{k,\pm}| \le 1$. If

(7.2.33) $$\lambda_k\mu - 4 \le 0$$

then it is easy to verify that $|\eta_{k,\pm}| = 1$, and if $\lambda_k\mu - 4 > 0$, then $\eta_{k,-} < -1$. Hence, (7.2.33) is the necessary and sufficient condition for stability. Since the eigenvalues λ_k satisfy $0 < \lambda_k < 4$, a sufficient condition for (7.2.33) is that $\mu \le 1$ or

(7.2.34) $$\Delta t \le \frac{\Delta x}{\sqrt{c}}$$

This is also essentially a necessary condition in the sense that $\lambda_n \to 4$ as $n \to \infty$, so any condition weaker than (7.2.34) would allow (7.2.33) to be violated for sufficiently large n. The stability condition (7.2.34) is much less stringent on Δt than was (7.2.23) for the heat equation. Indeed, (7.2.34) shows that Δt need decrease only proportionately to Δx, rather than as the square of Δx, as was the case with (7.2.23).

Although this section has dealt only with the simple heat and wave equations, the same principles of obtaining finite difference methods apply to more-general initial-boundary-value problems for either single equations or systems of equations. In all such cases, the user must be alert to the possibility of instability, although for most equations, a simple analysis of the form given in this section will not be possible.

Supplementary Discussion and References : 7.2

We have only touched the surface on finite difference methods for parabolic and hyperbolic equations. In particular, we have considered only first- and second-order methods, although a variety of higher-order methods have been developed. More importantly, most of the useful methods for parabolic equations are implicit, and these will be dealt with in the next section. Books by Ames [1977], Forsythe and Wasow [1960], and Mitchell [1969] discuss many additional methods. See also Isaacson and Keller [1966] and Richtmyer and Morton [1967] for a discussion of methods as well as a rigorous analysis of discretization error and stability criteria.

The separation-of-variables analysis leading to (7.2.17) can also be viewed in matrix-theoretic terms. The matrix-vector formulation of (7.2.5) is

$$\mathbf{u}^{m+1} = \mathbf{u}^m - \mu \mathrm{A}\mathbf{u}^m, \qquad m = 0, 1, \ldots$$

where A is the matrix (7.2.14) and $\mathbf{u}^m$ is the vector with components $u_1^m, \ldots, u_n^m$. The matrix $\mathrm{H} = \mathrm{I} - \mu\mathrm{A}$ has eigenvalues $1 - \mu\lambda_k$ and eigenvectors $\mathbf{w}_k$, where the λ_k and $\mathbf{w}_k$ are the eigenvalues and eigenvectors of A. Therefore, if

$$\mathbf{u}^0 = \sum_{k=1}^{n} a_k \mathbf{w}_k$$

is the expansion of $\mathbf{u}^0$ in terms of the eigenvectors, then

$$\mathbf{u}^m = \mathrm{H}\mathbf{u}^{m-1} = \cdots = \mathrm{H}^m\mathbf{u}^0 = \sum_{k=1}^{n} a_k(1 - \mu\lambda_k)^m \mathbf{w}_k$$

which is simply (7.2.17).

EXERCISES 7.2

7.2.1. Use (7.2.5) to approximate a solution to $u_t = u_{xx}$ for the boundary and initial conditions $u(t, 0) = 0$, $u(t, 1) = 1$, $u(0, x) = \sin \pi x + x$. Use different values of Δt and Δx and discuss your approximate solutions. For what ratios of Δt and Δx do you conclude that your approximate solution is stable?

7.2.2. Substitute (7.2.17) into (7.2.5) and verify that it is, indeed, a solution. Verify also that (7.2.19) holds if the a_k are given by (7.2.18).

7.2.3. Repeat and verify the calculation of Table 7.1.

7.2.4. Use the approach discussed in the text for the heat equation to conclude that the method (7.2.26) for the wave equation is second-order accurate in both time and space.

7.2.5. Write a computer program to solve the wave equation (7.2.24) with the initial and boundary conditions (7.2.25) by the difference method (7.2.26). Apply your program to the case $c = 1$, $f(x) = \sin \pi x$ for various values of Δt and Δx. In particular, conclude that the calculation is stable if (7.2.34) is satisfied.

7.3 Implicit Methods

The finite difference method (7.2.5) discussed in the previous section is called *explicit* because the values of u_j^{m+1} at the next time level are obtained by an explicit formula in terms of the values at the previous time level. In contrast, consider again the heat equation

(7.3.1) $$u_t = cu_{xx}, \qquad 0 \le x \le 1, \qquad t \ge 0$$

and the difference analog

(7.3.2) $$\frac{u_j^{m+1} - u_j^m}{\Delta t} = \frac{c}{(\Delta x)^2}(u_{j+1}^{m+1} - 2u_j^{m+1} + u_{j-1}^{m+1}), \qquad j = 1, \ldots, n$$

This is similar in form to (7.2.4) but has the important difference that the values of u_j on the right side are now evaluated at the $(m + 1)$st time level rather than the mth. Consequently, if we know u_j^m, $j = 1, \ldots, n$, and are ready to compute u_j^{m+1}, $j = 1, \ldots, n$, we see that the variables u_j on the right-hand side of (7.3.2) are all unknown. Thus, we must view (7.3.2) as a system of equations that implicitly defines the values u_j^{m+1}, $j = 1, \ldots, n$. This is one of the basic differences between implicit and explicit methods: in an explicit method, we have an explicit formula for u_j^{m+1}, such as (7.2.5), in terms of known values of u_j at previous time levels, whereas with implicit methods, we must solve a system of equations to advance to the next time level.

Let us examine the system (7.3.2) more closely. If, as in the previous section, we set $\mu = c\Delta t/(\Delta x)^2$, then we can rewrite (7.3.2) as

(7.3.3) $$(1 + 2\mu)u_j^{m+1} - \mu(u_{j+1}^{m+1} + u_{j-1}^{m+1}) = u_j^m, \qquad j = 1, \ldots, n$$

or in matrix-vector form,

(7.3.4)
$$\begin{bmatrix} 1+2\mu & -\mu & & & \\ -\mu & 1+2\mu & -\mu & & \\ & -\mu & \ddots & \ddots & \\ & & \ddots & \ddots & -\mu \\ & & & -\mu & 1+2\mu \end{bmatrix} \times \begin{bmatrix} u_1^{m+1} \\ u_2^{m+1} \\ \cdot \\ \cdot \\ \cdot \\ u_n^{m+1} \end{bmatrix} = \begin{bmatrix} u_1^m + \mu\alpha \\ u_2^m \\ \cdot \\ \cdot \\ \cdot \\ u_{n-1}^m \\ u_n^m + \mu\beta \end{bmatrix}$$

In deriving (7.3.4), we have assumed the same boundary conditions

(7.3.5) $$u(t, 0) = \alpha \qquad u(t, 1) = \beta$$

used in the previous section, so, as before, $u_0^k = \alpha$ and $u_{n+1}^k = \beta$ for $k = 0, 1, \ldots$; these values then go to the right-hand side in the first and last equations of (7.3.4) as indicated. We also assume the initial condition

(7.3.6) $$u(0, x) = f(x), \qquad 0 \le x \le 1$$

so, as before, $u_j^0 = f(x_j)$, $j = 1, \ldots, n$.

The implicit method (7.3.4) is now carried out by solving the linear system of equations (7.3.4) at each time step to obtain the u_j^{m+1} from the u_j^m. The matrix in (7.3.4) is tridiagonal and also diagonally dominant (Section 3.2) since $c > 0$, and thus $\mu > 0$. Therefore, as we saw in Section 3.4, the system of equations can be efficiently solved by Gaussian elimination without pivoting. In the particular case of (7.3.3), we could compute the L and U factors once and for all, although we may not be able to do this for more general problems.

Even though each time step of (7.3.4) can be carried out relatively efficiently, this method is more costly per time step than the explicit method (7.2.5). However, in payment for this additional cost, we obtain a substantial benefit in the stability properties of the method, which, in many cases, will allow us to use a much larger time step than for the explicit method and thus greatly cut the overall computing costs. We will now indicate the stability analysis following the lines of the previous section.

We assume now, as before, that $\alpha = \beta = 0$. Then, corresponding to (7.2.17),

(7.3.7)
$$u_j^m = \sum_{k=1}^{n} a_k \gamma_k^m \sin(k\pi j \Delta x)$$

identically satisfies the difference scheme (7.3.3) for any constants a_k provided that

(7.3.8)
$$\gamma_k = \frac{1}{1 + 2\mu\left(1 + \cos\dfrac{k\pi}{n+1}\right)}, \qquad k = 1, \ldots, n$$

Also, u_j^0 satisfies the initial condition if

(7.3.9)
$$a_k = \sum_{\ell=1}^{n} f(x_\ell)\sin(k\pi\ell\Delta x)$$

The verification of these results is left to exercise 7.3.2.

Now, recall from our discussion in the previous section that we require that the approximate solution $u_j^m \to 0$ as $m \to \infty$ if it is to mirror the solution of the differential equation itself. From (7.3.7), we see that this will be the case, in general, if and only if

(7.3.10)
$$|\gamma_k| < 1, \qquad k = 1, \ldots, n$$

But from (7.3.8), since $\mu > 0$,

(7.3.11)
$$0 < \gamma_k < 1, \qquad k = 1, \ldots, n$$

so (7.3.10) indeed holds. Most importantly, we see that (7.3.11) is true for *any* $\mu > 0$; thus, since $\mu = c\Delta t/(\Delta x)^2$, (7.3.11) is true for *any* ratio of Δt and Δx. We say in this case that the method is *unconditionally stable*, meaning that it is stable without restrictions on the relative size of Δt and Δx.

The fact that the method (7.3.4) is unconditionally stable does *not* mean that we can expect to obtain a good approximate solution for any Δt and Δx. As usual, these must be chosen sufficiently small to control discretization error. Now, it is the case (see exercise 7.3.3) that (7.3.4), like the corresponding explicit method (7.2.5), is first-order accurate in time and second-order accurate in space; that is, the discretization error will be

$$e(\Delta t, \Delta x) = 0[(\Delta t), (\Delta x)^2]$$

Suppose that

$$e(\Delta t, \Delta x) = c_1\Delta t + c_2(\Delta x)^2$$

Then, for the contributions to the total error from the discretization in time and the discretization in space to be commensurate, we require that

$$\Delta t \doteq c_3(\Delta x)^2$$

which is reminiscent of the stability condition (7.2.23) for the explicit method. Thus, we see that although the stability requirements for our implicit method do not impose any restrictions on the relative sizes of Δt and Δx, the accuracy requirements may.

A potentially better implicit method in this regard is the famous *Crank–Nicolson method*, which is essentially an average of the explicit method (7.2.4) and the implicit method (7.3.2). In fact, if we indeed average the right-hand sides of (7.2.4) and (7.3.2), we obtain

$$\textbf{(7.3.12)} \quad u_j^{m+1} - u_j^m = \frac{c\Delta t}{2(\Delta x)^2}(u_{j+1}^{m+1} - 2u_j^{m+1} + u_{j-1}^{m+1} + u_{j+1}^m - 2u_j^m + u_{j-1}^m)$$

If we now let $\mu = c\Delta t/2(\Delta x)^2$, (7.3.12) in matrix-vector form is identical to (7.3.4) on the left-hand side, and the right-hand side becomes

$$\textbf{(7.3.13)} \quad \begin{array}{ll} \mu u_2^m - (2\mu - 1)u_1^m + 2\mu\alpha & \\ \mu u_{j+1}^m - (2\mu - 1)u_j^m + \mu u_{j-1}^m, & j = 2, \ldots, n-1 \\ 2\mu\beta - (2\mu - 1)u_n^m + \mu u_{n-1}^m & \end{array}$$

Hence, again, (7.3.12) is carried out by solving a tridiagonal system of equations at each time step. The coefficient matrix of these linear systems is given in (7.3.4), whereas the right-hand side, given by (7.3.13), is somewhat more complicated than that of (7.3.4), so (7.3.12) takes slightly more work per time step. The advantage of (7.3.12), however, is that it is not only unconditionally stable, as is (7.3.4), but it is second-order accurate in time as well as in space. (The verification of these assertions is left to exercise 7.3.5). These properties have made it one of the most often used methods for parabolic equations.

One easy way of keeping in mind the three different methods (7.2.5), (7.3.4), and (7.3.12) is by their "stencils" of grid points as illustrated in Figure 7.5. These show which grid points enter into the difference method.

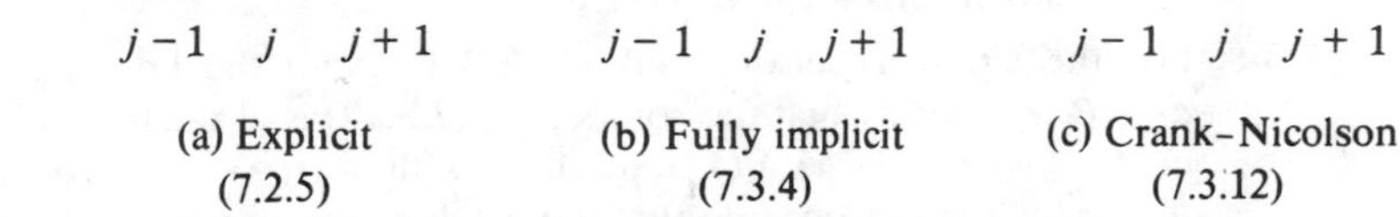

(a) Explicit (7.2.5) (b) Fully implicit (7.3.4) (c) Crank–Nicolson (7.3.12)

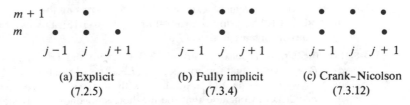

FIGURE 7.5 *Stencils for the Methods.*

It has become common practice in the numerical solution of parabolic-type partial differential equations to use implicit methods since their good stability properties outweigh the additional work required per time step. Most of the methods in actual use are more complicated than the Crank–Nicolson method, but the principles are the same. However, for problems involving more than one space dimension, straightforward extensions of the implicit methods of this section are not satisfactory, and additional techniques are required. One such technique will be discussed in Section 8.2.

It is possible to formulate implicit methods for hyperbolic equations—such as the wave equation of the previous section—in much the same way. However, as was seen with the wave equation, the stability requirements of explicit methods typically do not impose a stringent restriction on the time step. Consequently, implicit methods for hyperbolic equations are rather little used in practice, and we shall not discuss them further.

Supplementary Discussion and References: 7.3

The references given in Section 7.2 are also relevant for implicit methods. In particular, Richtmyer and Morton [1967, pp. 189–91] summarize graphically a number of implicit finite difference methods for parabolic equations in terms of their stencils.

EXERCISES 7.3

7.3.1. Write a program to carry out (7.3.4) and apply it to the problem of exercise 7.2.1. Use various values of Δt and Δx and verify numerically the stability of the method. Discuss your results compared to those for exercise 7.2.1, including the relative ease and efficiency of carrying out the two methods.

7.3.2. Proceed along the lines of the previous section to verify that (7.3.7) satisfies (7.3.3).

7.3.3. Proceed along the lines of the analysis of the previous section to show that the local discretization error for the method (7.3.3) satisfies (7.2.9).

7.3.4. Modify your program of exercise 7.3.1 to carry out the Crank–Nicolson method (7.3.12) by using the right-hand side (7.3.13). Discuss your results and compare this method to (7.3.4).

7.3.5. For the Crank–Nicolson method (7.3.12) with the boundary conditions $\alpha = \beta = 0$, verify that the solution of (7.3.12) is of the form (7.3.7), where now $\gamma_k = (1 - \mu\lambda_k)/(1 + \mu\lambda_k)$, with $\lambda_k = 2 - 2\cos[k\pi/(n+1)]$, $\mu = c\Delta t/2(\Delta x)^2$. Conclude that the method is unconditionally stable. Show also that the method is second-order accurate in both space and time.

7.3.6. The Dufort–Frankel method for the heat equation is $u_j^{m+1} - u_j^{m-1} = [\Delta tc/(\Delta x)^2]\,(u_{j+1}^m - u_j^{m+1} - u_j^{m-1} + u_{j-1}^m)$. Show that this method is unconditionally stable. Give an explicit formulation of it.

7.4 Semidiscrete Methods

We now consider another approach to initial-boundary-value problems which utilizes the projection principles of Chapter 5 and reduces the partial differential equation to an approximating system of ordinary differential equations. This approach can be applied in principle to both parabolic- and hyperbolic-type equations. We will first illustrate it for the heat equation

(7.4.1) $$u_t = cu_{xx}, \qquad 0 \le x \le 1,\ t \ge 0$$

with the initial and boundary conditions

(7.4.2) $$u(0, x) = f(x) \qquad u(t, 0) = 0 \qquad u(t, 1) = 0$$

As in Section 5.1, let $\phi_1(x), \ldots, \phi_n(x)$ be a set of basis functions that satisfy the boundary conditions; that is,

(7.4.3) $$\phi_k(0) = 0 \qquad \phi_k(1) = 0, \qquad k = 1, \ldots, n$$

We attempt to find an approximate solution $\hat{u}$ of (7.4.1) of the form

(7.4.4) $$\hat{u}(t, x) = \sum_{i=1}^{n} \alpha_i(t)\phi_i(x)$$

where the α_i are to be determined. Note that this is the same approach taken in Chapter 5, with the exception that now we allow the coefficients α_i of the linear combination of the basis functions to be functions of t to reflect the time-dependent nature of the problem.

In order to determine the unknown coefficients α_i, we can apply any of the criteria of Section 5.1, and we will consider first collocation in the following way. We again let $0 < x_1 < \cdots < x_n < 1$ be (not necessarily equally spaced) grid points in the x variable, and we require that the approximate solution (7.4.4) satisfy the differential equation at these points; that is, since

$$\hat{u}_t(t, x) = \sum_{i=1}^{n} \alpha_i'(t)\phi_i(x) \qquad \hat{u}_{xx}(t, x) = \sum_{i=1}^{n} \alpha_i(t)\phi_i''(x)$$

we require that

(7.4.5) $$\sum_{i=1}^{n} \alpha_i'(t)\phi_i(x_j) = c\sum_{i=1}^{n} \alpha_i(t)\phi_i''(x_j), \qquad j = 1, \ldots, n$$

If we introduce the $n \times n$ matrices

$$\text{(7.4.6)} \qquad \mathrm{A} = (\phi_j(x_i)) \qquad \mathrm{B} = c(\phi_j''(x_i))$$

and the n vectors

$$\boldsymbol{\alpha}(t) = (\alpha_1(t), \ldots, \alpha_n(t)) \qquad \boldsymbol{\alpha}'(t) = (\alpha_1'(t), \ldots, \alpha_n'(t))$$

we can write (7.4.5) as

$$\text{(7.4.7)} \qquad \mathrm{A}\boldsymbol{\alpha}'(t) = \mathrm{B}\boldsymbol{\alpha}(t)$$

or, if we assume that A is nonsingular and set $\mathrm{C} = \mathrm{A}^{-1}\mathrm{B}$,

$$\text{(7.4.8)} \qquad \boldsymbol{\alpha}'(t) = \mathrm{C}\boldsymbol{\alpha}(t)$$

Equation (7.4.8) is a system of n ordinary differential equations for the α_i. In order to solve this system, we still need an initial condition for (7.4.8). If we require that the approximate solution $\hat{u}$ satisfy the initial condition (7.4.2) at the points $x_1, \ldots, x_n$, we have

$$\sum_{i=1}^{n} \alpha_i(0)\phi_i(x_j) = f(x_j), \qquad j = 1, \ldots, n$$

or

$$\text{(7.4.9)} \qquad \mathrm{A}\boldsymbol{\alpha}(0) = \mathbf{f}$$

where $\mathbf{f} = (f(x_1), \ldots, f(x_n))$. By our assumption that A is nonsingular, we then have

$$\text{(7.4.10)} \qquad \alpha(0) = \mathrm{A}^{-1}\mathbf{f}$$

The conceptual problem is then to solve the system of ordinary differential equations (7.4.8) with the initial condition (7.4.10). If we could do this exactly, then $\hat{u}$ as given by (7.4.4) would be the approximate solution. Such a method is called semidiscrete because we have discretized only in space by means of the basis functions ϕ_i and grid points x_i while leaving time as a continuous variable. In practice, however, the system of differential equations (7.4.8) must be solved numerically, so a discretization of time is introduced by that process, and the term *semidiscrete* is somewhat of a misnomer. Nevertheless, the conceptual viewpoint of considering a discretization of only the space variables and thus reducing the problem to a system of ordinary differential equations is useful.

Let us consider the simple Euler method discussed in Chapter 2 for the numerical integration of the system (7.4.8). If $t_0, t_1, \ldots$ are equally spaced points in time with spacing Δt, then Euler's method is

$$\text{(7.4.11)} \qquad \boldsymbol{\alpha}^{k+1} = \boldsymbol{\alpha}^k + \Delta t \mathrm{C}\boldsymbol{\alpha}^k, \qquad k = 0, 1, \ldots$$

where $\boldsymbol{\alpha}^k$ denotes the approximate solution at the kth time step. In practice, we would not carry out (7.4.11) in the manner indicated since we will not actually form $\mathrm{C} = \mathrm{A}^{-1}\mathrm{B}$. Rather, we will work directly with the differential equation (7.4.7) and the corresponding Euler method

(7.4.12) $$A\boldsymbol{\alpha}^{k+1} = A\boldsymbol{\alpha}^k + \Delta t B\boldsymbol{\alpha}^k, \qquad k = 0, 1, \ldots$$

Thus, at each time step, we will solve the linear system of equations (7.4.12) with coefficient matrix A. The LU decomposition of A can, in this case, be done once and for all and the factors saved to be used at each time step.

In principle, one could apply any of the higher-order methods discussed in Chapter 2 for initial-value problems for ordinary differential equations; the explicit formulation of some of these methods in the case of (7.4.8) is left to exercise 7.4.2. However, the equations (7.4.8) are typically rather "stiff," in the sense discussed in Chapter 2, and the use of explicit methods will require a rather small time step. Hence, it may be advantageous to use a method such as the trapezoid rule. Applied to (7.4.7), the trapezoid rule (2.5.38) becomes

$$\boldsymbol{\alpha}^{k+1} = \boldsymbol{\alpha}^k + \frac{\Delta t}{2}(A^{-1}B\boldsymbol{\alpha}^{k+1} + A^{-1}B\boldsymbol{\alpha}^k)$$

or, multiplying through by A and collecting coefficients of $\boldsymbol{\alpha}^{k+1}$ and $\boldsymbol{\alpha}^k$,

(7.4.13) $$\left(A - \frac{\Delta t}{2}B\right)\boldsymbol{\alpha}^{k+1} = \left(A + \frac{\Delta t}{2}B\right)\boldsymbol{\alpha}^k$$

To carry out this method requires the solution at each time step of a linear system similar to (7.4.12) but with the coefficient matrix A replaced by $A - (\Delta t/2)B$. Assuming that this latter matrix is nonsingular, we may, in principle, proceed as before to compute the LU factors once and for all and use these in subsequent solutions of (7.4.13) at the different time steps. If the subtraction of the matrix $(\Delta t/2)B$ from A does not materially affect the difficulty of computing the LU decomposition, then the work in carrying out (7.4.13) will be not much more than for Euler's method. However, the trapezoid method is second-order accurate in time, as discussed in Chapter 2, and allows a larger time step for stiff equations; it should, therefore, be more suitable for this problem.

The same approach can be applied to hyperbolic equations, and we illustrate this for the wave equation

(7.4.14) $$u_{tt} = cu_{xx}, \qquad 0 \le x \le 1, \qquad t \ge 0$$

with the initial and boundary conditions

(7.4.15) $$u(0, x) = f(x) \qquad u_t(0, x) = g(x) \qquad u(t, 0) = 0 \qquad u(t, 1) = 0$$

It is common practice to reduce a hyperbolic equation like (7.4.14) to a system of equations in which only the first derivative with respect to time appears. This is quite analogous to the situation for ordinary differential equations: recall that in Chapter 2, we reduced higher-order equations to first-order systems of ordinary differential equations. In the case of (7.4.14), we will use a reduction made by introducing a function $v(t, x)$ such that

(7.4.16) $$u_t = av_x \qquad v_t = au_x$$

where $a = \sqrt{c}$. If u and v are a solution of the system (7.4.16), and are sufficiently differentiable, then by differentiating the first equation of (7.4.16) with respect to t and the second with respect to x, we obtain

$$u_{tt} = av_{xt} = av_{tx} = a^2u_{xx} = cu_{xx}$$

so u is a solution of (7.4.14). Moreover, the initial and boundary conditions (7.4.15) for (7.4.14) go over to

(7.4.17) $$u(0, x) = f(x) \qquad v(0, x) = \frac{1}{a}\int_0^x g(s)\, ds$$

$$u(t, 0) = 0 \qquad u(t, 1) = 0$$

Now, let $\phi_1(x), \ldots, \phi_n(x)$ and $\psi_1(x), \ldots, \psi_n(0)$ be two sets of basis functions that satisfy

(7.4.18) $$\phi_i(0) = \phi_i(1) = \psi_i(0) = \psi_i(1) = 0, \qquad i = 1, \ldots, n$$

We shall seek approximate solutions $\hat{u}$ and $\hat{v}$ of (7.4.16) of the form

(7.4.19) $$\hat{u}(x, t) = \sum_{i=1}^{n} \alpha_i(t)\phi_i(x) \qquad \hat{v}(x, t) = \sum_{i=1}^{n} \beta_i(t)\psi_i(x)$$

If we require that these approximate solutions satisfy the equations (7.4.16) at the grid points $x_1, \ldots, x_n$, we obtain

(7.4.20)
$$\sum_{i=1}^{n} \alpha_i'(t)\phi_i(x_j) = a\sum_{i=1}^{n} \beta_i(t)\psi_i'(x_j), \qquad j = 1, \ldots, n$$
$$\sum_{i=1}^{n} \beta_i'(t)\psi_i(x_j) = a\sum_{i=1}^{n} \alpha_i(t)\phi_i'(x_j), \qquad j = 1, \ldots, n$$

which is a coupled system of ordinary differential equations for the unknown functions $\alpha_1, \ldots, \alpha_n$ and $\beta_1, \ldots, \beta_n$. As before, the initial conditions are obtained from (7.4.17) by

$$\sum_{i=1}^{n} \alpha_i(0)\phi_i(x_j) = f(x_j) \qquad \sum_{i=1}^{n} \beta_i(0)\psi_i(x_j) = \frac{1}{a}\int_0^x g(s)\, ds, \qquad j = 1, \ldots, n$$

where we will assume again that the $n \times n$ matrices $(\phi_i(x_j))$ and $(\psi_i(x_j))$ are nonsingular. Thus, the semidiscrete method for the wave equation (7.4.14) is entirely analogous to that for the heat equation, with the exception that there are now twice as many unknown functions in the system of ordinary differential equations.

We have used the collocation principle for the discretization of the space variable in both of the preceding examples, but the Galerkin principle discussed in Chapter 5 could also be used.

Finite difference discretizations can also be used in the same fashion, as we now discuss briefly for the heat equation (7.4.1). If u is the exact solution of (7.4.1), then the approximate relation

$$\textbf{(7.4.21)} \qquad u_t(t, x_i) \doteq \frac{c}{(\Delta x)^2}[u(t, x_{i+1}) - 2u(t, x_i) + u(t, x_{i-1})]$$

holds at the grid points $x_1, \ldots, x_n$. This suggests the following procedure. We seek to find n functions $v_1(t), \ldots, v_n(t)$ such that

$$v_i(t) \doteq u(t, x_i), \qquad i = 1, \ldots, n$$

The approximate relationship (7.4.21) suggests attempting to find these functions as the solution of the system of ordinary differential equations

$$\textbf{(7.4.22)} \quad v_i'(t) = \frac{c}{h^2}[v_{i+1}(t) - 2v_i(t) + v_{i-1}(t)], \qquad i = 1, \ldots, n$$

in which the functions v_0 and v_{n+1} are taken to be identically zero from the boundary conditions (7.4.2). Also, from the initial condition (7.4.2), we will take

$$\textbf{(7.4.23)} \qquad v_i(0) = f(x_i), \qquad i = 1, \ldots, n$$

The system (7.4.22) is conveniently written in matrix form as

$$\textbf{(7.4.24)} \qquad \mathbf{v}'(t) = \frac{-c}{(\Delta x)^2} \mathrm{A}\mathbf{v}(t)$$

where now A is simply the $(2, -1)$ tridiagonal matrix (7.2.14). If we apply Euler's method to this system, we have

$$\mathbf{v}^{m+1} = \mathbf{v}^m - \frac{c\Delta t}{(\Delta x)^2} \mathrm{A}\mathbf{v}^0, \qquad m = 0, 1, \ldots$$

Written out in component form, this is

$$v_i^{m+1} = v_i^m + \frac{c\Delta t}{(\Delta x)^2}(v_{i+1}^m - 2v_i^m + v_{i-1}^m), \qquad i = 1, \ldots, n, \; m = 0, 1, \ldots$$

which is simply the explicit method (7.2.5). Similarly, the implicit method (7.3.2) is obtained by applying the backward Euler method to (7.4.24), and the Crank–Nicolson method (7.3.12) arises by applying the trapezoid rule (2.5.38) to (7.4.24).

The preceding procedure leading to the system of ordinary differential equations (7.4.24) is sometimes called the *method of lines* and potentially has wide applicability.

Supplementary Discussion: 7.4

The use of semidiscrete methods is still an active research area and it is not clear at this time what their ultimate utility will be vis-à-vis other methods. See Mitchell and Wait [1977] for a further discussion.

Most general-purpose software for the numerical solution of time-dependent partial differential equations is based on the method of iines (see Madsen and Sincovec [1974]). The advantage to this approach is that one can use high-quality software that has been developed for solving ordinary differential equations (Hindmarsh [1972]). General partial differential equation software based on the method of lines includes Sincovec and Madsen [1975], Madsen and Sincovec [1979], Melgaard and Sincovec [1981], and Schiesser [1976].

EXERCISES 7.4

7.4.1. **a.** Write out the system of equations (7.4.7) explicitly for the basis functions $\phi_k(x) = \sin k\pi x$, $k = 1, \ldots, n$, assuming that the grid points $x_1, \ldots, x_n$ are equally spaced. Write a program to carry out Euler's method (7.4.12) with $n = 10$ and $\Delta t = 0.1$. Run the program for 20 time steps, and for different initial conditions.

b. Do the same if the ϕ_k are quadratic splines as discussed in Section 5.2.

7.4.2. Write down explicitly the second- and fourth-order Runge–Kutta methods and the second- and fourth-order Adams–Bashforth methods for (7.4.8).

7.4.3. Write a program to carry out the trapezoid method (7.4.13) for the problems of exercise 7.4.1.

7.4.4. Repeat exercise 7.4.1 for the equations (7.4.20) for the wave equation, assuming that the ϕ_i and ψ_i are both trigonometric functions in part a, and quadratic splines in part b.

8 The Curse of Dimensionality

8.1 Problems in Two and Three Space Dimensions

In the previous chapter, we considered partial differential equations in two independent variables: time and one space variable. Since physical phenomena occur in a three-dimensional world, mathematical models in only one space dimension are usually considerable simplifications of the actual physical situation although, in many cases, they are sufficient for phenomena that exhibit various symmetries or in which events are happening in two of the three space directions at such a slow rate that those directions can be ignored. However, large-scale scientific computing is now increasingly concerned with more detailed analyses of problems in which all three space directions, or at least two, are of concern. This chapter, then, will be concerned with problems in more than one space dimension, although for simplicity of exposition, we will confine any considerations of detail to only two dimensions.

In the previous chapter, we derived the heat equation

$$u_t = cu_{xx} \tag{8.1.1}$$

as a mathematical model of the temperature in a long, thin rod. Consider now the corresponding problem where the body of interest is a three-dimensional cube as shown in Figure 8.1.

The method of derivation of (8.1.1) extends to three dimensions, except that, now, partial derivatives in all three variables x, y, and z will occur. Thus, the extension of (8.1.1) to three space variables is

$$u_t = c(u_{xx} + u_{yy} + u_{zz}) \tag{8.1.2}$$

where the constant c is again the ratio of the thermal conductivity and the

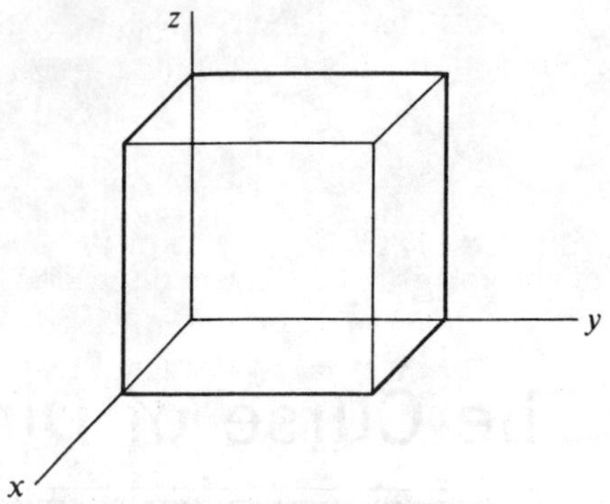

FIGURE 8.1 *Three-Dimensional Cube.*

product of the specific heat and mass density under the assumption that these quantities are not functions of space or time.

Equation (8.1.2) is a model of the temperature u as a function of time and at points within the interior of the body. As usual, to complete the model, we need to specify boundary conditions, and for this purpose, it is simplest for exposition to treat the corresponding problem in two space dimensions:

(8.1.3) $$u_t = c(u_{xx} + u_{yy})$$

We can consider (8.1.3) to be the mathematical model of the temperature in a flat, thin plate as shown in Figure 8.2, where we have taken the plate to be the unit square.

The simplest boundary conditions are where the temperature is prescribed on the four sides of the plate:

(8.1.4) $$u(t, x, y) = g(x, y), \quad \text{on sides of plate}$$

where g is a given function. Another possibility is to assume that one of

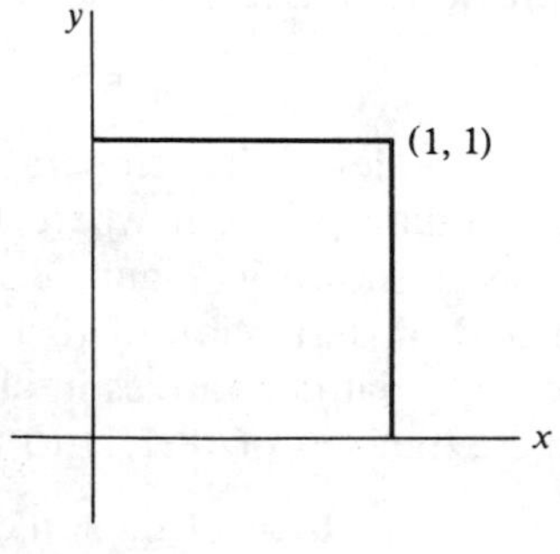

FIGURE 8.2 *Flat, Thin Plate.*

the sides, say $x = 0$, is perfectly insulated; thus, there is no heat loss across that side and no change in temperature, so the boundary condition is

(8.1.5) $$u_x(t, 0, y) = 0, \qquad 0 \le y \le 1$$

combined with the specification (8.1.4) on the other sides. A boundary condition of the form (8.1.5) is usually called a *Neumann condition*, and that of (8.1.4) is a *Dirichlet condition*. Clearly, various other such combinations are possible, including a specified temperature change (other than zero) across a boundary. Boundary conditions for the three-dimensional problem can be specified in a similar fashion. We also have to specify a temperature distribution at some time which we take to be $t = 0$; such an initial condition for (8.1.3) is of the form

(8.1.6) $$u(0, x, y) = f(x, y)$$

Given the initial condition (8.1.6) and boundary conditions of the form (8.1.4) and/or (8.1.5), it is intuitively clear that the temperature distribution should evolve in time to a final steady state that is determined only by the boundary conditions. In many situations, it is this steady-state solution that is of primary interest. Since this steady-state solution no longer depends on time, it should satisfy the equation (8.1.3) with $u_t = 0$; that is, the equation

(8.1.7) $$u_{xx} + u_{yy} = 0$$

which is Laplace's equation and, as mentioned in the previous chapter, is the prototype example of an elliptic equation. If we wish only the steady-state solution of the temperature distribution problem that we have been discussing, we can proceed, in principle, in two ways: solve equation (8.1.3) for u as a function of time until convergence to a steady state is reached, or solve (8.1.7) for only the steady-state solution.

Laplace's equation is also a mathematical model for a variety of other physical phenomena. In particular, it is sometimes called the *potential equation* since the electrostatic potential ϕ in the theory of electrostatics satisfies the equation

(8.1.8) $$\phi_{xx} + \phi_{yy} + \phi_{zz} = 0$$

that is, the Laplace equation in three dimensions. Similarly, the magnetic potential in the theory of magnetostatics and the gravitational potential in the Newtonian theory of gravity satisfy the same equation.

We will now sketch briefly the derivation of (8.1.8) for the gravitational potential. Recall that in the Newtonian theory of gravity, if m and m_1 are point masses with coordinates (x, y, z) and (x_1, y_1, z_1), then the vector describing the attractive force between these masses is given by

(8.1.9) $$\mathbf{F} = \frac{gmm_1}{r^3}(x - x_1, y - y_1, z - z_1)$$

where g is the gravitational constant and r is the (Euclidean) distance between the points. As is easily verified (exercise 8.1.1), the vector **F** is the gradient of the *potential function*

(8.1.10)
$$\phi(x, y, z) = \frac{-gmm_1}{r}$$

That is,

(8.1.11)
$$\mathbf{F} = (\phi_x, \phi_y, \phi_z)$$

More generally, if $m_1, \ldots, m_n$ are a number of point masses with coordinates (x_i, y_i, z_i), then the force vector at a point (x, y, z), which we assume has unit mass with no loss of generality, is again given by (8.1.11) if we now define the potential function by

(8.1.12)
$$\phi(x, y, z) = g \sum_{i=1}^{n} \frac{m_i}{r_i}$$

where

(8.1.13)
$$r_i = [(x - x_i)^2 + (y - y_i)^2 + (z - z_i)^2]^{\frac{1}{2}}$$

In many situations, however, the assumption of point masses is not sufficiently realistic, and it is necessary to extend (8.1.12) to an integral formulation. That is, if $\rho(\hat{x}, \hat{y}, \hat{z})$ is the mass-density function in some volume V, then the potential function ϕ at a point (x, y, z) can be defined as the continuous analog of (8.1.12), namely

(8.1.14)
$$\phi(x, y, z) = g \iiint_V \frac{\phi(\hat{x}, \hat{y}, \hat{z})\, dx\, dy\, dz}{r}$$

where

$$r = r(x, y, z; \hat{x}, \hat{y}, \hat{z}) = [(x - \hat{x})^2 + (y - \hat{y})^2 + (z - \hat{z})^2]^{\frac{1}{2}}$$

Again, the gravitational force at the point (x, y, z) due to the continuous mass distribution defined by ρ is given by (8.1.11). Thus, by differentiating under the integral in (8.1.14), we obtain

$$\phi_x = -g \iiint_V \frac{\rho(\hat{x}, \hat{y}, \hat{z})(x - \hat{x})}{r^3}\, d\hat{x}\, d\hat{y}\, d\hat{z}$$

and similarly for ϕ_y and ϕ_z. If we also calculate the second partial derivatives, we find

$$\phi_{xx} = g \iiint_V \rho(\hat{x}, \hat{y}, \hat{z}) \left[\frac{3(x - \hat{x})^2}{r^5} - \frac{1}{r^3}\right] dx\, dy\, dz$$

with similar expressions for ϕ_{yy} and ϕ_{zz}. Thus, if we add these, we obtain

$$\phi_{xx} + \phi_{yy} + \phi_{zz} = 0$$

That is, ϕ satisfies the Laplace equation (8.1.8).

The Laplace equation is the simplest example of an elliptic equation. More generally, the equation

$$\textbf{(8.1.15)} \qquad au_{xx} + bu_{xy} + cu_{yy} + du_x + eu_y + fu = g$$

where all of the coefficients $a, b, \ldots$ can be functions of x and y, is elliptic provided that

$$\textbf{(8.1.16)} \qquad [b(x, y)]^2 < a(x, y)c(x, y)$$

for all x, y in the region of interest; the equation is hyperbolic if $b^2 > ac$ and parabolic if $b^2 = ac$. An important special case of (8.1.15) is the equation

$$\textbf{(8.1.17)} \qquad (a(x, y)u_x)_x + (c(x, y)u_y)_y = 0$$

which is elliptic if a and c are positive and differentiable.

The methods we discuss in the following sections are usually applicable for general elliptic equations defined on rather general domains. For ease of exposition, however, we shall largely confine details of the exposition to Laplace's equation in two dimensions on a square region.

Supplementary Discussion and References: 8.1

The derivation and theory of elliptic partial differential equations as well as additional examples are discussed in all of the references given in the Supplementary Discussion of Section 7.1.

Higher-order equations of elliptic type arise in many important applications. For example, the biharmonic equation

$$u_{xxxx} + 2u_{xxyy} + u_{yyyy} = 0$$

models stress distribution in the theory of elasticity.

Very interesting, important, and difficult problems occur for equations of *mixed type* in which the condition (8.1.16) holds for x, y in part of the domain while the opposite inequality holds in another part; that is, the equation is elliptic in part of the domain and hyperbolic in another part. Such problems arise, for example, in transonic airflow in which the airflow is subsonic in part of the region (the elliptic part) and supersonic in another part (the hyperbolic part). A potential type equation for this problem is given by

$$(a^2 - \phi_x^2)\phi_{xx} - 2\phi_x\phi_y\phi_{xy} + (a^2 - \phi_y^2)\phi_{yy} = 0$$

Here, a, which may be a function of x, y, is the speed of sound, and ϕ_x

and ϕ_y represent velocities in the x and y directions. If $a^2 > \phi_x^2 + \phi_y^2$, the equation is elliptic, whereas if $a^2 = \phi_x^2 + \phi_y$ or $a^2 < \phi_x^2 + \phi_y^2$, the equation is parabolic and hyperbolic, respectively.

EXERCISE 8.1

8.1.1. Show that the vector **F** of (8.1.9) is the gradient of the function ϕ of (8.1.10); that is, **F** is the vector (ϕ_x, ϕ_y, ϕ_z).

8.2 Discretization of Problems in Two Space Dimensions

We now begin the study of methods for the numerical solution of elliptic equations. The two-point boundary-value problem

$$u'' + au' + bu = f, \qquad u(0) = \alpha, \qquad u(1) = \beta \tag{8.2.1}$$

treated in Chapters 3 and 5 may be considered an elliptic equation in one variable, and we wish to extend to equations in two independent variables the finite difference methods previously developed for (8.2.1).

We will consider first the finite difference method for *Poisson's equation*

$$u_{xx} + u_{yy} = f \tag{8.2.2}$$

which is Laplace's equation if the given right-hand side f is identically zero. We assume that the domain of the problem is the unit square $0 \le x, y \le 1$ in the x, y plane and that Dirichlet boundary conditions

$$u(x, y) = g(x, y), \qquad (x, y) \text{ on boundary} \tag{8.2.3}$$

are given on the boundary of the domain where g is a given function. We impose a mesh of grid points on the unit square with spacing h between the points in both the horizontal and vertical directions; this is illustrated in Figure 8.3.

Now, consider a typical grid point $(\hat{x}, \hat{y})$. We approximate u_{xx} and u_{yy} at this point by the usual centered difference approximations

$$u_{xx}(\hat{x}, \hat{y}) \doteq \frac{1}{h^2}[u(\hat{x} + h, \hat{y}) - 2u(\hat{x}, \hat{y}) + u(\hat{x} - h, \hat{y})] \tag{8.2.4a}$$

$$u_{yy}(\hat{x}, \hat{y}) \doteq \frac{1}{h^2}[u(\hat{x}, \hat{y} + h) - 2u(\hat{x}, \hat{y}) + u(\hat{x}, \hat{y} - h)] \tag{8.2.4b}$$

If we put these approximations into the differential equation (8.2.2), we

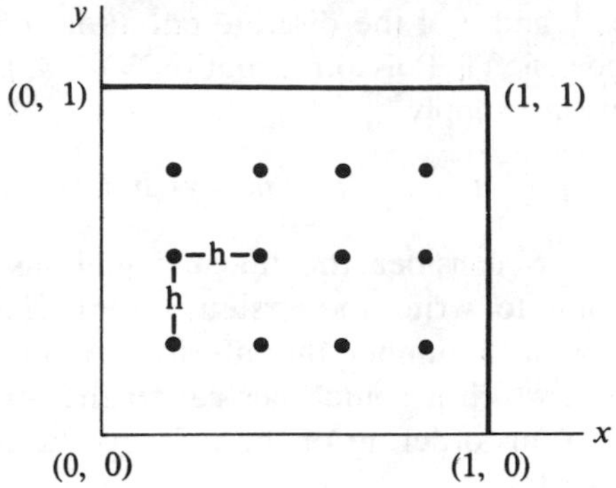

FIGURE 8.3 *Mesh Points on the Unit Square.*

obtain

(8.2.5) $$u(\hat{x} + h, \hat{y}) + u(\hat{x} - h, \hat{y}) + u(\hat{x}, \hat{y} + h) + u(\hat{x}, \hat{y} - h) - 4u(\hat{x}, \hat{y}) \doteq h^2 f(\hat{x}, \hat{y})$$

which is an approximate relationship that the exact solution u of (8.2.2) satisfies at any grid point in the interior of the domain.

The interior grid points are given by

(8.2.6) $$(x_i, y_j) = (ih, jh), \qquad i, j = 1, \ldots, N$$

where $(N + 1)h = 1$, and we now define approximations u_{ij} to the exact solution $u(x_i, y_j)$ at the N^2 interior grid points by requiring that they satisfy exactly the relationship (8.2.5); that is,

(8.2.7) $$u_{i+1,j} + u_{i-1,j} + u_{i,j+1} + u_{i,j-1} - 4u_{ij} = h^2 f_{ij}, \qquad i, j = 1, \ldots, N$$

This is a linear system of equations in the $(N + 2)^2$ variables u_{ij}. Note, however, that the variables $u_{0,j}$, $u_{N+1,j}$, $j = 0, \ldots, N + 1$, and $u_{i,0}$, $u_{i,N+1}$, $i = 0, \ldots, N + 1$, correspond to the grid points on the boundary and, hence, are fixed by the boundary condition (8.2.3); that is,

(8.2.8) $$\begin{aligned} u_{0,j} &= g(0, y_j) & u_{N+1,j} &= g(1, y_j), & j &= 0, 1, \ldots, N + 1 \\ u_{i,0} &= g(x_i, 0) & u_{i,N+1} &= g(x_i, 1), & i &= 0, 1, \ldots, N + 1 \end{aligned}$$

Therefore, (8.2.7) is a linear system of equations in the N^2 unknowns u_{ij}, $i, j = 1, \ldots, N$, corresponding to the interior grid points. The computational task at hand is to solve this linear system, and then u_{ij} will be our approximation at the point (x_i, y_i) to the solution of the differential equation (8.2.2). Note that (8.2.7) is simply the natural extension to two variables x and y of the discrete equations obtained in Chapter 3 for the "one-dimensional Poisson equation" $u'' = f$. In that case, the discrete equations are simply

$$u_{i+1} - 2u_i + u_{i-1} = h^2 f_i, \qquad i = 1, \ldots, N$$

Let us consider the linear equations (8.2.7) more closely. It is illuminating to write the system in matrix-vector form, and for this purpose, we will number the interior grid points in the manner shown in Figure 8.4, which is sometimes called the *lexicographic ordering*. Corresponding to this ordering of the grid points, we order the unknowns $\{u_{ij}\}$ into the vector

$$(u_{11}, \ldots, u_{N1}, u_{12}, \ldots, u_{N2}, \ldots, u_{1N}, \ldots, u_{NN}) \tag{8.2.9}$$

and write the equations (8.2.7) in the same order (where we have changed the sign in (8.2.7) and also have put the known boundary values on the right-hand side of the equation). Thus, the equations in matrix form become

$$\begin{bmatrix}
4 & -1 & 0 & \cdot & \cdot & \cdot & 0 & -1 & 0 & \cdot & \cdot & \cdot & & & & & & \\
-1 & 4 & -1 & 0 & \cdot & \cdot & \cdot & 0 & -1 & 0 & \cdot & \cdot & \cdot & & & & & \\
 & & \cdot & & & & & & & & & & & & & & & \\
 & & & \cdot & & & & & & & & & & & & & & \\
 & & & & \cdot & & & & & & & & & & & & & \\
0 & \cdot & \cdot & 0 & -1 & 4 & -1 & 0 & \cdot & \cdot & \cdot & 0 & -1 & \cdot & \cdot & \cdot & & \\
0 & \cdot & \cdot & \cdot & 0 & -1 & 4 & 0 & 0 & \cdot & \cdot & \cdot & 0 & -1 & 0 & \cdot & \cdot & \cdot \\
-1 & 0 & \cdot & \cdot & \cdot & 0 & 0 & 4 & -1 & 0 & \cdot & \cdot & \cdot & 0 & -1 & 0 & \cdot & \cdot & \cdot \\
0 & -1 & \cdot & \cdot & \cdot & \cdot & 0 & -1 & 4 & -1 & 0 & \cdot & \cdot & \cdot & 0 & -1 & 0 & \cdot & \cdot & \cdot \\
0 & & & & & & & & & & & & & & & & & \\
 & & & & & & & & & \vdots & & & & & & & &
\end{bmatrix} \tag{8.2.10}$$

$$\times \begin{bmatrix} u_{11} \\ u_{21} \\ \cdot \\ \cdot \\ \cdot \\ u_{N-1,1} \\ u_{N1} \\ u_{12} \\ u_{22} \\ \cdot \\ \cdot \\ \cdot \end{bmatrix} = \begin{bmatrix} u_{01} + u_{10} - h^2 f_{11} \\ u_{20} - h^2 f_{21} \\ \cdot \\ \cdot \\ \cdot \\ u_{N-1,0} - h^2 f_{N-1,1} \\ u_{N+1,1} + u_{N,0} - h^2 f_{N,1} \\ u_{02} - h^2 f_{12} \\ -h^2 f_{22} \\ \cdot \\ \cdot \\ \cdot \end{bmatrix}$$

The pattern of these equations should be clear. In particular, for each interior grid point that is not adjacent to a boundary grid point, the corresponding equation will involve only other unknowns (except for f), while for those interior points adjacent to a boundary grid point, at least

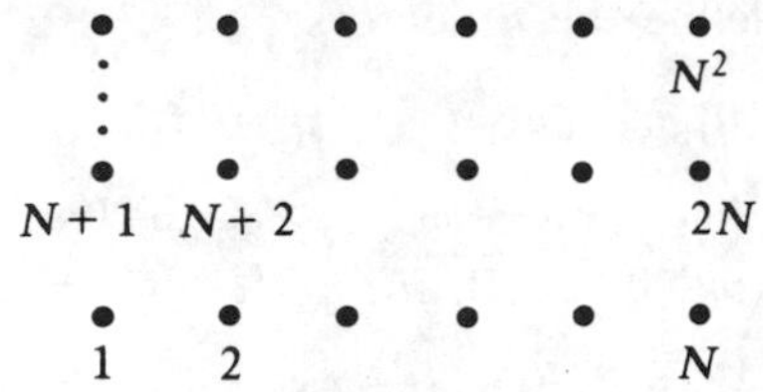

FIGURE 8.4 *Ordering of the Grid Points.*

one value of a u_{ij} will be known by the boundary condition and is put on the right-hand side of the equation.

Although (8.2.10) exhibits the structure of the matrix equation, it is rather cumbersome. It is much easier to write the system (8.2.10) in *block matrix* form, where, in general, we mean by this, writing a matrix A as

$$A = \begin{bmatrix} A_{11} & \cdots & A_{1p} \\ \vdots & & \vdots \\ A_{p1} & \cdots & A_{pp} \end{bmatrix}$$

where each A_{ij} is itself a matrix. To do this in a very natural way for the coefficient matrix of (8.2.10), we define the $N \times N$ tridiagonal matrix

$$T_N = \begin{bmatrix} 4 & -1 & & \\ -1 & \ddots & \ddots & \\ & \ddots & \ddots & -1 \\ & & -1 & 4 \end{bmatrix}$$

and let I_N denote the $N \times N$ identity matrix. Then, the $N^2 \times N^2$ coefficient matrix of (8.2.10) is simply the *block tridiagonal matrix*

$$A = \begin{bmatrix} T_N & -I_N & & & \\ -I_N & T_N & \ddots & & \\ & -I_N & \ddots & \ddots & \\ & & \ddots & \ddots & -I_N \\ & & & -I_N & T_N \end{bmatrix}$$

If we also define the n vectors

$$\mathbf{u}_i = (u_{1i}, \ldots, u_{Ni})^T \qquad \mathbf{f}_i = (f_{1i}, \ldots, f_{Ni})^T, \qquad i = 1, \ldots, N$$
$$\mathbf{b}_1 = (u_{01} + u_{10}, u_{20}, \ldots, u_{N-1,0}, u_{N,0} + u_{N+1,1})^T$$
$$\mathbf{b}_i = (u_{0i}, 0, \ldots, 0, u_{N+1,i})^T, \qquad i = 2, \ldots, N-1$$
$$\mathbf{b}_N = (u_{0,N} + u_{1,N+1}, u_{2,N+1}, \ldots, u_{N-1,N+1}, u_{N,N+1} + u_{N+1,N})^T$$

then we can write the complete system (8.2.10) in the compact block tridiagonal form

(8.2.11)
$$\begin{bmatrix} T_N & -I_N & & & \\ -I_N & \cdot & \cdot & & \\ & \cdot & \cdot & \cdot & \\ & & \cdot & \cdot & -I_N \\ & & & -I_N & T_N \end{bmatrix} \begin{bmatrix} \mathbf{u}_1 \\ \mathbf{u}_2 \\ \cdot \\ \cdot \\ \cdot \\ \mathbf{u}_N \end{bmatrix} = \begin{bmatrix} \mathbf{b}_1 - h^2\mathbf{f}_1 \\ \mathbf{b}_2 - h^2\mathbf{f}_2 \\ \cdot \\ \cdot \\ \cdot \\ \mathbf{b}_N - h^2\mathbf{f}_N \end{bmatrix}$$

We now make several comments about this system of equations. If N is of moderate size, say $N = 100$, then there are $N^2 = 10^4$ unknowns, and the matrix in (8.2.11) is $10{,}000 \times 10{,}000$. On the other hand, in each row of the matrix, there are at most five nonzero elements, regardless of the size of N, so the distribution of nonzero to zero elements is very "sparse" if N is at all large. Such matrices are called *large sparse matrices* and arise in a variety of ways besides the numerical solution of partial differential equations.

It is the property of being sparse that allows such large systems of equations to be solved on today's computers with relative ease. Recall that in Chapter 3, we saw that Gaussian elimination requires on the order of n^3 arithmetic operations to solve an $n \times n$ linear system. Hence, if a $10^4 \times 10^4$ linear system were "dense," that is, few of its elements were zero, and Gaussian elimination were used to solve the system, then on the order of 10^{12} operations would be required. At a rate of 10^8 operations per second, which is about what can be achieved on today's fastest computers, it would still require several hours to solve such a system. However, by utilizing the special structure and sparsity of systems such as (8.2.11), we shall see later in this chapter that they can be solved, despite their large size, relatively quickly and easily.

We end this section by applying the discretization of Poisson's equation to the heat equation (8.1.3) in two space variables—

(8.2.12)
$$u_t = c(u_{xx} + u_{yy})$$

where, again for simplicity in exposition, we will assume that the x, y domain is the unit square of Figure 8.3 and that the Dirichlet boundary conditions (8.2.3) are given on the sides of the square. We also assume the initial condition

(8.2.13) $$u(0, x, y) = f(x, y)$$

Corresponding to the method (7.2.5) in the case of a single space variable, we can easily formulate an explicit method for (8.2.12):

(8.2.14) $$u_{ij}^{m+1} = u_{ij}^m + \frac{c\Delta t}{h^2}(u_{i,j+1}^m + u_{i,j-1}^m + u_{i+1,j}^m + u_{i-1,j}^m - 4u_{ij}^m),$$

$$m = 0, 1, \ldots, \qquad i, j = 1, \ldots, N$$

Here, u_{ij}^m denotes the approximate solution at the i, j gridpoint and at the mth time level $m\Delta t$, and u_{ij}^{m+1} is the approximate solution at the next time level. The terms in parentheses on the right-hand side of (8.2.14) correspond exactly to the discretization (8.2.7) with $f_{ij} = 0$. The prescription (8.2.14) has the same properties as its one-dimensional counterpart (7.2.5): it is first-order accurate in time and second-order accurate in space, and it is easy to carry out. It is also subject to a similar stability condition

(8.2.15) $$\Delta t \leq \frac{h^2}{4c}$$

and thus has the problem that if h is small, very small time steps are required.

We can attempt to circumvent this restriction on the time step in the same way that we did in Section 7.3 by the use of implicit methods. For example, the implicit method (7.3.2) now becomes

(8.2.16) $$u_{ij}^{m+1} = u_{ij}^m + \frac{c\Delta t}{h^2}(u_{ij+1}^{m+1} + u_{ij-1}^{m+1} + u_{i+1,j}^{m+1} + u_{i-1,j}^{m+1} - 4u_{ij}^{m+1})$$

which is unconditionally stable. However, to carry out this method requires the solution at each time step of the system of linear equations

(8.2.17) $$\left(4 + \frac{h^2}{c\Delta t}\right)u_{ij}^{m+1} - u_{ij+1}^{m+1} - u_{ij-1}^{m+1} - u_{i+1,j}^{m+1} - u_{i-1,j}^{m+1}$$

$$= \frac{h^2}{c\Delta t}u_{ij}^m, \qquad i, j = 1, \ldots, N$$

This system has the same form as the system (8.2.7) for Poisson's equation, with the exception that the coefficient of u_{ij}^{m+1} is modified. Indeed, the left-hand sides of the equations (8.2.17) have exactly the same form as the finite difference equations for the *Helmholtz equation* $u_{xx} + u_{yy} - \sigma u = 0$ where σ is a given nonnegative function of x and y. The term $-\sigma u$ in this differential equation goes over to $-h^2\sigma_{ij}u_{ij}$ in the difference equations (8.2.7), with $\sigma_{ij} = \sigma(x_i, y_i)$. The particular constant function $\sigma = -1/(c\Delta t)$ then corresponds to the left-hand side of (8.2.17).

In the case of a single space variable, the use of an implicit method such as (7.3.2) does not cause much computational difficulty since the solution of tridiagonal systems of equations can be accomplished so rapidly. However, each time step of (8.2.17) requires the solution of a two-dimensional Poisson-type equation, which is a harder computational problem for which methods will be discussed in the next two sections. The Crank–Nicolson method (7.3.12) can also be easily extended to the equation (8.2.12) (exercise 8.2.3) but suffers from the same difficulty that Poisson-type equations must be solved at each time step. We shall consider, instead, a different class of methods, in which the basic computational step is, again, the solution of tridiagonal systems of equations. These are the *alternating direction implicit* (*ADI*) *methods.*

Perhaps the simplest such method is that of *Peaceman–Rachford,* which has the form

(8.2.18a) $$u_{ij}^{m+1/2} = u_{ij}^{m} + \frac{1}{2}\frac{c\Delta t}{h^2}\left(u_{i+1,j}^{m+1/2} + u_{i-1,j}^{m+1/2} - 2u_{ij}^{m+1/2} + u_{i,j+1}^{m} + u_{i,j-1}^{m} - 2u_{ij}^{m}\right)$$

(8.2.18b) $$u_{ij}^{m+1} = u_{ij}^{m+1/2} + \frac{1}{2}\frac{c\Delta t}{h^2}\left(u_{i,j+1}^{m+1} + u_{i,j-1}^{m+1} - 2u_{ij}^{m+1} + u_{i+1,j}^{m+1/2} + u_{i-1,j}^{m+1/2} - 2u_{ij}^{m+1/2}\right)$$

This is to be viewed as a two-step method in which at the first step—(8.2.18a)—intermediate values $u_{ij}^{m+1/2}$, $i, j = 1, \ldots, N$, are computed. These $u_{ij}^{m+1/2}$ are to be interpreted as approximate values of the solution at the intermediate time level $m + \frac{1}{2}$; thus, the factor $\frac{1}{2}$ appears on the right-hand side of (8.2.18a) because the time step is $\frac{1}{2}\Delta t$. The computation in (8.2.18a) involves the solution of the N tridiagonal systems of equations

(8.2.19) $$(2 + \alpha)u_{ij}^{m+1/2} - u_{i+1,j}^{m+1/2} - u_{i-1,j}^{m+1/2} = (\alpha - 2)u_{ij}^{m} + u_{i,j+1}^{m} + u_{i,j-1}^{m}, \qquad i = 1, \ldots, N$$

for $j = 1, \ldots, N$ where $\alpha = 2h^2/(c\Delta t)$; that is, for each fixed j, (8.2.19) is a tridiagonal system whose solution is $u_{ij}^{m+1/2}$, $i = 1, \ldots, N$. The coefficient matrix of each of these systems is simply $\alpha \mathrm{I} + \mathrm{A}$, where A is the tridiagonal matrix (7.2.14). Thus $\alpha \mathrm{I} + \mathrm{A}$ is strictly diagonally dominant, and hence these systems can be rapidly solved by Gaussian elimination without interchanges.

Once the intermediate values $u_{ij}^{m+1/2}$ have been computed, the final values u_{ij}^{m+1} are obtained from (8.2.18b) by solving the N tridiagonal systems

(8.2.20) $$(2 + \alpha)u_{ij}^{m+1} - u_{i,j+1}^{m+1} - u_{i,j-1}^{m+1} = (\alpha - 2)u_{ij}^{m+1/2} + u_{i+1,j}^{m+1/2} + u_{i-1,j}^{m+1/2}, \qquad j = 1, \ldots, N$$

for $i = 1, \ldots, N$. Again, the coefficient matrices of these systems are $\alpha \mathrm{I} + \mathrm{A}$.

Thus, the computational process requires the solution of $2N$ tridiagonal systems of dimension N to move from the mth time level to the $(m + 1)$st. It can be shown that this method is unconditionally stable.

The term *alternating direction* derives from the paradigm that we are, in some sense, approximating values of the solution in the x-direction by (8.2.18a), and then in the y-direction by (8.2.18b). There are many variants of the Peaceman–Rachford method that employ this basic idea of alternating direction, and this class of methods has been one of the most widely used for parabolic-type equations. The same idea can also be used to obtain iterative methods for elliptic equations, which will be discussed in Section 8.4.

Supplementary Discussion and References: 8.2

The discussion of this section has been restricted to Poisson's equation in two variables on a square domain, and the corresponding heat equation. However, problems that arise in practice will generally deviate considerably from these ideal conditions: the domain may not be square; the equation may have nonconstant coefficients or even be nonlinear; the boundary conditions may be a mixture of Dirichlet and Neumann conditions; there may be more than a single equation—that is, there may be a coupled system of partial differential equations; and there may be three or more independent variables. The general principles of finite difference discretization of this section still apply, but each of the preceding factors causes complications.

One of the classical references for the discretization of elliptic equations by finite difference methods is Forsythe and Wasow [1960]. See also Roache [1972] for problems that arise in fluid dynamics, and Ames [1977]. Discussions and analyses of alternating direction methods, and of related methods such as the method of fractional steps, are given in a number of books; see, for example, Varga [1962] and Richtmyer and Morton [1967].

In the last several years, finite element and other projection-type methods have played an increasingly important role in the solution of elliptic- and parabolic-type equations. Although the mathematical basis of the finite element method goes back to the 1940s, its development into a viable procedure was carried out primarily by engineers in the 1950s and 1960s, especially for problems in structural analysis. Since then, the mathematical basis has been extended and broadened and its applicability to general elliptic and parabolic equations well demonstrated. One of the method's main advantages is its ability to handle curved boundaries. For introductions to the finite element method, see Strang and Fix [1973] and Mitchell and Wait [1977].

EXERCISES 8.2

8.2.1. Assume that the function u is as many times continuously differentiable as needed. Expand u in a Taylor series about $(\hat{x}, \hat{y})$ and show that the difference approximations (8.2.4) are second-order accurate; that is, $u_{xx}(\hat{x}, \hat{y}) - (1/h^2)[u(\hat{x} + h, \hat{y}) - 2u(\hat{x}, \hat{y}) + u(\hat{x} - h, \hat{y})] = 0(h^2)$, and similarly for the approximation to u_{yy}.

8.2.2. Write out equations (8.2.7), (8.2.10), and (8.2.11) explicitly for $N = 3$.

8.2.3. Formulate the Crank–Nicolson method for equation (8.2.12).

8.3 Direct Methods for Large Sparse Systems

In Section 8.2, we derived equation (8.2.10), a system of linear equations that we shall denote in matrix form by $A\mathbf{x} = \mathbf{b}$. The matrix A consisted primarily of zero elements—each row and each column contained at most five nonzero elements. Furthermore, the nonzero elements were arranged in a very regular pattern—they were all contained in five diagonals. Considerable computer time and space could be saved if storage of the zero elements and operations involving the zero elements were avoided. For our purposes, a *sparse* matrix or system will be one for which advantage can be taken of the zero elements, both their number and their location or distribution. This and the next section will be concerned with methods for solving sparse linear systems.

There are two basic approaches to solving sparse systems of linear equations. The first approach is to use a direct method—Gaussian elimination—under the constraint of avoiding operating on and storing all or most of the zero elements. By Gaussian elimination, we include triangular factorization and Cholesky's algorithm. Two important considerations include the order in which unknowns are eliminated and the data structure used for storing information concerning the matrix elements. This method is discussed in this section. The second approach to solving sparse linear systems is to use iterative methods. Primary considerations are convergence and rates of convergence. This topic is covered in Section 8.4.

As discussed in Chapter 3, and again in Section 8.2, to solve a general $n \times n$ linear system of equations by Gaussian elimination requires $0(n^3)$ arithmetic operations and $0(n^2)$ storage locations. Thus, the two main goals of a sparse variant of Gaussian elimination are:

1. Reduce the operation count of $0(n^3)$ by not performing operations involving zeros.
2. Reduce storage requirements of $0(n^2)$ by storing only the nonzero elements and information describing their locations.

The remainder of this section will address these goals.

	1	2	3	4	5	6	7	8	9	10	11	12	13	14	15	16
1	4	−1			−1											
2	−1	4	−1			−1										
3		−1	4	−1			−1									
4			−1	4				−1								
5	−1				4	−1			−1							
6		−1			−1	4	−1			−1						
7			−1			−1	4	−1			−1					
8				−1			−1	4				−1				
9					−1				4	−1			−1			
10						−1			−1	4	−1			−1		
11							−1			−1	4	−1			−1	
12								−1			−1	4				−1
13									−1				4	−1		
14										−1			−1	4	−1	
15											−1			−1	4	−1
16												−1			−1	4

FIGURE 8.5 *Matrix Representation of Figure* 8.4, *for* $N = 4$.

First, let us consider the matrix given by equation (8.2.10), which is based on the lexicographic ordering given in Figure 8.4. For $N = 4$, the banded matrix given in Figure 8.5 is generated.

If the ordering is chosen differently, the corresponding matrix is different. For example, if the ordering is based on numbering every other grid point, as is demonstrated by Figure 8.6, the matrix displayed in Figure 8.7 results. This ordering is called the *red-black ordering* because of the analogous arrangement of the red and black squares on a chess-board. This matrix has a very unusual characteristic: it is a block matrix

o 15 B	o 7 R	o 16 B	o 8 R
o 5 R	o 13 B	o 6 R	o 14 B
o 11 B	o 3 R	o 12 B	o 4 R
o 1 R	o 9 B	o 2 R	o 10 B

FIGURE 8.6 *Grid for* $N = 4$ *and Red-Black Ordering.*

	1	2	3	4	5	6	7	8	9	10	11	12	13	14	15	16
1	4								−1		−1					
2		4							−1	−1		−1				
3			4						−1		−1	−1	−1			
4				4						−1		−1		−1		
5					4						−1		−1		−1	
6						4						−1	−1	−1		−1
7							4						−1		−1	−1
8								4						−1		−1
9	−1	−1	−1						4							
10		−1		−1						4						
11	−1		−1		−1						4					
12		−1	−1	−1		−1						4				
13			−1		−1	−1	−1						4			
14				−1		−1		−1						4		
15					−1		−1								4	
16						−1	−1	−1								4

FIGURE 8.7 *Matrix Representation of Figure 8.6.*

composed of four blocks with the two diagonal blocks being diagonal and the off-diagonal blocks containing all of the -1 values. The two matrices given by Figures 8.5 and 8.7 are important in the analysis of iterative methods—the subject of Section 8.4.

The matrix generated by approximating the differential equation (8.2.2) depends on several things. The value of h, the mesh size, determines n, the order of the matrix. The ordering of the grid points determines the locations of the nonzero values in the matrix. The contrast between Figures 8.5 and 8.7 demonstrates this point. Furthermore, the difference approximation [see equation (8.2.4)] determines the values of the nonzero entries in the matrix as well as influences how sparse the matrix is. For example, if the difference approximation given by the equation (3.2.36) is used instead of (8.2.4), the values of the nonzeros in the matrix will be different, and there will be up to nine nonzeros per row (exercise 8.3.4).

Let us consider another sparse matrix, one with much less regularity and structure than the ones given by Figures 8.5 and 8.7. This matrix has as its basis a Department of Transportation study concerning automobile safety. The object in Figure 8.8 crudely models a person known as "dynamic stickman." Such a graph has a corresponding sparse matrix structure if every node or vertex is numbered as is shown in Figure 8.8.

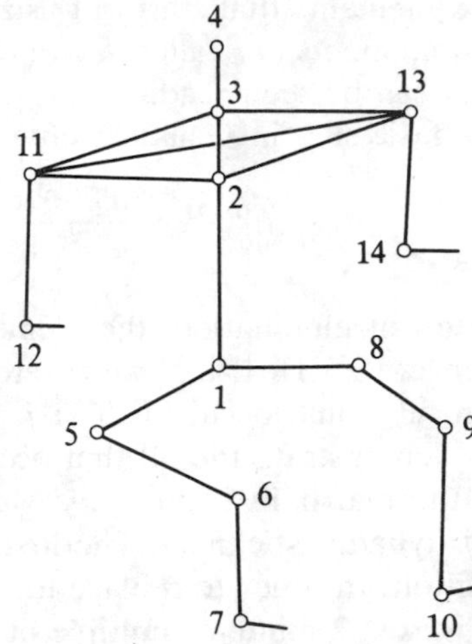

FIGURE 8.8 *Dynamic Stickman.*

The sparse matrix structure is determined as follows: if node i is connected to node j by an edge, then the i, j element, a_{ij}, is nonzero. Thus, the matrix representation of dynamic stickman for the numbering indicated in Figure 8.8 is shown in Figure 8.9. For now, we will not be concerned with the nonzero values, only their locations.

The key difference between the application of Gaussian elimination to a sparse matrix and the application to a full matrix is that for a

	1	2	3	4	5	6	7	8	9	10	11	12	13	14
1	X	X			X			X						
2	X	X	X								X		X	
3		X	X	X							X		X	
4			X	X										
5	X				X	X		X						
6					X	X	X							
7						X	X							
8	X				X			X	X					
9								X	X	X				
10									X	X				
11		X	X								X	X	X	
12											X	X		
13		X	X								X		X	X
14													X	X

FIGURE 8.9 *Matrix Representation of Figure* 8.8.

sparse matrix, elements that start out as zero can become nonzero. Such newly created elements are called *fill-in elements*, or simply *fill*. The way that fill occurs can be seen readily by examining the elimination process. Consider the basic step in Gaussian elimination [see equation (3.3.11)]:

(8.3.1)
$$a_{ij}^{(k+1)} = \frac{a_{ij}^{(k)} - a_{ik}^{(k)}a_{kj}^{(k)}}{a_{kk}^{(k)}}$$

At the kth step of elimination, the element $a_{ij}^{(k)}$ is modified to become $a_{ij}^{(k+1)}$ as given in (8.3.1). If $a_{ij}^{(k)}$ were zero while $a_{ik}^{(k)}$ and $a_{kj}^{(k)}$ were both nonzero, then fill would occur in the i, j position during step k.

Let us demonstrate the fill that occurs when Gaussian elimination is applied to the matrix in Figure 8.9, which corresponds to the original numbering of dynamic stickman. The first element to be eliminated is in the (2, 1) position. In order to replace that element with zero, we replace all of row 2 by row 2 minus a multiple of row 1. That would correspond to using equation (8.3.1) with $k = 1$, $i = 2$, and $j = 2, \ldots, n$. Fill will occur when $a_{2j}^{(1)} = 0$, but $a_{1j}^{(1)} \neq 0$. This is true for $j = 5$ and 8. Thus, $a_{25}^{(2)}$ and $a_{28}^{(2)}$ become nonzero during the first stage of Gaussian elimination. This is represented in Figure 8.10 by 1s in the (2, 5) and (2, 8) positions. Likewise, the (5, 2) and (8, 2) elements are filled when the (5, 1) and (8, 1) elements are eliminated. During the second stage of Gaussian elimination, the elimination of elements in column 2 leads to fill in row 3 and

	1	2	3	4	5	6	7	8	9	10	11	12	13	14
1	X	X			X			X						
2	X	X	X		1			1			X		X	
3		X	X	X	2			2			X		X	
4			X	X	3			3			3		3	
5	X	1	2	3	X	X		X			3		3	
6					X	X	X	5			5		5	
7						X	X	6			6		6	
8	X	1	2	3	X	5	6	X	X		3		3	
9								X	X	X	8		8	
10									X	X	9		9	
11		X	X	3	3	5	6	3	8	9	X	X	X	
12											X	X	11	
13		X	X	3	3	5	6	3	8	9	X	11	X	X
14													X	X

FIGURE 8.10 *Matrix Representation of Figure 8.8 after Gaussian Elimination. A number m in the (i, j) position indicates that a nonzero was created at stage m of elimination.*

column 3. These elements, as well as all fill elements during elimination, are indicated in Figure 8.10. A number m in Figure 8.10 indicates that an element filled in at that location at stage m of the elimination. Note that no fill occurred at stages 4, 7, 10, 12, 13, and 14. By inspection of Figure 8.10, one can see that the original matrix had 48 nonzeros, but the elimination has added 46 fill elements, for a total of 94—almost doubling the number of nonzero elements and the consequent storage requirements. The additional arithmetic operations required will be explored later. Compare these figures with 196, the number of elements in a dense 14×14 matrix.

The "sparse variants of Gaussian elimination" mentioned previously now come into play. The key question is, Can we perform the elimination in a different order and have fewer fill elements? Performing the elimination in a different order would correspond to permuting rows and corresponding columns of the original matrix. Thus, the sparse variants correspond to reordering rows and corresponding columns of the original matrix. To demonstrate the difference, let us reorder the nodes of dynamic stickman as is indicated in Figure 8.11. The corresponding matrix is given in Figure 8.12. Now, if we perform Gaussian elimination on this matrix, we will generate the fill indicated in Figure 8.13. As expected, the reordered matrix in Figure 8.12 still has 48 nonzeros. They have the same values as those in Figure 8.9, but they have been rearranged. However, there are differences in the fill. By inspecting Figure 8.13, we see that the amount of fill is only 28 elements—reduced from 46 for the original ordering. Thus, the required storage for the factored form of the reordered matrix is significantly less than for the factored form of the original matrix.

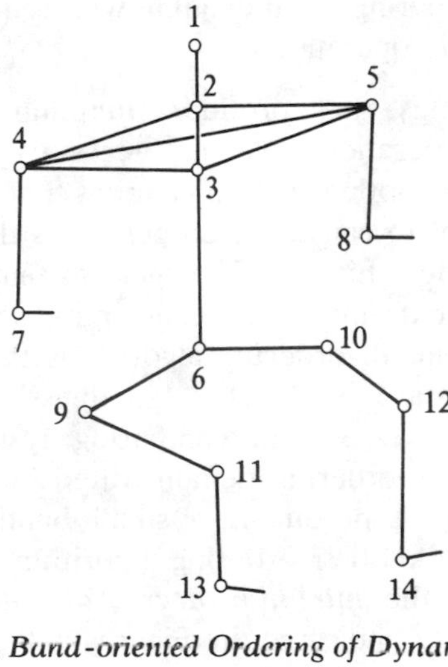

FIGURE 8.11 *A Band-oriented Ordering of Dynamic Stickman.*

	1	2	3	4	5	6	7	8	9	10	11	12	13	14
1	X	X												
2	X	X	X	X	X									
3		X	X	X	X	X								
4		X	X	X	X		X							
5		X	X	X	X			X						
6			X			X			X	X				
7				X			X							
8					X			X						
9						X			X	X	X			
10						X			X	X		X		
11									X		X		X	
12										X		X		X
13											X		X	
14												X		X

FIGURE 8.12 *Matrix Representation of Figure* 8.11.

By the preceding paragraph, we see that the order of elimination can affect the amount of fill considerably. It follows that the amount of computer storage for the matrix elements and the number of arithmetic operations during elimination depends heavily on the particular ordering used. Two questions that occur naturally are:

1. What ordering of the unknowns requires the minimum amount of fill?
2. What ordering of the unknowns requires the minimum number of arithmetic operations?

The orderings that produce minimum fill and those that produce minimum operations are not necessarily the same. This can be seen intuitively by noting that an element that fills early in the elimination has the potential to cause more operations than an element that fills late in the elimination. Finding the orderings that minimize fill or operations is a task that is extremely time-consuming, so much so that it is not done in practice. Instead, ordering algorithms that are relatively fast and do a "good" job are used. The "goodness" is subjectively determined by studying test cases and comparing results produced by different algorithms. The ordering demonstrated by Figures 8.11–8.13 is based on the concept of producing a small bandwidth (recall the definition in Chapter 3). Another ordering algorithm that we shall apply to dynamic stickman is the *minimum-degree algorithm*. Returning to the original numbering as indicated in Figures 8.8 and 8.9, the minimum-degree

	1	2	3	4	5	6	7	8	9	10	11	12	13	14
1	X	X												
2	X	X	X	X	X									
3		X	X	X	X	X								
4		X	X	X	X	3	X							
5		X	X	X	X	3	4	X						
6			X	3	3	X	4	5	X	X				
7				X	4	4	X	5	6	6				
8					X	5	5	X	6	6				
9						X	6	6	X	X	X			
10						X	6	6	X	X	9	X		
11									X	9	X	10	X	
12										X	10	X	11	X
13											X	11	X	12
14												X	12	X

FIGURE 8.13 *Matrix Representation of Figure* 8.11 *after Elimination.*

algorithm chooses a row, say row j, with the fewest number of nonzeros (or a node with the fewest number of immediate neighbors) and interchanges the first row and column with the jth row and column. Then, a stage of elimination is carried out. The algorithm repeats this step, using the reduced matrix. The number of nonzeros in a row is an upper bound on the number of elements that may fill in during that particular stage of

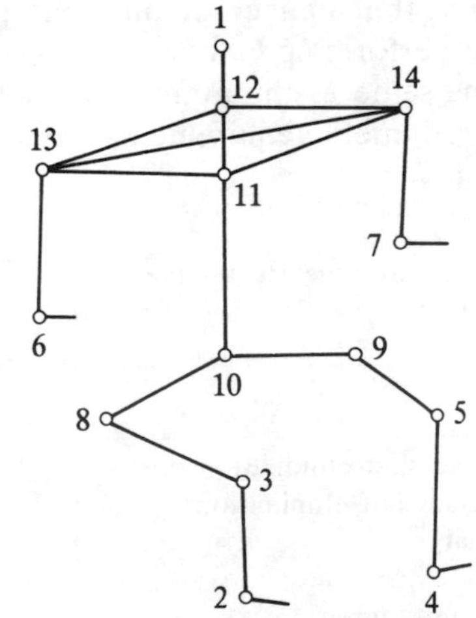

FIGURE 8.14 *A Minimum Degree Ordering of Dynamic Stickman.*

	1	2	3	4	5	6	7	8	9	10	11	12	13	14
1	X											X		
2		X	X											
3		X	X					X						
4				X	X									
5				X	X				X					
6						X							X	
7							X							X
8			X					X	X	X				
9					X			X	X	X				
10								X	X	X	X			
11										X	X	X	X	X
12	X										X	X	X	X
13						X					X	X	X	X
14							X				X	X	X	X

FIGURE 8.15 *Matrix Representation of Figure* 8.14.

Gaussian elimination. Thus, the minimum-degree algorithm is locally trying to minimize the fill. Figures 8.14 and 8.15 indicate the minimum-degree algorithm applied to dynamic stickman. Although not typical, the minimum-degree ordering results in absolutely no fill at all for this particular matrix. As a summary, Table 8.1 contains information concerning storage requirements for the various ordering algorithms.

Now, let us compare the various orderings in terms of the number of multiplicative operations required to carry out Gaussian elimination. Table 8.2 lists the number of multiplications required by each of the orderings for performing Gaussian elimination. The number of additions is roughly the same as the number of multiplications. As in the case of storage, the arithmetic requirements are strongly influenced by the ordering algorithm.

TABLE 8.1 *Storage Requirements for Various Orderings of Dynamic Stickman*: $n = 14$; *Number of Original Nonzeros* = 48

	Fill	Total
Dense Gaussian elimination		196
Sparse Gaussian elimination		
Original	46	94
Band	28	76
Minimum-degree	0	48

TABLE 8.2 *Requirements for Multiplicative Operations for Various Orderings of Dynamic Stickman*: $n = 14$; *Number of Original Nonzeros* = 48

	Factorization	Solution
Dense Gaussian elimination	546	210
Sparse Gaussian elimination		
Original	138	108
Band	117	84
Minimum-degree	39	62

Even though these data indicate that the minimum-degree algorithm is far superior to the other orderings for this problem, it would be unwarranted to conclude that minimum-degree is always the algorithm to use. The relative performances of different ordering algorithms are problem-dependent. There are cases for which other algorithms are superior to minimum-degree. Extensive testing on a collection of relevant matrices is necessary before deciding which algorithm to use.

Thus far, we have not been specific about the differences between sparse symmetric matrices and sparse nonsymmetric matrices, nor have we mentioned storage schemes or pivoting for maintaining numerical stability. The problem that is simplest and which has been the most analyzed is the problem of a symmetric matrix that requires no pivoting for numerical stability. Such matrices may be positive-definite or diagonally dominant and often arise in finite element and finite difference approximations. For this case, one can use the Cholesky algorithm or symmetric Gaussian elimination algorithms that are modifications of those for dense matrices given in Chapter 3. Some of the simpler ordering algorithms try to produce small bandwidths. The minimum-degree algorithm is often used on the problems. More complex algorithms are mentioned in the Supplementary Discussion. A common method of storing a sparse matrix is based on the fact that any fill that occurs to the left of the diagonal in any row must occur to the right of the first nonzero in that row. Thus, the storage scheme is to store, in contiguous locations in a one-dimensional array, all entries from the first nonzero to the diagonal. An additional n pointers are needed to record the positions of the diagonal elements of A. An example is shown in Figure 8.16.

A second class of practical problems that occur are sparse matrices that are not symmetric but have a symmetric sparse structure, that is, $a_{ij} \neq a_{ji}$ but $a_{ij} = 0$ if and only if $a_{ji} = 0$. These matrices often occur in electrical power network problems. It is common to ignore pivoting for numerical stability even though there is no guarantee of accurate results. The minimum-degree algorithm is often used for determining the ordering for these problems.

$$A = \begin{bmatrix} a_{11} & & & & & \\ a_{21} & a_{22} & & \text{Symmetric} & & \\ & & a_{33} & & & \\ a_{41} & & a_{43} & a_{44} & & \\ & & a_{53} & & a_{55} & \\ & & a_{63} & a_{64} & & a_{66} \end{bmatrix}$$

$$(a_{11}\ a_{21}\ a_{22}\ a_{33}\ a_{41}\ a_{42}\ a_{43}\ a_{44}\ a_{53}\ a_{54}\ a_{55}\ a_{63}\ a_{64}\ a_{65}\ a_{66})$$

$$(1\ \ 3\ \ 4\ \ 8\ \ 11\ \ 15)$$

FIGURE 8.16 *An Example of a Row-oriented Symmetric Storage Scheme.*

For general nonsymmetric sparse problems, there are variations of the minimum-degree algorithm that are often used in conjunction with a modification of numerical stability pivoting, called *threshold pivoting.* In partial pivoting, an element can be used as the pivot if it is the largest, in modulus, of the elements in its column. In threshold pivoting, an element may be used as the pivot if it is not too small compared to the largest, say 10%–20% as large. This strategy may present several candidates for the pivot element. Then, the algorithm can choose that element which is best for sparsity considerations. This strategy is a compromise between maintaining sparsity and controlling loss of accuracy through round-off.

A straightforward method of storing the nonzero entries of a nonsymmetric matrix is to label each nonzero element with its row and column number. That is, use a triple (a_k, i_k, j_k), where a_k is a nonzero in the (i_k, j_k) position of the matrix and k runs from 1 to the number of nonzeros. This is a simple way of entering data to a program, but not the best way for efficient execution of Gaussian elimination. Instead, more-complicated structures are used in high-quality software.

Supplementary Discussion and References: 8.3

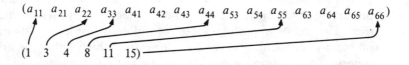

Literally hundreds of articles have been written on the subject of solving sparse linear systems with direct methods. It is a very active area of current research. Accordingly, this section can in no way be comprehensive. The authors do not expect that the reader will be able to program a high-quality sparse linear equations code after reading this section. Instead, the purpose of this section is to give a basic understanding of the primary concepts and techniques of the field.

Three books that address direct sparse matrix algorithms are Tewarson [1973], Erisman and Reid [1981], and George and Liu [1980]. A sequence of sparse matrix conferences with published proceedings is Willoughby [1969], Reid [1971], Rose and Willoughby [1972], Bunch and Rose [1976], and Duff and Stewart [1979]. Two pioneering articles in direct methods for sparse matrix problems were Parter [1961] and Rose [1971]. A more recent comprehensive survey article is Duff [1977].

Dynamic stickman comes from a Department of Transportation study and is discussed extensively in Erisman and Reid [1981]. For the symmetric positive-definite matrices that arise in finite element calculations, several special ordering algorithms have been developed. Included are profile reduction, one-way dissection, nested dissection, and the refined quotient tree algorithm. The book by George and Liu [1980] contains considerable information on these algorithms. For the nonsymmetric problem, there also are special algorithms, some of which go by the names of their developers: Markowitz and Tinney. Erisman and Reid [1981] discuss several of these algorithms.

Data structure considerations in sparse matrix implementations are discussed in Duff [1977], Erisman and Reid [1981], and George and Liu [1980].

Software for direct methods in sparse matrix computations that is documented and well tested is described in Duff and Reid (the "Harwell codes") [1979], George and Liu (SPARSPAK) [1979], and Eisenstat et al. (YSMP) [1977].

EXERCISES 8.3

8.3.1. Carry out Gaussian elimination on the matrix in Figure 8.15 to show that the minimum-degree algorithm produces an ordering with no fill for dynamic stickman.

8.3.2. Consider the original numbering for dynamic stickman in Figure 8.8. First of all, reverse the numbering; that is, the node numbered 1 becomes node 14, node 2 becomes node 13, and so on. Now, carry out the minimum-degree algorithm on dynamic stickman (whenever there is a tie, use the node with the smaller original number). Compare the permuted matrix and its fill with that for the matrix in Figure 8.15.

8.3.3. Consider a sparse variant of Cholesky's algorithm (see Chapter 3) applied to a symmetric positive-definite matrix. Show that the fill is identical to the fill for symmetric Gaussian elimination.

8.3.4. Consider the boundary-value problem given by (8.2.2) and (8.2.3). Use (3.2.36) to approximate the second derivatives. Write the matrix equation analogous to (8.2.10). You will need to use (8.2.4) for grid points adjacent to the boundary. Write the matrix for the lexicographic ordering and the red-black ordering.

8.4 Iterative Methods

An alternative to the Gaussian elimination methods discussed in the previous section is an iterative method. Iterative methods will generally be more effective than direct methods for elliptic equations in three space dimensions, although which type of method to use will depend upon several factors, including the computer, the particular equation to be solved, and the accuracy required in the solution. However, for nonlinear equations, iterative methods are a necessity.

We consider the linear system $A\mathbf{x} = \mathbf{b}$ and make no assumptions about A at this time except that

(8.4.1) $$a_{ii} \neq 0, \qquad i = 1, \ldots, n$$

That is, the diagonal elements are nonzero. Perhaps the simplest iterative procedure is *Jacobi's method.* Assume that an initial approximation $\mathbf{x}^0$ to the solution is chosen. Then, the next iterate is given by

(8.4.2) $$x_i^{(1)} = \frac{1}{a_{ii}}\left(b_i - \sum_{j \neq i} a_{ij} x_j^{(0)}\right), \qquad i = 1, \ldots, n$$

It will be useful to write this in matrix-vector notation, and for this purpose, we let

$$D = \begin{bmatrix} a_{11} & & & & \bigcirc \\ & a_{22} & & & \\ & & \cdot & & \\ & & & \cdot & \\ \bigcirc & & & & \cdot \\ & & & & a_{nn} \end{bmatrix}$$

(8.4.3)

$$B = -\begin{bmatrix} 0 & a_{12} & \cdot & \cdot & \cdot & a_{1n} \\ \cdot & \cdot & & & & \cdot \\ a_{21} & & \cdot & & & \cdot \\ \cdot & \cdot & & \cdot & & \cdot \\ \cdot & & \cdot & & & a_{n-1,n} \\ \cdot & & & \cdot & & \\ a_{n1} & \cdot & \cdot & \cdot & a_{n,n-1} & 0 \end{bmatrix}$$

so A = D − B. Then, it is easy to verify that (8.4.2) may be written as

$$\mathbf{x}^1 = D^{-1}(\mathbf{b} + B\mathbf{x}^0)$$

and the entire sequence of Jacobi iterates is defined by

(8.4.4)
$$\mathbf{x}^{k+1} = D^{-1}(\mathbf{b} + B\mathbf{x}^k), \qquad k = 0, 1, \ldots$$

A closely related iteration is derived from the following observation. After $x_1^{(1)}$ is computed in (8.4.2), it is available to use in the computation of $x_2^{(1)}$, and it would seem natural to use this updated value rather than the original estimate $x_1^{(0)}$. If we use updated values as soon as they are available, then (8.4.2) becomes

(8.4.5)
$$x_i^{(1)} = \frac{1}{a_{ii}}\left(b_i - \sum_{j<i} a_{ij}x_j^{(1)} - \sum_{j>i} a_{ij}x_j^{(0)}\right), \qquad i = 1, \ldots, n$$

which is the first step in the *Gauss–Seidel iteration.* In order to write this iteration in matrix-vector form, we introduce the upper- and lower-triangular matrices

(8.4.6)
$$U = -\begin{bmatrix} 0 & a_{12} & \cdots & a_{1n} \\ & 0 & & \cdot \\ & & \ddots & \cdot \\ & & 0 & a_{n-1,n} \\ & & & 0 \end{bmatrix}$$

$$L = -\begin{bmatrix} 0 & & & \\ a_{21} & 0 & & \\ \cdot & & \ddots & \\ a_{n1} & & & 0 \\ a_{n1} & \cdots & a_{n,n-1} & 0 \end{bmatrix}$$

If we multiply (8.4.5) through by a_{ii}, then it is easy to verify that the n equations in (8.4.5) can be written as

(8.4.7)
$$D\mathbf{x}^1 - L\mathbf{x}^1 = b + U\mathbf{x}^0$$

Since D − L is a lower-triangular matrix with nonzero diagonal elements, it is nonsingular. Hence, (8.4.7) can be written as $\mathbf{x}^1 = (D - L)^{-1}(U\mathbf{x}^0 + b)$, and the entire sequence of Gauss–Seidel iterates is defined by

(8.4.8)
$$\mathbf{x}^{k+1} = (D - L)^{-1}[U\mathbf{x}^k + \mathbf{b}], \qquad k = 0, 1, \ldots$$

The representations (8.4.4) and (8.4.8) of the Jacobi and Gauss–Seidel iterations are useful for theoretical purposes, but the actual computations would be done using the componentwise representations (8.4.2) and (8.4.5).

Let us consider the application of these iterative methods to a discrete analog of Laplace's equation on a square. The simplest difference equations for this problem were given by (8.2.7) (with $f_{ij} = 0$) in the form

(8.4.9) $$u_{i+1,j} + u_{i-1,j} + u_{i,j+1} + u_{i,j-1} - 4u_{ij} = 0, \qquad i, j = 1, \ldots, N$$

Here, the unknowns are the u_{ij}, $i, j = 1, \ldots, N$, and the remaining values of the u's are assumed known from the boundary conditions. Given initial approximations $u_{ij}^{(0)}$, a Jacobi step applied to (8.4.9) is simply

$$u_{ij}^{(1)} = \tfrac{1}{4}(u_{i+1,j}^{(0)} + u_{i-1,j}^{(0)} + u_{i,j+1}^{(0)} + u_{i,j-1}^{(0)})$$

That is, the new Jacobi approximation to the solution at the (i, j) grid point is simply the average of the previous approximations at the four surrounding grid points $(i \pm 1, j)$, $(i, j \pm 1)$. It is for this reason that the Jacobi method is sometimes known as the *method of simultaneous displacements.* Note that for the Jacobi method, the order in which the equations are processed is immaterial. For the Gauss–Seidel method, the situation is reversed, and each different ordering of the equations actually corresponds to a different iterative process. If we order the grid points left to right and bottom to top, as was done in Section 8.1, then a typical Gauss–Seidel step is

$$u_{ij}^{(1)} = \tfrac{1}{4}(u_{i-1,j}^{(1)} + u_{i,j-1}^{(1)} + u_{i+1,j}^{(0)} + u_{i,j+1}^{(0)})$$

That is, the new approximation at the (i, j) grid point is again an average of the approximations at the four surrounding grid points, but now using two old values and two new values. The difference in the two methods is shown schematically in Figure 8.17.

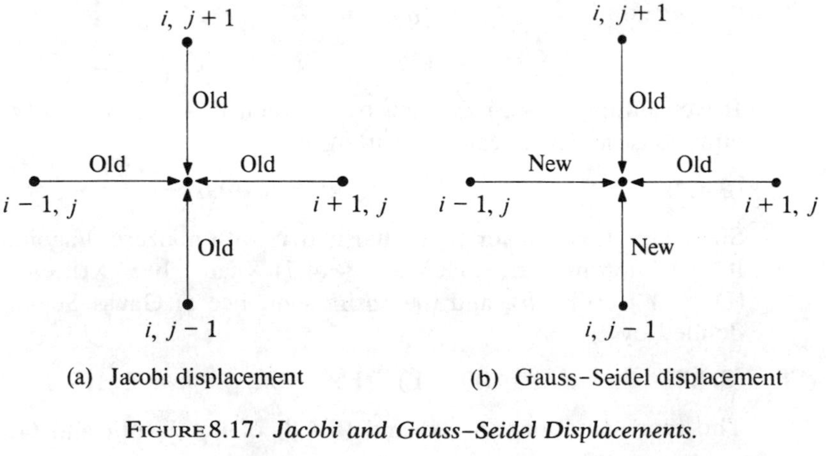

FIGURE 8.17. *Jacobi and Gauss–Seidel Displacements.*

We consider next the question of convergence of iterative methods. Both the Jacobi and Gauss–Seidel methods can be written in the general form

$$\mathbf{x}^{k+1} = \mathrm{H}\mathbf{x}^k + \mathbf{d}, \qquad k = 0, 1, \ldots \tag{8.4.10}$$

where the choice of the matrix H and the vector **d** determines the iterative process; in particular, $\mathrm{H} = \mathrm{D}^{-1}\mathrm{B}$ and $\mathbf{d} = \mathrm{D}^{-1}\mathbf{b}$ for the Jacobi process, whereas $\mathrm{H} = (\mathrm{D} - \mathrm{L})^{-1}\mathrm{U}$ and $\mathbf{d} = (\mathrm{D} - \mathrm{L})^{-1}\mathbf{b}$ for Gauss–Seidel. Now, assume that $\mathbf{x}^*$ is the exact solution of the system $\mathrm{A}\mathbf{x} = \mathbf{b}$. For the Jacobi method, we then have

$$(\mathrm{D} - \mathrm{B})\mathbf{x}^* = \mathbf{b} \quad \text{or} \quad \mathbf{x}^* = \mathrm{D}^{-1}\mathrm{B}\mathbf{x}^* + \mathrm{D}^{-1}\mathbf{b}$$

and for Gauss–Seidel,

$$(\mathrm{D} - \mathrm{L} - \mathrm{U})\mathbf{x}^* = \mathbf{b} \quad \text{or} \quad \mathbf{x}^* = (\mathrm{D} - \mathrm{L})^{-1}\mathrm{U}\mathbf{x}^* + (\mathrm{D} - \mathrm{L})^{-1}\mathbf{b}$$

so, in both cases,

$$\mathbf{x}^* = \mathrm{H}\mathbf{x}^* + \mathbf{d} \tag{8.4.11}$$

If we subtract (8.4.11) from (8.4.10), we have

$$\mathbf{e}^{k+1} = \mathrm{H}\mathbf{e}^k, \qquad k = 0, 1, \ldots \tag{8.4.12}$$

where $\mathbf{e}^k = \mathbf{x}^k - \mathbf{x}^*$ is the error at the kth step.

Equation (8.4.12) is the basic error relation for iterative methods of the form (8.4.10). We have already analyzed this equation in another context in Chapter 6 (see theorem 6.1.4) and concluded that the vectors $\mathbf{e}^k$ will tend to zero as k tends to infinity if and only if the spectral radius of H, $\rho(\mathrm{H})$, is less than 1. We restate this basic result in terms of the iterative method (8.4.10).

THEOREM 8.4.1 *The iterates* (8.4.10) *converge to the solution* $\mathbf{x}^*$ *for any starting vector* $\mathbf{x}^0$ *if and only if* $\rho(\mathrm{H}) < 1$.

Theorem 8.4.1 is not restricted to the Jacobi and Gauss–Seidel methods but applies to any iterative process of the form (8.4.10) under the assumption that (8.4.11) holds, and is the basic theoretical result for such iterative methods. On the other hand, it does not immediately tell us if a particular iterative method is convergent; we need to ascertain if the spectral radius of the iteration matrix for the method is less than 1. In general, this is a very difficult problem, for which one might have to resort to computing all the eigenvalues of the iteration matrix. But for some iterative methods and for certain classes of matrices, it is relatively easy to determine that the convergence criterion is satisfied. We next give some examples of this for the Jacobi and Gauss–Seidel methods.

THEOREM 8.4.2 *Assume that the matrix* A *is strictly diagonally dominant, that is,*

$$|a_{ii}| > \sum_{j \neq i} |a_{ij}|, \qquad i = 1, \ldots, n \tag{8.4.13}$$

Then both the Jacobi and Gauss–Seidel iterations converge to the unique solution of $\mathrm{A}\mathbf{x} = \mathbf{b}$ *for any starting vector* $\mathbf{x}^0$.

The proof of this is very simple for the Jacobi method. Since $\mathrm{H} = \mathrm{D}^{-1}\mathrm{B}$, the condition (8.4.13) implies that the sums of the absolute values of the elements in each row of H are less than 1. Hence, $\|\mathrm{H}\|_\infty < 1$, and therefore all eigenvalues of H are less than 1 in absolute value, so theorem 8.4.1 applies. The proof for the Gauss–Seidel method is somewhat more involved, and we do not give it here.

The condition of strict diagonal dominance is a rather stringent one and does not apply, in particular, to the difference equations (8.4.9) for Laplace's equation: in most rows of the coefficient matrix, there are four coefficients of absolute value 1 in the off-diagonal positions, so strict inequality does not hold in (8.4.13). However, by using different techniques (see the Supplementary Discussion), it can be shown that both methods indeed converge for the difference equations (8.4.9).

The coefficient matrix of equations (8.4.9) is clearly symmetric [see equation (8.2.10)], and it can be shown that it is also positive-definite. Indeed, it is the case that for many, if not most, discrete analogs of elliptic partial differential equations, the coefficient matrix will be symmetric and positive-definite. In this case, the Gauss–Seidel iteration will always converge, although symmetry and positive-definiteness is not necessarily sufficient for the Jacobi method to converge. We state the following theorem without proof:

THEOREM 8.4.3 *Assume that the matrix* A *is symmetric and positive-definite. Then, the Gauss–Seidel iterates converge to the unique solution of* $\mathrm{A}\mathbf{x} = \mathbf{b}$ *for any starting vector* $\mathbf{x}^0$.

Even when the Jacobi and Gauss–Seidel methods are convergent, the rate of convergence may be so slow as to preclude their usefulness; this is particularly so for discrete analogs of elliptic partial differential equations. For example, for equation (8.4.9) with $N = 44$, the error in each iteration of the Gauss–Seidel method will decrease asymptotically by only a factor of about 0.995. Moreover, the Jacobi method is about twice as slow on this problem, and the rate of convergence of both methods becomes worse as N increases.

In certain cases, it is possible to accelerate considerably the rate of convergence of the Gauss–Seidel method. Given the current approximation $\mathbf{x}^k$, we first compute the Gauss–Seidel iterate

(**8.4.14**) $$\hat{x}_i^{(k+1)} = \frac{1}{a_{ii}}\left(b_i - \sum_{j<i} a_{ij}x_j^{(k+1)} - \sum_{j>i} a_{ij}x_j^{(k)}\right)$$

as an intermediate value, and then take the final value of the new approximation to the ith component to be

(**8.4.15**) $$x_i^{(k+1)} = x_i^{(k)} + \omega(\hat{x}_i^{(k+1)} - x_i^{(k)})$$

Here ω is a parameter that has been introduced to accelerate the rate of convergence.

We can rewrite (8.4.14) and (8.4.15) in the following way. First, substitute (8.4.14) into (8.4.15):

(**8.4.16**) $$x_i^{(k+1)} = (1-\omega)x_i^{(k)} + \frac{\omega}{a_{ii}}\left(b_i - \sum_{j<i} a_{ij}x_j^{(k+1)} - \sum_{j>i} a_{ij}x_j^{(k)}\right)$$

and then rearrange into the form

$$a_{ii}x_i^{(k+1)} + \omega \sum_{j<i} a_{ij}x_i^{(k+1)} = (1-\omega)a_{ii}x_i^{(k)} - \omega \sum_{j>i} a_{ij}x_j^{(k)} + \omega b_i$$

This relationship between the new iterates $x_i^{(k+1)}$ and the old $x_i^{(k)}$ holds for $i = 1, \ldots, n$, and using the decomposition $A = D - L - U$ as before, we can write it in matrix-vector terms as

$$D\mathbf{x}^{k+1} - \omega L\mathbf{x}^{k+1} = (1-\omega)D\mathbf{x}^k + \omega U\mathbf{x}^k + \omega\mathbf{b}$$

Since the matrix $D - \omega L$ is again lower-triangular and, by assumption, has nonzero diagonal elements, it is nonsingular, so we may write

(**8.4.17**) $$\mathbf{x}^{k+1} = (D-\omega L)^{-1}[(1-\omega)D + \omega U]\mathbf{x}^k + \omega(D-\omega L)^{-1}\mathbf{b}$$

This defines the *successive overrelaxation* (*SOR*) *method*, although, as with Gauss–Seidel, the componentwise prescription (8.4.14)/(8.4.15), would be used for the actual computation. Note that if $\omega = 1$, (8.4.17) reduces to the Gauss–Seidel iteration.

We restrict ourselves to real values of the parameter ω. Then, a necessary condition that the *SOR* iteration (8.4.17) even be convergent is that $0 < \omega < 2$. In general, a choice of ω in this range will *not* give convergence, but in the important case that the coefficient matrix A is symmetric and positive-definite, we have the following extension of theorem 8.4.3, which we also state without proof:

THEOREM 8.4.4 (Ostrowski–Reich) *Assume that* A *is symmetric and positive-definite. Then, for any* $\omega \in (0, 2)$ *and any starting vector* $\mathbf{x}^0$, *the* SOR *iterates* (8.4.17) *converge to the solution of* $A\mathbf{x} = \mathbf{b}$.

We would like to be able to choose the parameter ω so as to optimize the rate of convergence of the iteration (8.4.17). In general, this is a very difficult problem, and we will attempt to summarize, without proofs, a few of the things that are known about its solution. For a class of matrices that are called *consistently ordered with property* A, there is a rather complete theory that relates the rate of convergence of the SOR method to that of the Jacobi method and gives important insights into how to choose the optimum value of ω. We will not define this class of matrices precisely; suffice it to say that it includes the matrix (8.2.10) of equations (8.4.9) as well as many other matrices that arise as discrete analogs of elliptic partial differential equations.

The fundamental result that holds for this class of matrices is a relationship between the eigenvalues λ_i of the SOR iteration matrix $H_\omega = (D - \omega L)^{-1}[(1 - \omega)D + \omega U]$ and the eigenvalues of the Jacobi iteration matrix $J = D^{-1}(L + U)$. Corresponding to a zero eigenvalue of J of multiplicity p, there are p eigenvalues of H_ω equal to $\omega - 1$. For this class of matrices, the nonzero eigenvalues of J necessarily occur in plus and minus pairs $\pm\mu_i$ and are related to corresponding eigenvalues of H_ω by

(8.4.18)
$$(\lambda_i + \omega - 1)^2 = \lambda_i\omega^2\mu_i^2$$

This is a quadratic equation for λ_i that defines two values of λ_i for each μ_i^2. Under the assumption that the μ_i are all real and less than 1 in absolute value, (8.4.18) can be used to obtain the optimum value of ω that minimizes the spectral radius, $\rho(H_\omega)$, of H_ω, and it is the spectral radius that governs the ultimate rate of convergence of the method. The optimum value of ω, denoted by ω_0, is given in terms of the spectral radius of J by

(8.4.19)
$$\omega_0 = \frac{2}{1 + \sqrt{1 - \rho^2}}, \qquad \rho = \rho(J)$$

and is always between 1 and 2. The corresponding value of $\rho(H_\omega)$ is

(8.4.20)
$$\rho(H_{\omega_0}) = \omega_0 - 1$$

Moreover, from (8.4.18), we can obtain the behavior of $\rho(H_\omega)$ as a function of ω, as is shown in Figure 8.18.

We can obtain an idea of the acceleration of convergence that is possible by considering equations (8.4.9). For the corresponding matrix, it is possible to compute the eigenvalues of the Jacobi iteration matrix J explicitly, and the largest turns out to be

(8.4.21)
$$\rho(J) = \cos \pi h \doteq 1 - \frac{\pi^2 h^2}{2}, \qquad h = \frac{1}{N + 1}$$

where the approximate relationship holds very well for large N. If we put

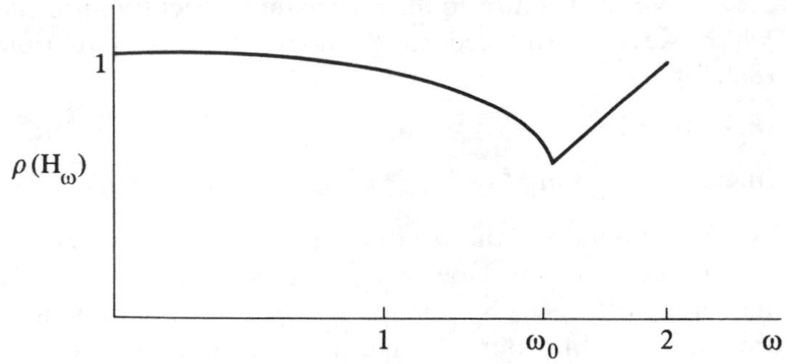

FIGURE 8.18 $\rho(H_\omega)$ *as a Function of* ω.

this in (8.4.19), we obtain

$$\textbf{(8.4.22)} \quad \omega_0 = \frac{2}{1 + \sqrt{1 - \cos^2 \pi h}} \qquad \rho(H_{\omega_0}) = \frac{1 - \sqrt{1 - \cos^2 \pi h}}{1 + \sqrt{1 - \cos^2 \pi h}}$$

If, again for illustration, we take $N = 44$, then

$$\textbf{(8.4.23)} \quad p(J) \doteq 0.9976 \qquad \rho(H) \doteq 0.995 \qquad \omega_0 \doteq 1.87 \qquad \rho(H_{\omega_0}) \doteq 0.87$$

This shows that, asymptotically, the error in Jacobi's method will decrease by a factor of 0.9976 at each step, and that of the Gauss–Seidel method by a factor of 0.995, which is twice as fast. But the error in the SOR method will decrease by a factor of 0.87, which is about thirty times as fast as the Gauss–Seidel method. Moreover, the improvement becomes more marked as N increases (see exercise 8.4.9).

The preceding discussion indicates that dramatic improvements in the rate of convergence of the Gauss–Seidel method are possible. However, a number of caveats are in order. First of all, many—perhaps most—large sparse matrices that arise in practice do not enjoy being "consistently ordered with property A," and the preceding theory will not hold. It is still possible that introduction of the parameter ω into the Gauss–Seidel method will produce a substantial increase in the rate of convergence, but this will not be known in advance, nor will it be known how to choose a good value of ω except by trial and error. However, even in the case that the coefficient matrix is "consistently ordered with property A," it still may be difficult to obtain a good estimate of ω_0. It was possible to compute explicitly the quantities of (8.4.23) only because of the very special nature of the equations (8.4.9), which allowed an exact computation of $\rho(J)$. In general, this will not be possible, and to use (8.4.22) will require estimating $\rho(J)$, which is itself a difficult problem. Thus, even in those cases where the preceding theory holds, it may be necessary to use a trial-and-error process to obtain a suitable value of ω_0.

We next return to the alternating direction implicit (ADI) methods, which were introduced in Section 8.2. The equations (8.2.19) and (8.2.20)

$$\textbf{(8.4.24)}\quad (2+\alpha)u_{ij}^{m+1/2} - u_{i+1,j}^{m+1/2} - u_{i-1,j}^{m+1/2} = (\alpha - 2)u_{i,j}^{m} + u_{i,j+1}^{m} + u_{i,j-1}^{m}$$

$$\textbf{(8.4.25)}\quad (2+\alpha)u_{ij}^{m+1} - u_{i,j+1}^{m+1} - u_{i,j-1}^{m+1} = (\alpha - 2)u_{i,j}^{m+1/2} + u_{i+1,j}^{m+1/2} + u_{i-1,j}^{m+1/2}$$

were developed for the heat equation, and the superscripts indicated the various time levels. However, we can interpret (8.4.24)/(8.4.25) as an iteration for Laplace's equation with the superscripts indicating the iteration number. In order to make this interpretation, let **u** be the vector of (8.2.9) in which the unknowns u_{ij} are ordered in terms of the grid points from left to right and bottom to top. Then, (8.4.24) can be written as

$$\textbf{(8.4.26)}\qquad (\alpha\mathrm{I} + \mathrm{H})\mathbf{u}^{m+1/2} = (\alpha\mathrm{I} - \mathrm{V})\mathbf{u}^{m} + \mathbf{b}$$

Here, H is the $N^2 \times N^2$ matrix

$$\mathrm{H} = \begin{bmatrix} \mathrm{A} & & & & \\ & \mathrm{A} & & & \\ & & \cdot & & \\ & & & \cdot & \\ & & & & \cdot \\ & & & & & \mathrm{A} \end{bmatrix}$$

where A is again the $(2, -1)$ tridiagonal matrix of (7.2.14), V is a permutation of H such that the action of V on **u** does the differencing on the j index as indicated in (8.4.24), and **b** contains the u_{ij} from (8.4.24) that are known from the boundary values, and also values of the f_{ij} if we are dealing with Poisson's equation. Note that the equation

$$(\alpha\mathrm{I} + \mathrm{H})\mathbf{u} = (\alpha\mathrm{I} - \mathrm{V})\mathbf{u} + \mathbf{b}$$

or, cancelling $\alpha\mathrm{I}$ on each side,

$$(\mathrm{H} + \mathrm{V})\mathbf{u} = \mathbf{b}$$

is exactly the equation (8.2.10). Indeed, if $\mathcal{A}$ is the coefficient matrix of (8.2.10), then $\mathcal{A} = \mathrm{H} + \mathrm{V}$, and V consists of 2s on the main diagonal and the -1s in the "outrigger" positions as shown in (8.2.10).

Similarly, (8.4.25) may be written as

$$\textbf{(8.4.27)}\qquad (\alpha\mathrm{I} + \mathrm{V})\mathbf{u}^{m+1} = (\alpha\mathrm{I} - \mathrm{H})\mathbf{u}^{m+1/2} + \mathbf{b}$$

and the combination of (8.4.26) and (8.4.27) is the *Peaceman–Rachford ADI method.* The quantity α, which was a function of Δx and Δt for the heat equation, now plays the role of a positive parameter to be chosen to enhance the rate of convergence.

The ADI iteration is carried out by solving the tridiagonal systems of (8.4.24) and (8.4.25), while the matrix representations (8.4.26)/(8.4.27) are useful for theoretical purposes. If we substitute in (8.4.27) the representation of $\mathbf{u}^{m+1/2}$ from (8.4.26) and then multiply through by $(\alpha I + V)^{-1}$, we have

(8.4.28) $$\mathbf{u}^{m+1} = B\mathbf{u}^m + \mathbf{d}, \qquad m = 0, 1, \ldots$$

where

(8.4.29) $$B = (\alpha I + V)^{-1}(\alpha I - H)(\alpha I + H)^{-1}(\alpha I - V)$$

and

$$\mathbf{d} = (\alpha I + V)^{-1}(\alpha I + H)^{-1}\mathbf{b}$$

The inverses that appear in (8.4.29) exist provided that $\alpha > 0$; also, under this assumption on α, it can be shown that the spectral radius of B is less than 1, and therefore the iterates (8.4.28) converge for any starting $\mathbf{u}^0$. The rate of convergence will depend on the parameter α. Indeed, it turns out that the rate of convergence can be greatly accelerated if one uses a number of different parameters $\alpha_1, \ldots, \alpha_m$ repeated cyclically. With these α_i properly chosen, which is beyond our scope to describe, the Peaceman–Rachford iteration converges very rapidly.

The Peaceman–Rachford iteration can be applied to more general elliptic problems than we have considered. The convergence of the iteration (8.4.28) will be ensured provided only that the matrices H and V are positive-definite and $\alpha > 0$. However, the possibility of being able to choose a sequence of parameters to give rapid convergence is very strongly dependent on the domain of the differential equation being a rectangle and the equation itself being of the form $u_{xx} + u_{yy} + \sigma u = 0$.

We end this section by briefly describing an increasingly important method which is actually direct (that is, the solution of the linear system is obtained in a finite number of arithmetic operations) but is used in practice as an iterative method. This is the *conjugate gradient method.* We first describe the method and then discuss its rationale.

We assume that the coefficient matrix A of the linear system is symmetric and positive-definite and we let $(\mathbf{x}, \mathbf{y}) \equiv \mathbf{x}^T\mathbf{y}$ denote the Euclidean inner product. Then, the conjugate gradient algorithm is

1. a. Choose a starting approximation $\mathbf{x}^0$.
b. Compute $\mathbf{r}^0 = \mathbf{b} - A\mathbf{x}^0$.
c. Set $\mathbf{p}^0 = \mathbf{r}^0$ and $k = 0$.
2. a. Compute $\alpha_k = (\mathbf{r}^k, \mathbf{p}^k)/(\mathbf{p}^k, A\mathbf{p}^k)$.
b. Compute $\mathbf{x}^{k+1} = \mathbf{x}^k + \alpha_k \mathbf{p}^k$.
c. Compute $\mathbf{r}^{k+1} = \mathbf{r}^k - \alpha_k A\mathbf{p}^k$.
d. Test for convergence. Is $\|\mathbf{r}^{k+1}\| \le \varepsilon$? If not, continue.
3. a. Compute $\beta_k = (\mathbf{r}^{k+1}, A\mathbf{p}^k)/(\mathbf{p}^k, A\mathbf{p}^k)$
b. Compute $\mathbf{p}^{k+1} = \mathbf{r}^{k+1} - \beta_k \mathbf{p}^k$.
c. Increase k by 1 and return to step 2a.

We now make several comments about this method. First, it is perhaps most naturally viewed as a minimization method. Since A is positive-definite, the quadratic form

(8.4.30) $$\tfrac{1}{2}\mathbf{x}^T A\mathbf{x} - \mathbf{x}^T\mathbf{b}$$

will have a minimum, and the vector $\mathbf{x}^*$ for which that minimum is achieved is the solution of the linear system $A\mathbf{x} = \mathbf{b}$. Given the current approximation $\mathbf{x}^k$ and a "direction" vector $\mathbf{p}^k$, the next approximation, $\mathbf{x}^{k+1}$, is computed so as to minimize the quadratic form (8.4.30) in the direction $\mathbf{p}^k$ emanating from $\mathbf{x}^k$ as illustrated in Figure 8.19. This is simply the one-dimensional minimization problem

(8.4.31) $$\underset{\alpha}{\text{Minimize}}\ \tfrac{1}{2}(\mathbf{x}^k + \alpha\mathbf{p}^k)^T A(\mathbf{x}^k + \alpha\mathbf{p}^k) - (\mathbf{x}^k + \alpha\mathbf{p}^k)^T\mathbf{b}$$

If the quadratic form in (8.4.31) is expanded, it is readily seen to be simply a quadratic in α, and the value of α that minimizes this quadratic is given in step 2a of the algorithm.

Next, the residual $\mathbf{r}^{k+1} = \mathbf{b} - A\mathbf{x}^{k+1}$ is to be computed. This could be done directly, but since

$$\mathbf{b} - A\mathbf{x}^{k+1} = \mathbf{b} - A(\mathbf{x}^k + \alpha_k\mathbf{p}^k) = \mathbf{r}^k - \alpha_k A\mathbf{p}^k$$

it can be computed without forming $A\mathbf{x}^{k+1}$ since $A\mathbf{p}^k$ is already known. We now test for convergence by seeing if $\|\mathbf{r}^{k+1}\|$ is less than some prescribed tolerance ε, although a variety of other convergence tests could be applied if desired. If we have not converged, we compute a new direction vector $\mathbf{p}^{k+1}$ in step 3b, and then return to step 2a to compute the next approximation.

The computation of the direction vectors $\mathbf{p}^k$ is the key part of the algorithm. These are to be computed so as to satisfy

(8.4.32) $$(\mathbf{p}^i, A\mathbf{p}^j) = 0, \qquad i \neq j,\ i, j = 0, 1, \ldots, n-1$$

Indeed, β_k is chosen so that $(\mathbf{p}^{k+1}, A\mathbf{p}^k) = 0$ since

$$(\mathbf{p}^{k+1}, A\mathbf{p}^k) = (\mathbf{r}^{k+1} - \beta_k\mathbf{p}^k, A\mathbf{p}^k) = (\mathbf{r}^{k+1}, A\mathbf{p}^k) - \beta_k(\mathbf{p}^k, A\mathbf{p}^k)$$

To show that (8.4.32) holds for other values of i and j requires an

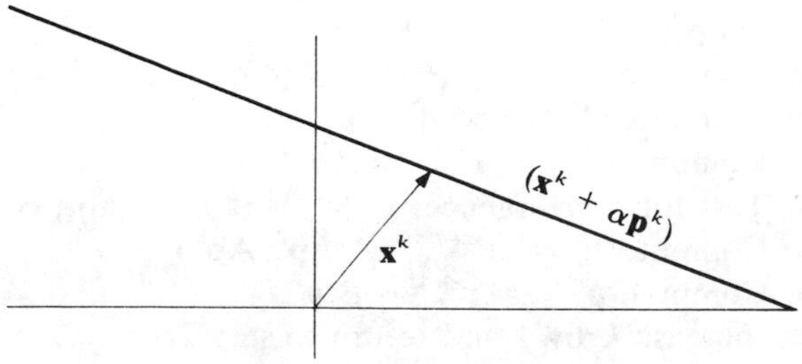

FIGURE 8.19 *Minimize the Quadratic Form in the Direction* $\mathbf{p}^k$.

induction argument and some manipulations, the details of which are left to exercise 8.4.10.

A set of vectors $\{\mathbf{p}^k\}$ that satisfy (8.4.32) are said to be *conjugate* with respect to A. Whenever the corresponding set of $\{\mathbf{x}^k\}$ is computed by steps 2a, b, and c, the exact solution of the linear system $A\mathbf{x} = \mathbf{b}$ will be obtained in, at most, n steps. It is this property that makes the conjugate gradient algorithm a direct method. In practice, however, two factors tend to override this property. First, because of rounding error, the exact solution will not be obtained in n steps, and it is usually not sufficient to stop the process at that point. Second, for very large matrices, say $n = 10{,}000$, termination of the algorithm in n steps is not a desirable property since we need to obtain an approximate solution in many fewer steps if the method is to be competitive with other iterative methods. It turns out that for many problems of interest, we can indeed achieve convergence in far fewer than n steps, and the conjugate gradient algorithm or one of its many variants is an attractive alternative to the other iterative methods of this section.

In this section, we have given an introduction to some of the simplest iterative methods for large sparse systems of linear equations, especially those that arise from elliptic partial differential equations. There are a variety of other iterative methods, some of which are mentioned in the Supplementary Discussion, and which method to use on a given problem is usually not clear. Moreover, direct methods, as discussed in the previous section, have proved to be more efficient on large sparse matrices than was previously assumed to be possible. For elliptic equations in two space dimensions, direct methods are probably now to be preferred, whereas for three-dimensional problems, iterative methods are probably the best.

Supplementary Discussion: 8.4

The Jacobi and Gauss–Seidel iterations are classical methods that go back to the last century. The SOR method grew out of heuristic relaxation methods that were brought to a high degree of sophistication by R. Southwell and his co-workers during World War II. The basic theory of the method was developed by S. Frankel and D. Young during the late 1940s. For a complete discussion of the Jacobi, Gauss–Seidel, SOR, and ADI methods and their many variants, see Forsythe and Wasow [1960], Varga [1962], and Young [1971].

Theorem 8.4.2 can be extended to a form suitable to handle equations such as (8.4.9) by the concept of *irreducible matrices*. A matrix A is said to be *reducible* if there is a permutation matrix P such that

$$P^T A P = \begin{bmatrix} A_1 & A_2 \\ 0 & A_3 \end{bmatrix}$$

Otherwise, it is irreducible. Theorem 8.4.2 then extends as follows. Assume that A is irreducible and diagonally dominant with strict inequality for at least one of the relations $|a_{ii}| \geq \sum_{j \neq i} |a_{ij}|$, $i = 1, \ldots, n$. Then, the system of equations $A\mathbf{x} = \mathbf{b}$ has a unique solution $\mathbf{x}^*$, and both the Jacobi and Gauss–Seidel iterates converge to $\mathbf{x}^*$ for any starting vector $\mathbf{x}^0$. It can be shown that the coefficient matrix of equation (8.4.9) is irreducible and that this theorem then applies.

The conjugate gradient algorithm was developed in the early 1950s by Hestenes and Stiefel [1952] and has enjoyed a resurgence of interest in the last several years as an iterative method for large sparse systems of equations. For a recent discussion of this method and many of its variants, see Chandra [1978].

Many elliptic equations that arise in practice are nonlinear. The methods of the section do not apply immediately in this case, although extensions of them to nonlinear equations have been developed (see Ortega and Rheinboldt [1970]). On the other hand, if a method such as Newton's is used (Section 4.3), then at each stage of Newton's method, a large sparse linear system must be solved approximately, and iterative methods can be used for this purpose.

EXERCISES 8.4

8.4.1. Apply the Jacobi and Gauss–Seidel iterations to the system of equations $A\mathbf{x} = \mathbf{b}$ where

$$A = \begin{bmatrix} 3 & 1 & 1 \\ 1 & 3 & 1 \\ 1 & 1 & 3 \end{bmatrix} \qquad \mathbf{b} = \begin{bmatrix} 1 \\ 2 \\ 3 \end{bmatrix}$$

Use the starting approximation $\mathbf{x}^0 = (1, 1, 1)$ and take enough steps of the iterative processes so that the pattern of convergence is becoming clear.

8.4.2. Write computer programs for the Jacobi and Gauss–Seidel methods. Test them on the problem of exercise 8.4.1.

8.4.3. Write out in detail the Jacobi and Gauss–Seidel iterations for equations (8.4.9) for $N = 3$.

8.4.4. Prove theorem 8.4.1 in detail under the assumption that H has n linearly independent eigenvectors.

8.4.5. Consider the elliptic equation $u_{xx} + u_{yy} + cu = 0$ with the values of u prescribed on the boundary of a square domain. Derive the difference equations corresponding to (8.4.9). If c is a negative constant, show that the resulting coefficient matrix is strictly diagonally dominant.

8.4.6. Let A be a real $n \times n$ symmetric positive-definite matrix.

a. Show that the diagonal elements of A are necessarily positive.

b. If C is any real $n \times n$ nonsingular matrix, show that $C^T AC$ is also positive-definite.

8.4.7. Carry out several steps of the SOR iteration for the problem of exercise 8.4.1. Use the values $\omega = 0.6$ and $\omega = 1.4$ and compare the rates of convergence to the Gauss–Seidel iteration.

8.4.8. Write a computer program to apply the SOR iteration to equation (8.4.9).

8.4.9. Use the relations (8.4.21) and (8.4.22) to compute $\rho(\mathrm{J})$, $\rho(\mathrm{H}_1)$, ω_0, and $\rho(\mathrm{H}_{\omega_0})$ for equation (8.4.9) for $N = 99$ and $N = 999$.

8.4.10. Prove that the relationship (8.4.32) holds by using the following induction argument. As the induction hypothesis, assume that $(\mathbf{p}^k, \mathrm{A}\mathbf{p}^j) = (\mathbf{r}^k, \mathbf{r}^j) = 0$, $j = 0, \ldots, k-1$. (We have shown in the text that $(\mathbf{p}^1, \mathrm{A}\mathbf{p}^0) = 0$; $(\mathbf{r}^1, \mathbf{r}^0) = (\mathbf{r}^0 - \alpha_0\mathrm{A}\mathbf{p}^0, \mathbf{p}^0) = 0$ by the definition of α_0). Then, show that $(\mathbf{p}^{k+1}, \mathrm{A}\mathbf{p}^j) = (\mathbf{r}^{k+1}, \mathbf{r}^j) = 0$ for $j = 0, 1, \ldots, k$. (Hint: Show first that the second relationship is true.)

Epilogue

We have attempted to cover some of the major areas of elementary numerical analysis in the context of the numerical solution of differential equations. But many important areas have not been dealt with or have been mentioned only too briefly, for example, optimization (i.e., minimization or maximization) of a function of n variables, possibly subject to constraints; the solution of integral and integral-differential equations; and the approximation of functions including many beautiful parts of aproximation theory. We also have scratched only the surface in our treatment of partial differential equations. However, we hope that we have been able to give a sufficient background in basic numerical methods so that the reader can proceed to more advanced and comprehensive treatments of areas of interest, and we have attempted to indicate sufficient references for this purpose.

Appendixes

1 Basic Results from Analysis

In the appendix, we review briefly and without proofs some of the basic results from the calculus that are used in the text.

MEAN-VALUE THEOREM: *If the function f is continuously differentiable on an interval $[a, b]$, then there is a point ξ between a and b such that*

$$f(b) - f(a) = f'(\xi)(b - a) \tag{A.1.1}$$

TAYLOR EXPANSION: *If the function f is k times continuously differentiable on an interval $[a, b]$, then for any x and x_0 between a and b, there is a ξ between x and x_0 such that*

$$\begin{aligned} f(x) = f(x_0) + f'(x_0)(x - x_0) + \tfrac{1}{2}f''(x_0)(x - x_0)^2 + \cdots \\ + \frac{1}{(k-1)!}f^{(k-1)}(x_0)(x - x_0)^{k-1} + \frac{1}{k!}f^{(k)}(\xi)(x - x_0)^k \end{aligned} \tag{A.1.2}$$

Note that the mean-value theorem can be considered to be the special case of the Taylor expansion for $k = 1$ and $a = x_0$, $b = x$.

CHAIN RULE: *If f and g are two differentiable functions, then the* composite function $h(x) = f(g(x))$ *is differentiable, and*

$$h'(x) = f'(g(x))g'(x) \tag{A.1.3}$$

SECOND MEAN-VALUE THEOREM OF THE INTEGRAL CALCULUS: *If u and v are continuous functions on the interval $[a, b]$ and v does not change* *sign in* $[a, b]$, *then there is a* $\xi \in [a, b]$ *such that*

$$\int_a^b u(x)v(x)\,dx = u(\xi)\int_a^b v(x)\,dx \tag{A.1.4}$$

The remaining results deal with functions of several variables $f(x_1, \ldots, x_n)$, or $f(\mathbf{x})$ where $\mathbf{x}$ is the vector with components $x_1, \ldots, x_n$. The partial derivative of f with respect to the ith variable is defined at a point $\mathbf{x}$ by

$$\frac{\partial f}{\partial x_i}(\mathbf{x}) = \lim_{h \to 0} \frac{1}{h}[f(x_1, \ldots, x_{i-1}, x_i + h, x_{i+1}, \ldots, x_n) - f(\mathbf{x})] \tag{A.1.5}$$

and similarly for partial derivatives of higher order. The *derivative* of f at a point $\mathbf{x}$ is defined by

$$f'(\mathbf{x}) = \left(\frac{\partial f}{\partial x_1}(\mathbf{x}), \ldots, \frac{\partial f}{\partial x_n}(\mathbf{x})\right) \tag{A.1.6}$$

and is considered to be a row vector. The transpose of this vector is sometimes called the *gradient* of f and is denoted by ∇f. In this context, it is often convenient to view ∇ as the vector operator of partial derivatives:

$$\nabla = \left(\frac{\partial}{\partial x_1}, \ldots, \frac{\partial}{\partial x_n}\right)$$

Then, the operator ∇^2, often denoted by Δ, is the dot product of ∇ with itself, so

$$\Delta f = \nabla^2 f = \frac{\partial^2 f}{\partial x_1^2} + \cdots + \frac{\partial^2 f}{\partial x_n^2}$$

This sum of second partial derivatives is very important in the study of partial differential equations (see Chapters 7 and 8).

The function f is said to be continuously differentiable in some region of n space if each (first) partial derivative of f exists and is continuous within that region. For functions of several variables, the mean-value theorem again holds, as follows.

MEAN-VALUE THEOREM FOR FUNCTIONS OF SEVERAL VARIABLES *If f is a continuously differentiable function of n variables in some region, and if* $\mathbf{x}$ *and* $\mathbf{y}$ *are two points such that the points*

$$t\mathbf{x} + (1 - t)\mathbf{y}, \qquad 0 \le t \le 1$$

are all in the region, then there is a ξ between 0 and 1 such that

$$f(\mathbf{y}) - f(\mathbf{x}) = f'(\xi\mathbf{x} + (1 - \xi)\mathbf{y})(\mathbf{y} - \mathbf{x}) \tag{A.1.7}$$

We note that this mean-value theorem is simply the usual one for functions of a single variable as applied to the function

$$\hat{f}(t) = f(t\mathbf{x} + (1 - t)\mathbf{y})$$

If $f_1, \ldots, f_m$ are all functions of n variables, then we denote the vector-valued function with components $f_1, \ldots, f_m$ by $\mathbf{F}$. For such vector-valued functions, there is a natural derivative defined by

(A.1.8)
$$\mathbf{F}'(\mathbf{x}) = \left(\frac{\partial f_i(\mathbf{x})}{\partial x_j}\right)$$

where the notation means that $\mathbf{F}'(\mathbf{x})$ is an $m \times n$ matrix, usually called the *Jacobian matrix*, whose i, j element is the partial derivative of the ith component of $\mathbf{F}$ with respect to the jth variable. For example, if $m = n = 2$, then

$$\mathbf{F}'(\mathbf{x}) = \begin{bmatrix} \dfrac{\partial f_1(\mathbf{x})}{\partial x_1} & \dfrac{\partial f_1(\mathbf{x})}{\partial x_2} \\ \dfrac{\partial f_2(\mathbf{x})}{\partial x_1} & \dfrac{\partial f_2(\mathbf{x})}{\partial x_2} \end{bmatrix}$$

Note that in the special case $m = 1$, $\mathbf{F}$ is simply the single function f_1, and the Jacobian matrix reduces to the row vector as given by (A.1.6).

2 Ordinary Differential Equations

If y is a function of a single variable t, then an ordinary differential equation for y is a relation of the form

$$F(t, y(t), y'(t), \ldots, y^{(n)}(t)) = 0 \tag{A.2.1}$$

for some given function F of $n + 2$ variables, and where the independent variable t ranges over some finite or infinite interval. Equation (A.2.1) is the most general nth-order ordinary differential equation, where the *order* is determined by the highest-order derivative of the unknown function y that appears in the equation. Usually, the equation is assumed to be explicit in the highest derivative and is written as

$$y^{(n)}(t) = f(t, y(t), y'(t), \ldots, y^{(n-1)}(t)) \tag{A.2.2}$$

If the function f is linear in y and its derivatives, then the equation is called linear and can be written in the form

$$y^{(n)}(t) = a_0(t) + a_1(t)y(t) + \cdots + a_n(t)y^{(n-1)}(t) \tag{A.2.3}$$

for given functions $a_0, \ldots, a_n$.

The equation (A.2.2) can also be considered for vector-valued functions $\mathbf{y}$ and $\mathbf{f}$, in which case we would have a system of nth-order equations. The simplest such possibility is a system of first-order equations

$$\mathbf{y}'(t) = \mathbf{f}(t, \mathbf{y}(t)) \tag{A.2.4}$$

where we assume that $\mathbf{y}$ and $\mathbf{f}$ are n vectors with components $y_1, \ldots, y_n$ and $f_1, \ldots, f_n$.

A system of first-order equations is, in principle, all that we need to consider since a single nth-order equation can be reduced to a system of n first-order equations (and, consequently, a system of m nth-order equations to a system of nm first-order equations). This reduction can be achieved, for example, as follows. Define new variables

$$y_i(t) \equiv y^{(i-1)}(t), \qquad i = 1, \ldots, n \tag{A.2.5}$$

In terms of these variables, (A.2.2) becomes

$$y_n' = f(t, y_1, y_2, \ldots, y_{n-1}) \tag{A.2.6}$$

whereas from (A.2.5), we obtain

$$y_i' = y_{i+1}, \qquad i = 1, \ldots, n-1 \tag{A.2.7}$$

Equations (A.2.6)/(A.2.7) give a first-order system of equations in the unknowns $y_1, \ldots, y_n$, where the component y_1 is the original unknown y of equation (A.2.2).

A very important special case of (A.2.4) is when $\mathbf{f}$ is linear in $\mathbf{y}$, and the equation takes the form

$$\mathbf{y}'(t) = \mathrm{A}(t)\mathbf{y}(t) + \mathbf{b}(t) \tag{A.2.8}$$

where A is a given $n \times n$ matrix whose elements are functions of t, and $\mathbf{b}$ is a given vector function of t. An important special case of (A.2.8), in turn, is when A is independent of t, and $\mathbf{b} = 0$, so that the equation is

$$\mathbf{y}' = \mathrm{A}\mathbf{y} \tag{A.2.9}$$

Such a *linear homogeneous* system with *constant coefficients* can, in principle, be solved explicitly by the series expansion

$$\mathbf{y}(t) = (\mathrm{I} + \mathrm{A}t + \tfrac{1}{2}\mathrm{A}^2t^2 + \cdots)\mathbf{c} \tag{A.2.10}$$

where $\mathbf{c}$ is an arbitrary constant vector. The series expansion is simply that of the exponential of a matrix, and (A.2.10) can be written in the compact form

$$\mathbf{y}(t) = e^{\mathrm{A}t}\mathbf{c} \tag{A.2.11}$$

Equation (A.2.11) shows that the general solution of (A.2.9) depends on n arbitrary constants—the n components of the vector $\mathbf{c}$. Thus, in order to obtain a unique solution of the system (A.2.9), n additional conditions must be specified, and these are usually given in terms of *initial* or *boundary conditions.* For example, suppose that we desire a solution of (A.2.9) for $t \geq 0$ such that at $t = 0$, the solution takes on the initial condition $\mathbf{y}_0$. The solution is then given by (A.2.11) as $\mathbf{y}(t) = e^{\mathrm{A}t}\mathbf{y}_0$.

For more complicated equations, the initial condition will not be represented in the solution in such a straightforward fashion. Indeed, it is not immediately obvious under what conditions the general *initial-value problem*

$$\mathbf{y}'(t) = \mathbf{f}(t, \mathbf{y}(t)), \qquad \mathbf{y}(0) = \mathbf{y}_0 \tag{A.2.12}$$

will even have a unique solution, but a number of basic theorems in this regard are known and may be found in any book on ordinary differential equations.

If all n conditions are not given at a single point, then the situation is more complicated and gives rise to *boundary-value problems.* The simplest such problem is the following. Consider the single second-order equation

$$y'' = f(t, y) \tag{A.2.13}$$

where we specify that y takes on prescribed values at the end points of some interval $[a, b]$; that is,

$$y(a) = \alpha \qquad y(b) = \beta \tag{A.2.14}$$

for given constants α and β. In this situation, we are usually interested in a solution of (A.2.13) only between a and b, and the equation (A.2.13) together with the boundary conditions (A.2.14) is called a *two-point boundary-value problem.* Again, there is the basic question—more difficult than for initial-value problems—of when a unique solution exists for such a problem and various results are known.

In (A.2.14), we could require a condition on the first derivative, in place of the function value, such as

$$y'(a) = \alpha \qquad y(b) = \beta$$

More generally, for the nth-order equation (A.2.2), we need to specify n conditions on y and/or its first $n - 1$ derivatives, and a large number of variations are possible. Viewed in terms of the first-order system (A.2.4), we need to specify values for p of the components $y_1, \ldots, y_n$ at a, and another $n - p$ values at b.

3 Linear Algebra and Matrix Theory

The most important tool in many areas of scientific computing is linear algebra and matrix theory, and we review here some of the basic results that will be used.

If $A = (a_{ij})$ is a real $n \times n$ matrix, we denote the transpose of A by A^T, the inverse by A^{-1}, and the determinant by det A. If the inverse of A exists, then A is *nonsingular.* The following basic result gives various other ways of stating this.

THEOREM A.3.1 *The following are equivalent*:

1. A *is nonsingular.*
2. $\det A \neq 0$.
3. *The linear system* $A\mathbf{x} = 0$ *has only the solution* $\mathbf{x} = 0$.
4. *For any vector* $\mathbf{b}$, *the linear system* $A\mathbf{x} = \mathbf{b}$ *has a unique solution.*
5. *The columns (rows) of* A *are linearly independent*; *that is, if* $\mathbf{a}_1, \ldots, \mathbf{a}_n$ *are the columns of* A *and* $\alpha_1\mathbf{a}_1 + \cdots + \alpha_n\mathbf{a}_n = 0$, *then the scalars* α_i *are necessarily zero.*

The last condition (5) may be rephrased to say that A has rank n where, in general, the rank is defined as the number of linearly independent columns (or rows) of the matrix.

A (real or complex) scalar λ and a vector $\mathbf{x} \neq 0$ are an *eigenvalue* and *eigenvector*, respectively, of the matrix A if

(A.3.1)
$$A\mathbf{x} = \lambda\mathbf{x}$$

By theorem A.3.1, it follows that λ is an eigenvalue if and only if

(A.3.2)
$$\det(A - \lambda I) = 0$$

This is the *characteristic equation* of A and is a polynomial of degree n in λ. (Here, as always, I is the identity matrix.) Consequently, A has precisely n (not necessarily distinct) eigenvalues—the n roots of (A.3.2). The collection of these n eigenvalues $\lambda_1, \ldots, \lambda_n$ is called the *spectrum* of A, and

(A.3.3)
$$\rho(A) = \max_{1 \leq i \leq n} |\lambda_i|$$

is the *spectral radius* of A.

Eigenvalues are, in general, difficult to compute, but there is an important class of matrices in which they are available by inspection. These are upper- or lower- *triangular matrices*—

$$A = \begin{bmatrix} a_{11} & \cdot & \cdot & \cdot & a_{1n} \\ & \cdot & & & \cdot \\ & & \cdot & & \cdot \\ & \bigcirc & & \cdot & \cdot \\ & & & & a_{nn} \end{bmatrix} \quad A = \begin{bmatrix} a_{11} & & & & \bigcirc \\ \cdot & \cdot & & & \\ \cdot & & \cdot & & \\ \cdot & & & \cdot & \\ a_{n1} & \cdot & \cdot & \cdot & a_{nn} \end{bmatrix}$$

for which the eigenvalues are simply the main diagonal elements. An important special case of triangular matrices are *diagonal matrices*—

$$D = \begin{bmatrix} d_1 & & & \bigcirc \\ & \cdot & & \\ & & \cdot & \\ \bigcirc & & & d_n \end{bmatrix}$$

which we will usually denote by $D = \text{diag}(d_1, \ldots, d_n)$.

Even if the matrix A is real, the eigenvalues of A may be complex. However, if A is *symmetric*, that is, $A = A^T$, then its eigenvalues are necessarily real. Moreover, if A is also *positive-definite*, which means that $\mathbf{x}^T A\mathbf{x} > 0$ for all $\mathbf{x} \neq 0$, then its eigenvalues are also positive. The converse also holds; that is, if all the eigenvalues of a symmetric matrix are positive, then the matrix is positive-definite.

One of the most important operations in matrix theory is the *similarity transformation*. Two $n \times n$ matrices A and B are *similar* if there is a nonsingular matrix P such that $B = PAP^{-1}$. An important property of the similarity transformation is that it preserves eigenvalues.

THEOREM A.3.2 *If* A *and* B *are similar matrices, they have the same eigenvalues.*

The Euclidean length of a vector $\mathbf{x}$ is defined by

(A.3.4)
$$\|\mathbf{x}\|_2 = \left(\sum_{i=1}^{n} x_i^2\right)^{1/2}$$

This is a special case of a *vector norm*, which is a real-valued function that satisfies the following distancelike properties:

(A.3.5)
1. $\|\mathbf{x}\| \geq 0$ for any vector $\mathbf{x}$ and $\|\mathbf{x}\| = 0$ only if $\mathbf{x} = 0$
2. $\|\alpha\mathbf{x}\| = |\alpha|\,\|\mathbf{x}\|$ for any scalar α
3. $\|\mathbf{x} + \mathbf{y}\| \leq \|\mathbf{x}\| + \|\mathbf{y}\|$ for all vectors $\mathbf{x}$ and $\mathbf{y}$

Property 3 is known as the *triangle inequality.*

The Euclidean length (A.3.4) satisfies these properties and is usually called the Euclidean norm, or ℓ_2 norm. Other commonly used norms are defined by

$$\text{(A.3.6)} \qquad \|\mathbf{x}\|_1 = \sum_{i=1}^{n} |x_i| \qquad \|\mathbf{x}\|_\infty = \max_{1 \leq i \leq n} |x_i|$$

which are known as the ℓ_1 norm, and the ℓ_∞ or max norm, respectively. The three norms (A.3.4) and (A.3.6) are special cases of the general class of ℓ_p norms

$$\text{(A.3.7)} \qquad \|\mathbf{x}\|_p = \left(\sum_{i=1}^{n} |x_i^p| \right)^{1/p}$$

defined for any real number $p \in [1, \infty)$. The ℓ_∞ norm is the limiting case of (A.3.7) as $p \to \infty$.

Another important class of norms are the *elliptic norms* defined by

$$\|\mathbf{x}\| = (\mathbf{x}^T B \mathbf{x})^{1/2}$$

for some given symmetric positive-definite matrix B; the Euclidean norm is the special case B = I.

These various norms can be visualized geometrically in terms of the set of vectors of norm 1, that is, $\{\mathbf{x} : \|\mathbf{x}\| = 1\}$, which is known as the *unit sphere.* These are shown in Figure A.3.1 for vectors in the plane. Note that only for the Euclidean norm are the unit vectors on the circle of radius 1.

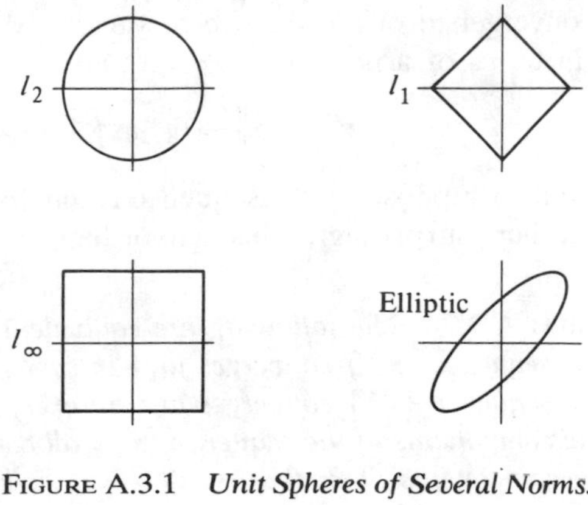

FIGURE A.3.1 *Unit Spheres of Several Norms.*

The elliptic norms play a particularly central role in matrix theory because they arise in terms of an *inner product*, which in turn defines orthogonality of vectors. An inner product is a real-valued function of two vector variables that satisfies the following conditions (stated only for real vectors):

(A.3.8)
1. $(\mathbf{x}, \mathbf{x}) \geq 0$ for all vectors x; $(\mathbf{x}, \mathbf{x}) = 0$ only if $\mathbf{x} = 0$
2. $(\alpha\mathbf{x}, \mathbf{y}) = \alpha(\mathbf{x}, \mathbf{y})$ for all vectors $\mathbf{x}$ and $\mathbf{y}$ and scalars α
3. $(\mathbf{x}, \mathbf{y}) = (\mathbf{y}, \mathbf{x})$ for all vectors $\mathbf{x}$ and $\mathbf{y}$
4. $(\mathbf{x} + \mathbf{z}, \mathbf{y}) = (\mathbf{x}, \mathbf{y}) + (\mathbf{z}, \mathbf{y})$ for all vectors $\mathbf{x}$, $\mathbf{y}$, and $\mathbf{z}$

For any inner product, a norm may be defined by

$$\|\mathbf{x}\| = (\mathbf{x}, \mathbf{x})^{1/2}$$

and the elliptic norms then derive from the inner product

(A.3.9)
$$(\mathbf{x}, \mathbf{y}) \equiv \mathbf{x}^T B \mathbf{y}$$

Two nonzero vectors $\mathbf{x}$ and $\mathbf{y}$ are *orthogonal* with respect to some inner product if

$$(\mathbf{x}, \mathbf{y}) = 0$$

If the inner product is the Euclidean one defined by (A.3.9) with $B = I$, then this gives the usual and intuitive concept of orthogonality. A set of nonzero vectors $\mathbf{x}_1, \ldots, \mathbf{x}_m$ is *orthogonal* if

$$(\mathbf{x}_i, \mathbf{x}_j) = 0, \qquad i \neq j$$

A set of orthogonal vectors is necessarily linearly independent, and a set of n such vectors is said to be an *orthogonal basis.*

If the columns of a matrix A are orthogonal and also of length unity in the Euclidean inner product, then the matrix is *orthogonal.* Orthogonal matrices have the important property that they preserve the length of a vector; that is, $\|A\mathbf{x}\|_2 = \|\mathbf{x}\|_2$.

Convergence of a sequence of vectors $\{\mathbf{x}^{(k)}\}$ to a limit vector $\mathbf{x}$ is defined in terms of a norm by

$$\|\mathbf{x}^{(k)} - \mathbf{x}\| \to 0 \quad \text{as} \quad k \to \infty$$

It is natural to suppose that a sequence might converge in one norm but not in another. Surprisingly, this cannot happen.

THEOREM A.3.3 *The following are equivalent:*
1. *The sequence* $\{\mathbf{x}^{(k)}\}$ *converges to* $\mathbf{x}$ *in some norm.*
2. *The sequence* $\{\mathbf{x}^{(k)}\}$ *converges to* $\mathbf{x}$ *in every norm.*
3. *The components of the sequence* $\{\mathbf{x}^{(k)}\}$ *all converge to the corresponding components of* $\mathbf{x}$; *that is,* $x_i^{(k)} \to x_i$, *as* $k \to \infty$ *for* $i = 1, \ldots, n$.

As a consequence of this result—sometimes known as the *norm equivalence theorem*—when we speak of the convergence of a sequence of vectors, it is immaterial whether we specify the norm or not.

Any vector norm gives rise to a corresponding matrix norm by means of the definition

(A.3.10)
$$\|A\| = \max_{\mathbf{x} \neq 0} \frac{\|A\mathbf{x}\|}{\|\mathbf{x}\|}$$

The properties (A.3.5) also hold for a matrix norm; in addition, there is the multiplicative property $\|AB\| \leq \|A\| \, \|B\|$.

As with vectors, the convergence of a sequence of matrices may be defined componentwise or, equivalently, in terms of any matrix norm. That is, we write $A_k \to A$ as $k \to \infty$ if, in some norm, $\|A_k - A\| \to 0$ as $k \to \infty$. Again, convergence in some norm implies convergence in any norm.

The powers A^k, $k = 1, 2, \ldots$, of a given matrix form a particularly important sequence of matrices. The basic result on the convergence of such a sequence is given in terms of the spectral radius of A by the following theorem:

THEOREM A.3.4 *The sequence* $\{A^k\}$, $k = 1, 2, \ldots$, *converges to zero if and only if* $\rho(A) < 1$.

The geometric interpretation of a matrix norm is that $\|A\|$ is the maximum length of a unit vector after transformation by A; this is depicted in Figure A.3.2 for the ℓ_2 norm.

The matrix norms corresponding to the ℓ_1 and ℓ_∞ vector norms are easily computed by

(A.3.11)
$$\|A\|_1 = \max_{1 \leq j \leq n} \sum_{i=1}^{n} |a_{ij}| \qquad \|A\|_\infty = \max_{1 \leq i \leq n} \sum_{j=1}^{n} |a_{ij}|$$

That is, $\|A\|_1$ is the maximum column sum of the elements of A, and $\|A\|_\infty$ is the maximum row sum. The Euclidean matrix norm is given in terms of the spectral radius of A^TA by

(A.3.12)
$$\|A\|_2 = [\rho(A^TA)]^{1/2}$$

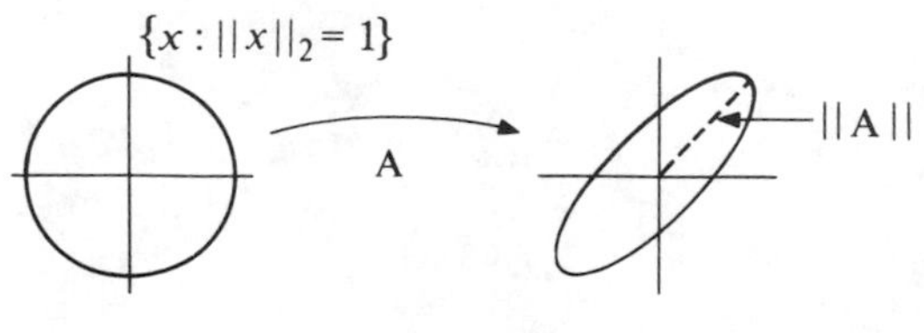

FIGURE A.3.2 *The l_2 Norm.*

and is much more difficult to compute. In case A is symmetric, (A.3.12) reduces to

(A.3.13) $$\|A\|_2 = \rho(A)$$

which is still difficult to compute but is more directly related to the matrix A.

We note that it follows immediately from (A.3.10) that if λ is any eigenvalue of A and $\mathbf{x}$ a corresponding eigenvector, then

$$|\lambda|\,\|\mathbf{x}\| = \|\lambda\mathbf{x}\| = \|A\mathbf{x}\| \leq \|A\|\,\|\mathbf{x}\|$$

so $|\lambda| \leq \|A\|$; that is, any norm of the matrix A gives a bound on all eigenvalues of A. In general, however, the property (A.3.13) of the ℓ_2 norm will not hold.

Bibliography

ALLGOWER, E.; GEORG, K. [1980]. *Simplicial and Continuation Methods for Approximating Fixed Points and Solutions to Systems of Equations.* SIAM Review 22, pp. 28–85.

AMES, W. [1977]. *Numerical Methods for Partial Differential Equations.* Academic Press, New York.

ANONYMOUS [1977]. *The MACSYMA Reference Manual.* Version 9, Mathlab Group Laboratory for Computer Science, M.I.T., Cambridge, MA.

AZIZ, A. (Editor) [1975]. *Numerical Solutions of Boundary Value Problems in Ordinary Differential Equations.* Academic Press, New York.

BAILEY, P.; SHAMPINE, L.; WALTMAN, P. [1968]. *Nonlinear Two Point Boundary Value Problems.* Academic Press, New York.

BATHE, K. J.; WILSON, E. [1976]. *Numerical Methods in Finite Element Analysis.* Prentice-Hall, Englewood Cliffs, N.J.

BERG, P.; MCGREGOR, J. [1966]. *Elementary Partial Differential Equations.* Holden-Day.

BROWN, W. [1973]. *ALTRAN User's Manual.* Third Edition, Bell Laboratories, Murray Hill, N.J.

BUNCH, J.; ROSE, D. (Editors) [1976]. *Sparse Matrix Computations.* Academic Press, New York.

CARRIER, G.; PEARSON, C. [1976]. *Partial Differential Equations: Theory and Technique.* Academic Press, New York.

CHANDRA, R. [1978]. *Conjugate Gradient Methods for Partial Differential Equations.* Dept. of Computer Science Research Rpt., No. 129, Yale University.

CHASEN, S. [1978]. *Geometric Principles and Procedures for Computer Graphics.* Prentice-Hall, Englewood Cliffs, N.J.

CODDINGTON, E.; LEVINSON, N. [1955]. *Theory of Ordinary Differential Equations.* McGraw-Hill, New York.

COLE, J. [1968]. *Perturbation Methods in Applied Mathematics.* Blaisdell (Ginn).

COURANT, R.; HILBERT, D. [1953, 1962]. *Methods of Mathematical Physics.* Volumes 1 and 2. Interscience, New York.

DANIEL, J.; MOORE, R. [1970]. *Computation and Theory in Ordinary Differential Equations.* Freeman, San Francisco.

DAVIS, P.; RABINOWITZ, P. [1975]. *Methods of Numerical Integration.* Academic Press, New York.

DENNEMEYER, R. [1968]. *Introduction to Partial Differential Equations and Boundary Value Problems.* McGraw-Hill, New York.

DENNIS, J.; MORE, J. [1977]. *Quasi-Newton Methods, Motivation and Theory.* SIAM Review 19, pp. 46–89.

DE BOOR, C. [1978]. *A Practical Guide to Splines.* Springer-Verlag, New York.

DONGARRA, J.; BUNCH, J.; MOLER, C.; STEWART, G. [1979]. *LINPACK Users' Guide.* SIAM, Philadelphia.

DUFF, I. [1977]. *A Survey of Sparse Matrix Research.* Proceedings of the IEEE. 65, pp. 500–535.

DUFF, I.; REID, J. [1979]. *Some Design Features of a Sparse Matrix Code.* ACM Trans. on Math Soft. 5, pp. 18–35.

DUFF, I.; STEWART, G. (Editors) [1979]. *Sparse Matrix Proceedings 1978* SIAM, Philadelphia.

EISENSTAT, S.; GURSKY, M. C.; SCHULTZ, M. H. and SHERMAN, A. H. [1977]. *Yale Sparse Matrix Package I: The Symmetric Codes.* Rpt. 112, Dept. of Computer Science, Yale University.

ERISMAN, A.; REID, J. [1981]. *Direct Methods for Sparse Matrices,* Oxford University Press, Oxford.

FORSYTHE, G.; MOLER, C. [1967]. *Computer Solution of Linear Algebraic Systems.* Prentice-Hall, Englewood Cliffs, N.J.

FORSYTHE, G.; WASOW, W. [1960]. *Finite Difference Methods for Partial Differential Equations.* Wiley, New York.

FRANCIS, J. G. F. [1961, 1962]. *The QR Transformation, Parts I & II.* Computer Journal 4, pp. 265–271, 332–345.

GARABEDIAN, P. [1964]. *Partial Differential Equations.* Wiley, New York.

GARBOW, B.; BOYLE, J.; DONGARRA, J.; MOLER, C. [1977]. *Matrix Eigensystem Routines—EISPACK Guide Extension.* vol. 51, Springer-Verlag, New York.

GEAR, C. W. [1971]. *Numerical Initial Value Problems in Ordinary Differential Equations.* Prentice-Hall, Englewood Cliffs, N.J.

GEORGE, A.; LIU, J. [1979]. *The Design of a User Interface for a Sparse Matrix Package.* ACM Trans. on Math. Software 5, pp. 139–162.

GEORGE, A.; LIU, J. [1981]. *Computer Solution of Large Sparse Positive Definite Systems.* Prentice-Hall, Englewood Cliffs, N.J.

GILOI, W. [1978]. *Interactive Computer Graphics: Data Structures, Algorithms, Languages.* Prentice-Hall, Englewood Cliffs, N.J.

HEARN, A. [1973]. REDUCE User's Manual, Second Edition, University of Utah, Salt Lake City.

HEARN, A. [1976]. Scientific Applications of Symbolic Computation. In Computer Science and Scientific Computing. J. Ortega, Editor. Academic Press, New York.

HENRICI, P. [1962]. *Discrete Variable Methods in Ordinary Differential Equations.* Wiley, New York.

HESTENES, M.; STIEFEL, E. [1952]. *Methods of Conjugate Gradients for Solving Linear Systems.* Journal of Research of the National Bureau of Standards, 49, pp. 409–436.

HINDMARSH, A. C. [1972]. GEAR: *Ordinary Differential Equation System Solver.* Lawrence Livermore Laboratory Rpt. UCID-30001, rev. 2, Livermore, California.

HIRT, C.; COOK, J. [1975]. *Perspective Displays for 3-Dimensional Finite Difference Calculations.* Computers and Fluids 3, pp. 293–304.

HOPPENSTEADT, F. [1975]. *Mathematical Theories of Populations: Demographics, Genetics and Epidemics.* SIAM, Philadelphia.

HOUSEHOLDER, A. [1964]. *The Theory of Matrices in Numerical Analysis.* Ginn (Blaisdell), Boston.

ISAACSON, E.; KELLER, H. [1966]. *Analysis of Numerical Methods.* Wiley, New York.

JENKS, R. [1974]. *The SCRATCHPAD Language.* SIGPLAN Notices, ACM, New York, pp. 101–111.

JENNINGS, A. [1977]. *Matrix Computation for Engineers and Scientists.* John Wiley, New York.

KAHAN, W.; PARLETT, B. [1968]. *On the Convergence of a Practical QR Algorithm.* Proceedings of the IFIP Congress, pp. A25–A30.

KAUFMAN, L. [1974]. *The LZ Algorithm to Solve the Generalized Eigenvalue Problem,* SIAM Journal on Numerical Analysis 11, pp. 997–1024.

KELLER, H. [1968]. *Numerical Methods for Two-Point Boundary Value Problems.* Ginn (Blaisdell), New York.

KELLER, H. [1975]. *Numerical Solution of Boundary Value Problems for Ordinary Differential Equations: Survey and some recent results on difference methods, in Numerical Solutions of Boundary Value Problems for Ordinary Differential Equations.* A. Aziz (Editor), Academic Press, New York.

KEYFITZ, N. [1968]. *Introduction to the Mathematics of Population.* Addison-Wesley, Reading, Mass.

KUBLANOVSKAYA, V. [1961]. *On Some Algorithms for the Solution of the Complete Eigenvalue Problem.* Zh. vych. Mat. 1, pp. 555–570.

LAIDLER, J. [1958]. *The Chemical Kinetics of Enzyme Action.* Oxford Univ. Press (Clarendon), London and New York.

LAMBERT, J. [1973]. *Computational Methods in Ordinary Differential Equations.* Wiley, New York.

LAPIDUS, L.; SEINFELD, J. [1971]. *Numerical Solution of Ordinary Differential Equations.* Academic Press, New York.

LASALLE, J.; LEFSCHETZ, S. [1961]. *Stability by Liapunov's Direct Method.* Academic Press, New York.

LOTKA, A. [1925]. *Elements of Physical Biology.* Williams & Williams, Baltimore (Reprinted as *Elements of Mathematical Biology* by Dover, New York, 1956).

LUCUS, T. R.; REDDIEN, G. W. [1972]. *Some Collocation Methods for Nonlinear Boundary Value Problems.* SIAM Journal on Numerical Analysis 9, pp. 341–356.

MADSEN, N. K.; SINCOVEC, R. F. [1974]. *The Numerical Method of Lines for the Solution of Nonlinear Partial Differential Equations.* In Computational Methods in Nonlinear Mechanics, J. T. Oden, et al, Editors. Texas Inst. for Computational Mechanics, Austin, Texas, pp. 371–380.

MADSEN, N. K.; SINCOVEC, R. F. [1979]. *PDECOL: General Collocation Software for Partial Differential Equations.* ACM Trans. Math. Software 5, pp. 326–351.

MELGAARD, D. K.; SINCOVEC, R. F. [1981]. *Algorithms PDETWO and PSETM for the Solution of Two Dimensional Nonlinear Partial Differential Equations.* ACM Trans. Math. Software 7, to appear.

MEYER, G. [1973]. *Initial Value Methods for Boundary Value Problems; Theory and Application of Invariant Imbedding.* Academic Press, New York.

MITCHELL, A. [1969]. *Computational Methods in Partial Differential Equations.* Wiley, New York.

MITCHELL, A.; WAIT, R. [1977]. *The Finite Element Method in Partial Differential Equations.* Wiley, New York.

MOLER, C.; STEWART, G. [1973]. *An Algorithm for Generalized Matrix Eigenvalue Problems.* SIAM Journal on Numerical Analysis 10, pp. 241–256.

MURRAY, J. [1968]. *A Simple Method for Obtaining Approximate Solutions for a Large Class of Diffusion-Kinetic Enzyme Problems.* Math. Biosciences 2.

NEWMAN, W.; SPROUL, R. [1979]. *Principles of Interactive Computer Graphics* (2nd edition). McGraw-Hill, New York.

ORTEGA, J. [1972]. *Numerical Analysis: A Second Course.* Academic Press, New York.

ORTEGA, J. (Editor) [1976]. *Scientific Computing and Computer Science.* Academic Press, New York.

ORTEGA, J.; RHEINBOLDT, W. [1970]. *Iterative Solution of Nonlinear Equations in Several Variables.* Academic Press, New York.

OSTROWSKI, A. [1973]. *Solution of Equations in Euclidean and Banach Spaces.* Academic Press, New York.

PARLETT, B. [1980]. *The Symmetric Eigenvalue Problem.* Prentice-Hall, Englewood Cliffs, N.J.

PARTER, S. [1961]. *The Use of Linear Graphs in Gauss Elimination.* SIAM Review 3, pp. 119–130.

POWERS, D. [1972]. *Boundary Value Problems.* Academic Press, New York.

PRENTER, P. [1975]. *Splines and Variational Methods.* Wiley, New York.

REID, J. (Editor) [1971]. *Large Sparse Sets of Linear Equations.* Academic Press, London and New York.

RICHTMYER, R.; MORTON, K. [1967]. *Difference Methods for Initial Value Problems.* Interscience-Wiley, New York.

ROACHE, P. [1972]. *Computational Fluid Dynamics.* Hermosa Publishers, Albuquerque, N.M.

ROBERTS, S.; SHIPMAN, J. [1972]. *Two-Point Boundary Value Problems: Shooting Methods.* American Elsevier, New York.

ROGERS, D.; ADAMS, J. [1976]. *Mathematical Elements for Computer Graphics.* McGraw-Hill, New York.

ROSE, D. [1971]. *A Graph-theoretic Study of the Numerical Solution of Sparse Positive Definite Systems of Linear Equations.* in Graph Theory and Computing, R. Read, Editor, pp. 183–217.

ROSE, D.; WILLOUGHBY, R. (Editors) [1972]. *Sparse Matrices and Their Applications.* Plenum Press, New York.

ROSSER, J.; NEWTON, R.; GROSS, G. [1974]. *The Mathematical Theory of Rocket Flight.* McGraw-Hill, New York.

RUBINOW, S. [1975]. *Introduction to Mathematical Biology,* Wiley-Interscience, New York.

RUSSELL, R. [1977]. *A Comparison of Collocation and Finite Differences for Two-Point Boundary Value Problems.* SIAM Journal on Numerical Analysis 14, pp. 19–39.

RUSSELL, R.; SHAMPINE, L. [1972]. *A Collocation Method for Boundary Value Problems.* Numerische Mathematik 19, pp. 1–28.

RUSSELL, R.; SHAMPINE, L. [1975]. *Numerical Methods for Singular Boundary Value Problems.* SIAM Journal of Numerical Analysis 12, pp. 13–36.

SCHIESSER, W. [1976]. *DSS/2 Introductory Programming Manual.* Lehigh University, Bethlehem, Pennsylvania.

SCHULTZ, M. [1973]. *Spline Analysis.* Prentice-Hall, Englewood Cliffs, N.J.

SHAMPINE, L.; ALLEN, R. [1973]. *Numerical Computing: An Introduction.* Saunders, Philadelphia.

SHAMPINE, L.; GEAR, C. [1979]. *A User's View of Solving Stiff Ordinary Differential Equations.* SIAM Review 21, pp. 1–17.

SHAMPINE, L.; WATTS, H.; DAVENPORT, S. [1976]. *Solving Nonstiff Ordinary Differential Equations—The State of the Art.* SIAM Review 18, pp. 376–411.

SINCOVEC, R.; MADSEN, N. [1975]. *Software for Nonlinear Partial Differential Equations.* ACM Trans. Math. Software 1, pp. 232–260.

SMITH, B.; BOYLE, J.; DONGARRA, J.; GARBOW, B.; IKUBI, Y.; KLEEMA, V.; MOLER, C. [1977]. *Matrix Eigensystem Routines—EISPACK Guide*, vol. 6, Second Edition, Springer-Verlag, Berlin.

STETTER, H.; AKTAS, Z. [1977]. *A Classification and Survey of Numerical Methods for Boundary Value Problems for Ordinary Differential Equations.* International Journal for Numerical Methods in Engineering 11, pp. 771–796.

STEWART, G. W. [1973]. *Introduction to Matrix Computations.* Academic Press, New York.

STRANG, G.; FIX, G. [1973]. *An Analysis of the Finite Element Method.* Prentice-Hall, Englewood Cliffs, N.J.

STRASSEN, V. [1969]. *Gaussian elimination is not optimal.* Numerische Mathematik 13, 1969, pp. 354–56.

STROUD, A. [1971]. *Approximate Calculation of Multiple Integrals.* Prentice-Hall, Englewood Cliffs, N.J.

TEWARSON, R. [1973]. *Sparse Matrices.* Academic Press, New York.

TOBEY, R. et al [1969]. *PL/I—FORMAC Symbolic Mathematics Interpreter* IBM Program Information Department, Hawthorne, New York.

TRAUB, J. [1964]. *Iterative Methods for the Solution of Equations.* Prentice-Hall, Englewood Cliffs, N.J.

VARGA, R. [1962]. *Matrix Iterative Analysis.* Prentice-Hall, Englewood Cliffs, N.J.

WALKER, B.; GURD, J.; DRAWNEEK, E. [1976]. *Interactive Computer Graphics.* Crane Russak.

WARD, R. [1975]. *The Combination Shift QZ Algorithm.* SIAM Journal on Numerical Analysis 12, pp. 835–853.

WILKINSON, J. [1963]. *Rounding Errors in Algebraic Processes.* Prentice-Hall, Englewood Cliffs, N.J.

WILKINSON, J. [1961]. *Error Analysis of Direct Methods of Matrix Inversion.* Journal ACM 8, pp. 281–330.

WILKINSON, J. [1965]. *The Algebraic Eigenvalue Problem.* Oxford University Press (Clarendon), London and New York.

WILLOUGHBY, R. (Editor) [1969]. *Sparse Matrix Proceedings.* RA 1 (#11707). IBM Thomas J. Watson Research Center, Yorktown Heights, New York.

YOUNG, D. [1971]. *Iterative Solution of Large Linear Systems.* Academic Press, New York.

YOUNG, D.; GREGORY, R. [1972, 1973]. *A Survey of Numerical Mathematics.* Volumes 1 and 2. Addison-Wesley, Reading, MA.

Author Index

Subject Index